1 concent
2. volentory
3. Personaly
4. Dom.

CIVIL PROCEDURE COURSE SUPPLEMENT:
RULES, STATUTES and ADDITIONAL MATERIALS

2019 Edition

CIVIL PROCEDURE COURSE SUPPLEMENT: RULES, STATUTES and ADDITIONAL MATERIALS

2019 Edition

Lawrence Friedman

CIVIL PROCEDURE COURSE SUPPLEMENT:
RULES, STATUTES and ADDITIONAL MATERIALS
2019 Edition

13:31 Q
13:32 D
13:67
13:32

Contents

Chapter One
The Federal Court System and Adjudication Basics

Students encountering civil procedure for first time often experience frustration with the course and the material. While you likely came to law school having at least a passing familiarity with the concepts that animate other first-year courses, like property, contracts, and torts, unless you were either a plaintiff or a defendant in a civil case, or a paralegal assisting in the litigation of such a case, civil procedure may at first appear impenetrable. It is not unlike learning a foreign language: there is a rule for everything, and many of the rules are neither clear nor intuitive. It is important to remember that these rules are what make civil procedure a *system*—a system specifically designed to promote the orderly resolution of civil disputes.

The introductory materials in this chapter are intended to ease your transition into the world of civil procedure. Think about it this way: in each of the cases you will be studying in this course, there lies a dispute derived from an area of substantive law—indeed, the underlying dispute may be one grounded in property, contracts, or torts. But we are not concerned here with the substantive outcome of that dispute. Rather, we will focus on its procedural aspects—how and why the parties make their respective strategic and tactical moves, from the plaintiff's selection of the court in which to file his or her complaint to the various responses the defendant can make to end the litigation short of a trial. For trial is, theoretically, the plaintiff's goal—and, in a sense, all that we discuss in civil procedure is about the road to trial. You should know at the outset that we will not get there, at least not in this course; the trial and what happens at trial are the subject of other courses you may take in law school, including evidence and trial practice.

It's also important to remember that, in the real world outside the classroom walls, most litigation of civil disputes occurs in state trial courts. But here we will be studying the federal rules of civil procedure, which apply in all the federal district courts. Though there are local variations, for the most part the rules are similar in the majority of the states. And, that said, it might be helpful to begin with an overview of the federal and state court systems, before turning to the business of the courts.

A. The Federal Court System

The Federal Rules of Civil Procedure apply in the federal trial courts, which are called district courts. There are 94 federal judicial districts, at least one in each state, with several in the larger and more populated states. For example, New York has four judicial districts. Each district court has at least one judge and may have several subordinate judicial officers, known as magistrates, who are hired for defined terms by the court and who have more limited authority.

Above the federal district courts are the United States Circuit Courts of Appeals. There are 13 federal judicial circuits; 11 are numbered and refer to territorial areas of the United States. For instance, the United States Court of Appeals for the First Circuit includes Maine, New Hampshire, Massachusetts, Rhode Island, and Puerto Rico. The United States Court of Appeals for the District of Columbia Circuit only hears appeals from the District Court for the District of Columbia, where many challenges to federal laws and regulations are litigated. The only non-territorial appeals court is the Court of Appeals for the Federal Circuit; that court's jurisdiction is defined by the kinds of cases it hears, which include appeals under patent laws and certain damage suits against fed government.

Judges of the federal district and appeals courts are, pursuant to the U.S. Constitution, nominated by the President and must be confirmed by a majority vote of the Senate. They enjoy life tenure. Congress enjoys plenary authority to establish the number and kind of lower federal courts, as well as the number of judges for each court.

Above the circuit courts is the United States Supreme Court, the only court for which the U.S. Constitution specifically provides. Congress sets number of justices and the Supreme Court's jurisdiction in accordance with the limits contained in Article III of the Constitution. Currently, and for many years, the court has had nine justices, one of whom serves as the chief justice. As with the lower federal court judges, all must be nominated by the President and confirmed by a majority of the Senate. The Supreme Court has jurisdiction to review all decisions of the federal courts of appeals, as well as decisions of the state supreme courts that involve the interpretation of federal law.

Importantly, the Supreme Court has the discretion to determine its own docket. While five justices are needed to comprise a majority to decide a case, it takes only four justices to grant certiorari and take a case for argument. Many hundreds more petitions for certiorari are filed than the court will accept; these days, the court will rarely hear argument and issue written decisions in more than 70 or so cases a term. A Supreme Court term begins the first Monday of October and ends the last day of June the following calendar year. When the Supreme Court declines to take a case, the lower court decision stands.

B. State Court Systems

Most state court systems resemble their federal counterpart, though smaller and less populous states may lack an intermediate appellate court. Consider, for example, the Massachusetts court system. The Massachusetts trial court department includes courts with limited civil jurisdiction, typically defined by the amount in controversy, which are known as either district or municipal courts. Above these trial courts sits the Massachusetts Superior Court, which is the trial court of general jurisdiction in the Commonwealth and the equivalent of the federal district courts we will be focusing on in civil procedure. The Massachusetts trial court department also includes several specialty courts, the jurisdiction of which is indicated by their names: the juvenile court, the land court, the housing court, and the family and probate court.

Above the trial court is the Massachusetts Appeals Court, the court to which all appeals from the trial courts are made. And atop the Appeals court sits the oldest appellate court in the United States, the Massachusetts Supreme Judicial Court. The SJC's docket is almost purely discretionary, but differs substantively from the U.S. Supreme Court's docket given the breadth of issues the state courts deal with. One of the primary reasons that most civil litigation in the United States occurs in the state courts is because the jurisdiction of the federal districts is, as we shall see, relatively limited. It's worth noting that, unlike the U.S. Supreme Court, the SJC has seven justices— there is nothing magical about the number nine, and states vary in the number of judges who serve on the state's appellate tribunals as well as in the methods of appointment and retention. Judges in Massachusetts, as in the other New England states and the federal government, are appointed, but most state judges are either elected or appointed and then subject to some kind of retention vote.

C. The Business of Courts

As noted above, most state trial courts at the level of the Massachusetts Superior Court are courts of general jurisdiction, while the federal district courts are courts of limited jurisdiction. While litigants may seek to file complaints involving a wide range of disputes in the Massachusetts Superior Court, down the road at the federal district court, litigants are generally limited to two kinds of cases: those involving disputes that arise under federal law, and those that involve citizens of different states where the amount in controversy exceeds $75,000. The former are called federal question cases and the latter diversity cases, and we will be exploring these two categories of cases in far greater detail later in the first semester when we reach subject-matter jurisdiction.

As you might imagine, there are many instances in which a litigant could choose to pursue an action in a federal district court or in a state trial court. We will periodically touch on this strategic decision, but for now, keep in mind some of the considerations that plaintiffs might be entertaining, including the speed with which they will get to trial (or stated, differently, how crowded the court's docket is), and whether there are other advantages to be gained by litigating the matter before a state tribunal or a federal tribunal in terms.

D. Deciding Cases

Cases are the embodiment of a dispute or disputes between a plaintiff and a defendant, or multiple plaintiffs and multiple defendants. The dispute is not just about the facts—though the parties will disagree about the facts. It is about whether one party or the other has the law on his or her side. Most of the law that controls our lives is found in state and federal statutes and regulations—these are enacted rules, in the sense that they represent laws that have been enacted by legislative or administrative bodies with the authority for regulating some aspect of our lives. Though enacted rules are the primary sources of regulation, in law school we devote the bulk of the first year to studying appellate decisions. We do this to learn how judges and lawyers reason—how they apply generalized rules to specific situations. And we need to know how judges reason because, even though most rules are written down in statutes or formal regulations, the indeterminacy of the English language means there is almost inevitably some interpretive question that must be answered.

Before discussing the ways in which courts give meaning to rules, you should know that there is a hierarchy of enacted rules and a hierarchy of courts that interpret them. First the rules: at the top is the U.S. Constitution. The rules contained in our founding document are often far more ambiguous and uncertain than we realize until a specific question arises under them. The U.S. Supreme Court has the primary responsibility for interpreting the constitution. Below the constitution are federal statutes, the laws passed by Congress. Below that are federal administrative rules and executive (presidential) orders. Below that are state constitutions, about the meaning of which state supreme courts have the final say. Below that are state statutes and state administrative regulations and executive orders. And below that is state common law—the rules of property, contracts, and torts that you study in your other first year courses.

Just as there is hierarchy of laws, there is hierarchy of courts and of the precedential value of the decisions that those courts reach. When it comes to federal statutory and administrative law, the U.S. Supreme Court's understanding is paramount. When it comes to state statutory and administrative law, the state supreme court's understanding is paramount.

It might surprise you to learn that the U.S. Supreme Court and the state supreme courts have not addressed a vast array of issues. In such cases, the lower courts must adjust their sights. In the absence of a definitive answer from the highest court in the jurisdiction, the intermediate appellate court's understanding will control. Thus, in Massachusetts, the federal district courts will follow the precedent set by the United States Court of Appeals for the First Circuit, and the state superior courts will follow the precedent set by the Massachusetts Appeals Court.

In the absence of relevant intermediate court precedent, the trial courts will often look to each other, or outside the jurisdiction for guidance. For example, faced with a novel issue, the Massachusetts Superior Court will look to decisions of other Superior Court judges, even though those decisions are not binding because a higher court did not issue them. Judges and lawyers must rely on whatever guidance they can find to help them to interpret and apply enacted law and common law principles—this is how adjudication works in the United States. Every case is not a case of first impression, and like cases must be decided alike—this is the rule of stare decisis.

Consider that the enacted rules we have been discussing, like statutes and regulations, are often nothing more than general statements of what the law permits or requires of certain classes of persons in certain circumstances. They are abstract and can suffer from vagueness and ambiguity until further defined by courts through litigation. When they seek to give meaning to statutes and regulations, judges and lawyers may consider, for example, the ordinary meaning of words, judicial precedent regarding the law in question, cases governed by other rules in same statute or regulation, historical events linked to the rule's enactment, and legislative history—all in an effort to determine what is the best interpretation of the law in question. When common law rules are at issue, judicial precedent will be the primary consideration.

You have likely figured out that, in fulfilling their obligation to make sense of enacted and common law rules, courts at all levels wield a great deal of power. Where enacted rules are concerned, the process of interpretation shifts power from the enacting body to the judiciary. This is another reason courts abide by the rule of stare decisis: to ensure some consistency in their decisions. Of course, the facts in different cases are seldom identical, which means that much of legal reasoning is reasoning by analogy. Here is what lawyers and judges do when using precedent to figure out the meaning of an enacted or common law rule:

(1)   identify the controlling case(s);

(2)   identify the similar or dissimilar facts; and

(3)   determine whether the similarities are more important than the differences in relation to object of the rule.

At all times, you should keep in mind that this reasoning process will not always result in answers that are one hundred percent certain. But in interpreting rules and legal precedents, and in advocating for and counseling clients, we must learn to live with indeterminacy. As the saying goes, less than 100 percent certainty is not uncertainty.

What happens when the trial court gets the law wrong? In general, this happens in relatively few instances, and it is the main reason we have appellate courts in the federal and state systems—to correct the lower courts and clarify the controlling law. Appellate courts in the United States do not decide or revisit facts; that is the work of either the judge or jury in the appropriate trial court. When the trial court makes any ruling of law – on, say, an evidentiary issue, or when it instructs the jury about the law that applies to the dispute about which it has heard competing stories regarding the facts – it may be subject to review and reversal. Of course, the legislature may also correct a judicial misapprehension of a statute, and a new statute supersedes all prior versions of that statute and all prior cases interpreting the statute. Appellate courts can affirm, reverse or remand a case, depending on the issue under consideration.

E. An Illustration: No Vehicles

Let's consider an illustration of the process of reasoning from precedent before proceeding. This is a famous illustration, stemming from the central problem identified above: the English language being what it is, there is often room for some kind of interpretation. The illustration asks you to imagine a municipal ordinance—perhaps in the City of Cambridge, posted on a park gate near Harvard Square. The sign reads, in its entirety: "NO VEHICLES ALLOWED IN THE PARK." A simple enough rule, yes? Maybe. It depends.[1]

If this rule were to become the subject of a lawsuit, its various meanings and permutations would have to be resolved. In other words, the trial court would have to give the rule meaning. Let's suppose the court had some precedents before it. Here are the trial court's ground rules in resolving a dispute involving these rules: trial court judges decide cases, but they do not have the authority to enact rules. They must give deference to enactments of

---

[1] This is among the most well-known hypotheticals in the common law world, first advanced by H.L.A. Hart in *Positivism and the Separation of Law and Morals*, 71 HARV. L. REV. 593, 606-15 (1958). Hart argued that "[t]here must be a core of settled meaning, but there will be, as well, a penumbra of debatable cases in which words are neither obviously applicable nor obviously ruled out." *Id.* at 607.

lawmaking bodies and cannot reformulate or ignore enacted rules—this is the principle of legislative supremacy. Trial court judges must adhere to precedent: a rule of law developed by a higher court within the same jurisdiction must be applied in a case with similar facts.

So, let's examine three cases in which the Massachusetts Supreme Judicial Court interpreted this rule. In the first, *Doe v. O'Brien*, the plaintiff claims she was injured when struck by the defendant driving his car through the park in order to save time on his way home from work. The court concluded, in a summary opinion, that the defendant's actions were negligence per se, because a car is a "vehicle" for purposes of the rule.

In the second case, *Smith v. Greenberg*, the plaintiff alleged she was injured when struck by the defendant riding a bicycle through the park. The court concluded, also in a summary opinion, that a bicycle is not a "vehicle" for purposes of the rule.

Finally, in the third precedent case, *Brown v. Monserud*, the plaintiff alleged she was injured when struck by the defendant skateboarding through the park. The court concluded, again in a summary opinion, that a skateboard is not a "vehicle" for purposes of the rule.

What is it that links these three rulings? What is the connection between them that leads to a common understanding of what, in the context of the rule, the term "vehicle" might mean? What is it, in other words, that the court has concluded the local legislature meant by this term? Will that understanding of the term transfer neatly to other cases?

F. A Second Illustration: *Fast-Fish and Loose-Fish*

It's worth remembering that, while studying civil procedure may at times feel like learning a foreign language, it is at its heart no different than the study of property, contracts, or torts. The goal is to extract from the cases the doctrine—the sub-rules that help us to understand the main rules. The main rules are sometimes referred to as "black letter rules." The value lawyers add to dispute resolution is their ability to understand the sub-rules are and how to apply them.

To illustrate the extent to which we need sub-rules to understand and apply the black letter rules, consider the excerpt that follows, Chapter 89 from Herman Melville's novel, *Moby-Dick; or the Whale* (1851). Melville, the son-in-law of the great Massachusetts Chief Justice Lemuel Shaw, wrote of the law in many of his works, including *Moby-Dick*. He saw that the law and legal principles were everywhere at play, and in the chapter on the distinction between "fast-fish" and "loose-fish," he captured, in his own inimitable style, the critical task judges and lawyers face in seeking to articulate the rules that help us to apply and understand the black letter rules, particularly when a case raised new or idiosyncratic facts.

Fast-Fish and Loose-Fish

The allusion to the waif and waif-poles in the last chapter but one, necessitates some account of the laws and regulations of the whale fishery, of which the waif may be deemed the grand symbol and badge.

It frequently happens that when several ships are cruising in company, a whale may be struck by one vessel, then escape, and be finally killed and captured by another vessel; and herein are indirectly comprised many minor contingencies, all partaking of this one grand feature. For example,—after a weary and perilous chase and capture of a whale, the body may get loose from the ship by reason of a violent storm; and drifting far away to leeward, be retaken by a second whaler, who, in a calm, snugly tows it alongside, without risk of life or line. Thus the most vexatious and violent disputes would often arise between the fishermen, were there not some written or unwritten, universal, undisputed law applicable to all cases.

Perhaps the only formal whaling code authorized by legislative enactment, was that of Holland. It was decreed by the States-General in A.D. 1695. But though no other nation has ever had any written whaling law, yet the American fishermen have been their own legislators and lawyers in this matter. They have provided a system which for terse comprehensiveness surpasses Justinian's Pandects and the By-laws of the Chinese Society for the Suppression of Meddling with other People's Business. Yes; these laws might be engraven on a Queen Anne's farthing, or the barb of a harpoon, and worn round the neck, so small are they.

I. A Fast-Fish belongs to the party fast to it.

II. A Loose-Fish is fair game for anybody who can soonest catch it.

But what plays the mischief with this masterly code is the admirable brevity of it, which necessitates a vast volume of commentaries to expound it.

First: What is a Fast-Fish? Alive or dead a fish is technically fast, when it is connected with an occupied ship or boat, by any medium at all controllable by the occupant or occupants,—a mast, an oar, a nine-inch cable, a telegraph wire, or a strand of cobweb, it is all the same. Likewise a fish is technically fast when it bears a waif, or any other recognised symbol of possession; so long as the party waifing it plainly evince their ability at any time to take it alongside, as well as their intention so to do.

These are scientific commentaries; but the commentaries of the whalemen themselves sometimes consist in hard words and harder knocks—the Coke-upon-Littleton of the fist. True, among the more upright and honourable whalemen allowances are always made for peculiar cases, where it would be an outrageous moral injustice for one party to claim possession of a whale previously chased or killed by another party. But others are by no means so scrupulous.

Some fifty years ago there was a curious case of whale-trover litigated in England, wherein the plaintiffs set forth that after a hard chase of a whale in the Northern seas; and when indeed they (the plaintiffs) had succeeded in harpooning the fish; they were at last, through peril of their lives, obliged to forsake not only their lines, but their boat itself. Ultimately the defendants (the crew of another ship) came up with the whale, struck, killed, seized, and finally appropriated it before the very eyes of the plaintiffs. And when those defendants were remonstrated with, their captain snapped his fingers in the plaintiffs' teeth, and assured them that by way of doxology to the deed he had done, he would now retain their line, harpoons, and boat, which had remained attached to the whale at the time of the seizure. Wherefore the plaintiffs now sued for the recovery of the value of their whale, line, harpoons, and boat.

Mr. Erskine was counsel for the defendants; Lord Ellenborough was the judge. In the course of the defence, the witty Erskine went on to illustrate his position, by alluding to a recent crim. con. case, wherein a gentleman, after in vain trying to bridle his wife's viciousness, had at last abandoned her upon the seas of life; but in the course of years, repenting of that step, he instituted an action to recover possession of her. Erskine was on the other side; and he then supported it by saying, that though the gentleman had originally harpooned the lady, and had once had her fast, and only by reason of the great stress of her plunging viciousness, had at last abandoned her; yet abandon her he did, so that she became a loose-fish; and therefore when a subsequent gentleman re-harpooned her, the lady then became that subsequent gentleman's property, along with whatever harpoon might have been found sticking in her.

Now in the present case Erskine contended that the examples of the whale and the lady were reciprocally illustrative of each other.

These pleadings, and the counter pleadings, being duly heard, the very learned Judge in set terms decided, to wit,—That as for the boat, he awarded it to the plaintiffs, because they had merely abandoned it to save their lives; but that with regard to the controverted whale, harpoons, and line, they belonged to the defendants; the whale, because it was a Loose-Fish at the time of the final capture; and the harpoons and line because when the fish made off with them, it (the fish) acquired a property in those articles; and hence anybody who afterwards took the fish had a right to them. Now the defendants afterwards took the fish; ergo, the aforesaid articles were theirs.

A common man looking at this decision of the very learned Judge, might possibly object to it. But ploughed up to the primary rock of the matter, the two great principles laid down in the twin whaling laws previously quoted, and applied and elucidated by Lord Ellenborough in the above cited case; these two laws touching Fast-Fish and Loose-Fish, I say, will, on reflection, be found the fundamentals of all human jurisprudence; for notwithstanding its complicated tracery of sculpture, the Temple of the Law, like the Temple of the Philistines, has but two props to stand on.

Is it not a saying in every one's mouth, Possession is half of the law: that is, regardless of how the thing came into possession? But often possession is the whole of the law. What are the sinews and souls of Russian serfs and Republican slaves but Fast-Fish, whereof possession is the whole of the law? What to the rapacious landlord is the widow's last mite but a Fast-Fish? What is yonder undetected villain's marble mansion with a door-plate for a waif; what is that but a Fast-Fish? What is the ruinous discount which Mordecai, the broker, gets from poor Woebegone, the bankrupt, on a loan to keep Woebegone's family from starvation; what is that ruinous discount but a Fast-Fish? What is the Archbishop of Savesoul's income of £100,000 seized from the scant bread and cheese of hundreds of thousands of broken-backed laborers (all sure of heaven without any of Savesoul's help) what is that globular £100,000 but a Fast-Fish? What are the Duke of Dunder's hereditary towns and hamlets but Fast-Fish? What to that redoubted harpooneer, John Bull, is poor Ireland, but a Fast-Fish? What to that apostolic lancer, Brother Jonathan, is Texas but a Fast-Fish? And concerning all these, is not Possession the whole of the law?

But if the doctrine of Fast-Fish be pretty generally applicable, the kindred doctrine of Loose-Fish is still more widely so. That is internationally and universally applicable.

What was America in 1492 but a Loose-Fish, in which Columbus struck the Spanish standard by way of waifing it for his royal master and mistress? What was Poland to the Czar? What Greece to the Turk? What India to England? What at last will Mexico be to the United States? All Loose-Fish.

What are the Rights of Man and the Liberties of the World but Loose-Fish? What all men's minds and opinions but Loose-Fish? What is the principle of religious belief in them but a Loose-Fish? What to the ostentatious smuggling verbalists are the thoughts of thinkers but Loose-Fish? What is the great globe itself but a Loose-Fish? And what are you, reader, but a Loose-Fish and a Fast-Fish, too?

Notes and Questions

1.   Melville's narrator (Ishmael) notes that, among the more upright and honorable whalers, "allowances are always made for peculiar cases, where it would be an outrageous moral injustice for one party to claim possession of a whale previously claimed or killed by another party." But other whalers are not so scrupulous. Who did the rules evolve to govern—the upright and the honorable, or those whalers less so? Or, does the nature of the rules suggest we may not always know which whaler ultimately might fall into each category?

2.   The ultimate question is: what do the rules mean? By themselves, the rules the narrator explicates do not answer many questions—hence the commentaries offering some guidance as to how they should be applied in particular instances. But even the interpretations — the sub-rules, if you will, or rules about the rules — are not always clear. What does it mean, for example, for a whale to be connected to a boat? Can a whale really be held fast by a cobweb? Is the symbol of possession and control more important than actual possession and control? Was it that the whalers simply needed a way to resolve disputes—just as we do today? And what counts as a tag, anyway—does it have to look like a tag or announce itself as one?

3.   And what of the case the narrator describes? He suggests a common man might object to it. Why? Was the decision a fair one? Did it reflect an appropriate application of the rules? In what ways might it be considered unfair? Should defendants have been permitted to retain their harpoons and lines when the whale made off with them? What incentives and disincentives to action does this rule create?

4.   What do you think the narrator thinks about the fairness of these rules? Does he see them as indicative of the rules that pervade all societies, regarding those who have possession—or the symbols of possession—and those who do not? Are the rules regarding Fast-fish and Loose-fish unduly formalistic? Recall who the rules were intended to govern: wouldn't plaintiffs have been entitled to the same result had the situation been reversed? Is that a kind of fairness? A kind of justice?

5.   The narrator is talking in this chapter about rules that are nominally substantive—that accord rights and control expectations. Throughout civil procedure, we will be discussing and examining rules that are nominally procedural. But procedural rules raise many of the same issues: is the goal of a particular rule a fair or just result? Or is it to enhance efficiency and the efficient resolution of disputes? Can procedural rules accomplish both of these goals, or neither, at the same time? Should courts, in interpreting and applying these rules, favor one goal or the other?

Chapter Two
Alternative Dispute Resolution

Many civil disputes are not resolved by courts. Increasingly, they are resolved through less formal means of dispute resolution, including arbitration and mediation. Arbitration is usually a kind of private, informal trial, in which each side pleads its case before a panel of arbitrators (or, sometimes, a single arbitrator), which considers the evidence and arguments and then issues a decision. The arbitration ruling typically binds the parties, and there are limited grounds to appeal an arbitral decision. You have likely committed yourself to dispute resolution through arbitration many times over as a result of signing standard form contracts and click-through agreements.

Mediation, by contrast, is typically conducted by a neutral individual who tries to help the disputants to resolve their dispute. Mediation may be court-ordered, and it typically is not binding—which means the parties to a failed mediation may then pursue litigation.

The cases that follow explore various aspects of arbitration and mediation as alternatives to litigation. As you read them, consider the costs and benefits of these alternatives, and whether they provide the same benefits to parties – or the system of civil dispute resolution – in terms of fairness and efficiency.

GILMER v. INTERSTATE/JOHNSON LANE CORP.
500 U.S. 20 (1991)

JUSTICE WHITE delivered the opinion of the Court.

The question presented in this case is whether a claim under the Age Discrimination in Employment Act of 1967 (ADEA), 29 U. S. C. § 621 *et seq.,* can be subjected to compulsory arbitration pursuant to an arbitration agreement in a securities registration application. The Court of Appeals held that it could, and we affirm.

I

Respondent Interstate/Johnson Lane Corporation (Interstate) hired petitioner Robert Gilmer as a Manager of Financial Services in May 1981. As required by his employment, Gilmer registered as a securities representative with several stock exchanges, including the New York Stock Exchange (NYSE). His registration application, entitled "Uniform Application for Securities Industry Registration or Transfer," provided, among other things, that Gilmer "agree[d] to arbitrate any dispute, claim or controversy" arising between him and Interstate "that is required to be arbitrated under the rules, constitutions or by-laws of the organizations with which I register." Of relevance to this case, NYSE Rule 347 provides for arbitration of "[a]ny controversy between a registered representative and any member or member organization arising out of the employment or termination of employment of such registered representative."

Interstate terminated Gilmer's employment in 1987, at which time Gilmer was 62 years of age. After first filing an age discrimination charge with the Equal Employment Opportunity Commission (EEOC), Gilmer subsequently brought suit in the United States District Court for the Western District of North Carolina, alleging that Interstate had discharged him because of his age, in violation of the ADEA. In response to Gilmer's complaint, Interstate filed in the District Court a motion to compel arbitration of the ADEA claim. In its motion, Interstate relied upon the arbitration agreement in Gilmer's registration application, as well as the Federal Arbitration Act (FAA), 9 U. S. C. § 1 *et seq.* The District Court denied Interstate's motion, ... because it concluded that "Congress intended to protect ADEA claimants from the waiver of a judicial forum." The United States Court of Appeals for the Fourth Circuit reversed. We granted certiorari to resolve a conflict among the Courts of Appeals regarding the arbitrability of ADEA claims.

II

The FAA was originally enacted in 1925, and then reenacted and codified in 1947 as Title 9 of the United States Code. Its purpose was to reverse the longstanding judicial hostility to arbitration agreements that had existed at English common law and had been adopted by American courts, and to place arbitration agreements upon the same footing as other contracts. Its primary substantive provision states that "[a] written provision in any maritime transaction or a contract evidencing a transaction involving commerce to settle by arbitration a controversy thereafter arising out of such contract or transaction. . . shall be valid, irrevocable, and enforceable, save upon such grounds as exist at law or in equity for the revocation of any contract." 9 U. S. C. § 2. The FAA also provides for stays of proceedings in federal district courts when an issue in the proceeding is referable to arbitration, § 3, and for orders compelling arbitration when one party has failed, neglected, or refused to comply with an arbitration agreement, § 4. These provisions manifest a "liberal federal policy favoring arbitration agreements." *Moses H. Cone Memorial Hospital v. Mercury Construction Corp.* (1983).

It is by now clear that statutory claims may be the subject of an arbitration agreement, enforceable pursuant to the FAA. Indeed, in recent years we have held enforceable arbitration agreements relating to claims arising under the Sherman Act of the Securities Exchange Act of 1934; the civil provisions of the Racketeer Influenced and Corrupt Organizations Act (RICO); and the Securities Act of 1933. In these cases we recognized that "[b]y agreeing to arbitrate a statutory claim, a party does not forgo the substantive rights afforded by the statute; it only submits to their resolution in an arbitral, rather than a judicial, forum." *Mitsubishi Motors Corp. v. Soler Chrysler-Plymouth, Inc.* (1985).

Although all statutory claims may not be appropriate for arbitration, "[h]aving made the bargain to arbitrate, the party should be held to it unless Congress itself has evinced an intention to preclude a waiver of judicial remedies for the statutory rights at issue." *Id.* In this regard, we note that the burden is on Gilmer to show that Congress intended to preclude a waiver of a judicial forum for ADEA claims. If such an intention exists, it will be discoverable in the text of the ADEA, its legislative history, or an "inherent conflict" between arbitration and the ADEA's underlying purposes. Throughout such an inquiry, it should be kept in mind that "questions of arbitrability must be addressed with a healthy regard for the federal policy favoring arbitration." *Moses H. Cone.*

III

Gilmer concedes that nothing in the text of the ADEA or its legislative history explicitly precludes arbitration. He argues, however, that compulsory arbitration of ADEA claims pursuant to arbitration agreements would be inconsistent with the statutory framework and purposes of the ADEA. Like the Court of Appeals, we disagree.

A

Congress enacted the ADEA in 1967 "to promote employment of older persons based on their ability rather than age; to prohibit arbitrary age discrimination in employment; [and] to help employers and workers find ways of meeting problems arising from the impact of age on employment." 29 U. S. C. § 621(b). To achieve those goals, the ADEA, among other things, makes it unlawful for an employer "to fail or refuse to hire or to discharge any individual or otherwise discriminate against any individual with respect to his compensation, terms, conditions, or privileges of employment, because of such individual's age." § 623(a)(1). This proscription is enforced both by private suits and by the EEOC. In order for an aggrieved individual to bring suit under the ADEA, he or she must first file a charge with the EEOC and then wait at least 60 days. § 626(d). An individual's right to sue is extinguished, however, if the EEOC institutes an action against the employer. § 626(c)(1). Before the EEOC can bring such an action, though, it must "attempt to eliminate the discriminatory practice or practices alleged, and to effect voluntary compliance with the requirements of this chapter through informal methods of conciliation, conference, and persuasion." § 626(b).

As Gilmer contends, the ADEA is designed not only to address individual grievances, but also to further important social policies. We do not perceive any inherent inconsistency between those policies, however, and enforcing agreements to arbitrate age discrimination claims. It is true that arbitration focuses on specific disputes between the parties involved. The same can be said, however, of judicial resolution of claims. Both of these dispute resolution mechanisms nevertheless also can further broader social purposes. The Sherman Act, the Securities Exchange Act of 1934, RICO, and the Securities Act of 1933 all are designed to advance important public policies, but, as noted above, claims under those statutes are appropriate for arbitration. "[S]o long as the prospective litigant effectively may vindicate [his or her] statutory cause of action in the arbitral forum, the statute will continue to serve both its remedial and deterrent function." *Mitsubishi*.

We also are unpersuaded by the argument that arbitration will undermine the role of the EEOC in enforcing the ADEA. An individual ADEA claimant subject to an arbitration agreement will still be free to file a charge with the EEOC, even though the claimant is not able to institute a private judicial action. Indeed, Gilmer filed a charge with the EEOC in this case. In any event, the EEOC's role in combating age discrimination is not dependent on the filing of a charge; the agency may receive information concerning alleged violations of the ADEA "from any source," and it has independent authority to investigate age discrimination. Moreover, nothing in the ADEA indicates that Congress intended that the EEOC be involved in all employment disputes. Such disputes can be settled, for example, without any EEOC involvement. Finally, the mere involvement of an administrative agency in the enforcement of a statute is not sufficient to preclude arbitration. For example, the Securities Exchange Commission is heavily involved in the enforcement of the Securities Exchange Act of 1934 and the Securities Act of 1933, but we have held that claims under both of those statutes may be subject to compulsory arbitration.

Gilmer also argues that compulsory arbitration is improper because it deprives claimants of the judicial forum provided for by the ADEA. Congress, however, did not explicitly preclude arbitration or other nonjudicial resolution of claims, even in its recent amendments to the ADEA. "[I]f Congress intended the substantive protection afforded [by the ADEA] to include protection against waiver of the right to a judicial forum, that intention will be deducible from text or legislative history." *Mitsubishi*. Moreover, Gilmer's argument ignores the ADEA's flexible approach to resolution of claims. The EEOC, for example, is directed to pursue "informal methods of conciliation, conference, and persuasion," 29 U. S. C. § 626(b), which suggests that out-of-court dispute resolution, such as arbitration, is consistent with the statutory scheme established by Congress. In addition, arbitration is consistent with Congress' grant of concurrent jurisdiction over ADEA claims to state and federal courts, because arbitration agreements, "like the provision for concurrent jurisdiction, serve to advance the objective of allowing [claimants] a broader right to select the forum for resolving disputes, whether it be judicial or otherwise." *Rodriguez de Quijas v. Shearson/American Express, Inc.* (1989).

B

In arguing that arbitration is inconsistent with the ADEA, Gilmer also raises a host of challenges to the adequacy of arbitration procedures. Initially, we note that in our recent arbitration cases we have already rejected most of these arguments as insufficient to preclude arbitration of statutory claims. Such generalized attacks on arbitration "res[t] on suspicion of arbitration as a method of weakening the protections afforded in the substantive law to would-be complainants," and as such, they are "far out of step with our current strong endorsement of the federal statutes favoring this method of resolving disputes." *Rodriguez de Quijas.* Consequently, we address these arguments only briefly.

Gilmer first speculates that arbitration panels will be biased. However, "[w]e decline to indulge the presumption that the parties and arbitral body conducting a proceeding will be unable or unwilling to retain competent, conscientious and impartial arbitrators." *Mitsubishi.* In any event, we note that the NYSE arbitration rules, which are applicable to the dispute in this case, provide protections against biased panels. The rules require, for example, that the parties be informed of the employment histories of the arbitrators, and that they be allowed to make further inquiries into the arbitrators' backgrounds. In addition, each party is allowed one peremptory challenge and unlimited challenges for cause. Moreover, the arbitrators are required to disclose "any circumstances which might preclude [them] from rendering an objective and impartial determination." The FAA also protects against bias, by providing that courts may overturn arbitration decisions "[w]here there was evident partiality or corruption in the arbitrators." There has been no showing in this case that those provisions are inadequate to guard against potential bias.

Gilmer also complains that the discovery allowed in arbitration is more limited than in the federal courts, which he contends will make it difficult to prove discrimination. It is unlikely, however, that age discrimination claims require more extensive discovery than other claims that we have found to be arbitrable, such as RICO and antitrust claims. Moreover, there has been no showing in this case that the NYSE discovery provisions, which allow for document production, information requests, depositions, and subpoenas will prove insufficient to allow ADEA claimants such as Gilmer a fair opportunity to present their claims. Although those procedures might not be as extensive as in the federal courts, by agreeing to arbitrate, a party "trades the procedures and opportunity for review of the courtroom for the simplicity, informality, and expedition of arbitration." *Mitsubishi.* Indeed, an important counterweight to the reduced discovery in NYSE arbitration is that arbitrators are not bound by the rules of evidence.

A further alleged deficiency of arbitration is that arbitrators often will not issue written opinions, resulting, Gilmer contends, in a lack of public knowledge of employers' discriminatory policies, an inability to obtain effective appellate review, and a stifling of the development of the law. The NYSE rules, however, do require that all arbitration awards be in writing, and that the awards contain the names of the parties, a summary of the issues in controversy, and a description of the award issued. In addition, the award decisions are made available to the public. Furthermore, judicial decisions addressing ADEA claims will continue to be issued because it is unlikely that all or even most ADEA claimants will be subject to arbitration agreements. Finally, Gilmer's concerns apply equally to settlements of ADEA claims, which, as noted above, are clearly allowed.

It is also argued that arbitration procedures cannot adequately further the purposes of the ADEA because they do not provide for broad equitable relief and class actions. As the court below noted, however, arbitrators do have the power to fashion equitable relief. Indeed, the NYSE rules applicable here do not restrict the types of relief an arbitrator may award, but merely refer to "damages and/or other relief." The NYSE rules also provide for collective proceedings. But "even if the arbitration could not go forward as a class action or class relief could not be granted by the arbitrator, the fact that the [ADEA] provides for the possibility of bringing a collective action does not mean that individual attempts at conciliation were intended to be barred." *Nicholson v. CPC Int'l Inc.* (CA3 1989) (Becker, J., dissenting). Finally, it should be remembered that arbitration agreements will not preclude the *EEOC* from bringing actions seeking class-wide and equitable relief.

C

An additional reason advanced by Gilmer for refusing to enforce arbitration agreements relating to ADEA claims is his contention that there often will be unequal bargaining power between employers and employees. Mere inequality in bargaining power, however, is not a sufficient reason to hold that arbitration agreements are never enforceable in the employment context. Relationships between securities dealers and investors, for example, may involve unequal bargaining power, but we nevertheless [have] held ... that agreements to arbitrate in that context are enforceable. As discussed above, the FAA's purpose was to place arbitration agreements on the same footing as other contracts. Thus, arbitration agreements are enforceable "save upon such grounds as exist at law or in equity for the revocation of any contract." 9 U. S. C. § 2. "Of course, courts should remain attuned to well-supported claims that the agreement to arbitrate resulted from the sort of fraud or overwhelming economic power that would provide grounds 'for the revocation of any contract.'" *Mitsubishi*. There is no indication in this case, however, that Gilmer, an experienced businessman, was coerced or defrauded into agreeing to the arbitration clause in his registration application. As with the claimed procedural inadequacies discussed above, this claim of unequal bargaining power is best left for resolution in specific cases.

V

We conclude that Gilmer has not met his burden of showing that Congress, in enacting the ADEA, intended to preclude arbitration of claims under that Act. Accordingly, the judgment of the Court of Appeals is

Affirmed.

JUSTICE STEVENS, with whom JUSTICE MARSHALL joins, dissenting.

... Not only would I find that the FAA does not apply to employment-related disputes between employers and employees in general, but also I would hold that compulsory arbitration conflicts with the congressional purpose animating the ADEA, in particular. As this Court previously has noted, authorizing the courts to issue broad injunctive relief is the cornerstone to eliminating discrimination in society. *Albermarle Paper Co. v. Moody* (1975). The ADEA, like Title VII of the Civil Rights Act of 1964, authorizes courts to award broad, class-based injunctive relief to achieve the purposes of the Act. Because commercial arbitration is typically limited to a specific dispute between the particular parties and because the available remedies in arbitral forums generally do not provide for class-wide injunctive relief, I would conclude that an essential purpose of the ADEA is frustrated by compulsory arbitration of employment discrimination claims. ...

In my opinion the same concerns expressed by Chief Justice Burger with regard to compulsory arbitration of Title VII claims may be said of claims arising under the ADEA. The Court's holding today clearly eviscerates the important role played by an independent judiciary in eradicating employment discrimination.

When the FAA was passed in 1925, I doubt that any legislator who voted for it expected it to apply to statutory claims, to form contracts between parties of unequal bargaining power, or to the arbitration of disputes arising out of the employment relationship. In recent years, however, the Court "has effectively rewritten the statute," and abandoned its earlier view that statutory claims were not appropriate subjects for arbitration. Although I remain persuaded that it erred in doing so, the Court has also put to one side any concern about the inequality of bargaining power between an entire industry, on the one hand, and an individual customer or employee, on the other. Until today, however, the Court has not read § 2 of the FAA as broadly encompassing disputes arising out of the employment relationship. I believe this additional extension of the FAA is erroneous. Accordingly, I respectfully dissent.

Notes and Questions

1. Why did the Court not see any inconsistencies between litigation and arbitration as means of enforcing the ADEA?

2. On what basis did the plaintiff argue that arbitration panels might be biased? Why does the Court reject that argument? How does the Court address the plaintiff's arguments that the panels will limit discovery and may not issue written opinions?

3. Do arbitration panels have the authority to award the same kind of relief that a court could?

4. Arbitration agreements are contracts, and contract law allows a number of challenges to an agreement's validity—like, for example, a claim of unequal bargaining power. The next case illustrates some contract-based challenges to the enforcement of an arbitration agreement.

EMERONYE v. CACI INTERNATIONAL, INC.
141 F.Supp.2d 82 (D. D.C. 2001)
MEMORANDUM OPINION

HUVELLE, District Judge.

Before the Court is defendant's motion to dismiss, plaintiff's opposition, and defendant's reply. Plaintiff Charity Emeronye filed this suit against her former employer, CACI International, Inc., alleging discrimination under 42 U.S.C. § 1981, *et seq.*, and Title VII of the Civil Rights Act of 1964, as amended, 42 U.S.C. § 2000e, *et seq.* Plaintiff contends that she was denied promotions because of her race and/or national origin, and that her employer engaged in retaliatory conduct. Defendant moves to dismiss under Fed.R.Civ.P. 12(b)(1), arguing that under plaintiff's employment agreement her discrimination claims are subject to mandatory arbitration and cannot be pursued in this Court. In response, plaintiff argues that: (1) the Federal Arbitration Act, 9 U.S.C. § 1, *et seq.*, ("FAA"), does not apply to employment contracts; (2) the employment contract was an adhesion contract that plaintiff did not assent to; (3) the contract here does not contain a clear waiver of statutory rights; and (4) under the FAA, a court can stay a case pending arbitration, but cannot dismiss. The Court finds that the parties' dispute is covered by the Employment Agreement, thus subject to mediation and then binding arbitration, and that this arbitration provision is enforceable. Accordingly, defendant's motion to dismiss and to compel arbitration is granted.

BACKGROUND

Plaintiff is a Nigerian female with a law degree from the University of London and an L.L.M. degree from DePaul University, majoring in health law. Plaintiff began working for defendant in May 1997 as a "temporary coder." On August 6, 1997, defendant offered plaintiff a permanent position as a paralegal. The offer letter, which was signed by both plaintiff and defendant, requested that plaintiff return a signed copy of the standard "Employee Agreement," which was attached. Def. Reply Ex. A. The offer letter also stated that "[y]our signature on [the Employee Agreement] acknowledges your understanding of the requirements contained therein, and your agreement to abide by them." Plaintiff signed the Employee Agreement on August 6, 1997. This two page agreement provides in relevant part that:

> Any controversy or claim arising out of, or relating to this Agreement, or its breach, or otherwise arising out of or relating to my CACI employment (including without limitation to any claim of discrimination whether based on race, color, ... [or] national origin ... or any other legally protected status, and whether based on federal or State law, or otherwise) shall be settled first by resort to mediation by CACI's Ombudsman and then, if mediation fails to resolve the matter, by arbitration. This arbitration shall be held ... in accordance with ... arbitration procedures of the American Arbitration Association. Judgment upon award rendered by the arbitrator shall be binding upon both parties and may be entered and enforced in any court of competent jurisdiction.

Plaintiff thereafter began work as a paralegal. Plaintiff alleges that in late 1997, her supervisor, a white female, began a course of disparate treatment toward her because of her race (black) and national origin (African/Nigerian). Between March and October 1998, plaintiff applied for several open "senior paralegal" and "supervisory paralegal" positions that she alleges she was qualified for. Plaintiff contends that she was denied these promotions as a result of discrimination, and was retaliated against after filing an EEO complaint with CACI's EEO Office in August 1999. Plaintiff filed this suit against defendant on September 21, 2000, claiming violations of Title VII and 42 U.S.C. § 1981.

LEGAL ANALYSIS

I. The Federal Arbitration Act Applies to Employment Contracts

Plaintiff initially argued that the FAA does not apply to employment contracts, under the exclusion set forth in Section 1, which provides that "contracts of employment of seamen, railroad employees, or any other class of workers engaged in foreign or interstate commerce" are excluded from the Act's coverage. 9 U.S.C. § 1. Plaintiff argued that employment contracts fall within the category of "workers engaged in foreign or interstate commerce" and therefore are not covered by the FAA. Plaintiff concedes, however, that after the present motion was filed, the Supreme Court rejected such a broad interpretation of the exclusion in *Circuit City v. Adams* (2001), stating that "[w]e now decide that the better interpretation is to construe the statute ... to confine the exemption to transportation workers." Therefore, as plaintiff must now admit, her employment agreement is within the scope of the FAA.

II. The Arbitration Clause is Enforceable

Plaintiff also contends that the arbitration clause is not enforceable because 1) the Employee Agreement was a contract of adhesion to which she did not assent, and 2) she cannot waive her statutory rights in the absence of a clear and explicit waiver, which the Agreement did not contain.

Plaintiff argues that there was no agreement to arbitrate because there was no "meeting of the minds" as to the arbitration clause. Plaintiff contends that at the commencement of her employment she was presented with a number of forms to sign, that she does not recall signing the Employee Agreement or having discussions with anyone at CACI about the agreement, does not recall agreeing to arbitration, and does not recall reading the arbitration policy or having a copy given to her. None of these claims renders the arbitration clause unenforceable.

The court in *Maye v. Smith Barney, Inc.* (S.D.N.Y. 1995), rejected similar claims in ruling that the arbitration agreement at issue was enforceable. Plaintiffs in *Maye* alleged that during a two-hour orientation meeting with 28 other new employees they were asked to sign their names to documents approximately 75 times, that no one explained the contents of the documents to them, and that they did not have an adequate opportunity to read most of them. In particular, no one pointed out the arbitration clause in the documents they signed. The court found that because applicable state law provided that one who signs a written contract is conclusively presumed to know and assent to its contents, absent fraud or coercion, plaintiffs' signatures were sufficient to render the agreements enforceable.

Similarly, the arbitration clause in plaintiff's "Employee Agreement" is enforceable under both District of Columbia and Virginia law. In both the District of Columbia and Virginia, a signature on a contract indicates "mutuality of assent" and a party is bound by the contract unless he or she can show special circumstances relieving him or her of such an obligation. *See Ayers v. Mosby* (Va. 1998) ("In the absence of fraud, duress, or mutual mistake, a person having the capacity to understand a written instrument who reads it, or without reading it or having it read to her, signs it, is bound by her signature"); *First Virginia Bank-Colonial v. Masri* (Va. 1993) ("While [defendant] testified that he did not read the language on the reverse side of the wire transfer agreement, he is nevertheless bound by that language. In the absence of fraud, duress, or mutual mistake, an individual having the capacity to understand a written document, who signs that document without reading it, is bound by his signature."); *Mueller v. Commonwealth* (Va. 1993) ("[I]t is hornbook law that one who signs a contract ... will normally be bound by its terms and that ignorance ... of its terms will not ordinarily affect the liability of such person under the contract." (citations and internal quotations omitted)).

Plaintiff has failed to show any special circumstances that would negate her assent to the contract. The offer of employment letter signed by plaintiff states that the Employee Agreement is attached, and that "[y]our signature on these documents acknowledges your understanding of the requirements contained therein, and your agreement to abide by them." The "Employment Agreement" was only two pages long. The fact that plaintiff does not recall signing the agreement, that she had other paperwork to complete, or that the arbitration provision was not explained to her is insufficient to render the contract unenforceable.[5]

Plaintiff's argument that the arbitration clause is unenforceable because it does not contain a clear waiver of statutory rights is also unavailing. Plaintiff cites *Bailey v. Federal National Mortgage Ass'n*, for the proposition that "an employee does not waive a statutorily protected right unless the undertaking is 'explicitly stated' and any such 'waiver must be clear and unmistakable.'" 209 F.3d 740, 747 (quoting *Wright v. Universal Maritime Serv. Corp.* (1998)). The question in *Bailey* was whether an agreement to arbitrate existed between an employer and an existing employee when the employer unilaterally implemented a Dispute Resolution Policy requiring arbitration of job-related claims, but the employee had never indicated that he agreed to the policy or signed any agreement to that effect. The Court found that no meeting of the minds, and therefore no enforceable contract, existed. In its discussion of this issue, the Court noted in a parenthetical citation that in *Wright*, the Supreme Court held that a general arbitration clause *in a collective bargaining agreement* does not waive an employee's right to a judicial forum for a claim of employment discrimination unless such a waiver is clear and unmistakable.

Here, plaintiff is not waiving any substantive rights but simply subjecting her claims to a different forum. It is "clear" that statutory claims are fully subject to binding arbitration outside of the context of collective bargaining. *Cole v. Burns Int'l Sec. Servs.* (D.D.C. 1996), *aff'd,* (D.C. Cir. 1997). "[B]y agreeing to arbitrate a statutory claim, a party does not forego the substantive rights afforded by the statute; it only submits to their resolution in an arbitral, rather than judicial, forum." *Id.* (quoting *Gilmer v. Interstate/Johnson Lane Corp.* (1991) (citations omitted). As discussed above, plaintiff's waiver of the judicial forum is valid under applicable contract law and is not subject to any additional requirements.

III. The FAA Does Not Preclude Dismissal of an Action Pending Arbitration When All Issues Before the Court Are Subject to Arbitration

The FAA provides that once arbitration is compelled, the court "shall on application of one of the parties stay the trial of the terms of the agreement, providing that applicant for the stay is not in default in proceeding with such arbitration." 9 U.S.C. § 3. However, a court is not precluded from dismissing a claim after compelling arbitration "in the proper circumstances," including when all issues raised in the complaint must be submitted to arbitration. *Cole* (citation omitted). Plaintiff does not dispute that all of her claims fall within the *scope* of the agreement, but asks that a stay be entered to allow plaintiff to exercise her post-arbitration appeal rights without having to refile the action. The Courts finds, however, that because all of plaintiffs claims are subject to arbitration, dismissal of this action is within the discretion of the Court and is appropriate.

CONCLUSION

For the foregoing reasons, defendant's motion to dismiss and to compel arbitration is granted.

ORDER

It is hereby ORDERED that defendant's motion to dismiss and to compel arbitration ... is GRANTED.

Plaintiff's complaint is dismissed with prejudice.

[5] Moreover, the fact that plaintiff had a legal education and two law degrees supports that plaintiff should be bound by the terms of the contract she signed. *See Cremin v. Merrill Lynch Pierce Fenner & Smith, Inc.* (N.D.Ill. 1997) (holding because "[plaintiff] is well-educated, with an MBA in finance from Northwestern University, and intelligent," and the arbitration clause was conspicuous and clear, "it is fair to apply the elementary rule of contract law that one is presumed to know the contents of a signed agreement.").

Notes and Questions

1. The plaintiff focuses on the validity of the arbitration clause and fundamental contract arguments. Why does the court conclude the clause is enforceable? How do the precedents cited by the court help to guide its consideration?

2. Do you think the fact that the plaintiff had been trained in the law influenced the court's analysis?

3. Why does the court not to stay this matter, as the plaintiff requested?

4. This case concerns a challenge to arbitration compelled by a contractual agreement; the next addresses alternative dispute resolution mandated by state law.

WOODS v. HOLY CROSS HOSPITAL
591 F.2d 1164 (5th Cir. 1979)

TJOFLAT, Circuit Judge:

In this case we are called upon to examine portions of Florida's Medical Malpractice Law and determine whether its mandate that a medical malpractice claimant participate in a mediation process prior to bringing an action in court must be enforced by a federal district court in a diversity case. For the reasons set forth below, we find that this requirement meets federal constitutional standards and must be applied in such an action.

On July 21, 1975, Nellie Woods, a citizen of Ohio and the administratrix of the estate of her late husband, John N. Woods, filed an action in federal district court in which she claimed damages pursuant to Florida's Wrongful Death Act for Mr. Woods's death. The alleged cause of death was medical malpractice committed by two physicians and a hospital, all named as defendants. Their malpractice insurers were later added as parties-defendant. Jurisdiction was based upon diversity of citizenship, 28 U.S.C. § 1332 (1976). The defendants separately moved to dismiss Mrs. Woods's complaint, alleging that her failure to abide by the mediation panel requirement of Florida Statutes section 768.44 precluded her action. The district court granted the motions to dismiss on the ground that Mrs. Woods had failed to perform a condition precedent to her suit by not proceeding before a Florida malpractice mediation panel. This appeal was taken by Mrs. Woods from the final judgment dismissing her complaint.

Mrs. Woods has raised various issues in this appeal. [She argues that] Florida Medical Malpractice Law violates federal ... right to jury trial standards. We dismiss her other arguments as nonmeritorious. We will discuss Mrs. Woods's major arguments seriatim after we set forth the relevant Florida statutory scheme.

In 1975 the Florida Legislature found as follows:

> WHEREAS, the cost of purchasing medical professional liability insurance for doctors and other health care providers has skyrocketed in the past few months; and

> WHEREAS, it is not uncommon to find physicians in high-risk categories paying premiums in excess of $20,000 annually; and

> WHEREAS, the consumer ultimately must bear the financial burdens created by the high cost of insurance; and

> WHEREAS, without some legislative relief, doctors will be forced to curtail their practices, retire, or practice defensive medicine at increased cost to the citizens of Florida; and

> WHEREAS, the problem has reached crisis proportion in Florida . . ..

Preamble to 1975 Fla.Laws ch. 75-9. Accordingly, it adopted the Medical Malpractice Reform Act of 1975. The predecessor to sections 768.44 and .47 was contained in that provision.

Florida Statutes section 768.44 creates a system under which prior to bringing an action against a medical or osteopathic physician, podiatrist, hospital or health maintenance organization in any court of the state a medical malpractice claimant must submit his claim to a medical liability mediation panel by filing the claim on special forms with the clerk of a state circuit court. If he fails so to file he is precluded from bringing any action based on medical malpractice in "any court of [the state of Florida]."

After a claim is properly filed all defendants must answer within twenty days or else a claimant may proceed in court. If answers are timely filed a claim is heard by a mediation panel consisting of a state circuit judge, an attorney, and a licensed physician. The circuit judge is chosen in a "blind" system; the attorney and physician are chosen from lists compiled by the chief judge of each judicial circuit in Florida. The attorney and physician panel members are each paid one hundred dollars for each day they spend on the panel; both parties to a claim are assessed equally for the payment of these fees. A hearing must be held within ten months of the filing of a claim with the circuit court clerk or else the mediation panel's jurisdiction terminates and a normal lawsuit may be filed; any applicable statute of limitations is tolled from the filing of a claim until at least sixty days after a mediation panel either mails its decision to the parties or has its jurisdiction otherwise terminated. Discovery rules of the Florida Rules of Civil Procedure are applied at panel hearings, and procedural and evidentiary rules are less formal than in ordinary civil litigation. Parties may subpoena and cross-examine witnesses at hearings; counsel for the parties may make opening and closing statements. The judge presiding over a hearing is precluded from presiding over any subsequent judicial proceedings arising out of the claim at issue, and other panel members may act as neither counsel nor witnesses at any subsequent trial of the claim.

Within thirty days of the completion of any hearing a panel files a written decision in which, using specified language, it finds the defendant was or was not negligent and accordingly is or is not liable to the plaintiff. A panel member may concur or dissent to the decision in writing. If liability is found and the parties so agree the panel may proceed to help the parties reach a settlement. In this regard, the panel may recommend a reasonable range of damages, but may not recommend punitive damages. Any damage recommendation is not admissible into evidence at any subsequent trial.

Section 768.47 provides that if any party rejects the decision of a mediation panel he may institute litigation based on his claim in an appropriate court. The panel findings are admissible into evidence in any subsequent litigation, but specific findings of fact are inadmissible. Parties may comment upon panel findings in opening statement or closing argument just as on any other evidence introduced at trial. If there was a dissenting opinion to the panel's decision the numerical vote of the panel is also admissible into evidence. If a defendant fails to participate in the mediation panel process the plaintiff may disclose this fact in any subsequent civil action. Panel members may not be called to testify as witnesses concerning the merits of a case. The jury is instructed that a panel's finding is not binding upon it but should be accorded such weight as the jury chooses to ascribe to it.

...

Mrs. Woods [contends] sections 768.44 and .47 ... combine unconstitutionally to restrict her seventh amendment right to a jury trial. Two seventh amendment questions are presented: (1) does making screening a condition precedent to a jury trial unduly burden the right to such a trial; and (2) does the admission into evidence of a mediation panel's finding on liability usurp the function of a jury.

1. *Mandatory Screening and the Seventh Amendment:*

Mrs. Woods argues that the delay incident to the mediation prerequisite unconstitutionally infringes upon her seventh amendment right. This contention is without merit. The seventh amendment "does not prescribe at what stage of an action a trial by jury must, if demanded, be had, or what conditions may be imposed upon the demand of such a trial, consistently with preserving the right to it." *Capital Traction Co. v. Hof* (1899). Nothing in the seventh amendment requires that a jury make its findings at the earliest possible moment in the course of civil litigation; the requirement is only that the jury *ultimately* determine the issues of fact if they cannot be settled by the parties or determined as a matter of law. ... If a federal court may constitutionally refer a complicated matter to an auditor or special master, it may certainly utilize a medical liability mediation panel without violating the dictates of the seventh amendment. Once the panel has considered the evidence and rendered its decision either party to the claim is free to proceed to a jury trial; the jury will remain the ultimate arbiter of the case. So long as Mrs. Woods's right to have her claim fully and finally determined by a jury is preserved, she cannot be heard to complain that her right to a jury trial has been unconstitutionally restricted.

2. *Admission of Panel Findings in Evidence at Subsequent Trial and the Seventh Amendment:*

Mrs. Woods maintains that the presentation of panel findings on liability at a subsequent jury trial will so influence the jury that it will be unable independently to examine the question of liability, particularly since section 768.47 precludes the calling of panel members to testify regarding the merits of the case. We are unable to accept this contention. Section 768.47(2) specifically provides that "[t]he jury shall be instructed that the conclusion of the hearing panel shall not be binding, but shall be accorded such weight as they choose to ascribe to it." The panel finding is a particularly relevant, but not conclusive, form of evidence. The parties to a malpractice dispute are free to present the same witnesses and exhibits before the trial jury that they presented to the mediation panel, and the jury may draw its own conclusions from their testimony, even if in so doing it rejects the panel's finding. We observe that the United States Supreme Court has on several occasions approved the admission of expert findings into evidence before a jury and has consistently rejected seventh amendment challenges to such a procedure. In *Meeker v. Lehigh Valley Railroad* (1915), the Supreme Court held that a provision in the Interstate Commerce Act providing that findings and orders of the Interstate Commerce Commission were admissible as prima facie evidence of the facts stated therein in a suit brought to enforce a reparation award did not violate the seventh amendment. The Court observed that:

> This provision only establishes a rebuttable presumption. It cuts off no defense, interposes no obstacle to a full contestation of all the issues, and takes no question of fact from either court or jury. At most, therefore, it is merely a rule of evidence. It does not abridge the right of trial by jury, or take away any of its incidents. Nor does it anywise work a denial of due process of law.

Id. Unlike the provision upheld in *Meeker,* section 768.47 establishes no prima facie rule of evidence; it merely states that the jury should give panel findings such weight as it feels appropriate. ...

Mrs. Woods relies heavily on two state court decisions, *Wright v. Du Page Hospital Association* (Ill. 1976), and *Simon v. St. Elizabeth Medical Center* (Ohio 1976), for her proposition that the admissibility requirement is invalid. ... *Wright* does not in fact stand for this point. *Simon* may be disregarded as an aberrational decision — its holding on the jury trial issue has been implicitly or specifically rejected in a number of other state cases. We join in their rejection of *Simon* and accordingly hold that the admissibility provision of section 768.47 does not unconstitutionally usurp the function of a seventh amendment-required jury.

For the reasons set forth above, we find that the district court correctly held that Florida Statutes sections 768.44 and .47 are constitutional, that they must be applied by a federal court in a diversity case, and that Mrs. Woods's complaint must be dismissed for failure to abide by the mediation requirement of section 768.44.

AFFIRMED.

Notes and Questions

1. Why does the court conclude the delay occasioned by mandatory mediation did not result in a violation of the plaintiff's Seventh Amendment right to a jury trial? What does the Seventh Amendment require?

2. Does the admission into evidence at trial of the mediation panel's conclusions interfere with the role of the jury? How does the statute seek to ameliorate any potential prejudice? Do you believe such an effort is likely to be successful? Does your answer depend upon the extent to which the court's instructions are clear and the individual jurors receptive to those instructions?

3. Federal constitutional arguments are not the only means by which procedural matters can be challenged. Each state has its own constitution and, while many state constitutional provisions mirror their federal counterparts, others may be unique to a particular state. In fact, several state constitutions protect an individual's right to have access to the courts of the state, and the question in the next case is whether such a right is violated by compelling the parties to participate in some kind of alternate dispute resolution process before proceeding to litigate their dispute.

COMMONWEALTH OF KENTUCKY v. CLAYCOMB
___ S.W.3d ___ (Ky. 2018)

OPINION OF THE COURT BY CHIEF JUSTICE MINTON.

Of all the rights guaranteed by state constitutions but absent from the federal Bill of Rights, the guarantee of a right of access to the courts to obtain a remedy for injury is possibly the most important. Kentucky's version of this guarantee, referred to in our jurisprudence as the open-courts provision, appears in the Bill of Rights, Section 14, of the Kentucky Constitution, which states: "All courts shall be open, and every person for an injury done him in his lands, goods, person or reputation, shall have remedy by due course of law, and right and justice administered without sale, denial or delay."

The Kentucky General Assembly in its 2017 regular session enacted Kentucky Revised Statutes ("KRS") Chapter 216C, the Medical Review Panel Act, establishing a mandatory process to delay certain medical-malpractice claimants' ability to access immediately the courts of the Commonwealth by creating medical-review panels and requiring a panel's opinion about the merits of the claimant's proposed complaint against health-care providers before the claimant may file suit. This case presents to us on discretionary review a legal challenge to KRS Chapter 216C in which the trial court declared the Act unconstitutional on several grounds. We hold that because the Act delays access to the courts of the Commonwealth for the adjudication of common-law claims, Chapter 216C violates Section 14 of the Kentucky Constitution.

I. BACKGROUND.

A. The General Assembly enacts the Medical Review Panels Act.

KRS Chapter 216C "provides for the establishment of medical review panels to review proposed malpractice complaints against health care providers. . . ." KRS 216C.020(1) makes clear:

All malpractice and malpractice-related claims against a health care provider, other than claims validly agreed for submission to a binding arbitration procedure, shall be reviewed by a medical review panel. Such an action may not be commenced in a court in Kentucky before:

(a) The claimant's proposed complaint has been presented to a medical review panel established under this chapter; and

(b) An opinion is given by the panel. If the panel has not given its opinion within nine (9) months after the filing of the proposed complaint, the plaintiff may commence the action in court.

KRS 216C.010(4) defines *health care provider* to mean:

[A]ny health facility as defined in KRS 216B.015, or a provider, including natural persons, of health care or health services, including, but not limited to those licensed, certified, registered under, or subject to KRS 194A.700 to 194A.729 or KRS Chapter 310, 311, 311A, 311B, 312, 313, 314, 314A, 315, 319, 319A, 320, 327, 333, 334A, or 335 and the current and former officers, directors, administrators, agents, or employees of any such persons or entities acting within the course and scope of their office, employment, or agency.

In other words, as the trial court noted, the medical review panel must first review any malpractice or malpractice-related claim filed on or after June 29, 2017, against any individual or entity bearing some sort of relationship to the health care profession and industry, "other than claims validly agreed for submission to a binding arbitration procedure," before that claim is subject to adjudication:

Any action involving a dependent claim accruing after June 29, 2017, shall be immediately and automatically stayed until:

(a) The claimant's proposed complaint against the health care provider has been presented to a medical review panel established under this chapter and an opinion is given by the panel; or

(b) Nine (9) months after the filing of the proposed complaint if the panel has not given its opinion.

The panel does not engage in any adjudication of a claimant's claim. Rather, the entire purpose and function of the panel is to generate an opinion about the merits of the claim, an opinion that may or may not have any evidentiary usefulness in a court of law. Finally, Chapter 216C does allow the parties to bypass medical review panel review, but only if *all* parties involved in the action agree.

B. The trial court declares the Medical Review Panels Act unconstitutional.

Ezra Claycomb, a minor, by and through his next friend, natural guardian, and parent, Tonya Claycomb, individually and on behalf of all others similarly situated, sued the Commonwealth in the trial court, challenging the constitutionality of Chapter 216C. Ezra suffers from severe brain damage and cerebral palsy allegedly caused by medical malpractice. But for Chapter 216C, Claycomb could immediately file a medical-malpractice suit in circuit court.

... The trial court found the entirety of Chapter 216C unconstitutional and permanently enjoined the Commonwealth from enforcing any of its provisions.

The Commonwealth then requested in the Court of Appeals emergency relief from the trial court's order under Kentucky Rule of Civil Procedure ("CR") 65.08(7) and suspension of the enforcement of the permanent injunction under CR 65.08(2), which the Court of Appeals granted. This Court then accepted transfer to decide the merits of the case.

II. ANALYSIS.

[Having clarified that Section 14 applies] to all departments of government, we turn to evaluating its implications for the case at hand. In our review, we must remember our duty to presume that the statutes we address are constitutional. ...

We have held that Section 14 protects "[t]he right of every individual in society to access a system of justice to redress wrongs," *O'Bryan v. Hedgespeth* (Ky. 1995), and such protection "is basic and fundamental to our common law heritage." *Fireman's Fund Ins. Co. v. Government Emps. Ins. Co.* (Ky 1982). The right to a remedy protected in Section 14 applies to actions for death and personal injuries, among other types of actions. And medical-malpractice claims fall under this category of claims.

...

The General Assembly, through Chapter 216C, has created a mandatory delay affecting the ability of all medical-malpractice claimants to seek *any* redress, unless all parties either "validly agree[] . . . to a binding arbitration procedure" or agree to bypass the medical review panel process. Chapter 216C takes away the ability of medical-malpractice claimants to seek immediate redress in the forum of the claimant's choosing. Chapter 216C contravenes one of the main purposes of Section 14 — to prohibit legislatively created delays in the ability of a claimant to seek immediate redress in the courts of the Commonwealth for common-law personal injury....

Section 14 provides for courts to be "open." Section 14 affords "every person for an injury done him in his . . . person . . . remedy by due course of law, and right and justice administered without . . . delay." Forcing a medical-malpractice claimant seeking immediate redress for an alleged common-law personal-injury to be at the mercy of the other parties involved when attempting to bypass the panel process cannot satisfy Section 14's mandate that "[a]ll courts . . . be open" and every Kentuckian "shall have remedy by due course of law, and right and justice administered without . . . delay."

Admittedly, delays are inherent in every adjudicatory proceeding. What makes the delay imposed by Chapter 216C unconstitutional is the General Assembly's *usurpation* of a claimant's freedom to access the adjudicatory method of his or her choosing at the time of his or her choosing. Chapter 216C is in contravention of Section 14 because *no adjudication whatsoever* takes place of a medical-malpractice claimant's claim unless a valid agreement has been made to arbitrate or bypass the panel process. Claimants may only seek immediate redress for their common-law personal-injury claims through arbitration or the courts if, and only if, the adverse parties agree to proceed through arbitration or the courts. This is an untenable restriction on the exercise of the individual's right to receive "remedy by due course of law, and right and justice administered without . . . delay" from an "open" court system.

The mandatory imposition of a delay in seeking immediate redress for a common-law personal-injury claim in the adjudicatory forum of the claimant's choosing cannot amount to "due course of law," because it is as though *no* "course of law" is taking place whatsoever. No "right and justice" is being "administered" at all. And, not only have the courts become closed, in contravention of the mandate that they "shall be open," but seemingly every dispute-resolution process for malpractice claims has been closed, unless all parties agree to arbitrate or bypass the panel process.

Justice Keller suggests that we have failed to consider what the phrase "due course of law" was intended to entail, seemingly glancing over the wise words of the Kansas Supreme Court that we borrow:

> It is not an easy task to deduce either from reason or the authorities a satisfactory definition of . . . "due course of law." We feel safe, however, . . . in saying these terms do not mean any act that the Legislature may have passed if such act does not give to one opportunity to be heard before being deprived or property, liberty, or reputation, or having been deprived of either does not afford a like opportunity of showing the extent of his injury and give an adequate remedy to recover therefor. Whatever these terms may mean more than this, *they do mean due and orderly procedure of*

courts in the ascertainment of damages for injury, to the end that the injured one "shall have remedy" — that is, proper and adequate remedy — thus to be ascertained. *To refuse hearing and remedy for injury after its infliction is small remove from infliction of penalty before and without hearing.*

Hanson v. Krehbiel (Kan. 1904). Chapter 216C "refuse[s] hearing and remedy for injury after its infliction," *id.*, by forcing alleged wronged claimants to wait before they can begin the process of seeking redress. "Those terms . . . 'due course of law' . . . do not mean merely an act of the General Assembly. If they did, every restriction upon legislative authority would be at once abrogated." *Hoke v. Henderson* (N.C. 1833).

Chapter 216C is an unacceptable deviation from the "[t]he right of every individual in society to access a system of justice to redress wrongs." *O'Bryan.* Instead of affording claimants the ability to choose the process of redress they wish at the time they wish to exercise it, Chapter 216C forecloses all immediate access to any system of justice unless the other side agrees. Access to the adjudicatory method of their choice for *immediate* redress of common-law personal-injury claims is a constitutional right that all claimants have, unless they choose to give it up; the government cannot take away that right.

We do note, however, that proceeding through an alternative means of adjudication of a claim is not per se unconstitutional under Section 14. Whether through arbitration, mediation, administrative proceedings, or some other form of dispute-resolution process, if a claimant (1) has voluntarily agreed to seek redress of their common-law claims through that process and (2) has meaningfully waived access to the courts, then proceeding through a dispute-resolution process outside the court system that resulted in a delayed adjudication of a claim would, nevertheless, seem to pass constitutional muster under Section 14. But under Chapter 216C, common-law personal-injury claimants have no ability to seek *any immediate redress from the adjudicatory forum of their choosing* unless all parties agree to bypass the panel process. Under these circumstances, with their backs against the wall, claimants choosing to arbitrate cannot be said to have meaningfully waived their right to immediate access to the courts.

We must also point out that the remedy guarantee of Section 14 applies only to claims, "for an injury done [to a claimant] in his lands, goods, person or reputation." And the protections of Section 14 apply only to *claims originating out of the common law.* If the legislature affords a right to claimants outside the common law, then a delay in adjudication of that claim is not per se unconstitutional under Section 14. Section 14 only prevents the legislature from encroaching upon the realm of the judiciary, the creator of the common law, by imposing mandatory delays in the adjudication of common-law claims grounded in claims "for an injury done [to the claimant] in his lands, goods, person or reputation." Here, medical-malpractice claims, a subset of personal-injury and wrongful-death claims, have been a recognized part of the common law for centuries, and as such, the legislature cannot delay claimants from seeking immediate redress of such claims through the courts.

Lastly, there is no support, either from the text of Section 14, or from case law interpreting that provision, to interpose a "reasonableness" evaluation of the delay to determine if a delay can, in some circumstances, be constitutionally tolerable. ... "It is hornbook law that in interpreting Constitutions the words employed therein should be given the meaning and significance that they possessed at the time they were employed, and the one that the delegates of the convention that framed the instrument, and the people who voted their approval of it, intended to express and impart." *City of Lexington v. Thompson* (Ky. 1933). Section 14, originally written and adopted in 1792, does not proscribe the creation of "undue" or "unreasonable" delay on a Kentuckian's access to due course of law; Section 14 plainly proscribes delay.

...

III. CONCLUSION.

Because Chapter 216C violates Section 14 of the Kentucky Constitution, the Act is void in its entirety. Accordingly, we affirm, for the reasons stated in this opinion, the judgment of the trial court.

[Concurring opinion of Cunningham, J., omitted.]

KELLER, J., CONCURRING IN RESULT ONLY:

I concur in the result, here, because the MRPA clearly interferes with a fundamental right to access the courts in an unreasonably broad way. However, I cannot say that *any measure* the legislature may create to impose procedural steps *prior* to the bringing of an action under § 14 would *always* be unconstitutional. By thus holding, we begin to invade the role of the legislature and tie the General Assembly's hands. The MRPA overstepped constitutional bounds. But I do not agree that any similar measure will, *ipso facto,* violate § 14 because it creates *any* delay before bringing an action. Therefore, I concur in the majority's result only.

Cunningham and Wright, JJ., join.

Notes and Questions

1. What interest does Article 14 of the Kentucky Constitution protect? Why might the legislature have enacted the requirement that the parties appear before the medical-practice review panel or participate in binding arbitration?

2. In what way does the statute restrict the plaintiff's choice in this instance? How does this restriction differ from other delays that might occur in "due course"?

3. What are the conditions in which requiring litigants to proceed with an alternative dispute resolution process prior to adjudication will be constitutional under Article 14?

4. What are the limits of Article 14 on the legislature's ability to require claims that would be otherwise litigated to be subject to some kind of ex ante alternative dispute resolution?

Chapter Three
Notice: Constitutional and Statutory Dimensions

For a court to entertain a lawsuit, it must have valid jurisdiction over the defendant (personal jurisdiction), the authority to hear the kind of suit the plaintiff proposes (subject matter jurisdiction) and the defendant must be properly made aware of the impending suit—in other words, proper notice. Notice lies at the heart of due process, as you will read in *Mullane v. Central Hanover Bank & Trust Co.*, below, along with then opportunity to be heard. This chapter focuses on the constitutional and statutory dimensions of notice. We begin with the constitutional requirements for notice as initially explained by the Supreme Court in *Mullane* and then turn to the requirements in the litigation context as embodied in the Federal Rules of Civil Procedure.

A. Constitutional Dimensions

The constitutional sufficiency of notice arises in many contexts outside litigation, but in the basic question is the same: did someone receive adequate notice that he or she might be deprived of some property or liberty interest? You will study the nature of constitutionally protected property and liberty interests in your constitutional law course; for our purposes, the interests at stake are property in its fundamental forms—money, real estate, etc. Due process, as you will see, does not require that the means chosen to inform a party be 100 percent certain to work; rather, the adequacy of notice depends upon the circumstances of the case and the effectiveness of the means chosen as compared to other available alternatives, as you will see in the cases that follow.

MULLANE v. CENTRAL HANOVER BANK & TRUST CO.
339 U.S. 306 (1950)

MR. JUSTICE JACKSON delivered the opinion of the Court.

This controversy questions the constitutional sufficiency of notice to beneficiaries on judicial settlement of accounts by the trustee of a common trust fund established under the New York Banking Law. The New York Court of Appeals considered and overruled objections that the statutory notice contravenes requirements of the Fourteenth Amendment and that by allowance of the account beneficiaries were deprived of property without due process of law.

Common trust fund legislation is addressed to a problem appropriate for state action. Mounting overheads have made administration of small trusts undesirable to corporate trustees. In order that donors and testators of moderately sized trusts may not be denied the service of corporate fiduciaries, the District of Columbia and some thirty states other than New York have permitted pooling small trust estates into one fund for investment administration. The income, capital gains, losses and expenses of the collective trust are shared by the constituent trusts in proportion to their contribution. By this plan, diversification of risk and economy of management can be extended to those whose capital standing alone would not obtain such advantage.

Statutory authorization for the establishment of such common trust funds is provided in the New York Banking Law. Under this Act a trust company may, with approval of the State Banking Board, establish a common fund and, within prescribed limits, invest therein the assets of an unlimited number of estates, trusts or other funds of which it is trustee. Each participating trust shares ratably in the common fund, but exclusive management and control is in the trust company as trustee, and neither a fiduciary nor any beneficiary of a participating trust is deemed to have ownership in any particular asset or investment of this common fund. The trust company must keep fund assets separate from its own, and in its fiduciary capacity may not deal with itself or any affiliate. Provisions are made for accounting twelve to fifteen months after the establishment of a fund and triennially thereafter. The decree in each such judicial settlement of accounts is made binding and conclusive as to any matter set forth in the account upon everyone having any interest in the common fund or in any participating estate, trust or fund.

In January, 1946, Central Hanover Bank and Trust Company established a common trust fund in accordance with these provisions, and in March, 1947, it petitioned the Surrogate's Court for settlement of its first account as common trustee. During the accounting period a total of 113 trusts, approximately half *inter vivos* and half testamentary, participated in the common trust fund, the gross capital of which was nearly three million dollars. The record does not show the number or residence of the beneficiaries, but they were many and it is clear that some of them were not residents of the State of New York.

The only notice given beneficiaries of this specific application was by publication in a local newspaper in strict compliance with the minimum requirements of N.Y. Banking Law § 100-c (12).... [The] only notice required, and the only one given, was by newspaper publication setting forth merely the name and address of the trust company, the name and the date of establishment of the common trust fund, and a list of all participating estates, trusts or funds.

At the time the first investment in the common fund was made on behalf of each participating estate, however, the trust company, pursuant to the requirements of § 100-c (9), had notified by mail each person of full age and sound mind whose name and address were then known to it and who was "entitled to share in the income therefrom. . . [or] . . . who would be entitled to share in the principal if the event upon which such estate, trust or fund will become distributable should have occurred at the time of sending such notice." Included in the notice was a copy of those provisions of the Act relating to the sending of the notice itself and to the judicial settlement of common trust fund accounts.

Upon the filing of the petition for the settlement of accounts, appellant was, by order of the court pursuant to § 100-c (12), appointed special guardian and attorney for all persons known or unknown not otherwise appearing who had or might thereafter have any interest in the income of the common trust fund....

Appellant appeared specially, objecting that notice and the statutory provisions for notice to beneficiaries were inadequate to afford due process under the Fourteenth Amendment, and therefore that the court was without jurisdiction to render a final and binding decree. Appellant's objections were entertained and overruled, the Surrogate holding that the notice required and given was sufficient. A final decree accepting the accounts has been entered, affirmed by the Appellate Division of the Supreme Court, and by the Court of Appeals of the State of New York.

The effect of this decree, as held below, is to settle "all questions respecting the management of the common fund." We understand that every right which beneficiaries would otherwise have against the trust company, either as trustee of the common fund or as trustee of any individual trust, for improper management of the common trust fund during the period covered by the accounting is sealed and wholly terminated by the decree.

[Next we address] the opportunity [the State] must give beneficiaries to contest. Many controversies have raged about the cryptic and abstract words of the Due Process Clause but there can be no doubt that at a minimum they require that deprivation of life, liberty or property by adjudication be preceded by notice and opportunity for hearing appropriate to the nature of the case.

In two ways this proceeding does or may deprive beneficiaries of property. It may cut off their rights to have the trustee answer for negligent or illegal impairments of their interests. Also, their interests are presumably subject to diminution in the proceeding by allowance of fees and expenses to one who, in their names but without their knowledge, may conduct a fruitless or uncompensatory contest. Certainly the proceeding is one in which they may be deprived of property rights and hence notice and hearing must measure up to the standards of due process.

Personal service of written notice within the jurisdiction is the classic form of notice always adequate in any type of proceeding. But the vital interest of the State in bringing any issues as to its fiduciaries to a final settlement can be served only if interests or claims of individuals who are outside of the State can somehow be determined. A construction of the Due Process Clause which would place impossible or impractical obstacles in the way could not be justified.

Against this interest of the State we must balance the individual interest sought to be protected by the Fourteenth Amendment. This is defined by our holding that "The fundamental requisite of due process of law is the opportunity to be heard." *Grannis v. Ordean* (1914). This right to be heard has little reality or worth unless one is informed that the matter is pending and can choose for himself whether to appear or default, acquiesce or contest.

The Court has not committed itself to any formula achieving a balance between these interests in a particular proceeding or determining when constructive notice may be utilized or what test it must meet. Personal service has not in all circumstances been regarded as indispensable to the process due to residents, and it has more often been held unnecessary as to nonresidents. We disturb none of the established rules on these subjects. No decision constitutes a controlling or even a very illuminating precedent for the case before us. But a few general principles stand out in the books.

An elementary and fundamental requirement of due process in any proceeding which is to be accorded finality is notice reasonably calculated, under all the circumstances, to apprise interested parties of the pendency of the action and afford them an opportunity to present their objections. The notice must be of such nature as reasonably to convey the required information, and it must afford a reasonable time for those interested to make their appearance. But if with due regard for the practicalities and peculiarities of the case these conditions are reasonably met, the constitutional requirements are satisfied....

But when notice is a person's due, process which is a mere gesture is not due process. The means employed must be such as one desirous of actually informing the absentee might reasonably adopt to accomplish it. The reasonableness and hence the constitutional validity of any chosen method may be defended on the ground that it is in itself reasonably certain to inform those affected, or, where conditions do not reasonably permit such notice, that the form chosen is not substantially less likely to bring home notice than other of the feasible and customary substitutes.

It would be idle to pretend that publication alone, as prescribed here, is a reliable means of acquainting interested parties of the fact that their rights are before the courts. It is not an accident that the greater number of cases reaching this Court on the question of adequacy of notice have been concerned with actions founded on process constructively served through local newspapers. Chance alone brings to the attention of even a local resident an advertisement in small type inserted in the back pages of a newspaper, and if he makes his home outside the area of the newspaper's normal circulation the odds that the information will never reach him are large indeed. The chance of actual notice is further reduced when, as here, the notice required does not even name those whose attention it is supposed to attract, and does not inform acquaintances who might call it to attention. In weighing its sufficiency on the basis of equivalence with actual notice, we are unable to regard this as more than a feint.

Nor is publication here reinforced by steps likely to attract the parties' attention to the proceeding. It is true that publication traditionally has been acceptable as notification supplemental to other action which in itself may reasonably be expected to convey a warning. The ways of an owner with tangible property are such that he usually arranges means to learn of any direct attack upon his possessory or proprietary rights. ... A state may indulge the assumption that one who has left tangible property in the state either has abandoned it, in which case proceedings against it deprive him of nothing, or that he has left some caretaker under a duty to let him know that it is being jeopardized. ...

In the case before us there is, of course, no abandonment. On the other hand these beneficiaries do have a resident fiduciary as caretaker of their interest in this property. But it is their caretaker who in the accounting becomes their adversary. Their trustee is released from giving notice of jeopardy, and no one else is expected to do so. Not even the special guardian is required or apparently expected to communicate with his ward and client, and, of course, if such a duty were merely transferred from the trustee to the guardian, economy would not be served and more likely the cost would be increased.

This Court has not hesitated to approve of resort to publication as a customary substitute in another class of cases where it is not reasonably possible or practicable to give more adequate warning. Thus it has been recognized that, in the case of persons missing or unknown, employment of an indirect and even a probably futile means of notification is all that the situation permits and creates no constitutional bar to a final decree foreclosing their rights.

Those beneficiaries represented by appellant whose interests or whereabouts could not with due diligence be ascertained come clearly within this category. As to them the statutory notice is sufficient. However great the odds that publication will never reach the eyes of such unknown parties, it is not in the typical case much more likely to fail than any of the choices open to legislators endeavoring to prescribe the best notice practicable.

Nor do we consider it unreasonable for the State to dispense with more certain notice to those beneficiaries whose interests are either conjectural or future or, although they could be discovered upon investigation, do not in due course of business come to knowledge of the common trustee. Whatever searches might be required in another situation under ordinary standards of diligence, in view of the character of the proceedings and the nature of the interests here involved we think them unnecessary. We recognize the practical difficulties and costs that would be attendant on frequent investigations into the status of great numbers of beneficiaries, many of whose interests in the common fund are so remote as to be ephemeral; and we have no doubt that such impracticable and extended searches are not required in the name of due process. The expense of keeping informed from day to day of substitutions among even current income beneficiaries and presumptive remaindermen, to say nothing of the far greater number of contingent beneficiaries, would impose a severe burden on the plan, and would likely dissipate its advantages. These are practical matters in which we should be reluctant to disturb the judgment of the state authorities.

Accordingly we overrule appellant's constitutional objections to published notice insofar as they are urged on behalf of any beneficiaries whose interests or addresses are unknown to the trustee.

As to known present beneficiaries of known place of residence, however, notice by publication stands on a different footing. Exceptions in the name of necessity do not sweep away the rule that within the limits of practicability notice must be such as is reasonably calculated to reach interested parties. Where the names and post office addresses of those affected by a proceeding are at hand, the reasons disappear for resort to means less likely than the mails to apprise them of its pendency.

The trustee has on its books the names and addresses of the income beneficiaries represented by appellant, and we find no tenable ground for dispensing with a serious effort to inform them personally of the accounting, at least by ordinary mail to the record addresses. Certainly sending them a copy of the statute months and perhaps years in advance does not answer this purpose. The trustee periodically remits their income to them, and we think that they might reasonably expect that with or apart from their remittances word might come to them personally that steps were being taken affecting their interests.

We need not weigh contentions that a requirement of personal service of citation on even the large number of known resident or nonresident beneficiaries would, by reasons of delay if not of expense, seriously interfere with the proper administration of the fund. Of course personal service even without the jurisdiction of the issuing authority serves the end of actual and personal notice, whatever power of compulsion it might lack. However, no such service is required under the circumstances. This type of trust presupposes a large number of small interests. The individual interest does not stand alone but is identical with that of a class. The rights of each in the integrity of the fund and the fidelity of the trustee are shared by many other beneficiaries. Therefore notice reasonably certain to reach most of those interested in objecting is likely to safeguard the interests of all, since any objection sustained would inure to the benefit of all. We think that under such circumstances reasonable risks that notice might not actually reach every beneficiary are justifiable....

The statutory notice to known beneficiaries is inadequate, not because in fact it fails to reach everyone, but because under the circumstances it is not reasonably calculated to reach those who could easily be informed by other means at hand. However it may have been in former times, the mails today are recognized as an efficient and inexpensive means of communication. Moreover, the fact that the trust company has been able to give mailed notice to known beneficiaries at the time the common trust fund was established is persuasive that postal notification at the time of accounting would not seriously burden the plan.

In some situations the law requires greater precautions in its proceedings than the business world accepts for its own purposes. In few, if any, will it be satisfied with less. Certainly it is instructive, in determining the reasonableness of the impersonal broadcast notification here used, to ask whether it would satisfy a prudent man of business, counting his pennies but finding it in his interest to convey information to many persons whose names and addresses are in his files. We are not satisfied that it would. Publication may theoretically be available for all the world to see, but it is too much in our day to suppose that each or any individual beneficiary does or could examine all that is published to see if something may be tucked away in it that affects his property interests. ...

We hold that the notice of judicial settlement of accounts required by the New York Banking Law § 100-c (12) is incompatible with the requirements of the Fourteenth Amendment as a basis for adjudication depriving known persons whose whereabouts are also known of substantial property rights. Accordingly the judgment is reversed and the cause remanded for further proceedings not inconsistent with this opinion.

Reversed.

MR. JUSTICE DOUGLAS took no part in the consideration or decision of this case.

[Dissenting opinion of MR. JUSTICE BURTON, omitted.]

Notes and Questions

1. What is the test for determining the constitutional sufficiency for notice? Is this test more rule or standard? Why might the Court prefer one over the other in the context of notice?

2. Why did the Court not require actual notice be provided to each of the beneficiaries? And why was notice by publication sufficient for the unknown beneficiaries when it seems unlikely actually to have afforded them any real notice?

3. In what way must notice be tailored to the defendant's needs? What factors might a court consider in reviewing the adequacy of notice in a particular case—the defendant's age? Competency? Ability to understand English?

MENNONITE BOARD OF MISSIONS v. ADAMS
462 U.S. 791 (1983)

JUSTICE MARSHALL delivered the opinion of the Court.

This appeal raises the question whether notice by publication and posting provides a mortgagee of real property with adequate notice of a proceeding to sell the mortgaged property for nonpayment of taxes.

I

To secure an obligation to pay $14,000, Alfred Jean Moore executed a mortgage in favor of appellant Mennonite Board of Missions (MBM) on property in Elkhart, Ind., that Moore had purchased from MBM. The mortgage was recorded in the Elkhart County Recorder's Office on March 1, 1973. Under the terms of the agreement, Moore was responsible for paying all of the property taxes. Without MBM's knowledge, however, she failed to pay taxes on the property.

Indiana law provides for the annual sale of real property on which payments of property taxes have been delinquent for 15 months or longer. Prior to the sale, the county auditor must post notice in the county courthouse and publish notice once each week for three consecutive weeks. The owner of the property is entitled to notice by certified mail to his last known address. Until 1980, however, Indiana law did not provide for notice by mail or personal service to mortgagees of property that was to be sold for nonpayment of taxes.

After the required notice is provided, the county treasurer holds a public auction at which the real property is sold to the highest bidder. The purchaser acquires a certificate of sale which constitutes a lien against the real property for the entire amount paid. This lien is superior to all other liens against the property which existed at the time the certificate was issued.

The tax sale is followed by a 2-year redemption period during which the "owner, occupant, lienholder, or other person who has an interest in" the property may redeem the property. To redeem the property an individual must pay the county treasurer a sum sufficient to cover the purchase price of the property at the tax sale and the amount of taxes and special assessments paid by the purchaser following the sale, plus an additional percentage specified in the statute. The county in turn remits the payment to the purchaser of the property at the tax sale.

If no one redeems the property during the statutory redemption period, the purchaser may apply to the county auditor for a deed to the property. Before executing and delivering the deed, the county auditor must notify the former owner that he is still entitled to redeem the property. No notice to the mortgagee is required. If the property is not redeemed within 30 days, the county auditor may then execute and deliver a deed for the property to the purchaser, who thereby acquires "an estate in fee simple absolute, free and clear of all liens and encumbrances."

After obtaining a deed, the purchaser may initiate an action to quiet his title to the property. The previous owner, lienholders, and others who claim to have an interest in the property may no longer redeem the property. They may defeat the title conveyed by the tax deed only by proving, *inter alia*, that the property had not been subject to, or assessed for, the taxes for which it was sold, that the taxes had been paid before the sale, or that the property was properly redeemed before the deed was executed.

In 1977, Elkhart County initiated proceedings to sell Moore's property for nonpayment of taxes. The county provided notice as required under the statute: it posted and published an announcement of the tax sale and mailed notice to Moore by certified mail. MBM was not informed of the pending tax sale either by the County Auditor or by Moore. The property was sold for $1,167.75 to appellee Richard Adams on August 8, 1977. Neither Moore nor MBM appeared at the sale or took steps thereafter to redeem the property. Following the sale of her property, Moore continued to make payments each month to MBM, and as a result MBM did not realize that the property had been sold. On August 16, 1979, MBM first learned of the tax sale. By then the redemption period had run and Moore still owed appellant $8,237.19.

In November 1979, Adams filed a suit in state court seeking to quiet title to the property. In opposition to Adams' motion for summary judgment, MBM contended that it had not received constitutionally adequate notice of the pending tax sale and of the opportunity to redeem the property following the tax sale. The trial court upheld the Indiana tax sale statute against this constitutional challenge. The Indiana Court of Appeals affirmed. We ... now reverse.

II

In *Mullane v. Central Hanover Bank & Trust Co.* (1950), this Court recognized that prior to an action which will affect an interest in life, liberty, or property protected by the Due Process Clause of the Fourteenth Amendment, a State must provide "notice reasonably calculated, under all the circumstances, to apprise interested parties of the pendency of the action and afford them an opportunity to present their objections." Invoking this "elementary and fundamental requirement of due process," the Court held that published notice of an action to settle the accounts of a common trust fund was not sufficient to inform beneficiaries of the trust whose names and addresses were known. The Court explained that notice by publication was not reasonably calculated to provide actual notice of the pending proceeding and was therefore inadequate to inform those who could be notified by more effective means such as personal service or mailed notice....

In subsequent cases, this Court has adhered unwaveringly to the principle announced in *Mullane*. ... Most recently, in *Greene v. Lindsey* (1982), we held that posting a summons on the door of a tenant's apartment was an inadequate means of providing notice of forcible entry and detainer actions.

This case is controlled by the analysis in *Mullane.* To begin with, a mortgagee possesses a substantial property interest that is significantly affected by a tax sale. Under Indiana law, a mortgagee acquires a lien on the owner's property which may be conveyed together with the mortgagor's personal obligation to repay the debt secured by the mortgage. A mortgagee's security interest generally has priority over subsequent claims or liens attaching to the property, and a purchase-money mortgage takes precedence over virtually all other claims or liens including those which antedate the execution of the mortgage. The tax sale immediately and drastically diminishes the value of this security interest by granting the tax-sale purchaser a lien with priority over that of all other creditors. Ultimately, the tax sale may result in the complete nullification of the mortgagee's interest, since the purchaser acquires title free of all liens and other encumbrances at the conclusion of the redemption period.

Since a mortgagee clearly has a legally protected property interest, he is entitled to notice reasonably calculated to apprise him of a pending tax sale. When the mortgagee is identified in a mortgage that is publicly recorded, constructive notice by publication must be supplemented by notice mailed to the mortgagee's last known available address, or by personal service. But unless the mortgagee is not reasonably identifiable, constructive notice alone does not satisfy the mandate of *Mullane.*

Neither notice by publication and posting, nor mailed notice to the property owner, are means "such as one desirous of actually informing the [mortgagee] might reasonably adopt to accomplish it." *Mullane.* Because they are designed primarily to attract prospective purchasers to the tax sale, publication and posting are unlikely to reach those who, although they have an interest in the property, do not make special efforts to keep abreast of such notices. Notice to the property owner, who is not in privity with his creditor and who has failed to take steps necessary to preserve his own property interest, also cannot be expected to lead to actual notice to the mortgagee. The county's use of these less reliable forms of notice is not reasonable where, as here, "an inexpensive and efficient mechanism such as mail service is available." *Greene.*

Personal service or mailed notice is required even though sophisticated creditors have means at their disposal to discover whether property taxes have not been paid and whether tax-sale proceedings are therefore likely to be initiated. In the first place, a mortgage need not involve a complex commercial transaction among knowledgeable parties, and it may well be the least sophisticated creditor whose security interest is threatened by a tax sale. More importantly, a party's ability to take steps to safeguard its interests does not relieve the State of its constitutional obligation. It is true that particularly extensive efforts to provide notice may often be required when the State is aware of a party's inexperience or incompetence. But it does not follow that the State may forgo even the relatively modest administrative burden of providing notice by mail to parties who are particularly resourceful. Notice by mail or other means as certain to ensure actual notice is a minimum constitutional precondition to a proceeding which will adversely affect the liberty or property interests of *any* party, whether unlettered or well versed in commercial practice, if its name and address are reasonably ascertainable. ...

We therefore conclude that the manner of notice provided to appellant did not meet the requirements of the Due Process Clause of the Fourteenth Amendment. Accordingly, the judgment of the Indiana Court of Appeals is reversed, and the cause is remanded for further proceedings not inconsistent with this opinion.

It is so ordered.

JUSTICE O'CONNOR, with whom JUSTICE POWELL and JUSTICE REHNQUIST join, dissenting.

...

It cannot be doubted that the State has a vital interest in the collection of its tax revenues in whatever reasonable manner that it chooses.... The State has an equally strong interest in avoiding the burden imposed by the requirement that it must exercise "reasonable" efforts to ascertain the identity and location of any party with a legally protected interest. In the instant case, that burden is not limited to mailing notice. Rather, the State must have someone check the records and ascertain with respect to each delinquent taxpayer whether there is a mortgagee, perhaps whether the mortgage has been paid off, and whether there is a dependable address.

Against these vital interests of the State, we must weigh the interest possessed by the relevant class—in this case, mortgagees. Contrary to the Court's approach today, this interest may not be evaluated simply by reference to the fact that we have frequently found constructive notice to be inadequate since *Mullane*. Rather, such interest "must be judged in the light of its practical application to the affairs of men as they are ordinarily conducted." *North Laramie Land Co. v. Hoffman* (1925).

[Here, there] is no doubt that the Board could have safeguarded its interest with a minimum amount of effort. The county auctions of property commence by statute on the second Monday of each year. The county auditor is required to post notice in the county courthouse at least three weeks before the date of sale. The auditor is also required to publish notice in two different newspapers once each week for three weeks before the sale. The Board could have supplemented the protection offered by the State with the additional measures suggested by the court below: The Board could have required that Moore provide it with copies of paid tax assessments, or could have required that Moore deposit the tax moneys in an escrow account, or could have itself checked the public records to determine whether the tax assessment had been paid.

When a party is unreasonable in failing to protect its interest despite its ability to do so, due process does not require that the State save the party from its own lack of care. The balance required by *Mullane* clearly weighs in favor of finding that the Indiana statutes satisfied the requirements of due process. Accordingly, I dissent.

Notes and Questions

1. What interest was at stake in this case? Did the weight of that interest affect the analysis in determining whether notice was constitutionally adequate?

2. You should begin to see that the constitutional adequacy of notice exists on a continuum, with publication at one end and in-person notice at the other. In between exists a range of options, including posting, regular mail, and certified or registered mail. What about e-mail?

JONES v. FLOWERS

547 U.S. 220 (2006)

Chief Justice ROBERTS delivered the opinion of the Court.

Before a State may take property and sell it for unpaid taxes, the Due Process Clause of the Fourteenth Amendment requires the government to provide the owner "notice and opportunity for hearing appropriate to the nature of the case." *Mullane v. Central Hanover Bank & Trust Co.* (1950). We granted certiorari to determine whether, when notice of a tax sale is mailed to the owner and returned undelivered, the government must take additional reasonable steps to provide notice before taking the owner's property.

I

In 1967, petitioner Gary Jones purchased a house at 717 North Bryan Street in Little Rock, Arkansas. He lived in the house with his wife until they separated in 1993. Jones then moved into an apartment in Little Rock, and his wife continued to live in the North Bryan Street house. Jones paid his mortgage each month for 30 years, and the mortgage company paid Jones' property taxes. After Jones paid off his mortgage in 1997, the property taxes went unpaid, and the property was certified as delinquent.

In April 2000, respondent Mark Wilcox, the Commissioner of State Lands (Commissioner), attempted to notify Jones of his tax delinquency, and his right to redeem the property, by mailing a certified letter to Jones at the North Bryan Street address. The packet of information stated that unless Jones redeemed the property, it would be subject to public sale two years later on April 17, 2002. Nobody was home to sign for the letter, and nobody appeared at the post office to retrieve the letter within the next 15 days. The post office returned the unopened packet to the Commissioner marked "unclaimed."

Two years later, and just a few weeks before the public sale, the Commissioner published a notice of public sale in the Arkansas Democrat Gazette. No bids were submitted, which permitted the State to negotiate a private sale of the property. Several months later, respondent Linda Flowers submitted a purchase offer. The Commissioner mailed another certified letter to Jones at the North Bryan Street address, attempting to notify him that his house would be sold to Flowers if he did not pay his taxes. Like the first letter, the second was also returned to the Commissioner marked "unclaimed." Flowers purchased the house, which the parties stipulated in the trial court had a fair market value of $80,000, for $21,042.15. Immediately after the 30-day period for postsale redemption passed, Flowers had an unlawful detainer notice delivered to the property. The notice was served on Jones' daughter, who contacted Jones and notified him of the tax sale.

Jones filed a lawsuit in Arkansas state court against the Commissioner and Flowers, alleging that the Commissioner's failure to provide notice of the tax sale and of Jones' right to redeem resulted in the taking of his property without due process. The Commissioner and Flowers moved for summary judgment on the ground that the two unclaimed letters sent by the Commissioner were a constitutionally adequate attempt at notice, and Jones filed a cross-motion for summary judgment. The trial court granted summary judgment in favor of the Commissioner and Flowers. It concluded that the Arkansas tax sale statute, which set forth the notice procedure followed by the Commissioner, complied with constitutional due process requirements.

Jones appealed, and the Arkansas Supreme Court affirmed the trial court's judgment. The court noted our precedent stating that due process does not require actual notice, and it held that attempting to provide notice by certified mail satisfied due process in the circumstances presented.

We granted certiorari to resolve a conflict among the Circuits and State Supreme Courts concerning whether the Due Process Clause requires the government to take additional reasonable steps to notify a property owner when notice of a tax sale is returned undelivered. We hold that when mailed notice of a tax sale is returned unclaimed, the State must take additional reasonable steps to attempt to provide notice to the property owner before selling his property, if it is practicable to do so. Under the circumstances presented here, additional reasonable steps were available to the State. We therefore reverse the judgment of the Arkansas Supreme Court.

II

A

Due process does not require that a property owner receive actual notice before the government may take his property. Rather, we have stated that due process requires the government to provide "notice reasonably calculated, under all the circumstances, to apprise interested parties of the pendency of the action and afford them an opportunity to present their objections." *Mullane*. The Commissioner argues that once the State provided notice reasonably calculated to apprise Jones of the impending tax sale by mailing him a certified letter, due process was satisfied. The Arkansas statutory scheme is reasonably calculated to provide notice, the Commissioner continues, because it provides for notice by certified mail to an address that the property owner is responsible for keeping up to date. The Commissioner notes this Court's ample precedent condoning notice by mail, and adds that the Arkansas scheme exceeds constitutional requirements by requiring the Commissioner to use certified mail.

It is true that this Court has deemed notice constitutionally sufficient if it was reasonably calculated to reach the intended recipient when sent. In each of these cases, the government attempted to provide notice and heard nothing back indicating that anything had gone awry, and we stated that "[t]he reasonableness and hence the constitutional validity of [the] chosen method may be defended on the ground that it is in itself reasonably certain to inform those affected." *Mullane*. We have never addressed whether due process entails further responsibility when the government becomes aware prior to the taking that its attempt at notice has failed. That is a new wrinkle, and we have explained that the "notice required will vary with circumstances and conditions." *Walker v. City of Hutchinson* (1956). The question presented is whether such knowledge on the government's part is a "circumstance and condition" that varies the "notice required."

The Courts of Appeals and State Supreme Courts have addressed this question on frequent occasions, and most have decided that when the government learns its attempt at notice has failed, due process requires the government to do something more before real property may be sold in a tax sale. Many States already require in their statutes that the government do more than simply mail notice to delinquent owners, either at the outset or as a follow-up measure if initial mailed notice is ineffective.

In *Mullane*, we stated that "when notice is a person's due . . . [t]he means employed must be such as one desirous of actually informing the absentee might reasonably adopt to accomplish it," and that assessing the adequacy of a particular form of notice requires balancing the "interest of the State" against "the individual interest sought to be protected by the Fourteenth Amendment." ... In this case, we evaluate the adequacy of notice prior to the State extinguishing a property owner's interest in a home.

We do not think that a person who actually desired to inform a real property owner of an impending tax sale of a house he owns would do nothing when a certified letter sent to the owner is returned unclaimed. If the Commissioner prepared a stack of letters to mail to delinquent taxpayers, handed them to the postman, and then watched as the departing postman accidentally dropped the letters down a storm drain, one would certainly expect the Commissioner's office to prepare a new stack of letters and send them again. No one "desirous of actually informing" the owners would simply shrug his shoulders as the letters disappeared and say "I tried." Failure to follow up would be unreasonable, despite the fact that the letters were reasonably calculated to reach their intended recipients when delivered to the postman.

By the same token, when a letter is returned by the post office, the sender will ordinarily attempt to resend it, if it is practicable to do so. This is especially true when, as here, the subject matter of the letter concerns such an important and irreversible prospect as the loss of a house. Although the State may have made a reasonable calculation of how to reach Jones, it had good reason to suspect when the notice was returned that Jones was no better off than if the notice had never been sent. ... Deciding to take no further action is not what someone "desirous of actually informing" Jones would do; such a person would take further reasonable steps if any were available.

In prior cases, we have required the government to consider unique information about an intended recipient regardless of whether a statutory scheme is reasonably calculated to provide notice in the ordinary case. In *Robinson v. Hanrahan* (1972), we held that notice of forfeiture proceedings sent to a vehicle owner's home address was inadequate when the State knew that the property owner was in prison. In *Covey v. Town of Somers* (1956), we held that notice of foreclosure by mailing, posting, and publication was inadequate when town officials knew that the property owner was incompetent and without a guardian's protection.

The Commissioner points out that in these cases, the State was aware of such information *before* it calculated how best to provide notice. But it is difficult to explain why due process would have settled for something less if the government had learned after notice was sent, but before the taking occurred, that the property owner was in prison or was incompetent. Under *Robinson* and *Covey*, the government's knowledge that notice pursuant to the normal procedure was ineffective triggered an obligation on the government's part to take additional steps to effect notice. That knowledge was one of the "practicalities and peculiarities of the case," *Mullane*, that the Court took into account in determining whether constitutional requirements were met. It should similarly be taken into account in assessing the adequacy of notice in this case. The dissent dismisses the State's knowledge that its notice was ineffective as "learned long after the fact" (opinion of Thomas, J.), but the notice letter was promptly returned to the State two to three weeks after it was sent, and the Arkansas statutory regime precludes the State from taking the property for two *years* while the property owner may exercise his right to redeem.

It is certainly true, as the Commissioner and Solicitor General contend, that the failure of notice in a specific case does not establish the inadequacy of the attempted notice; in that sense, the constitutionality of a particular procedure for notice is assessed *ex ante,* rather than *post hoc.* But if a feature of the State's chosen procedure is that it promptly provides additional information to the government about the effectiveness of notice, it does not contravene the *ex ante* principle to consider what the government does with that information in assessing the adequacy of the chosen procedure. After all, the State knew *ex ante* that it would promptly learn whether its effort to effect notice through certified mail had succeeded. It would not be inconsistent with the approach the Court has taken in notice cases to ask, with respect to a procedure under which telephone calls were placed to owners, what the State did when no one answered. Asking what the State does when a notice letter is returned unclaimed is not substantively different.

The Commissioner has three further arguments for why reasonable follow-up measures were not required in this case. First, notice was sent to an address that Jones provided and had a legal obligation to keep updated. Second, "after failing to receive a property tax bill and pay property taxes, a property holder is on inquiry-notice that his property is subject to governmental taking." Third, Jones was obliged to ensure that those in whose hands he left his property would alert him if it was in jeopardy. None of these contentions relieves the State of its constitutional obligation to provide adequate notice.

The Commissioner does not argue that Jones' failure to comply with a statutory obligation to keep his address updated forfeits his right to constitutionally sufficient notice, and we agree. In *Robinson*, we noted that Illinois law required each vehicle owner to register his address with the secretary of state, and that the State's vehicle forfeiture scheme provided for notice by mail to the address listed in the secretary's records. But we found that the State had not provided constitutionally sufficient notice, despite having followed its reasonably calculated scheme, because it knew that Robinson could not be reached at his address of record. Although Ark. Code Ann. § 26-35-705 provides strong support for the Commissioner's argument that mailing a certified letter to Jones at 717 North Bryan Street was reasonably calculated to reach him, it does not alter the reasonableness of the Commissioner's position that he must do nothing more when the notice is promptly returned "unclaimed."

As for the Commissioner's inquiry notice argument, the common knowledge that property may become subject to government taking when taxes are not paid does not excuse the government from complying with its constitutional obligation of notice before taking private property. ... It is at least as widely known that arrestees have the right to remain silent, and that anything they say may be used against them, but that knowledge does not excuse a police failure to provide *Miranda* warnings. Arkansas affords even a delinquent taxpayer the right to settle accounts with the State and redeem his property, so Jones' failure to pay his taxes in a timely manner cannot by itself excuse inadequate notice.

Finally, the Commissioner reminds us of a statement from *Mullane* that the State can assume an owner leaves his property in the hands of one who will inform him if his interest is in jeopardy. But in this passage, Justice Jackson writes of "libel of a ship, attachment of a chattel[,] or entry upon real estate in the name of law"—such "seiz[ures]" of property, he concluded, "may reasonably be expected to come promptly to the owner's attention." An occupant, however, is not charged with acting as the owner's agent in all respects, and it is quite a leap from Justice Jackson's examples to conclude that it is an obligation of tenancy to follow up with certified mail of unknown content addressed to the owner. In fact, the State makes it impossible for the occupant to learn why the Commissioner is writing the owner, because an occupant cannot call for a certified letter without first obtaining the owner's signature. For all the occupant knows, the Commissioner of State Lands might write to certain residents about a variety of matters he finds important, such as state parks or highway construction; it would by no means be obvious to an occupant observing a certified mail slip from the Commissioner that the owner is in danger of losing his property. In any event, there is no record evidence that notices of attempted delivery were left at 717 North Bryan Street.

...

Jones should have been more diligent with respect to his property, no question. People must pay their taxes, and the government may hold citizens accountable for tax delinquency by taking their property. But before forcing a citizen to satisfy his debt by forfeiting his property, due process requires the government to provide adequate notice of the impending taking.

B

In response to the returned form suggesting that Jones had not received notice that he was about to lose his property, the State did—nothing. For the reasons stated, we conclude the State should have taken additional reasonable steps to notify Jones, if practicable to do so. The question remains whether there were any such available steps. [I]f there were no reasonable additional steps the government could have taken upon return of the unclaimed notice letter, it cannot be faulted for doing nothing.

We think there were several reasonable steps the State could have taken. What steps are reasonable in response to new information depends upon what the new information reveals. The return of the certified letter marked "unclaimed" meant either that Jones still lived at 717 North Bryan Street, but was not home when the postman called and did not retrieve the letter at the post office, or that Jones no longer resided at that address. One reasonable step primarily addressed to the former possibility would be for the State to resend the notice by regular mail, so that a signature was not required. The Commissioner says that use of certified mail makes actual notice more likely, because requiring the recipient's signature protects against misdelivery. But that is only true, of course, when someone is home to sign for the letter, or to inform the mail carrier that he has arrived at the wrong address. Otherwise, "[c]ertified mail is dispatched and handled in transit as ordinary mail," United States Postal Service, Domestic Mail Manual § 503.3.2.1 (Mar. 16, 2006), and the use of certified mail might make actual notice less likely in some cases— the letter cannot be left like regular mail to be examined at the end of the day, and it can only be retrieved from the post office for a specified period of time. Following up with regular mail might also increase the chances of actual notice to Jones if — as it turned out — he had moved. Even occupants who ignored certified mail notice slips addressed to the owner (if any had been left) might scrawl the owner's new address on the notice packet and leave it for the postman to retrieve, or notify Jones directly.

Other reasonable follow-up measures, directed at the possibility that Jones had moved as well as that he had simply not retrieved the certified letter, would have been to post notice on the front door, or to address otherwise undeliverable mail to "occupant." Most States that explicitly outline additional procedures in their tax sale statutes require just such steps. Either approach would increase the likelihood that the owner would be notified that he was about to lose his property, given the failure of a letter deliverable only to the owner in person. That is clear in the case of an owner who still resided at the premises. It is also true in the case of an owner who has moved: Occupants who might disregard a certified mail slip not addressed to them are less likely to ignore posted notice, and a letter addressed to them (even as "occupant") might be opened and read. In either case, there is a significant chance the occupants will alert the owner, if only because a change in ownership could well affect their own occupancy. In fact, Jones first learned of the State's effort to sell his house when he was alerted by one of the occupants — his daughter — after she was served with an unlawful detainer notice.

Jones believes that the Commissioner should have searched for his new address in the Little Rock phonebook and other government records such as income tax rolls. We do not believe the government was required to go this far. As the Commissioner points out, the return of Jones' mail marked "unclaimed" did not necessarily mean that 717 North Bryan Street was an incorrect address; it merely informed the Commissioner that no one appeared to sign for the mail before the designated date on which it would be returned to the sender. An open-ended search for a new address — especially when the State obligates the taxpayer to keep his address updated with the tax collector — imposes burdens on the State significantly greater than the several relatively easy options outlined above.

The Commissioner complains about the burden of even those additional steps, but his argument is belied by Arkansas' current requirement that notice to homestead owners be accomplished by personal service if certified mail is returned, and the fact that Arkansas transfers the cost of notice to the taxpayer or the tax sale purchaser. The Commissioner has offered no estimate of how many notice letters are returned, and no facts to support the dissent's assertion that the Commissioner must now physically locate "tens of thousands of properties every year." ...

Though the Commissioner argues that follow-up measures are not constitutionally required, he reminds us that the State did make some attempt to follow up with Jones by publishing notice in the newspaper a few weeks before the public sale. Several decades ago, this Court observed that "[c]hance alone" brings a person's attention to "an advertisement in small type inserted in the back pages of a newspaper," *Mullane*, and that notice by publication is adequate only where "it is not reasonably possible or practicable to give more adequate warning." *Id*. Following up by publication was not constitutionally adequate under the circumstances presented here because, as we have explained, it was possible and practicable to give Jones more adequate warning of the impending tax sale.

     * * *

There is no reason to suppose that the State will ever be less than fully zealous in its efforts to secure the tax revenue it needs. The same cannot be said for the State's efforts to ensure that its citizens receive proper notice before the State takes action against them. In this case, the State is exerting extraordinary power against a property owner—taking and selling a house he owns. It is not too much to insist that the State do a bit more to attempt to let him know about it when the notice letter addressed to him is returned unclaimed.

The Commissioner's effort to provide notice to Jones of an impending tax sale of his house was insufficient to satisfy due process given the circumstances of this case. The judgment of the Arkansas Supreme Court is reversed, and the case is remanded for proceedings not inconsistent with this opinion.

It is so ordered.

JUSTICE ALITO took no part in the consideration or decision of this case.

JUSTICE THOMAS, with whom JUSTICE SCALIA and JUSTICE KENNEDY join, dissenting.

... The methods of notice employed by Arkansas were reasonably calculated to inform petitioner of proceedings affecting his property interest and thus satisfy the requirements of the Due Process Clause. The State mailed a notice by certified letter to the address provided by petitioner. The certified letter was returned to the State marked "unclaimed" after three attempts to deliver it. The State then published a notice of public sale containing redemption information in the Arkansas Democrat Gazette newspaper. After Flowers submitted a purchase offer, the State sent yet another certified letter to petitioner at his record address. That letter, too, was returned to the State marked "unclaimed" after three delivery attempts.

Arkansas' attempts to contact petitioner by certified mail at his "record address," without more, satisfy due process. Because the notices were sent to the address provided by petitioner himself, the State had an especially sound basis for determining that notice would reach him. Moreover, Arkansas exceeded the constitutional minimum by additionally publishing notice in a local newspaper. Due process requires nothing more—and certainly not here, where petitioner had a statutory duty to pay his taxes and to report any change of address to the state taxing authority.

My conclusion that Arkansas' notice methods satisfy due process is reinforced by the well-established presumption that individuals, especially those owning property, act in their own interest. ...

The meaning of the Constitution should not turn on the antics of tax evaders and scofflaws. Nor is the self-created conundrum in which petitioner finds himself a legitimate ground for imposing additional constitutional obligations on the State. The State's attempts to notify petitioner by certified mail at the address that he provided and, additionally, by publishing notice in a local newspaper satisfy due process. Accordingly, I would affirm the judgment of the Arkansas Supreme Court.

Notes and Questions

1. Why in this case were additional steps necessary in order to provide constitutionally adequate notice? In what circumstances, generally, might plaintiffs have to take such steps? What about a situation in which a defendant refused to accept some form of certified or registered mail?

2. *Jones* emphasizes the principle adopted in *Mullane*—that the standard for determining the constitutional adequacy of notice is a flexible one that very much depends upon the particular facts of the case, including the interest at stake, the likelihood that the selected means of notifying the defendant is likely to do so, and the potential alternatives that might provide a greater assurance that the defendant receives the notice to which he or she is constitutionally entitled. The dissenting opinions in *Adams* and *Jones* articulate the considerations that lie on the other side of the equation—both the extent to which the defendant has declined to act in his or her own interest when it comes to notice, and the burden that additional steps might create, both in terms of the cost and resources.

B. Statutory Dimensions

The notice with which we are most concerned in civil procedure is notice to the defendant that he or she has been made a party to a lawsuit. Such notice is known as service of process, which refers to the delivery of the complaint that starts a lawsuit to the defendant. Under the Federal Rules, service of process is governed by Rule 4; state rules are often similar to Rule 4. Rule 4 is technical and comprehensive; it's a good idea to refer to the specifics of the rule when reading the cases construing it.

MID-CONTINENT WOOD PRODUCTS, INC. v. HARRIS
936 F.2d 297 (7th Cir. 1991)

COFFEY, Circuit Judge.

Lawrence A. Harris appeals the district court's order denying his Rule 60(b)(4) motion to vacate and dismiss a default judgment on the grounds of improper service of process. We reverse.

I. FACTS AND DISPOSITION BELOW

Harris Plywood, Inc. ("Harris Plywood") purchased lumber from the plaintiff, Mid-Continent Wood Products, Inc. ("Mid-Continent") on three separate occasions between May and August of 1980. When Harris Plywood failed to make any payments on the three shipments, the parties entered into negotiations in October 1980 and Harris agreed that the amount due would bear interest at the rate of fourteen percent per annum and that payments would commence within a few weeks. After Harris Plywood failed to make any payments, Mid-Continent filed suit in April 1981 for breach of contract. The parties entered into negotiations for a second time and after these discussions proved fruitless, Mid-Continent filed a motion for a default judgment. On October 28, 1981, the district court granted Mid-Continent's motion for a default judgment in *Mid-Continent Wood Products, Inc. v. Harris Plywood, Inc.* in the amount of $28,544.75. Instead of executing on the default judgment, Mid-Continent accepted a promissory note for the judgment amount from the defendant Lawrence Harris, President of Harris Plywood, in December of 1981. When Harris failed to pay the amount due, Mid-Continent filed this action to collect on Harris' promissory note.

Mid-Continent makes clear that (to state it mildly) it had a rather difficult time locating Harris and serving him with the complaint and summons. Initially, Mid-Continent attempted to serve Harris personally through a U.S. Marshal in December 1982. One month later on January 5, 1983, the marshal again attempted service by certified mail at Harris' place of employment, Superb Realty Corporation. Harris denied receipt of this mailing.

Mid-Continent states it next attempted service in May 1983 through a private process server at what was thought to be Harris' residence at 13 Secor Drive, Port Washington, New York. On two separate occasions the server attempted personal service but found no one at the address. On the third attempt, the server left the complaint and summons attached to the door of the residence, and followed this up by mailing another copy addressed to Harris at the same address.

At the request of the district court, Mid-Continent's attorney sent a letter on June 3, 1983, to the residence at 13 Secor Drive in order to notify Harris of an upcoming status hearing. A copy of this letter was also sent to Harris' counsel of record in the previous lawsuit, Samuel Panzer. Neither the letter to Harris nor the copy sent to Harris' attorney included copies of the complaint and summons. Harris' attorney contacted Mid-Continent on June 9, 1983 and proposed a settlement in which Harris would pay the entire amount due on the note in monthly installments. Mid-Continent's attorney rejected the offer and stated instead that if the full amount was not received, Mid-Continent would seek a judgment order against Harris. Nevertheless, Harris' attorney confirmed in writing Harris' intention of forwarding a check and promissory notes in partial satisfaction of the amount due under Harris' guaranty. As promised by Harris' attorney, a mailing arrived from Superb Realty, Harris' place of business, containing a check for $1,000.00 signed on behalf of Superb Realty and three notes for $1,000.00 each, also signed by agents acting on behalf of Superb Realty. On June 16, 1983, Mid-Continent's attorney again informed Harris' attorney that no settlement for less than the full amount would suffice and that if full payment was not received before the next status hearing on June 28, 1983, Mid-Continent would seek a default judgment against Harris. When no further payments were made, Mid-Continent obtained a default judgment against Harris on July 20, 1983, in the amount of $24,549.92.

After securing the judgment, Mid-Continent alleges that it attempted but was unable to locate Harris' assets for some time for purposes of executing on the judgment. Six years later, in June of 1989, Mid-Continent located certain assets of Harris' in Massachusetts and attempted to execute upon the 1983 judgment. However, on August 31, 1989, Harris filed a motion for relief in the district court pursuant to Rule 60(b)(4) of the Federal Rules of Civil Procedure claiming that because service on him did not properly comply with Rule 4 of the Federal Rules of Civil Procedure, the district court lacked personal jurisdiction over him at the time of the entry of judgment in 1983 and further that he never received a copy of the complaint and summons in this action. In support of his motion, Harris offered exhibits and affidavits stating that he never resided at 13 Secor Drive, Port Washington, New York, but stated that he lived at 15 Secor Drive, Port Washington, New York in 1983. He further stated that no one at 13 Secor Drive ever brought any documents pertaining to the case to his house at 15 Secor Drive. The district court issued an opinion denying Harris' motion to vacate and dismiss the default judgment on the grounds of improper service of process on November 1, 1989. While the district court acknowledged in its opinion that service upon Harris did not strictly comply with Rule 4, it nonetheless determined that strict compliance was unnecessary because of: 1) Harris' "actual knowledge of the lawsuit" based on Harris' former attorney's negotiations with Mid-Continent; 2) Mid-Continent's diligent efforts 'to obtain technically proper service upon Harris"; and 3) Harris' evasive conduct in responding to the attempts at service of process.

II. ISSUE FOR REVIEW

The issue before us is whether a district court may formulate its own test to determine whether to assert personal jurisdiction over a defendant in the absence of service of the complaint and summons in accordance with Rule 4 of the Federal Rules of Civil Procedure.

III. DISCUSSION

We review a district court's application of a legal standard *de novo*.

The district court found that Mid-Continent's attempted service of process on Harris did not comply with Rule 4. The district court then proceeded to devise a three-part test and fashioned an exception to the usual requirements of strict compliance with Rule 4:

> When the cases are examined, three requirements present themselves as requisite to finding an exception to strict compliance. First, it is imperative to upholding faulty service that the defendant actually know of a lawsuit.... Second, the server must show that he duly tried to serve the defendant properly; in other words, show that

more than a minimum effort was made and that the service actually made on the defendant came reasonably close to satisfying the requirements. This is often stated in terms of the plaintiff having `substantially complied' with Rule 4's mandate.... Third, the equities of the situation must warrant an exception from the usual strict compliance requirement. Specifically, the focus here is on the conduct of the defendant in responding to the situation.

The district court determined that these three factors "point clearly toward an exception from strict compliance in this case."

Rule 4(d)(1) provides that the complaint and summons shall, with respect to an individual defendant who is not an infant or incompetent, be made:

> by delivering a copy of the summons and of the complaint to the individual personally or by leaving copies thereof at the individual's dwelling house or usual place of abode with some person of suitable age and discretion then residing therein or by delivering a copy of the summons and of the complaint to an agent authorized by appointment or by law to receive service of process.
>
> ...

This court has previously stated that a liberal construction of the rules of service of process "cannot be utilized as a substitute for the plain legal requirement as to the manner in which service of process may be had." *United States v. Mollenhauer Laboratories, Inc.* (7th Cir. 1959).

The district court has not cited, nor have we discovered, any cases in support of a judicially created three-part test for substantial compliance with Rule 4's requirements for service of process such as the one devised by the district court. Instead, the factors considered by the district court have questionable validity, and as a result, the district court's three-part test must fail.

The first factor the district court considered in determining the jurisdictional question concerning Harris was its finding that Harris had "actual knowledge of the lawsuit" based on Harris' former attorney's negotiations with Mid-Continent. The district court quotes *Armco, Inc. v. Penrod-Stauffer Building Systems, Inc.* (4th Cir. 1984), for the proposition that "[w]hen there is actual notice, every technical violation of the rule or failure of strict compliance may not invalidate the service of process." However, the appellate court in *Armco* found the service of process to be invalid despite the defendant's knowledge of the suit and thus, the trial court was without jurisdiction and the default judgment was void.

This court has long recognized that valid service of process is necessary in order to assert personal jurisdiction over a defendant. Moreover, it is well recognized that a "defendant's actual notice of the litigation ... is insufficient to satisfy Rule 4's requirements." *Way v. Mueller Brass Co.* (5th Cir. 1988).

[A]ctual knowledge of the existence of a lawsuit is insufficient to confer personal jurisdiction over a defendant in the absence of valid service of process. Even though Harris may have had knowledge of the lawsuit as a result of Harris' former attorney's negotiations with Mid-Continent, "actual notice alone is insufficient to give the court the jurisdiction necessary to allow it to enter a judgment against a defendant." *Bennett v. Circus U.S.A.* (N.D. Ind. 1985). Thus, the district court's reliance on actual notice in determining that it had personal jurisdiction over Harris is erroneous.

The second part of the district court's three-part test focused on whether "the service actually made on the defendant came reasonably close to satisfying the requirements [of Rule 4]." The district court characterized this factor as whether the plaintiff "substantially complied" with Rule 4's mandate. The district court determined that Mid-Continent "tried diligently to obtain technically proper service upon Harris." The court further noted that these attempts "were sufficient to result in settlement discussions between the parties."

This court is reluctant to find jurisdiction based upon whether Mid-Continent "tried diligently" to serve Harris. Indeed, the extent to which the plaintiff "tried" to serve process should not be a factor as to whether a federal court has personal jurisdiction over a defendant. Rather, the requirements of Rule 4 are satisfied only when the plaintiff is successful in serving the complaint and summons on the defendant.

...

Even if we agreed with the district court's interpretation of the "substantial compliance" doctrine (which we do not), the facts lead us to believe that ours is a case of "substantial *non*-compliance." The extent of Mid-Continent's efforts to obtain service on Harris consisted of the following: 1) one certified mailing of the complaint and summons to a business address of Harris (which Harris denies receiving), and neither the envelope containing the complaint and summons nor the return receipt evidencing delivery were ever returned; 2) three attempts at personal service by a private process server over a four-day period at an incorrect address; and 3) a non-certified mailing to the same incorrect address.

The district court also cites the settlement discussions between the parties' attorneys as proof that the above-cited attempts at service were sufficient. However, nowhere in Rule 4 is there an exception for settlement discussions in the absence of the usual requirements of proper service of process, nor does the district court cite any case law in support of this proposition. Settlement discussions with Harris cannot save Mid-Continent from its failure to "substantially comply" with Rule 4's requirements of service of process.

The third and final factor of the district court's three-part test is whether the "equities" of the case warrant an exception from the usual strict compliance requirement: "Specifically, the focus here is on the conduct of the defendant in responding to the situation." The court cites evasion of process by the defendant as "the most typical example" of this kind of conduct. ...

The cases cited by the district court involve clear-cut examples of evasion: ... defendants who specifically refused to acknowledge service and are thus distinguishable. The facts in the case before us fall short of establishing clear and convincing evidence of evasion on the part of the defendant. [T]here is no evidence that Harris either refused to accept his mail or actually received mail service but refused to acknowledge it. The district court infers evasion on the part of Harris because of the repeated, *though faulty*, attempts at service of process by Mid-Continent. As we stated *supra*, valid service of process is a must in order to assert personal jurisdiction over a defendant. Furthermore, the district court found that Harris had acted inequitably by allowing his attorney to engage in settlement discussions with Mid-Continent's attorney and then challenging the service of process six years after the judgment was entered: "Defendant in this case simply sat on his potential defense until the plaintiff finally found some of his assets and only then attempted to assert it." While we certainly do not condone Harris' or his attorney's conduct, we are of the opinion that the record falls short of supporting a finding of evasion or inequitable conduct by Harris.

IV. CONCLUSION

The three-part test devised by the district court to uphold the default judgment entered against Harris fails to support an exception to the service of process requirements of Rule 4. Therefore, the district court's order denying Harris' Rule 60(b)(4) motion to vacate and dismiss the default judgment on the grounds of improper service of process is reversed.

Notes and Questions

1. Why does the Seventh Circuit Court of Appeals reject the test formulated by the district court for determining whether Rule 4 has been satisfied? Why does the Appeals Court maintain that strict compliance with the rules governing service of process is necessary?

2. Why is the defendant's actual notice not sufficient to satisfy the rule? When, if ever, will substantial compliance with the rule be acceptable?

3. When should a reviewing court take account of a defendant's efforts to evade service? When might a defendant have an obligation to submit to proper service of process?

4. The Appeals Court's understanding of Rule 4 and how the rule applies in this case is decidedly technical. What purpose does an insistence on technical compliance with the rules of service – or any similar rule – serve?

5. To be clear, the courts do not tolerate certain conduct in a plaintiff's effort to effect service; a plaintiff cannot fraudulently induce a defendant to enter the jurisdiction for purposes of service. *See Wyman v. Newhouse*, 93 F.2d 313 (CA2 1937). This issue is further addressed below in *May Department Stores Co. v. Wilansky.*

REPUBLIC OF SUDAN v. HARRISON
___ U.S. ___ (2019)

Justice ALITO delivered the opinion of the Court.

This case concerns the requirements applicable to a particular method of serving civil process on a foreign state. Under the Foreign Sovereign Immunities Act of 1976 (FSIA), a foreign state may be served by means of a mailing that is "addressed and dispatched ... to the head of the ministry of foreign affairs of the foreign state concerned." 28 U.S.C. § 1608(a)(3). The question now before us is whether this provision is satisfied when a service packet that names the foreign minister is mailed to the foreign state's embassy in the United States. ...

I

Under the FSIA, a foreign state is immune from the jurisdiction of courts in this country unless one of several enumerated exceptions to immunity applies. If a suit falls within one of these exceptions, the FSIA provides subject-matter jurisdiction in federal district courts. § 1330(a). The FSIA also provides for personal jurisdiction "where service has been made under section 1608."

Section 1608(a) governs service of process on "a foreign state or political subdivision of a foreign state." [It sets out the methods] by which "[s]ervice ... shall be made." ... If service is not possible under either of the first two methods, the third method, which is the one at issue in this case, may be used. This method calls for

> sending a copy of the summons and complaint and a notice of suit, together with a translation of each into the official language of the foreign state, *by any form of mail requiring a signed receipt, to be addressed and dispatched* by the clerk of the court *to the head of the ministry of foreign affairs of the foreign state concerned.*"

§ 1608(a)(3) (emphasis added).

...

Once served, a foreign state or political subdivision has 60 days to file a responsive pleading. § 1608(d). If the foreign state or political subdivision does not do this, it runs the risk of incurring a default judgment. ...

On October 12, 2000, the USS *Cole*, a United States Navy guided-missile destroyer, entered the harbor of Aden, Yemen, for what was intended to be a brief refueling stop. While refueling was underway, a small boat drew along the side of the *Cole*, and the occupants of the boat detonated explosives that tore a hole in the side of the *Cole*. Seventeen crewmembers were killed, and dozens more were injured. Al Qaeda later claimed responsibility for the attack.

Respondents ... are victims of the USS *Cole* bombing and their family members. [They] sued the Republic of Sudan, alleging that Sudan had provided material support to al Qaeda for the bombing. Because respondents brought suit under the FSIA, they were required to serve Sudan with process under § 1608(a). It is undisputed that service could not be made under § 1608(a)(1) or § 1608(a)(2), and respondents therefore turned to § 1608(a)(3). At respondents' request, the clerk of the court sent the service packet, return receipt requested, to: "Republic of Sudan, Deng Alor Koul, Minister of Foreign Affairs, Embassy of the Republic of Sudan, 2210 Massachusetts Avenue NW, Washington, DC 20008." The clerk certified that the service packet had been sent and, a few days later, certified that a signed receipt had been returned. After Sudan failed to appear in the litigation, the District Court for the District of Columbia held an evidentiary hearing and entered a $314 million default judgment against Sudan. Again at respondents' request, the clerk of the court mailed a copy of the default judgment in the same manner that the clerk had previously used.

With their default judgment in hand, respondents turned to the District Court for the Southern District of New York, where they sought to register the judgment and satisfy it through orders requiring several banks to turn over Sudanese assets. [T]he District Court entered an order confirming that a sufficient period of time had elapsed following the entry and notice of the default judgment, and the court then issued three turnover orders.

At this point, Sudan made an appearance for the purpose of contesting jurisdiction. It filed a notice of appeal from each of the three turnover orders and contended on appeal ... that § 1608(a)(3) required that the service packet be sent to its foreign minister at his principal office in Khartoum, the capital of Sudan, and not to the Sudanese Embassy in the United States.

The Court of Appeals for the Second Circuit rejected this argument and affirmed the orders of the District Court. ...

Subsequent to the Second Circuit's decision, the Court of Appeals for the Fourth Circuit held in a similar case that § 1608(a)(3) "does not authorize delivery of service to a foreign state's embassy even if it correctly identifies the intended recipient as the head of the ministry of foreign affairs."

We granted certiorari to resolve this conflict.

Why they wanted the case
2* - 4*
disagred

II

The question before us concerns the meaning of § 1608(a)(3), and in interpreting that provision, "[w]e begin 'where all such inquiries must begin: with the language of the statute itself.'" *Caraco Pharmaceutical Laboratories, Ltd. v. Novo Nordisk A/S* (2012) (quoting *United States v. Ron Pair Enterprises, Inc.* (1989)). As noted, § 1608(a)(3) requires that service be sent "by any form of mail requiring a signed receipt, to be addressed and dispatched by the clerk of the court to the head of the ministry of foreign affairs of the foreign state concerned."

The most natural reading of this language is that service must be mailed directly to the foreign minister's office in the foreign state. Although this is not, we grant, the only plausible reading of the statutory text, it is the most natural one.

A key term in § 1608(a)(3) is the past participle "addressed." A letter or package is "addressed" to an intended recipient when his or her name and "address" is [sic] placed on the outside of the item to be sent. And the noun "address," in the sense relevant here, means "the designation of a place (as a residence or place of business) where a person or organization may be found or communicated with." Webster's Third New International Dictionary 25 (1971) (Webster's Third). Since a foreign nation's embassy in the United States is neither the residence nor the usual place of business of that nation's foreign minister and is not a place where the minister can customarily be found, the most common understanding of the minister's "address" is inconsistent with the interpretation of § 1608(a)(3) adopted by the court below and advanced by respondents.

We acknowledge that there are circumstances in which a mailing may be "addressed" to the intended recipient at a place other than the individual's residence or usual place of business. For example, if the person sending the mailing does not know the intended recipient's current home or business address, the sender might use the intended recipient's last known address in the hope that the mailing will be forwarded. Or a sender might send a mailing to a third party who is thought to be in a position to ensure that the mailing is ultimately received by the intended recipient. But in the great majority of cases, addressing a mailing to X means placing on the outside of the mailing both X's name and the address of X's residence or customary place of work.

Section 1608(a)(3)'s use of the term "dispatched" points in the same direction. To "dispatch" a communication means "to send [it] off or away (as to a special destination) with promptness or speed often as a matter of official business." Webster's Third 653. A person who wishes to "dispatch" a letter to X will generally send it directly to X at a place where X is customarily found. The sender will not "dispatch" the letter in a roundabout way, such as by directing it to a third party who, it is hoped, will then send it on to the intended recipient.

A few examples illustrate this point. Suppose that a person is instructed to "address" a letter to the Attorney General of the United States and "dispatch" the letter (*i.e.*, to "send [it] off post-haste") to the Attorney General. The person giving these instructions would likely be disappointed and probably annoyed to learn that the letter had been sent to, let us say, the office of the United States Attorney for the District of Idaho. And this would be so even though a U.S. Attorney's office is part of the Department headed by the Attorney General and even though such an office would very probably forward the letter to the Attorney General's office in Washington. Similarly, a person who instructs a subordinate to dispatch a letter to the CEO of a big corporation that owns retail outlets throughout the country would probably be irritated to learn that the letter had been mailed to one of those stores instead of corporate headquarters. To "dispatch" a letter to an addressee connotes sending it directly.

A similar understanding underlies the venerable "mailbox rule." As first-year law students learn in their course on contracts, there is a presumption that a mailed acceptance of an offer is deemed operative when "dispatched" if it is "properly addressed." Restatement (Second) of Contracts § 66, p. 161 (1979) (Restatement). But no acceptance would be deemed properly addressed and dispatched if it lacked, and thus was not sent to, the offeror's address (or an address that the offeror held out as the place for receipt of an acceptance).

It is also significant that service under § 1608(a)(3) requires a signed returned receipt, a standard method for ensuring delivery to the addressee. We assume that certified mail sent to a foreign minister will generally be signed for by a subordinate, but the person who signs for the minister's certified mail in the foreign ministry itself presumably has authority to receive mail on the minister's behalf and has been instructed on how that mail is to be handled. The same is much less likely to be true for an employee in the mailroom of an embassy.

For all these reasons, we think that the most natural reading of § 1608(a)(3) is that the service packet must bear the foreign minister's name and customary address and that it be sent to the minister in a direct and expeditious way. And the minister's customary office is the place where he or she generally works, not a far-flung outpost that the minister may at most occasionally visit.

...

The ordinary meaning of the "addressed and dispatched" requirement in § 1608(a)(3) ... has the virtue of avoiding potential tension with the Federal Rules of Civil Procedure ...

At the time of the FSIA's enactment, Rule 4(i), entitled "Alternative provisions for service in a foreign-country," set out certain permissible methods of service on "part[ies] in a foreign country." Fed. Rule Civ. Proc. 4(i)(1) (1976). One such method was "by any form of mail, requiring a signed receipt, to be addressed and dispatched by the clerk of the court *to the party to be served*." Rule 4(i)(1)(D) (emphasis added). Rule 4(i)(2) further provided that "proof of service" pursuant to that method "shall include a receipt *signed by the addressee* or other evidence of *delivery to the addressee* satisfactory to the court." (Emphasis added.) The current version of Rule 4 is similar.

The virtually identical methods of service outlined in Rule 4 and § 1608(a)(3) pose a problem for respondents' position: If mailing a service packet to a foreign state's embassy in the United States were sufficient for purposes of § 1608(a)(3), then it would appear to be easier to serve the foreign state than to serve a person in that foreign state. This is so because a receipt signed by an embassy employee would not necessarily satisfy Rule 4 since such a receipt would not bear the signature of the foreign minister and might not constitute evidence that is sufficient to show that the service packet had actually been delivered to the minister. It would be an odd state of affairs for a foreign state's inhabitants to enjoy more protections in federal courts than the foreign state itself, particularly given that the foreign state's immunity from suit is at stake. The natural reading of § 1608(a)(3) avoids that oddity.

III

[A]s respondents' counsel acknowledged at oral argument, holding that Sudan was not properly served under § 1608(a)(3) is not the end of the road. Respondents may attempt service once again under § 1608(a)(3), and if that attempt fails, they may turn to § 1608(a)(4). When asked at argument to provide examples of any problems with service under § 1608(a)(4), respondents' counsel stated that he was unaware of any cases where such service failed.

* * *

We interpret § 1608(a)(3) as it is most naturally understood: A service packet must be addressed and dispatched to the foreign minister at the minister's office in the foreign state. We therefore reverse the judgment of the Court of Appeals and remand the case for further proceedings consistent with this opinion.

It is so ordered.

Justice THOMAS, dissenting.

The Court holds that service on a foreign state by certified mail under the Foreign Sovereign Immunities Act (FSIA) is defective unless the packet is "addressed and dispatched to the foreign minister *at the minister's office in the foreign state*." This bright-line rule may be attractive from a policy perspective, but the FSIA neither specifies nor precludes the use of any particular address. Instead, the statute requires only that the packet be sent to a particular person—"the head of the ministry of foreign affairs." 28 U.S.C. § 1608(a)(3).

Given the unique role that embassies play in facilitating communications between states, a foreign state's embassy in Washington, D. C., is, absent an indication to the contrary, a place where a U.S. litigant can serve the state's foreign minister. Because there is no evidence in this case suggesting that Sudan's Embassy declined the service packet addressed to its foreign minister—as it was free to do—I would hold that respondents complied with the FSIA when they addressed and dispatched a service packet to Sudan's Minister of Foreign Affairs at Sudan's Embassy in Washington, D. C. Accordingly, I respectfully dissent.

Notes and Questions

1.   Proper service of process is governed by statutes. The Federal Rules contemplate service on foreigners; in this case, the rules regarding service are governed by a federal statute, the Foreign Sovereign Immunities Act. What provision of that statute is at issue here? Why does this dispute arise?

2.   This case demonstrates, once again, how the indefiniteness of language can lead to confusion and litigation. The courts have a number of tools at their disposal to resolve these conflicts. With what approach does the Court begin here? And how does it proceed to support the conclusion to which use of that approach leads? What lessons can be drawn from the Court's analysis to aid lower courts and lawyers litigating similar issues in the future?

3.   What is the basis for Justice Thomas's dissent? Isn't the resolution he is suggesting in a real sense narrower in scope than the one the majority adopts? Why might the Court have preferred a broader analysis here, as opposed to, say, a case involving the constitutionality of a particular form of notice?

MAY DEPARTMENT STORES CO. v. WILANSKY
900 F. Supp. 1154 (E.D. Missouri 1995)
MEMORANDUM AND ORDER

SHAW, District Judge.

This matter is before the Court on defendant Heywood L. Wilansky's motion to dismiss the complaint for ... insufficiency of service of process....

Background. Plaintiff filed a two-count Complaint on Saturday, August 19, 1995, alleging that defendant Wilansky breached an employment agreement with plaintiff (Count I), and that defendant Bon-Ton tortiously interfered with the Wilansky-May employment agreement (Count II). ...

Plaintiff filed a motion for a temporary restraining order on August 25, 1995, and the Court conducted a hearing on the motion the same day.

asking someone
to come to a Jur
for one reason
but to actually
serve them.

Following the hearing, the parties requested the Court to delay entry of an order on the motion for temporary relief, and then submitted a proposed Stipulated Order which provided, *inter alia,* that Wilansky and his agents not use or disclose any of May's confidential data, information or documents. The Court issued the Stipulated Order on August 29, 1995. The Court issued an order for expedited discovery and a protective order on September 5, 1995, and began an evidentiary hearing on May's motion for preliminary injunction on September 14, 1995, which was not concluded.

Facts. Plaintiff May is a New York corporation with its principal place of business in St. Louis, Missouri. May is in the retail store business and operates eight regional department store divisions in much of the United States. Defendant Wilansky is an individual who was a citizen and resident of the State of Texas until late August or early September 1995, and is now a citizen and resident of the State of Pennsylvania. Wilansky had been in plaintiff's employ in various executive-level positions since 1977. ...

May and Wilansky entered into an Employment Agreement under which Wilansky would become the President and Chief Executive Officer of May's Filene's store division in Boston, Massachusetts (the "Employment Agreement"). The Employment Agreement was dated December 14, 1990, but was signed by Wilansky and Richard Battram, an officer of May, during the week of January 7, 1991, while on an airplane flying from New York to Boston. At that time, Wilansky was a resident of New York but was in the process of moving to Massachusetts to assume his new position. The term of the Employment Agreement was from January 15, 1991 through April 14, 1994.

Section 3 of the Employment Agreement requires that Wilansky devote his undivided time and attention to May's business. Section 4 prohibits Wilansky from engaging in any competing business during the contract term. Section 7 requires Wilansky to hold May's confidential data and information in the strictest confidence. Section 11 provides that any question or matter arising under the agreement shall be determined by the laws of the state of Wilansky's domicile.

The Employment Agreement was amended on April 7, 1992 to increase Wilansky's compensation. All other terms of the Employment Agreement remained the same. On September 16, 1992, Wilansky and Battram signed an Amendment of Employment Agreement (the "Foley's Amendment") in St. Louis, Missouri. Foley's Amendment provides, *inter alia,* that Wilansky would become President and Chief Executive Officer of May's Foley's store division in Houston, Texas; the contract term was extended to April 30, 1997; and Wilansky's compensation was changed. Section 7 of the Foley's Amendment states, "Except as provided herein, all of the terms, conditions and provisions of the Employment Agreement shall remain in full force and effect." In connection with Wilansky's duties under the Foley's Amendment, Wilansky and his family moved from Massachusetts to Texas.

On Friday, August 18, 1995, Wilansky accepted the position of President and Chief Executive Officer of Bon-Ton in Pennsylvania, and on the same day announced his resignation from May effective immediately. As noted above, the instant litigation commenced the day after Wilansky's resignation, on Saturday, August 19, 1995. Later on the same day, Bon-Ton and Wilansky filed a declaratory judgment action against May in the United States District Court for the District of Pennsylvania. Wilansky has now moved to Pennsylvania.

...

The Court must ... determine whether sufficient service of process was obtained on defendant Wilansky. Wilansky moves to dismiss pursuant to Fed.R.Civ.P. 12(b)(5), or to quash service of process, on the basis that he was improperly served by means of fraud and trickery.

The record shows Wilansky notified May he intended to resign from its employ by telephone call to Richard Battram on August 18, 1995. Battram called Wilansky back and asked him to come to St. Louis to discuss the issues. At some point thereafter, May had its attorneys prepare the instant Complaint. On Saturday morning, August 19, 1995, May sent a company airplane to Texas to pick up Wilansky and bring him to St. Louis. Also on Saturday morning, counsel for May persuaded the Clerk of the Court to open the Clerk's office and file the Complaint.

Wilansky met with Battram in Battram's office. The men discussed whether Wilansky's decision was final, and when it became clear to Battram that it was, Battram asked May's Secretary and General Counsel and one of May's attorneys from the Bryan Cave LLP firm, to come into the office. One of the attorneys handed Wilansky a summons and a copy of the Complaint, which had already been filed.

It is well-established law that if a person is induced by fraud or trickery to come within the jurisdiction of a court for the purpose of procuring service of process, service should be set aside. This rule has been applied for more than 100 years and emanates from a court's discretion not to exercise its power over a defendant. ...

When service is made following settlement negotiations or business meetings, courts have recognized the potential for dispute over whether the negotiations or meetings were instituted and carried out in good faith prior to service. It has been held in various cases that a plaintiff's real purpose was to serve the defendant with process and process should be quashed where there were prior arrangements for a process service to be present at the meeting, where the plaintiff's lawyers were preparing the lawsuit at the same time the plaintiff was urging the defendant to enter the jurisdiction, where a plaintiff failed to clearly warn a defendant before he entered the jurisdiction that the defendant would be served if talks failed, and where a plaintiff failed to give the defendant an opportunity to leave the jurisdiction before service is made.

Several courts which have addressed this issue have adopted a bright-line rule prohibiting service of process where a plaintiff has induced a defendant to enter the jurisdiction for talks, unless the plaintiff first warns the defendant before he enters the jurisdiction that he may subject himself to service, or gives the defendant an opportunity to leave the jurisdiction before service is made if settlement talks fail.

The bright-line rule "promotes good faith settlement, is efficient from a judicial standpoint, and serves to distance the courts from the possibility of trickery. A bright-line rule also obviates a determination of whether the plaintiff intended to file a complaint at the time the parties were arranging the settlement meeting." *K Mart Corp. v. Gen-Star* (F.R.D. 1986). ...

This Court finds the reasoning of the cases which have adopted a bright-line rule persuasive, and concludes that such a rule best serves the orderly administration of justice. Thus, service should be quashed when a defendant enters a jurisdiction for talks at a plaintiff's instigation, and the plaintiff has not either clearly and unequivocally informed the defendant that service of process may occur, or given the defendant a chance to leave the jurisdiction before service is made.

The factors courts have relied on in quashing service as improperly obtained are present in this case. It is undisputed that May, through Battram, initiated the August 19, 1995 meeting in St. Louis for the purpose of discussing Wilansky's decision to leave May's employ. Assuming that Battram and May intended to discuss the issue in good faith at the meeting, it is undisputed that May had filed its Complaint and had attorneys ready to serve Wilansky with process when it became clear he would not remain with May. May does not contend that it clearly warned Wilansky he might be served with process if he came to St. Louis, or that it gave him an opportunity to leave the jurisdiction before service was made. Applying the bright-line rule, the Court concludes the service of process on Wilansky should be quashed.

The Court still must determine whether the action against Wilansky should be dismissed. A leading treatise on federal procedure notes that courts "have broad discretion to dismiss the action or retain the case but quash the service that has been made on defendant." *See* 5A C. Wright & A. Miller, Federal Practice and Procedure: Civil 2d § 1354 (1990). "Service generally will be quashed and the action preserved in those cases in which there is a reasonable prospect that plaintiff ultimately will be able to serve defendant properly." *Id.* The courts, however, have more often dismissed a complaint without discussing alternative means of service where trickery or bad faith has been found.

The Court concludes that plaintiff's action against Wilansky should not be dismissed. In adopting the bright-line rule, this Court has made no findings of bad faith or trickery on the part of plaintiff May. There is little substantive difference between dismissal for improper service and quashing of service. A dismissal would require plaintiff to refile its Complaint and use proper means to serve Wilansky, while quashing of service merely requires new service. *See* 5A Wright & Miller, *supra,* § 1354. There is nothing in the record which suggests that May will not able to properly serve Wilansky. The Court concludes a dismissal would serve no purpose in this case and will order that service upon defendant Wilansky be quashed.

Notes and Questions

1. As noted above, persons cannot be induced by fraud or trickery to enter a jurisdiction for the purpose of serving process. What about when settlement discussions or negotiations are proposed?

2. The court here adopts a bright-line rule regarding invitation to enter a jurisdiction "for talks" absent a warning that the person may be subjected to service. Why was no such warning given in this case?

3. Notwithstanding the deficiencies in service here, the court concludes the action against Wilansky should not be dismissed. Why not?

4. Note that this case, and the others you have read so far, generally concern service of process on individuals. Rule 4 also contemplates the need to effect service of process on corporate entities, partnerships and associations, as discussed in the next case.

AMERICAN INSTITUTE OF CERTIFIED PUBLIC ACCOUNTANTS, v. AFFINITY CARD, INC.
8 F.Supp.2d 372 (S.D.N.Y. 1998)
OPINION AND ORDER

SCHEINDLIN, District Judge.

Plaintiff, The American Institute of Certified Public Accountants ("AICPA"), filed a complaint sounding in breach of contract against defendant, Affinity Card, Inc. ("Affinity"), on March 24, 1998. An affidavit of service was filed on April 7, 1998. The defendant did not move or answer in the time permitted, and the plaintiff applied for a default judgment pursuant.... On May 11, 1998, a default judgment was entered against the defendant. The defendant now moves pursuant to ... to vacate the judgment of default as void for lack of personal jurisdiction due to ineffective service of process. For the reasons stated below, the motion is granted.

I. Background

This action arises out of a tripartite contract entered into on November 5, 1992 by the plaintiff, defendant, and Marine Midland Bank. The contract established a Visa credit card marketed to AICPA members with Affinity's promotional assistance and issued by Marine Midland. AICPA and Affinity are entitled to a share in the fees collected from the program's participants. The plaintiff alleges that the defendant has improperly withheld information concerning these fees and has failed to make payments as obligated.

The plaintiff attempted service upon the defendant on March 30, 1998. Peter Murphy, a professional process server, handed the summons and complaint to one Patrick McDonald at Affinity's principal place of business in Wellesley, Massachusetts. The plaintiff subsequently filed an affidavit of service that identified McDonald as Assistant Vice-President of Affinity. McDonald, however, is not employed by Affinity. He is the Assistant Vice-President of Primecard Corporation ("Primecard").

Affinity shares a suite of offices with three other companies, including Primecard. The four companies share a receptionist's area, but the most significant link joining them is Greg Miller, president, treasurer, and at least a partial owner of all.

According to the plaintiff, Murphy entered the office and was greeted by McDonald at the receptionist's area. He asked McDonald "if Gregory Miller, Affinity Card's president, was there." After being informed that Miller was out, he told McDonald that he had some important legal papers for Affinity Card and Miller, and asked whether there was anyone there that could accept the papers for Affinity Card. McDonald said he could accept the papers and would make sure Miller received them that afternoon. Murphy then showed the summons and complaint to McDonald and asked for his name and title. McDonald said he was Assistant Vice-President, and Murphy assumed that McDonald meant Assistant Vice President of Affinity. After that exchange, Murphy handed the summons and complaint to McDonald. He is not certain if the documents were contained in an envelope as he handed them over, but is certain that if they were, he would have first shown them to McDonald.

The defendant's version of the events is slightly different. The defendant contends that after McDonald identified himself as Assistant Vice-President, Murphy said "that will do," or words to that effect, and handed over a sealed white envelope addressed to Miller. According to the defendant, Murphy did ask for Miller, but never asked McDonald if he could accept service for Affinity Card or Miller, never indicated the nature or purpose of the delivery, and never showed the documents to McDonald. McDonald placed the sealed, unopened envelope in Miller's box later that day.

II. Discussion

Defendant now moves for an order vacating the default judgment pursuant to Federal Rules of Civil Procedure 55(c) and 60(b)(4). After the entry of a default judgment, Rule 55(c) grants a litigant the right to petition a court to vacate the judgment upon a showing of good cause and in accordance with Rule 60(b). *See* 10 Charles A. Wright et al., *Federal Practice and Procedure* § 2692 at 464 (2d ed.1983). Subsection four of Rule 60(b) provides that a court may relieve a party from a final judgment if the judgment is void. Other grounds for relief provided by Rule 60(b) include mistake, surprise, excusable neglect, newly discovered evidence, fraud, satisfaction, or any other justifying reason. A motion predicated on subsection four is unique, however, in that relief is not discretionary and a meritorious defense is not necessary as on motions made pursuant to other 60(b) subsections.

Valid service of process is a prerequisite to a district court's assertion of personal jurisdiction over a defendant. A judgment entered against a party not subject to the personal jurisdiction of the court is a nullity. *Covington Indus., Inc. v. Resintex A.G.* (2nd Cir. 1980).Hence, a judgment obtained by way of defective service is void for lack of personal jurisdiction and must be set aside as a matter of law.

In a federal diversity action, service of process upon a corporation may be made pursuant to Fed.R.Civ.P. 4(h)(1), or pursuant to the law of either the state in which the district court sits, or in which service is effected. The issue raised here is therefore straightforward: was service of process effective pursuant to Fed.R.Civ.P. 4(h)(1), New York's long arm statute, or the laws of Massachusetts?

Before analyzing the sufficiency of the attempted service, it should be noted that the Second Circuit has expressed on numerous occasions its "preference that litigation disputes be resolved on the merits, not by default." *Cody v. Mello* (2d Cir. 1995). Default judgments have been described as "the most severe sanction which the court may apply, and its use must be tempered by the careful exercise of judicial discretion to assure that its imposition is merited." *Securities and Exch. Comm'n v. Management Dynamics, Inc.* (2d Cir. 1975) (quotation omitted). Although there is no judicial discretion when considering a jurisdictional question such as the sufficiency of process, when confronted with equally reliable but conflicting accounts, courts should resolve any doubts in favor of the party seeking relief under Rule 60(b). Accordingly, where the parties' accounts of the attempted service differ but both are inherently plausible, and there is nothing in the record upon which to judge the veracity of either version, a court should credit the version of the party seeking to vacate the default.

A. *Service of Process Under Federal Rule 4(h)(1)*

According to the Federal Rules of Civil Procedure, service of process may be made upon a corporation by delivering copies of the summons and complaint to an officer, a managing or general agent, or to any other agent authorized to receive service of process. The burden is on the plaintiff to show a basis for an inference that the defendant has authorized a particular person to accept service of process on its behalf.

McDonald does not come within the letter of the statute. He is neither employed by nor expressly authorized to accept service on behalf of the defendant. The plaintiff argues that service was nevertheless effective and cites to several cases that have construed service of process rules liberally. Indeed, Rule 4(h)(1) does not require rigid formalism, and there are many cases where courts have exercised personal jurisdiction over defendants although service of process was delivered to someone other than the persons listed in the rule.

The rule does not require that service be made solely on a restricted class of formally titled officials, but rather permits it to be made upon a representative so integrated with the organization that he will know what to do with the papers. Generally, service is sufficient when made upon an individual who stands in such a position as to render it fair, reasonable and just to imply the authority on his part to receive services.

In *Insurance Co. v. N.A. v. S/S Hellenic Challenger* (S.D.N.Y. 1980), the defendant sought to vacate a default judgment on the ground of defective service because the person served was not properly authorized to receive service and had misplaced and lost the summons and complaint. This Court ruled that service had nevertheless been properly effected, reasoning that the person served was "a representative of defendant 'well-integrated' into the organization and quite familiar with the formalities associated with the receipt of service of summonses and complaints...."

McDonald had been working at Primecard for just a few months, he had no responsibilities for Affinity, and had never even heard of it. He did not hold himself out as a representative of Affinity or authorized to receive service on its behalf. Nor did he learn that the envelope which he placed in Miller's mailbox contained important legal documents until several weeks later. He was not sufficiently "integrated" with Affinity to allow the inference that he had authority to receive service.

In every case cited by the plaintiff, the person served was employed by the defendant corporation. As stated, McDonald was not employed by Affinity. ...

The plaintiff places great weight on the fact that Greg Miller, the President of Affinity, actually received the summons and complaint on the very same day that the papers were delivered to McDonald. In *Durant v. Traditional Invs., Ltd.* (S.D.N.Y. 1990), this Court recognized the significance of actual notice. Citing to a procedural treatise, Judge Leisure wrote that "when a defendant receives actual notice of a lawsuit brought against him, technical imperfections with service will rarely invalidate the service." *Id.* at *3 (*citing* Wright & Miller, *Federal Practice & Procedure*, § 1063 at 225).

The actual receipt of the summons and complaint is an important factor in determining the effectiveness of service. However, actual notice of the action will not, in itself, cure an otherwise defective service.

Plaintiff attempts to salvage its opposition to this motion by arguing that Primecard and Affinity are the virtual alter egos of Greg Miller — as such, effective service upon Primecard should be deemed to constitute effective service upon Affinity. Because an alter ego is considered an indistinguishable entity, jurisdiction over one company constitutes jurisdiction over its alter egos.

Neither party raised choice of law as an issue, but it is well settled that federal district courts sitting in diversity apply the choice of law principles of the state in which they sit. Under New York choice of law principles, the law of the state of incorporation determines when the corporate form will be disregarded.

In Massachusetts, corporate form will be disregarded only i) when there is an active and direct exercise of pervasive control by the representatives of one corporation over the activities of another and there is some fraudulent or injurious consequence; or ii) when there is a confused intermingling of the activity of two or more corporations engaged in a common enterprise with substantial disregard of the separate nature of the corporate entities. The corporate veil will only be pierced if it is necessary to do so in order to prevent a gross inequity.

Plaintiff notes that Miller served as an officer and director of both corporations, and that the companies share some employees and a common address and phone number. These facts are insufficient to overcome the presumption of independence given to corporate entities. Absent additional evidence of the intermingling of corporate activities, or pervasive control of one entity by the other with fraudulent results, the Court must presume Primecard's independence and treat Affinity and Primecard as separate entities.

B. *Service Under New York's Long Arm Statute*

New York provides for specific jurisdiction over a foreign corporation that "transacts any business within the state or contracts anywhere to supply goods or services in the state," but only where the cause of action arises out of the aforesaid transaction. N.Y. C.P.L.R. § 302(a)(1) (McKinney 1998). If these conditions are met, service may be made outside New York in the same manner as service is made within the state. Under New York law, service may be made upon a corporation by delivering the summons to an officer, director, managing or general agent, cashier, or anyone authorized by appointment or law to receive service.

Affinity is amenable to service pursuant to New York's long arm statute, having contracted to provide services in New York. It is well settled under New York law that service is effective where the process server reasonably relies on an employee's representations that she is authorized to receive service of process on behalf of the defendant. As under the federal rules, service of process upon a non-employee who makes no representations as to authorization to receive service is not effective. Thus, plaintiff's service of process was ineffective under New York law.

C. Service Under Massachusetts Law

Massachusetts provides that service upon a corporation may be made by delivering a copy of the summons and complaint "to an officer, to a managing or general agent, or to a person in charge of the business at the principal place of business thereof within the Commonwealth, if any; or by delivering such copies to any other agent authorized by appointment or by law to receive service of process..." Mass. R. Civ. P. 4(d)(2). This language largely parallels the federal rules, but Massachusetts courts have construed the language narrowly. Given the relatively restrictive interpretation of the Massachusetts courts, service upon a non-employee is ineffective under Massachusetts standards.

III. Conclusion

The motion to vacate the default judgment is granted. The plaintiff technically has failed to effect proper service of process. Until proper service is effected, this Court has no jurisdiction over the defendant. However, as the Court may grant relief "upon such terms as are just," Fed.R.Civ.P. 60(b), and in light of the plaintiff's good faith belief that service had been properly effected, this vacatur is conditioned upon defendant's agreement to accept service on its attorney. Such service shall be made within seven (7) days of this Order. ...

SO ORDERED.

Notes and Questions

1. Why might a court express a preference that litigation disputes be resolved on the merits, and not be default?

2. How do the service provisions for corporations differ from the provisions for individuals?

3. Who has the burden to demonstrate that service was proper under the statute?

4. What significance does the court in this case attribute to the fact that a principal of the defendant corporation had actual notice of the lawsuit?

5. Having concluded that service was defective under the Federal Rules, the court goes on the analyze service under the New York and Massachusetts rules, as the Federal Rules allow. States can fashion their service rules as they like, so long as those rules do not violate due process.

6. Note the court's conclusion, acknowledging the ineffective service but conditioning vacatur on the defendant's agreement to accept service. If notice is required, and notice here was faulty, why allow the plaintiff a second chance in the circumstances of this case? Does your answer to this question connect to your answer to the first question, above?

Supplemental Materials:
Due Process and Personal Jurisdiction

A. The Post-*Pennoyer* World
HESS v. PAWLOSKI
274 U.S. 352 (1927)

MR. JUSTICE BUTLER delivered the opinion of the Court.

This action was brought by defendant ... to recover damages for personal injuries. The declaration alleged that plaintiff ... negligently and wantonly drove a motor vehicle on a public highway in Massachusetts and that by reason thereof the vehicle struck and injured defendant in error. Plaintiff ... is a resident of Pennsylvania. No personal service was made on him and no property belonging to him was attached. The service of process was made in compliance with c. 90, General Laws of Massachusetts, the material parts of which follow:

> The acceptance by a non-resident of the rights and privileges conferred by section three or four, as evidenced by his operating a motor vehicle thereunder, or the operation by a non-resident of a motor vehicle on a public way in the commonwealth other than under said sections, shall be deemed equivalent to an appointment by such non-resident of the registrar or his successor in office, to be his true and lawful attorney upon whom may be served all lawful processes in any action or proceeding against him, growing out of any accident or collision in which said non-resident may be involved while operating a motor vehicle on such a way, and said acceptance or operation shall be a signification of his agreement that any such process against him which is so served shall be of the same legal force and validity as if served on him personally. Service of such process shall be made by leaving a copy of the process with a fee of two dollars in the hands of the registrar, or in his office, and such service shall be sufficient service upon the said non-resident; provided, that notice of such service and a copy of the process are

forthwith sent by registered mail by the plaintiff to the defendant, and the defendant's return receipt and the plaintiff's affidavit of compliance herewith are appended to the writ and entered with the declaration. The court in which the action is pending may order such continuances as may be necessary to afford the defendant reasonable opportunity to defend the action.

Plaintiff ... appeared specially for the purpose of contesting jurisdiction and filed an answer in abatement and moved to dismiss on the ground that the service of process, if sustained, would deprive him of his property without due process of law in violation of the Fourteenth Amendment. The court ... denied the motion. The Supreme Judicial Court held the statute to be a valid exercise of the police power, and affirmed the order. ...

The question is whether the Massachusetts enactment contravenes the due process clause of the Fourteenth Amendment.

The process of a court of one State cannot run into another and summon a party there domiciled to respond to proceedings against him. Notice sent outside the State to a non-resident is unavailing to give jurisdiction in an action against him personally for money recovery. *Pennoyer v. Neff* (1878). ... A personal judgment rendered against a non-resident who has neither been served with process nor appeared in the suit is without validity. ...

Motor vehicles are dangerous machines; and, even when skillfully and carefully operated, their use is attended by serious dangers to persons and property. In the public interest the State may make and enforce regulations reasonably calculated to promote care on the part of all, residents and non-residents alike, who use its highways. The measure in question operates to require a non-resident to answer for his conduct in the State where arise causes of action alleged against him, as well as to provide for a claimant a convenient method by which he may sue to enforce his rights. Under the statute the implied consent is limited to proceedings growing out of accidents or collisions on a highway in which the non-resident may be involved. It is required that he shall actually receive ... notice of the service and a copy of the process. ... It makes no hostile discrimination against non-residents but tends to put them on the same footing as residents. [I]n advance of the operation of a motor vehicle on its highway by a non-resident, the State may require [the non-resident] to appoint one of its officials as his agent on whom process may be served in proceedings growing out of such use. [T]he State may declare that the use of the highway by the non-resident is the equivalent of the appointment of the registrar as agent on whom process may be served. The difference between the formal and implied appointment is not substantial so far as concerns the application of the due process clause of the Fourteenth Amendment.

Judgment affirmed.

B. Stream of Commerce and Purposeful Availment

ASAHI METAL INDUSTRY CO., LTD.
v.
SUPERIOR COURT OF CALIFORNIA
480 U.S. 102 (1987)

JUSTICE O'CONNOR announced the judgment of the Court and delivered the unanimous opinion of the Court with respect to Part I, the opinion of the Court with respect to Part II-B, in which THE CHIEF JUSTICE, JUSTICE BRENNAN, JUSTICE WHITE, JUSTICE MARSHALL, JUSTICE BLACKMUN, JUSTICE POWELL, and JUSTICE STEVENS join, and an opinion with respect to Parts II-A and III, in which THE CHIEF JUSTICE, JUSTICE POWELL, and JUSTICE SCALIA join.

This case presents the question whether the mere awareness on the part of a foreign defendant that the components it manufactured, sold, and delivered outside the United States would reach the forum State in the stream of commerce constitutes "minimum contacts" between the defendant and the forum State such that the exercise of jurisdiction "does not offend 'traditional notions of fair play and substantial justice.'" *International Shoe Co. v. Washington* (1945) (quoting *Milliken v. Meyer* (1940)).

I

On September 23, 1978, on Interstate Highway 80 in Solano County, California, Gary Zurcher lost control of his Honda motorcycle and collided with a tractor. Zurcher was severely injured, and his passenger and wife, Ruth Ann Moreno, was killed. In September 1979, Zurcher filed a product liability action in the Superior Court of the State of California in and for the County of Solano. Zurcher alleged that the 1978 accident was caused by a sudden loss of air and an explosion in the rear tire of the motorcycle, and alleged that the motorcycle tire, tube, and sealant were defective. Zurcher's complaint named, *inter alia,* Cheng Shin Rubber Industrial Co., Ltd. (Cheng Shin), the Taiwanese manufacturer of the tube. Cheng Shin in turn filed a cross-complaint seeking indemnification from its codefendants and from petitioner, Asahi Metal Industry Co., Ltd. (Asahi), the manufacturer of the tube's valve assembly. Zurcher's claims against Cheng Shin and the other defendants were eventually settled and dismissed, leaving only Cheng Shin's indemnity action against Asahi.

California's long-arm statute authorizes the exercise of jurisdiction "on any basis not inconsistent with the Constitution of this state or of the United States." Cal. Civ. Proc. Code Ann. § 410.10 (West 1973). Asahi moved to quash Cheng Shin's service of summons, arguing the State could not exert jurisdiction over it consistent with the Due Process Clause of the Fourteenth Amendment.

In relation to the motion, the following information was submitted by Asahi and Cheng Shin. Asahi is a Japanese corporation. It manufactures tire valve assemblies in Japan and sells the assemblies to Cheng Shin, and to several other tire manufacturers, for use as components in finished tire tubes. Asahi's sales to Cheng Shin took place in Taiwan. The shipments from Asahi to Cheng Shin were sent from Japan to Taiwan. Cheng Shin bought and incorporated into its tire tubes 150,000 Asahi valve assemblies in 1978; 500,000 in 1979; 500,000 in 1980; 100,000 in 1981; and 100,000 in 1982. Sales to Cheng Shin accounted for 1.24 percent of Asahi's income in 1981 and 0.44 percent in 1982. Cheng Shin alleged that approximately 20 percent of its sales in the United States are in California. Cheng Shin purchases valve assemblies from other suppliers as well, and sells finished tubes throughout the world.

In 1983 an attorney for Cheng Shin conducted an informal examination of the valve stems of the tire tubes sold in one cycle store in Solano County. The attorney declared that of the approximately 115 tire tubes in the store, 97 were purportedly manufactured in Japan or Taiwan, and of those 97, 21 valve stems were marked with the circled letter "A," apparently Asahi's trademark. Of the 21 Asahi valve stems, 12 were incorporated into Cheng Shin tire tubes. The store contained 41 other Cheng Shin tubes that incorporated the valve assemblies of other manufacturers. An affidavit of a manager of Cheng Shin whose duties included the purchasing of component parts stated: "In discussions with Asahi regarding the purchase of valve stem assemblies the fact that my Company sells tubes throughout the world and specifically the United States has been discussed. I am informed and believe that Asahi was fully aware that valve stem assemblies sold to my Company and to others would end up throughout the United States and in California." An affidavit of the president of Asahi, on the other hand, declared that Asahi "has never contemplated that its limited sales of tire valves to Cheng Shin in Taiwan would subject it to lawsuits in California." The record does not include any contract between Cheng Shin and Asahi.

Primarily on the basis of the above information, the Superior Court denied the motion to quash summons, stating: "Asahi obviously does business on an international scale. It is not unreasonable that they defend claims of defect in their product on an international scale."

The Court of Appeal of the State of California issued a peremptory writ of mandate commanding the Superior Court to quash service of summons. ... The Supreme Court of the State of California reversed and discharged the writ issued by the Court of Appeal. [T]he court found the exercise of jurisdiction over Asahi to be consistent with the Due Process Clause. It concluded that Asahi knew that some of the valve assemblies sold to Cheng Shin would be incorporated into tire tubes sold in California, and that Asahi benefited indirectly from the sale in California of products incorporating its components. The court considered Asahi's intentional act of placing its components into the stream of commerce — that is, by delivering the components to Cheng Shin in Taiwan — coupled with Asahi's awareness that some of the components would eventually find their way into California, sufficient to form the basis for state court jurisdiction under the Due Process Clause.

We granted certiorari, and now reverse.

II

A

The Due Process Clause of the Fourteenth Amendment limits the power of a state court to exert personal jurisdiction over a nonresident defendant. "[T]he constitutional touchstone" of the determination whether an exercise of personal jurisdiction comports with due process "remains whether the defendant purposefully established 'minimum contacts' in the forum State." *Burger King Corp. v. Rudzewicz* (1985) (quoting *International Shoe*). [M]inimum contacts must have a basis in "some act by which the defendant purposefully avails itself of the privilege of conducting activities within the forum State, thus invoking the benefits and protections of its laws." *Id.* "Jurisdiction is proper . . . where the contacts proximately result from actions by the defendant *himself* that create a 'substantial connection' with the forum State." *Id.* (quoting *McGee v. International Life Ins. Co.* (1957) (emphasis in original).

Applying the principle that minimum contacts must be based on an act of the defendant, the Court in *World-Wide Volkswagen Corp. v. Woodsen* (1980), rejected the assertion that a *consumer's* unilateral act of bringing the defendant's product into the forum State was a sufficient constitutional basis for personal jurisdiction over the defendant. It had been argued in *World-Wide Volkswagen* that because an automobile retailer and its wholesale distributor sold a product mobile by design and purpose, they could foresee being haled into court in the distant States into which their customers might drive. The Court rejected this concept of foreseeability as an insufficient basis for jurisdiction under the Due Process Clause. The Court disclaimed, however, the idea that "foreseeability is wholly irrelevant" to personal jurisdiction, concluding that "[t]he forum State does not exceed its powers under the Due Process Clause if it asserts personal jurisdiction over a corporation that delivers its products into the stream of commerce with the expectation that they will be purchased by consumers in the forum State." (citation omitted). ...

In *World-Wide Volkswagen* itself, the state court sought to base jurisdiction not on any act of the defendant, but on the foreseeable unilateral actions of the consumer. Since *World-Wide Volkswagen,* lower courts have been confronted with cases in which the defendant acted by placing a product in the stream of commerce, and the stream eventually swept defendant's product into the forum State, but the defendant did nothing else to purposefully avail itself of the market in the forum State. Some courts have understood the Due Process Clause, as interpreted in *World-Wide Volkswagen*, to allow an exercise of personal jurisdiction to be based on no more than the defendant's act of placing the product in the stream of commerce. Other courts have understood the Due Process Clause and the above-quoted language in *World-Wide Volkswagen* to require the action of the defendant to be more purposefully directed at the forum State than the mere act of placing a product in the stream of commerce.

The reasoning of the Supreme Court of California in the present case illustrates the former interpretation of *World-Wide Volkswagen*. The Supreme Court of California held that, because the stream of commerce eventually brought some valves Asahi sold Cheng Shin into California, Asahi's awareness that its valves would be sold in California was sufficient to permit California to exercise jurisdiction over Asahi consistent with the requirements of the Due Process Clause. The Supreme Court of California's position was consistent with those courts that have held that mere foreseeability or awareness was a constitutionally sufficient basis for personal jurisdiction if the defendant's product made its way into the forum State while still in the stream of commerce.

Other courts, however, have understood the Due Process Clause to require something more than that the defendant was aware of its product's entry into the forum State through the stream of commerce in order for the State to exert jurisdiction over the defendant. ...

We now find this latter position to be consonant with the requirements of due process. The "substantial connection," Burger King, between the defendant and the forum State necessary for a finding of minimum contacts must come about by *an action of the defendant purposefully directed toward the forum State*. The placement of a product into the stream of commerce, without more, is not an act of the defendant purposefully directed toward the forum State. Additional conduct of the defendant may indicate an intent or purpose to serve the market in the forum State, for example, designing the product for the market in the forum State, advertising in the forum State, establishing channels for providing regular advice to customers in the forum State, or marketing the product through a distributor who has agreed to serve as the sales agent in the forum State. But a defendant's awareness that the stream of commerce may or will sweep the product into the forum State does not convert the mere act of placing the product into the stream into an act purposefully directed toward the forum State.

Assuming, *arguendo*, that respondents have established Asahi's awareness that some of the valves sold to Cheng Shin would be incorporated into tire tubes sold in California, respondents have not demonstrated any action by Asahi to purposefully avail itself of the California market. Asahi does

Commers + Sub. Connections

not do business in California. It has no office, agents, employees, or property in California. It does not advertise or otherwise solicit business in California. It did not create, control, or employ the distribution system that brought its valves to California. There is no evidence that Asahi designed its product in anticipation of sales in California. On the basis of these facts, the exertion of personal jurisdiction over Asahi by the Superior Court of California exceeds the limits of due process.

holding

III

Because the facts of this case do not establish minimum contacts such that the exercise of personal jurisdiction is consistent with fair play and substantial justice, the judgment of the Supreme Court of California is reversed, and the case is remanded for further proceedings not inconsistent with this opinion.

It is so ordered.

JUSTICE BRENNAN, with whom JUSTICE WHITE, JUSTICE MARSHALL, and JUSTICE BLACKMUN join, concurring in part and concurring in the judgment.

I do not agree with the interpretation in Part II-A of the stream-of-commerce theory, nor with the conclusion that Asahi did not "purposely avail itself of the California market." ... I therefore join Parts I and II-B of the Court's opinion, and write separately to explain my disagreement with Part II-A.

... The stream of commerce refers not to unpredictable currents or eddies, but to the regular and anticipated flow of products from manufacture to distribution to retail sale. As long as a participant in this process is aware that the final product is being marketed in the forum State, the possibility of a lawsuit there cannot come as a surprise. Nor will the litigation present a burden for which there is no corresponding benefit. A defendant who has placed goods in the stream of commerce benefits economically from the retail sale of the final product in the forum State, and indirectly benefits from the State's laws that regulate and facilitate commercial activity. These benefits accrue regardless of whether that participant directly conducts business in the forum State, or engages in additional conduct directed toward that State. Accordingly, most courts and commentators have found that jurisdiction premised on the placement of a product into the stream of commerce is consistent with the Due Process Clause, and have not required a showing of additional conduct.

...

In this case, the facts found by the California Supreme Court support its finding of minimum contacts. The court found that "[a]lthough Asahi did not design or control the system of distribution that carried its valve assemblies into California, Asahi was aware of the distribution system's operation, and it knew that it would benefit economically from the sale in California of products incorporating its components." Accordingly, I cannot join the determination in Part II-A that Asahi's regular and extensive sales of component parts to a manufacturer it knew was making regular sales of the final product in California is insufficient to establish minimum contacts with California.

JUSTICE STEVENS, with whom JUSTICE WHITE and JUSTICE BLACKMUN join, concurring in part and concurring in the judgment.

The judgment of the Supreme Court of California should be reversed for the reasons stated in Part II-B of the Court's opinion. While I join Parts I and II-B, I do not join Part II-A for two reasons. First, it is not necessary to the Court's decision. ... Accordingly, I see no reason in this case for the plurality to articulate "purposeful direction" or any other test as the nexus between an act of a defendant and the forum State that is necessary to establish minimum contacts.

Second, even assuming that the test ought to be formulated here, Part II-A misapplies it to the facts of this case. The plurality seems to assume that an unwavering line can be drawn between "mere awareness" that a component will find its way into the forum State and "purposeful availment" of the forum's market. Over the course of its dealings with Cheng Shin, Asahi has arguably engaged in a higher quantum of conduct than "[t]he placement of a product into the stream of commerce, without more . . . ." Whether or not this conduct rises to the level of purposeful availment requires a constitutional determination that is affected by the volume, the value, and the hazardous character of the components. In most circumstances I would be inclined to conclude that a regular course of dealing that results in deliveries of over 100,000 units annually over a period of several years would constitute "purposeful availment" even though the item delivered to the forum State was a standard product marketed throughout the world.

C. Contracts and Purposeful Availment
McGEE v. INTERNATIONAL LIFE INSURANCE CO.
355 U.S. 220 (1957)

Opinion of the Court by MR. JUSTICE BLACK.

Petitioner, Lulu B. McGee, recovered a judgment in a California state court against respondent, International Life Insurance Company, on a contract of insurance. Respondent was not served with process in California but by registered mail at its principal place of business in Texas. The California court based its jurisdiction on a state statute which subjects foreign corporations to suit in California on insurance contracts with residents of that State even though such corporations cannot be served with process within its borders.

Unable to collect the judgment in California petitioner went to Texas where she filed suit on the judgment in a Texas court. But the Texas courts refused to enforce her judgment holding it was void under the Fourteenth Amendment because service of process outside California could not give the courts of that State jurisdiction over respondent. Since the case raised important questions, not only to California but to other States which have similar laws, we granted certiorari. It is not controverted that if the California court properly exercised jurisdiction over respondent the Texas courts erred in refusing to give its judgment full faith and credit.

The material facts are relatively simple. In 1944, Lowell Franklin, a resident of California, purchased a life insurance policy from the Empire Mutual Insurance Company, an Arizona corporation. In 1948 the respondent agreed with Empire Mutual to assume its insurance obligations. Respondent then mailed a reinsurance certificate to Franklin in California offering to insure him in accordance with the terms of the policy he held with Empire Mutual. He accepted this offer and from that time until his death in 1950 paid premiums by mail from his California home to respondent's Texas office. Petitioner, Franklin's mother, was the beneficiary under the policy. She sent proofs of his death to the respondent but it refused to pay claiming that he had committed suicide. It appears that neither Empire Mutual nor respondent has ever had any office or agent in California. And so far as the record before us shows, respondent has never solicited or done any insurance business in California apart from the policy involved here.

Since *Pennoyer v. Neff* (1878), this Court has held that the Due Process Clause of the Fourteenth Amendment places some limit on the power of state courts to enter binding judgments against persons not served with process within their boundaries. But just where this line of limitation falls has been the subject of prolific controversy, particularly with respect to foreign corporations. In a continuing process of evolution this Court accepted and then abandoned "consent," "doing business," and "presence" as the standard for measuring the extent of state judicial power over such corporations. More recently in *International Shoe v. Washington* (1945), the Court decided that "due process requires only that in order to subject a defendant to a judgment *in personam*, if he be not present within the territory of the forum, he have certain minimum contacts with it such that the maintenance of the suit does not offend 'traditional notions of fair play and substantial justice.'"

Looking back over this long history of litigation a trend is clearly discernible toward expanding the permissible scope of state jurisdiction over foreign corporations and other nonresidents. In part this is attributable to the fundamental transformation of our national economy over the years. Today many commercial transactions touch two or more States and may involve parties separated by the full continent. With this increasing nationalization of commerce has come a great increase in the amount of business conducted by mail across state lines. At the same time modern transportation and communication have made it much less burdensome for a party sued to defend himself in a State where he engages in economic activity.

Turning to this case we think it apparent that the Due Process Clause did not preclude the California court from entering a judgment binding on respondent. It is sufficient for purposes of due process that the suit was based on a contract which had substantial connection with that State. The contract was delivered in California, the premiums were mailed from there and the insured was a resident of that State when he died. It cannot be denied that California has a manifest interest in providing effective means of redress for its residents when their insurers refuse to pay claims. These residents would be at a severe disadvantage if they were forced to follow the insurance company to a distant State in order to hold it legally accountable. When claims were small or moderate individual claimants frequently could not afford the cost of bringing an action in a foreign forum—thus in effect making the company judgment proof. Often the crucial witnesses—as here on the company's defense of suicide—will be found in the insured's locality. Of course there may be inconvenience to the insurer if it is held amenable to suit in California where it had this contract but certainly nothing which amounts to a denial of due process. There is no contention that respondent did not have adequate notice of the suit or sufficient time to prepare its defenses and appear.

The California statute became law in 1949, after respondent had entered into the agreement with Franklin to assume Empire Mutual's obligation to him. Respondent contends that application of the statute to this existing contract improperly impairs the obligation of the contract. We believe that contention is devoid of merit. The statute was remedial, in the purest sense of that term, and neither enlarged nor impaired respondent's substantive rights or obligations under the contract. It did nothing more than to provide petitioner with a California forum to enforce whatever substantive rights she might have against respondent. At the same time respondent was given a reasonable time to appear and defend on the merits after being notified of the suit. Under such circumstances it had no vested right not to be sued in California.

The judgment is reversed and the cause is remanded to the Court of Civil Appeals of the State of Texas, First Supreme Judicial District, for further proceedings not inconsistent with this opinion.

It is so ordered.

HANSON v. DENCKLA
357 U.S. 235 (1958)

MR. CHIEF JUSTICE WARREN delivered the opinion of the Court.

This controversy concerns the right to $400,000, part of the corpus of a trust established in Delaware by a settlor who later became domiciled in Florida. One group of claimants, "legatees," urge that this property passed under the residuary clause of the settlor's will, which was admitted to probate in Florida. The Florida courts have sustained this position. Other claimants, "appointees" and "beneficiaries," contend that the property passed pursuant to the settlor's exercise of the *inter vivos* power of appointment created in the deed of trust. The Delaware courts adopted this position and refused to accord full faith and credit to the Florida determination because the Florida court had not acquired jurisdiction over an indispensable party, the Delaware trustee. We postponed the question of jurisdiction in the Florida appeal, and granted certiorari to the Delaware Supreme Court.

The trust whose validity is contested here was created in 1935. Dora Browning Donner, then a domiciliary of Pennsylvania, executed a trust instrument in Delaware naming the Wilmington Trust Co., of Wilmington, Delaware, as trustee. The corpus was composed of securities. Mrs. Donner reserved the income for life, and stated that the remainder should be paid to such persons or upon such trusts as she should appoint by *inter vivos* or testamentary instrument. The trust agreement provided that Mrs. Donner could change the trustee, and that she could amend, alter or revoke the agreement at any time. A measure of control over trust administration was assured by the provision that only with the consent of a trust "advisor" appointed by the settlor could the trustee (1) sell trust assets, (2) make investments, and (3) participate in any plan, proceeding, reorganization or merger involving securities held in the trust. A few days after the trust was established Mrs. Donner exercised her power of appointment. That appointment was replaced by another in 1939. Thereafter she left Pennsylvania, and in 1944 became domiciled in Florida, where she remained until her death in 1952. Mrs. Donner's will was executed Dec. 3, 1949. On that same day she executed the *inter vivos* power of appointment whose terms are at issue here. After making modest appointments in favor of a hospital and certain family retainers (the "appointees"), she appointed the sum of $200,000 to each of two trusts previously established with another Delaware trustee, the Delaware Trust Co. The balance of the trust corpus, over $1,000,000 at the date of her death, was appointed to her executrix. That amount passed under the residuary clause of her will and is not at issue here.

The two trusts with the Delaware Trust Co. were created in 1948 by Mrs. Donner's daughter, Elizabeth Donner Hanson, for the benefit of Elizabeth's children, Donner Hanson and Joseph Donner Winsor. In identical terms they provide that the income not required for the beneficiary's support should be accumulated to age 25, when the beneficiary should be paid 1/4 of the corpus and receive the income from the balance for life. Upon the death of the beneficiary the remainder was to go to such of the beneficiary's issue or Elizabeth Donner Hanson's issue as the beneficiary should appoint by *inter vivos* or testamentary instrument; in default of appointment to the beneficiary's issue alive at the time of his death, and if none to the issue of Elizabeth Donner Hanson.

Mrs. Donner died Nov. 20, 1952. Her will, which was admitted to probate in Florida, named Elizabeth Donner Hanson as executrix. She was instructed to pay all debts and taxes, including any which might be payable by reason of the property appointed under the power of appointment in the trust agreement with the Wilmington Trust Co. After disposing of personal and household effects, Mrs. Donner's will directed that the balance of her property (the $1,000,000 appointed from the Delaware trust) be paid in equal parts to two trusts for the benefit of her daughters Katherine N. R. Denckla and Dorothy B. R. Stewart.

This controversy grows out of the residuary clause that created the last-mentioned trusts. ... Residuary legatees Denckla and Stewart, already the recipients of over $500,000 each, urge that the power of appointment over the $400,000 appointed to sister Elizabeth's children was not "effectively exercised" and that the property should accordingly pass to them. Fourteen months after Mrs. Donner's death these parties petitioned a Florida chancery court for a declaratory judgment "concerning what property passes under the residuary clause" of the will. Personal service was had upon the following defendants: (1) executrix Elizabeth Donner Hanson, (2) beneficiaries Donner Hanson and Joseph Donner Winsor, and (3) potential beneficiary William Donner Roosevelt, also one of Elizabeth's children. Curtin Winsor, Jr., another of Elizabeth's children and also a potential beneficiary of the Delaware trusts, was not named as a party and was not served. About a dozen other defendants were nonresidents and could not be personally served. These included the Wilmington Trust Co. ("trustee"), the Delaware Trust Co. (to whom the $400,000 had been paid shortly after Mrs. Donner's death), certain individuals who were potential successors in interest to complainants Denckla and Stewart, and most of the named appointees in Mrs. Donner's 1949 appointment. A copy of the pleadings and a "Notice to Appear and Defend" were sent to each of these defendants by ordinary mail, and notice was published locally as required by the Florida statutes dealing with constructive service. With the exception of two individuals whose interests coincided with complainants Denckla and Stewart, none of the nonresident defendants made any appearance.

The appearing defendants (Elizabeth Donner Hanson and her children) moved to dismiss the suit because the exercise of jurisdiction over indispensable parties, the Delaware trustees, would offend Section 1 of the Fourteenth Amendment. The Chancellor ruled that he lacked jurisdiction over these nonresident defendants because no personal service was had and because the trust corpus was outside the territorial jurisdiction of the court. The cause was dismissed as to them. As far as parties before the court were concerned, however, he ruled that the power of appointment was testamentary and void under the applicable Florida law. In a decree dated Jan. 14, 1955, he ruled that the $400,000 passed under the residuary clause of the will.

After the Florida litigation began, but before entry of the decree, the executrix instituted a declaratory judgment action in Delaware to determine who was entitled to participate in the trust assets held in that State. Except for the addition of beneficiary Winsor and several appointees, the parties were substantially the same as in the Florida litigation. Nonresident defendants were notified by registered mail. All of the trust companies, beneficiaries, and legatees except Katherine N. R. Denckla, appeared and participated in the litigation. After the Florida court enjoined executrix Hanson from further participation, her children pursued their own interests. When the Florida decree was entered the legatees unsuccessfully urged it as *res judicata* of the Delaware dispute. In a decree dated Jan. 13, 1956, the Delaware Chancellor ruled that the trust and power of appointment were valid under the applicable Delaware law, and that the trust corpus had properly been paid to the Delaware Trust Co. and the other appointees.

... The Florida Supreme Court affirmed its Chancellor's conclusion that Florida law applied to determine the validity of the trust and power of appointment. ... The Chancellor's conclusion that there was no jurisdiction over the trust companies and other absent defendants was reversed. The court ruled that jurisdiction to construe the will carried with it "substantive" jurisdiction "over the persons of the absent defendants" even though the trust assets were not "physically in this state." ... In a motion for rehearing the beneficiaries and appointees urged for the first time that Florida should have given full faith and credit to the decision of the Delaware Chancellor. The motion was denied without opinion, Nov. 28, 1956.

The full faith and credit question was first raised in the Delaware litigation by an unsuccessful motion for new trial filed with the Chancellor Jan. 20, 1956. After the Florida Supreme Court decision the matter was renewed by a motion to remand filed with the Delaware Supreme Court. In a decision of Jan. 14, 1957, that court denied the motion and affirmed its Chancellor in all respects. The Florida decree was held not binding for purposes of full faith and credit because the Florida court had no personal jurisdiction over the trust companies and no jurisdiction over the trust *res*.

The issues for our decision are, *first*, whether Florida erred in holding that it had jurisdiction over the nonresident defendants, and *second*, whether Delaware erred in refusing full faith and credit to the Florida decree. ...

Appellants charge that this judgment is offensive to the Due Process Clause of the Fourteenth Amendment because the Florida court was without jurisdiction. ... Appellees ... urge that the circumstances of this case amount to sufficient affiliation with the State of Florida to empower its courts to exercise personal jurisdiction over this nonresident defendant. Principal reliance is placed upon *McGee v. International Life Ins. Co.* (1957). In *McGee* the Court noted the trend of expanding personal jurisdiction over nonresidents. As technological progress has increased the flow of commerce between States, the need for jurisdiction over nonresidents has undergone a similar increase. At the same time, progress in communications and transportation has made the defense of a suit in a foreign tribunal less burdensome. In response to these changes, the requirements for personal jurisdiction over nonresidents have evolved from the rigid rule of *Pennoyer v. Neff* to the flexible standard of *International Shoe Co. v. Washington*. But it is a mistake to assume that this trend heralds the eventual demise of all restrictions on the personal jurisdiction of state courts. Those restrictions are more than a guarantee of immunity from inconvenient or distant litigation. ... However minimal the burden of defending in a foreign tribunal, a defendant may not be called upon to do so unless he has had the "minimal contacts" with that State that are a prerequisite to its exercise of power over him.

We fail to find such contacts in the circumstances of this case. The defendant trust company has no office in Florida, and transacts no business there. None of the trust assets has ever been held or administered in Florida, and the record discloses no solicitation of business in that State either in person or by mail.

The cause of action in this case is not one that arises out of an act done or transaction consummated in the forum State. In that respect, it differs from *McGee*.... In *McGee*, the nonresident defendant solicited a reinsurance agreement with a resident of California. The offer was accepted in that State, and the insurance premiums were mailed from there until the insured's death. Nothing the interest California has in providing effective redress for its residents when nonresident insurers refuse to pay claims on insurance they have solicited in that State, the Court upheld jurisdiction because the suit "was based on a contract which had substantial connection with that State." In contrast, this action involves the validity of an agreement that was entered without any connection with the forum State. The agreement was executed in Delaware by a trust company incorporated in that State and a settlor domiciled in Pennsylvania. The first relationship Florida had to the agreement was years later when the settlor became domiciled there, and the trustee remitted the trust income to her in that State. From Florida Mrs. Donner carried on several bits of trust administration that may be compared to the mailing of premiums in *McGee*. But the record discloses no instance in which the *trustee* performed any acts in Florida that bear the same relationship to the agreement as the solicitation in *McGee*. Consequently, this suit cannot be said to be one to enforce an obligation that arose from a privilege the defendant exercised in Florida. ...

The execution in Florida of the powers of appointment under which the beneficiaries and appointees claim does not give Florida a substantial connection with the contract on which this suit is based. ... The unilateral activity of those who claim some relationship with a nonresident defendant cannot satisfy the requirement of contact with the forum State. The application of that rule will vary with the quality and nature of the defendant's activity, but it is essential in each case that there be some act by which the defendant purposefully avails itself of the privilege of conducting activities within the forum State, thus invoking the benefits and protections of its laws. The settlor's execution in Florida of her power of appointment cannot remedy the absence of such an act in this case.

It is urged that because the settlor and most of the appointees and beneficiaries were domiciled in Florida the courts of that State should be able to exercise personal jurisdiction over the nonresident trustees. This is a non sequitur. With personal jurisdiction over the executor, legatees, and appointees, there is nothing in federal law to prevent Florida from adjudicating concerning the respective rights and liabilities of those parties. But Florida has not chosen to do so. As we understand its law, the trustee is an indispensable party over whom the court must acquire jurisdiction before it is empowered to enter judgment in a proceeding affecting the validity of a trust. It does not acquire that jurisdiction by being the "center of gravity" of the controversy, or the most convenient location for litigation. The issue is personal jurisdiction, not choice of law. It is resolved in this case by considering the acts of the trustee. As we have indicated, they are insufficient to sustain the jurisdiction.

... As we have noted earlier, the Florida Supreme Court has repeatedly held that a trustee is an indispensable party without whom a Florida court has no power to adjudicate controversies affecting the validity of a trust. For that reason the Florida judgment must be reversed not only as to the nonresident trustees but also as to appellants, over whom the Florida court admittedly had jurisdiction.

... The same reasons that compel reversal of the Florida judgment require affirmance of the Delaware one. Delaware is under no obligation to give full faith and credit to a Florida judgment invalid in Florida because offensive to the Due Process Clause of the Fourteenth Amendment. ... Since Delaware was entitled to conclude that Florida law made the trust company an indispensable party, it was under no obligation to give the Florida judgment any faith and credit—even against parties over whom Florida's jurisdiction was unquestioned.

... *It is so ordered.*

MR. JUSTICE BLACK, whom MR. JUSTICE BURTON and MR. JUSTICE BRENNAN join, dissenting.

... [There] is nothing in the Due Process Clause which denies Florida the right to determine whether Mrs. Donner's appointment was valid as against its statute of wills. This disposition, which was designed to take effect after her death, had very close and substantial connections with that State. Not only was the appointment made in Florida by a domiciliary of Florida, but the primary beneficiaries also lived in that State. In my view it could hardly be denied that Florida had sufficient interest so that a court with jurisdiction might properly apply Florida law, if it chose, to determine whether the appointment was effectual. ... It seems to me that where a transaction has as much relationship to a State as Mrs. Donner's appointment had to Florida its courts ought to have power to adjudicate controversies arising out of that transaction, unless litigation there would impose such a heavy and disproportionate burden on a nonresident defendant that it would offend what this Court has referred to as "traditional notions of fair play and substantial justice." So far as the nonresident defendants here are concerned I can see nothing which approaches that degree of unfairness. Florida, the home of the principal contenders for Mrs. Donner's largess, was a reasonably convenient forum for all. Certainly there is nothing fundamentally unfair in subjecting the corporate trustee to the jurisdiction of the Florida courts. It chose to maintain business relations with Mrs. Donner in that State for eight years, regularly communicating with her with respect to the business of the trust including the very appointment in question.

Florida's interest in the validity of Mrs. Donner's appointment is made more emphatic by the fact that her will is being administered in that State. It has traditionally been the rule that the State where a person is domiciled at the time of his death is the proper place to determine the validity of his will, to construe its provisions and to marshal and distribute his personal property. Here Florida was seriously concerned with winding up Mrs. Donner's estate and with finally determining what property was to be distributed under her will. In fact this suit was brought for that very purpose.

...

[Dissenting opinion of Mr. JUSTICE DOUGLAS, omitted.]

D. The Effects Test

KULKO v. SUPERIOR COURT
436 U.S. 84 (1978)

MR. JUSTICE MARSHALL delivered the opinion of the Court.

The issue before us is whether, in this action for child support, the California state courts may exercise *in personam* jurisdiction over a nonresident, nondomiciliary parent of minor children domiciled within the State. For reasons set forth below, we hold that the exercise of such jurisdiction would violate the Due Process Clause of the Fourteenth Amendment.

Appellant Ezra Kulko married appellee Sharon Kulko Horn in 1959, during appellant's three-day stopover in California en route from a military base in Texas to a tour of duty in Korea. At the time of this marriage, both parties were domiciled in and residents of New York State. Immediately following the marriage, Sharon Kulko returned to New York, as did appellant after his tour of duty. Their first child, Darwin, was born to the Kulkos in New York in 1961, and a year later their second child, Ilsa, was born, also in New York. The Kulkos and their two children resided together as a family in New York City continuously until March 1972, when the Kulkos separated.

Following the separation, Sharon Kulko moved to San Francisco, Cal. A written separation agreement was drawn up in New York; in September 1972, Sharon Kulko flew to New York City in order to sign this agreement. The agreement provided, inter alia, that the children would remain with their father during the school year but would spend their Christmas, Easter, and summer vacations with their mother. While Sharon Kulko waived any claim for her own support or maintenance, Ezra Kulko agreed to pay his wife $3,000 per year in child support for the periods when the children were in her care, custody, and control. Immediately after execution of the separation agreement, Sharon Kulko flew to Haiti and procured a divorce there; the divorce decree incorporated the terms of the agreement. She then returned to California, where she remarried and took the name Horn.

The children resided with appellant during the school year and with their mother on vacations, as provided by the separation agreement, until December 1973. At this time, just before Ilsa was to leave New York to spend Christmas vacation with her mother, she told her father that she wanted to remain in California after her vacation. Appellant bought his daughter a one-way plane ticket, and Ilsa left, taking her clothing with her. Ilsa then commenced living in California with her mother during the school year and spending vacations with her father. In January 1976, appellant's other child, Darwin, called his mother from New York and advised her that he wanted to live with her in California. Unbeknownst to appellant, appellee Horn sent a plane ticket to her son, which he used to fly to California where he took up residence with his mother and sister.

Less than one month after Darwin's arrival in California, appellee Horn commenced this action against appellant in the California Superior Court. She sought to establish the Haitian divorce decree as a California judgment; to modify the judgment so as to award her full custody of the children; and to increase appellant's child-support obligations. Appellant appeared specially and moved to quash service of the summons on the ground that he was not a resident of California and lacked sufficient "minimum contacts" with the State under *International Shoe v. Washington* (1945) to warrant the State's assertion of personal jurisdiction over him.

The trial court summarily denied the motion to quash, and appellant sought review in the California Court of Appeal.... The appellate court affirmed the denial of appellant's motion to quash, reasoning that, by consenting to his children's living in California, appellant had "caused an effect in th[e] state" warranting the exercise of jurisdiction over him.

The California Supreme Court granted appellant's petition for review, and in a 4-2 decision sustained the rulings of the lower state courts. ... Agreeing with the court below, the Supreme Court stated that ... appellant had "purposely availed himself of the benefits and protections of the laws of California" by sending Ilsa to live with her mother in California. ...

...

The parties are in agreement that the constitutional standard for determining whether the State may enter a binding judgment against appellant here is that set forth in this Court's opinion in *International Shoe*: that a defendant "have certain minimum contacts with [the forum State] such that the maintenance of the suit does not offend 'traditional notions of fair play and substantial justice.'" [quotation omitted]. ...

[T]he "minimum contacts" test of *International Shoe* is not susceptible of mechanical application; rather, the facts of each case must be weighed to determine whether the requisite "affiliating circumstances" are present. *Hanson v. Denckla* (1958). We recognize that this determination is one in which few answers will be written "in black and white. The greys are dominant and even among them the shades are innumerable." *Estin v. Estin* (1948). But we believe that the California Supreme Court's application of the minimum-contacts test in this case represents an unwarranted extension of *International Shoe* ...

The "purposeful act" that the California Supreme Court believed ... warrant[ed] the exercise of personal jurisdiction over appellant in California was his "actively and fully consent[ing] to Ilsa living in California for the school year . . . and . . . sen[ding] her to California for that purpose." We cannot accept the proposition that appellant's acquiescence in Ilsa's desire to live with her mother conferred jurisdiction over appellant in the California courts in this action. A father who agrees, in the interests of family harmony and his children's preferences, to allow them to spend more time in California than was required under a separation agreement can hardly be said to have "purposefully availed himself" of the "benefits and protections" of California's laws.

Nor can we agree with the assertion of the court below that the exercise of *in personam* jurisdiction here was warranted by the financial benefit appellant derived from his daughter's presence in California for nine months of the year. This argument rests on the premise that, while appellant's liability for support payments remained unchanged, his yearly expenses for supporting the child in New York decreased. But this circumstance, even if true, does not support California's assertion of jurisdiction here. Any diminution in appellant's household costs resulted, not from the child's presence in California, but rather from her absence from appellant's home. ... Any ultimate financial advantage to appellant thus results not from the child's presence in California, but from appellee's failure earlier to seek an increase in payments under the separation agreement. The argument below to the contrary, in our view, confuses the question of appellant's liability with that of the proper forum in which to determine that liability.

In light of our conclusion that appellant did not purposefully derive benefit from any activities relating to the State of California, it is apparent that the California Supreme Court's reliance on appellant's having caused an "effect" in California was misplaced. This "effects" test is derived from the American Law Institute's Restatement (Second) of Conflict of Laws § 37 (1971), which provides:

> A state has power to exercise judicial jurisdiction over an individual who causes effects in the state by an act done elsewhere with respect to any cause of action arising from these effects unless the nature of the effects and of the individual's relationship to the state make the exercise of such jurisdiction unreasonable.

While this provision is not binding on this Court, it does not in any event support the decision below. As is apparent from the examples accompanying § 37 in the Restatement, this section was intended to reach wrongful activity outside of the State causing injury within the State, see, *e.g.*, Comment a, p. 157 (shooting bullet from one State into another), or commercial activity affecting state residents. Even in such situations, moreover, the Restatement recognizes that there might be circumstances that would render "unreasonable" the assertion of jurisdiction over the nonresident defendant.

[Here, there] is no claim that appellant has visited physical injury on either property or persons within the State of California. The cause of action herein asserted arises, not from the defendant's commercial transactions in interstate commerce, but rather from his personal, domestic relations. ... Furthermore, the controversy between the parties arises from a separation that occurred in the State of New York; appellee Horn seeks modification of a contract that was negotiated in New York and that she flew to New York to sign. As in *Hanson*, the instant action involves an agreement that was entered into with virtually no connection with the forum State.

... As noted above, appellant did no more than acquiesce in the stated preference of one of his children to live with her mother in California. This single act is surely not one that a reasonable parent would expect to result in the substantial financial burden and personal strain of litigating a child-support suit in a forum 3,000 miles away, and we therefore see no basis on which it can be said that appellant could reasonably have anticipated being "haled before a [California] court." ...

[We] conclude that the appellant's motion ... was erroneously denied by the California courts. The judgment of the California Supreme Court is, therefore,

Reversed.

[Dissenting opinion of Justice BRENNAN, omitted.]

CALDER v. JONES
465 U.S. 783 (1984)

effects test works.

JUSTICE REHNQUIST delivered the opinion of the Court.

Respondent Shirley Jones brought suit in California Superior Court claiming that she had been libeled in an article written and edited by petitioners in Florida. ... Petitioners were served with process by mail in Florida and caused special appearances to be entered on their behalf, moving to quash the service of process for lack of personal jurisdiction. The Superior Court granted the motion on the ground that First Amendment concerns weighed against an assertion of jurisdiction otherwise proper under the Due Process Clause. The California Court of Appeal reversed, rejecting the suggestion that First Amendment considerations enter into the jurisdictional analysis. We now affirm.

Respondent lives and works in California. She and her husband brought this suit against the National Enquirer, Inc., its local distributing company, and petitioners for libel, invasion of privacy, and intentional infliction of emotional harm. The Enquirer is a Florida corporation with its principal place of business in Florida. It publishes a national weekly newspaper with a total circulation of over 5 million. About 600,000 of those copies, almost twice the level of the next highest State, are sold in California. Respondent's and her husband's claims were based on an article that appeared in the Enquirer's October 9, 1979, issue. Both the Enquirer and the distributing company answered the complaint and made no objection to the jurisdiction of the California court.

Petitioner South is a reporter employed by the Enquirer. He is a resident of Florida, though he frequently travels to California on business. South wrote the first draft of the challenged article, and his byline appeared on it. He did most of his research in Florida, relying on phone calls to sources in California for the information contained in the article. Shortly before publication, South called respondent's home and read to her husband a draft of the article so as to elicit his comments upon it. Aside from his frequent trips and phone calls, South has no other relevant contacts with California.

Petitioner Calder is also a Florida resident. He has been to California only twice—once, on a pleasure trip, prior to the publication of the article and once after to testify in an unrelated trial. Calder is president and editor of the Enquirer. He "oversee[s] just about every function of the Enquirer." He reviewed and approved the initial evaluation of the subject of the article and edited it in its final form. He also declined to print a retraction requested by respondent. Calder has no other relevant contacts with California.

In considering petitioners' motion to quash service of process, the Superior Court surmised that the actions of petitioners in Florida, causing injury to respondent in California, would ordinarily be sufficient to support an assertion of jurisdiction over them in California. But the court felt that special solicitude was necessary because of the potential "chilling effect" on reporters and editors which would result from requiring them to appear in remote jurisdictions to answer for the content of articles upon which they worked. ... The Superior Court, therefore, granted the motion.

The California Court of Appeal reversed[, concluding] that a valid basis for jurisdiction existed on the theory that petitioners intended to, and did, cause tortious injury to respondent in California. The fact that the actions causing the effects in California were performed outside the State did not prevent the State from asserting jurisdiction over a cause of action arising out of those effects. The court rejected the Superior Court's conclusion that First Amendment considerations must be weighed in the scale against jurisdiction.

[Due Process] permits personal jurisdiction over a defendant in any State with which the defendant has "certain minimum contacts . . . such that the maintenance of the suit does not offend `traditional notions of fair play and substantial justice.'" *International Shoe Co. v. Washington* (1945) [quotation omitted]. In judging minimum contacts, a court properly focuses on "the relationship among the defendant, the forum, and the litigation." *Shaffer v. Heitner* (1977). The plaintiff's lack of "contacts" will not defeat otherwise proper jurisdiction, but they may be so manifold as to permit jurisdiction when it would not exist in their absence. Here, the plaintiff is the focus of the activities of the defendants out of which the suit arises.

The allegedly libelous story concerned the California activities of a California resident. It impugned the professionalism of an entertainer whose television career was centered in California. The article was drawn from California sources, and the brunt of the harm, in terms both of respondent's emotional distress and the injury to her professional reputation, was suffered in California. In sum, California is the focal point both of the story and of the harm suffered. Jurisdiction over petitioners is therefore proper in California based on the "effects" of their Florida conduct in California.

Petitioners argue that they are not responsible for the circulation of the article in California. A reporter and an editor, they claim, have no direct economic stake in their employer's sales in a distant State. Nor are ordinary employees able to control their employer's marketing activity. ... Petitioners liken themselves to a welder employed in Florida who works on a boiler which subsequently explodes in California. Cases which hold that jurisdiction will be proper over the manufacturer, should not be applied to the welder who has no control over and derives no direct benefit from his employer's sales in that distant State.

Petitioners' analogy does not wash. Whatever the status of their hypothetical welder, petitioners are not charged with mere untargeted negligence. Rather, their intentional, and allegedly tortious, actions were expressly aimed at California. Petitioner South wrote and petitioner Calder edited an article that they knew would have a potentially devastating impact upon respondent. And they knew that the brunt of that injury would be felt by respondent in the State in which she lives and works and in which the National Enquirer has its largest circulation. Under the circumstances, petitioners must "reasonably anticipate being haled into court there" to answer for the truth of the statements made in their article. An individual injured in California need not go to Florida to seek redress from persons who, though remaining in Florida, knowingly cause the injury in California.

Petitioners are correct that their contacts with California are not to be judged according to their employer's activities there. On the other hand, their status as employees does not somehow insulate them from jurisdiction. Each defendant's contacts with the forum State must be assessed individually. In this case, petitioners are primary participants in an alleged wrongdoing intentionally directed at a California resident, and jurisdiction over them is proper on that basis.

We also reject the suggestion that First Amendment concerns enter into the jurisdictional analysis. The infusion of such considerations would needlessly complicate an already imprecise inquiry. Moreover, the potential chill on protected First Amendment activity stemming from libel and defamation actions is already taken into account in the constitutional limitations on the substantive law governing such suits. To reintroduce those concerns at the jurisdictional stage would be a form of double counting. We have already declined in other contexts to grant special procedural protections to defendants in libel and defamation actions in addition to the constitutional protections embodied in the substantive laws.

We hold that jurisdiction over petitioners in California is proper because of their intentional conduct in Florida calculated to cause injury to respondent in California. The judgment of the California Court of Appeal is

Affirmed.

E. Relatedness: Specific Jurisdiction
BRISTOL–MYERS SQUIBB CO. v. SUPERIOR COURT
582 U.S. ___ (2017)

Justice ALITO delivered the opinion of the Court.

More than 600 plaintiffs, most of whom are not California residents, filed this civil action in a California state court against Bristol–Myers Squibb Company (BMS), asserting a variety of state-law claims based on injuries allegedly caused by a BMS drug called Plavix. The California Supreme Court held that the California courts have specific jurisdiction to entertain the nonresidents' claims. We now reverse.

I

BMS, a large pharmaceutical company, is incorporated in Delaware and headquartered in New York, and it maintains substantial operations in both New York and New Jersey. Over 50 percent of BMS's work force in the United States is employed in those two States.

BMS also engages in business activities in other jurisdictions, including California. Five of the company's research and laboratory facilities, which employ a total of around 160 employees, are located there. BMS also employs about 250 sales representatives in California and maintains a small state-government advocacy office in Sacramento.

One of the pharmaceuticals that BMS manufactures and sells is Plavix, a prescription drug that thins the blood and inhibits blood clotting. BMS did not develop Plavix in California, did not create a marketing strategy for Plavix in California, and did not manufacture, label, package, or work on the regulatory approval of the product in California. BMS instead engaged in all of these activities in either New York or New Jersey. But BMS does sell Plavix in California. Between 2006 and 2012, it sold almost 187 million Plavix pills in the State and took in more than $900 million from those sales. This amounts to a little over one percent of the company's nationwide sales revenue.

A group of plaintiffs—consisting of 86 California residents and 592 residents from 33 other States—filed eight separate complaints in California Superior Court, alleging that Plavix had damaged their health. All the complaints asserted 13 claims under California law, including products liability, negligent misrepresentation, and misleading advertising claims. The nonresident plaintiffs did not allege that they obtained Plavix through California physicians or from any other California source; nor did they claim that they were injured by Plavix or were treated for their injuries in California.

Asserting lack of personal jurisdiction, BMS moved to quash service of summons on the nonresidents' claims....

The California Supreme Court ... applied a "sliding scale approach to specific jurisdiction." Under this approach, "the more wide ranging the defendant's forum contacts, the more readily is shown a connection between the forum contacts and the claim." (internal quotation marks omitted). Applying this test, the majority concluded that "BMS's extensive contacts with California" permitted the exercise of specific jurisdiction "based on a less direct connection between BMS's forum activities and plaintiffs' claims than might otherwise be required." This attenuated requirement was met, the majority found, because the claims of the nonresidents were similar in several ways to the claims of the California residents (as to which specific jurisdiction was uncontested). The court noted that "[b]oth the resident and nonresident plaintiffs' claims are based on the same allegedly defective product and the assertedly misleading marketing and promotion of that product." And while acknowledging that "there is no claim that Plavix itself was designed and developed in [BMS's California research facilities]," the court thought it significant that other research was done in the State.

...

We granted certiorari to decide whether the California courts' exercise of jurisdiction in this case violates the Due Process Clause of the Fourteenth Amendment.

II

It has long been established that the Fourteenth Amendment limits the personal jurisdiction of state courts. Because "[a] state court's assertion of jurisdiction exposes defendants to the State's coercive power," it is "subject to review for compatibility with the Fourteenth Amendment's Due Process Clause," *Goodyear Dunlop Tires Operations, S.A. v. Brown* (2011), which "limits the power of a state court to render a valid personal judgment against a nonresident defendant," *World–Wide Volkswagen*. The primary focus of our personal jurisdiction inquiry is the defendant's relationship to the forum State.

Since our seminal decision in *International Shoe*, our decisions have recognized two types of personal jurisdiction: "general" (sometimes called "all-purpose") jurisdiction and "specific" (sometimes called "case-linked") jurisdiction. *Goodyear*. "For an individual, the paradigm forum for the exercise of general jurisdiction is the individual's domicile; for a corporation, it is an equivalent place, one in which the corporation is fairly regarded as at home." *Id.* A court with general jurisdiction may hear *any* claim against that defendant, even if all the incidents underlying the claim occurred in a different State. But "only a limited set of affiliations with a forum will render a defendant amenable to" general jurisdiction in that State. *Daimler AG v. Bauman* (2014).

non resedent + injury didn't happen in forum state

Specific jurisdiction is very different. In order for a state court to exercise specific jurisdiction, "the *suit*" must "aris[e] out of or relat[e] to the defendant's contacts with the *forum*." *Id.* (internal quotation marks omitted; emphasis added). In other words, there must be "an affiliation between the forum and the underlying controversy, principally, [an] activity or an occurrence that takes place in the forum State and is therefore subject to the State's regulation." *Goodyear* (internal quotation marks and brackets omitted). For this reason, "specific jurisdiction is confined to adjudication of issues deriving from, or connected with, the very controversy that establishes jurisdiction." *Id.* (internal quotation marks omitted).

III

A

Our settled principles regarding specific jurisdiction control this case. In order for a court to exercise specific jurisdiction over a claim, there must be an "affiliation between the forum and the underlying controversy, principally, [an] activity or an occurrence that takes place in the forum State." *Goodyear* (internal quotation marks and brackets in original omitted). When there is no such connection, specific jurisdiction is lacking regardless of the extent of a defendant's unconnected activities in the State.

For this reason, the California Supreme Court's "sliding scale approach" is difficult to square with our precedents. Under the California approach, the strength of the requisite connection between the forum and the specific claims at issue is relaxed if the defendant has extensive forum contacts that are unrelated to those claims. Our cases provide no support for this approach, which resembles a loose and spurious form of general jurisdiction. For specific jurisdiction, a defendant's general connections with the forum are not enough....

The present case illustrates the danger of the California approach. The State Supreme Court found that specific jurisdiction was present without identifying any adequate link between the State and the nonresidents' claims. As noted, the nonresidents were not prescribed Plavix in California, did not purchase Plavix in California, did not ingest Plavix in California, and were not injured by Plavix in California. The mere fact that *other* plaintiffs were prescribed, obtained, and ingested Plavix in California—and allegedly sustained the same injuries as did the nonresidents—does not allow the State to assert specific jurisdiction over the nonresidents' claims. As we have explained, "a defendant's relationship with a ... third party, standing alone, is an insufficient basis for jurisdiction." *Walden.* This remains true even when third parties (here, the plaintiffs who reside in California) can bring claims similar to those brought by the nonresidents. Nor is it sufficient—or even relevant—that BMS conducted research in California on matters unrelated to Plavix. What is needed—and what is missing here—is a connection between the forum and the specific claims at issue.

Our decision in *Walden v. Fiore* (2014) illustrates this requirement. In that case, Nevada plaintiffs sued an out-of-state defendant for conducting an allegedly unlawful search of the plaintiffs while they were in Georgia preparing to board a plane bound for Nevada. We held that the Nevada courts lacked specific jurisdiction even though the plaintiffs were Nevada residents and "suffered foreseeable harm in Nevada." *Id*. Because the "*relevant* conduct occurred entirely in Georgi[a] ... the mere fact that [this] conduct affected plaintiffs with connections to the forum State d[id] not suffice to authorize jurisdiction." *Id*. (emphasis added).

In today's case, the connection between the nonresidents' claims and the forum is even weaker. The relevant plaintiffs are not California residents and do not claim to have suffered harm in that State. In addition, as in *Walden*, all the conduct giving rise to the nonresidents' claims occurred elsewhere. It follows that the California courts cannot claim specific jurisdiction.

B

The nonresidents maintain that [*Keeton v. Hustler Magazine, Inc*. (1984) supports] the decision below, but they misinterpret [that precedent].

In *Keeton*, a New York resident sued Hustler in New Hampshire, claiming that she had been libeled in five issues of the magazine, which was distributed throughout the country, including in New Hampshire, where it sold 10,000 to 15,000 copies per month. Concluding that specific jurisdiction was present, we relied principally on the connection between the circulation of the magazine in New Hampshire and damage allegedly caused within the State. We noted that "[f]alse statements of fact harm both the subject of the falsehood and the readers of the statement." *Id*. (emphasis deleted). This factor amply distinguishes *Keeton* from the present case, for here the nonresidents' claims involve no harm in California and no harm to California residents.

The nonresident plaintiffs in this case point to our holding in *Keeton* that there was jurisdiction in New Hampshire to entertain the plaintiff's request for damages suffered outside the State, but that holding concerned jurisdiction to determine *the scope of a claim* involving in-state injury and injury to residents of the State, not, as in this case, jurisdiction to entertain claims involving no in-state injury and no injury to residents of the forum State. *Keeton* held that there was jurisdiction in New Hampshire to consider the full measure of the plaintiff's claim, but whether she could actually recover out-of-state damages was a merits question governed by New Hampshire libel law.

C

In a last ditch contention, respondents contend that BMS's "decision to contract with a California company [McKesson] to distribute [Plavix] nationally" provides a sufficient basis for personal jurisdiction. But as we have explained, "[t]he requirements of *International Shoe* ... must be met as to each defendant over whom a state court exercises jurisdiction." *Rush v. Savchuk* (1980). In this case, it is not alleged that BMS engaged in relevant acts together with McKesson in California. Nor is it alleged that BMS is derivatively liable for McKesson's conduct in California. And the nonresidents "have adduced no evidence to show how or by whom the Plavix they took was distributed to the pharmacies that dispensed it to them." The bare fact that BMS contracted with a California distributor is not enough to establish personal jurisdiction in the State.

IV

Our straightforward application in this case of settled principles of personal jurisdiction will not result in the parade of horribles that respondents conjure up. Our decision does not prevent the California and out-of-state plaintiffs from joining together in a consolidated action in the States that have general jurisdiction over BMS. BMS concedes that such suits could be brought in either New York or Delaware. Alternatively, the plaintiffs who are residents of a particular State—for example, the 92 plaintiffs from Texas and the 71 from Ohio—could probably sue together in their home States. In addition, since our decision concerns the due process limits on the exercise of specific jurisdiction by a State, we leave open the question whether the Fifth Amendment imposes the same restrictions on the exercise of personal jurisdiction by a federal court.

The judgment of the California Supreme Court is reversed, and the case is remanded for further proceedings not inconsistent with this opinion.

It is so ordered.

Justice SOTOMAYOR, dissenting.

... The majority's rule will make it difficult to aggregate the claims of plaintiffs across the country whose claims may be worth little alone. It will make it impossible to bring a nationwide mass action in state court against defendants who are "at home" in different States. And it will result in piecemeal litigation and the bifurcation of claims. None of this is necessary. A core concern in this Court's personal jurisdiction cases is fairness. And there is nothing unfair about subjecting a massive corporation to suit in a State for a nationwide course of conduct that injures both forum residents and nonresidents alike.

As the majority explains, since our pathmarking opinion in *International Shoe Co. v. Washington* (1945), the touchstone of the personal-jurisdiction analysis has been the question whether a defendant has "certain minimum contacts with [the State] such that the maintenance of the suit does not offend 'traditional notions of fair play and substantial justice.'" *Id.* (quoting *Milliken v. Meyer* (1940)). For decades this Court has considered that question through two different jurisdictional frames: "general" and "specific" jurisdiction. ...

If general jurisdiction is not appropriate, ... a state court can exercise only specific, or case-linked, jurisdiction over a dispute. Our cases have set out three conditions for the exercise of specific jurisdiction over a nonresident defendant. First, the defendant must have "purposefully avail[ed] itself of the privilege of conducting activities within the forum State" or have purposefully directed its conduct into the forum State. *J. McIntyre Machinery, Ltd. v. Nicastro* (2011) (plurality opinion) (quoting *Hanson v. Denckla* (1958)). Second, the plaintiff's claim must "arise out of or relate to" the defendant's forum conduct. *Helicopteros*. Finally, the exercise of jurisdiction must be reasonable under the circumstances. The factors relevant to such an analysis include "the burden on the defendant, the forum State's interest in adjudicating the dispute, the plaintiff's interest in obtaining convenient and effective relief, the interstate judicial system's interest in obtaining the most efficient resolution of controversies, and the shared interest of the several States in furthering fundamental substantive social policies." *Id.* (internal quotation marks omitted).

Viewed through this framework, the California courts appropriately exercised specific jurisdiction over respondents' claims.

First, there is no dispute that Bristol–Myers "purposefully avail[ed] itself," *Nicastro*, of California and its substantial pharmaceutical market. Bristol–Myers employs over 400 people in California and maintains half a dozen facilities in the State engaged in research, development, and policymaking. It contracts with a California-based distributor, McKesson, whose sales account for a significant portion of its revenue. And it markets and sells its drugs, including Plavix, in California, resulting in total Plavix sales in that State of nearly $1 billion during the period relevant to this suit.

Second, respondents' claims "relate to" Bristol–Myers' in-state conduct. A claim "relates to" a defendant's forum conduct if it has a "connect[ion] with" that conduct. *International Shoe*. So respondents could not, for instance, hale Bristol–Myers into court in California for negligently maintaining the sidewalk outside its New York headquarters—a claim that has no connection to acts Bristol–Myers took in California. But respondents' claims against Bristol–Myers look nothing like such a claim. Respondents' claims against Bristol–Myers concern conduct materially identical to acts the company took in California: its marketing and distribution of Plavix, which it undertook on a nationwide basis in all 50 States. That respondents were allegedly injured by this nationwide course of conduct in Indiana, Oklahoma, and Texas, and not California, does not mean that their claims do not "relate to" the advertising and distribution efforts that Bristol–Myers undertook in that State. All of the plaintiffs—residents and nonresidents alike—allege that they were injured by the same essential acts. Our cases require no connection more direct than that.

Finally, and importantly, there is no serious doubt that the exercise of jurisdiction over the nonresidents' claims is reasonable. Because Bristol–Myers already faces claims that are identical to the nonresidents' claims in this suit, it will not be harmed by having to defend against respondents' claims: Indeed, the alternative approach—litigating those claims in separate suits in as many as 34 different States—would prove far more burdensome. By contrast, the plaintiffs' "interest in obtaining convenient and effective relief," *Burger King Corp. v. Rudzewicz* (1985) (internal quotation marks omitted), is obviously furthered by participating in a consolidated proceeding in one State under shared counsel, which allows them to minimize costs, share discovery, and maximize recoveries on claims that may be too small to bring on their own. California, too, has an interest in providing a forum for mass actions like this one: Permitting the nonresidents to bring suit in California alongside the residents facilitates the efficient adjudication of the residents' claims and allows it to regulate more effectively the conduct of both nonresident corporations like Bristol–Myers and resident ones like McKesson.

Nothing in the Due Process Clause prohibits a California court from hearing respondents' claims—at least not in a case where they are joined to identical claims brought by California residents.

I fear the consequences of the majority's decision today will be substantial. Even absent a rigid requirement that a defendant's in-state conduct must actually cause a plaintiff's claim, the upshot of today's opinion is that plaintiffs cannot join their claims together and sue a defendant in a State in which only some of them have been injured. That rule is likely to have consequences far beyond this case.

First, and most prominently, the Court's opinion in this case will make it profoundly difficult for plaintiffs who are injured in different States by a defendant's nationwide course of conduct to sue that defendant in a single, consolidated action. The holding of today's opinion is that such an action cannot be brought in a State in which only some plaintiffs were injured. Not to worry, says the majority: The plaintiffs here could have sued Bristol–Myers in New York or Delaware; could "probably" have subdivided their separate claims into 34 lawsuits in the States in which they were injured; and might have been able to bring a single suit in federal court (an "open ... question"). Even setting aside the majority's caveats, what is the purpose of such limitations? What interests are served by preventing the consolidation of claims and limiting the forums in which they can be consolidated? The effect of the Court's opinion today is to eliminate nationwide mass actions in any State other than those in which a defendant is "essentially at home." Such a rule hands one more tool to corporate defendants determined to prevent the aggregation of individual claims, and forces injured plaintiffs to bear the burden of bringing suit in what will often be far flung jurisdictions.

Second, the Court's opinion today may make it impossible to bring certain mass actions at all. After this case, it is difficult to imagine where it might be possible to bring a nationwide mass action against two or more defendants headquartered and incorporated in different States. There will be no State where both defendants are "at home," and so no State in which the suit can proceed. What about a nationwide mass action brought against a defendant not headquartered or incorporated in the United States? Such a defendant is not "at home" in any State. Especially in a world in which defendants are subject to general jurisdiction in only a handful of States, the effect of today's opinion will be to curtail—and in some cases eliminate— plaintiffs' ability to hold corporations fully accountable for their nationwide conduct.

The majority chides respondents for conjuring a "parade of horribles," but says nothing about how suits like those described here will survive its opinion in this case. The answer is simple: They will not.

It "does not offend 'traditional notions of fair play and substantial justice,'" *International Shoe*, to permit plaintiffs to aggregate claims arising out of a single nationwide course of conduct in a single suit in a single State where some, but not all, were injured. But that is exactly what the Court holds today is barred by the Due Process Clause.

This is not a rule the Constitution has required before. I respectfully dissent.

NOWAK V. TAK HOW INVESTMENTS LTD.
94 F.3d 708 (CA1 1996)
[Note: internal sections re-ordered for clarity]

CUMMINGS, Circuit Judge.

A Massachusetts resident who accompanied her husband on a business trip to Hong Kong drowned in their hotel's swimming pool. Plaintiffs later brought this wrongful death diversity action against the Hong Kong corporation that owns the hotel—a corporation that has no place of business outside of Hong Kong. Defendant moved for dismissal, arguing that a Massachusetts court could not exercise personal jurisdiction consistently with due process.... The district court denied [the motion], and we now affirm.

I.

Tak How is a Hong Kong corporation with its only place of business in Hong Kong. Its sole asset is the Holiday Inn Crowne Plaza Harbour View in Hong Kong ("Holiday Inn"), where the accident in this case took place. Tak How has no assets, shareholders, or employees in Massachusetts. Sally Ann

removal - Δ take case out of State court an moves it to Fed. Court.

Nowak ("Mrs. Nowak") was at all relevant times married to plaintiff Ralph Nowak ("Mr. Nowak") and was the mother of their two children (collectively, the plaintiffs are "the Nowaks"). The Nowaks lived in Marblehead, Massachusetts, and Mr. Nowak was employed by Kiddie Products, Inc., which has its place of business in Avon, Massachusetts. Kiddie Products does extensive business in Hong Kong. As a Preliminary Design Manager in the Marketing Department, Mr. Nowak customarily made two business trips to Hong Kong each year, accompanied by his wife on one of those trips.

Kiddie Products employees had made trips to Hong Kong since at least 1982, but the company's relationship with Tak How and the Holiday Inn began only in 1992. John Colantuone, a vice-president, was one such employee who had travelled to Hong Kong since 1982 and had stayed at various other hotels. Colantuone was acquainted with the Holiday Inn through advertisements on Hong Kong radio in 1983 or 1984, but only decided to stay there in 1992 after becoming dissatisfied with the rates at other hotels. On his first visit, Colantuone met with the Holiday Inn's sales manager to negotiate a corporate discount for Kiddie Products employees. Holiday Inn agreed to the discount and wrote a letter confirming the arrangement based on a minimum number of room nights per year. Marie Burke, Colantuone's administrative assistant, made all hotel reservations for the company's employees. Although Kiddie Products regularly compared rates at other hotels, Burke was told to book all reservations at the Holiday Inn until instructed otherwise. Since 1992, Kiddie Products employees have stayed exclusively at the Holiday Inn.

In June 1993, the Holiday Inn telecopied Colantuone a message announcing new corporate rates and other promotional materials. Burke requested additional information, and the hotel promptly responded. In July 1993, after a series of exchanges by telecopier, Burke sent a reservation request to the Holiday Inn for several employees for September and October 1993. One of the reservations was for Mr. and Mrs. Nowak to arrive on September 16. On September 18, while the Nowaks were registered guests at the hotel, Mrs. Nowak drowned in the hotel swimming pool. The specific facts surrounding her death are not relevant here. It is uncontested that in 1992 and 1993, prior to Mrs. Nowak's death, Tak How advertised the Holiday Inn in certain national and international publications, some of which circulated in Massachusetts. In addition, in February 1993, Tak How sent direct mail solicitations to approximately 15,000 of its previous guests, including previous guests residing in Massachusetts.

The Nowaks filed this wrongful death action in Massachusetts state court in June 1994. Tak How then removed the case to federal district court and [moved] to dismiss ... for lack of personal jurisdiction under Fed.R.Civ.P. 12(b)(2).... The district court ..., after allowing time for jurisdictional discovery, issued a memorandum and order denying the Rule 12(b)(2) motion. The district court granted Tak How's motion for certification of the jurisdictional issue, but this Court denied Tak How's request for a stay of the district court proceeding pending appeal. Nonetheless, believing that a resulting judgment would not be enforceable in Hong Kong, Tak How did not answer the Nowaks' complaint. Accordingly, the district court entered a default judgment against Tak How for $3,128,168.33. Tak How appeals....

II.

[In] diversity cases such as this, the district court's personal jurisdiction over a nonresident defendant is governed by the forum state's long-arm statute. Under the Massachusetts statute, "[a] court may exercise personal jurisdiction over a person, who acts directly or by an agent, as to a cause of action in law or equity arising from the person's ... transacting any business in this Commonwealth." Mass. Gen. Laws Ann. ch. 223A, § 3(a) (1985). The statute imposes constraints on personal jurisdiction that go beyond those imposed by the Constitution. We must therefore find sufficient contacts between the defendant and the forum state to satisfy both the Massachusetts long-arm statute and the Constitution.

To satisfy the requirements of the long-arm statute, Section 3(a), the defendant must have transacted business in Massachusetts and the plaintiffs' claim must have arisen from the transaction of business by the defendant. In *Tatro v. Manor Care, Inc.* (Mass. 1994), a Massachusetts plaintiff sued a California hotel for injuries sustained in California. The Court concluded that the hotel's solicitation of business from Massachusetts residents satisfied the "transacting any business" requirement of Section 3(a), and that the "arising from" requirement was satisfied where, but for the hotel's solicitations and acceptance of reservations, the plaintiff would not have been injured in California. The factual scenario in the present case is analogous in all essential respects, and we therefore have little difficulty concluding that sufficient contacts exist to satisfy Section 3(a)'s requirements.

Turning to the constitutional restraints, this Court follows a tripartite analysis for determining the existence of specific personal jurisdiction: [The] defendant's forum-state contacts must represent a purposeful availment of the privilege of conducting activities in the forum state, thereby invoking the benefits and protections of that state's laws and making the defendant's involuntary presence before the state's court foreseeable[; the claim underlying the litigation must directly arise out of, or relate to, the defendant's forum-state activities; and,] the exercise of jurisdiction must, in light of the Gestalt factors, be reasonable.

[A].   Purposeful Availment

The [first] issue is whether Tak How's contacts with Massachusetts constitute purposeful availment. ... Our two focal points are voluntariness and foreseeability. The defendant's contacts with the forum state must be voluntary—that is, not based on the unilateral actions of another party or a third person. In addition, the defendant's contacts with the forum state must be such that he should reasonably anticipate being haled into court there.

We think that Tak How's unprompted June 1993 correspondence with Kiddie Products, which led directly to the ill-fated Hong Kong trip in September 1993, was at least minimally sufficient to satisfy this requirement. The June 1993 correspondence contained promotional materials from the Holiday Inn designed to further entice Kiddie Products employees to stay at the hotel. Even if it may be said that the materials were sent as part of an on-going relationship between the two companies that was originally instigated by Kiddie Products, the continued correspondence by Tak How to Massachusetts does not amount to the kind of unilateral action that makes the forum-state contacts involuntary. Tak How had an obvious financial interest in continuing business with Kiddie Products, and the June 1993 correspondence is the best example of an unprompted solicitation designed to facilitate that business relationship. In order to be subject to Massachusetts' jurisdiction, a defendant need only have one contact with the forum state, so long as that contact is meaningful.

Whether prompted or unprompted, Tak How's on-going correspondence and relationship with Kiddie Products, designed to bring Massachusetts residents into Hong Kong, rendered foreseeable the possibility of being haled into a Massachusetts court. That Tak How might have to defend itself in a Massachusetts court is certainly foreseeable based on its direct correspondence with Kiddie Products, but its other contacts with Massachusetts reveal an even more substantial attempt by Tak How to purposefully avail itself of the privilege of conducting business activities in the state: Tak How advertised its hotel in national and international publications that circulated in Massachusetts; it solicited by direct mail some of its previous guests residing in Massachusetts; and Tak How listed its hotel in various hotel guides used at travel agencies in Massachusetts. Exercising jurisdiction is appropriate where the defendant purposefully derives economic benefits from its forum-state activities.

[B].   Relatedness

... Tak How's principal argument on appeal is that relatedness requires a proximate cause relationship between its contacts with Massachusetts and the Nowaks' cause of action.

In arguing for a proximate cause relatedness test, Tak How relies on a series of First Circuit cases beginning with *Marino v. Hyatt Corp.* (CA1 1986). In each of these cases, this Court construed the language of a state long-arm statute requiring, as does the Massachusetts statute quoted above, that the cause of action "arise" from the forum-state contacts. Construing those statutes, we rejected plaintiffs' arguments that the injury at issue would not have occurred "but for" the forum-state contacts. Instead, we held that the defendant's conduct must be the legal or proximate cause of the injury.

At least for purposes of construing the Massachusetts long-arm statute, the Supreme Judicial Court of Massachusetts dealt our restrictive interpretation a fatal blow in *Tatro, supra*. The Court decided that the "but for" test is more consistent with the language of the long-arm statute and explicitly rejected our interpretation of the statute in the Marino line of cases. Personal jurisdiction was proper in *Tatro* because the California hotel had solicited business in Massachusetts and had agreed to provide the plaintiff with accommodations; but for those acts, the plaintiff would not have been injured.

Tak How contends that *Tatro* was not fatal to *Marino* and its progeny. It concedes, as it must, that *Tatro* is controlling insofar as it deals with the construction of the Massachusetts long-arm statute, but insists that the relatedness discussion in *Marino* had constitutional significance as well. ...

The requirement serves two purposes. First, relatedness is the divining rod that separates specific jurisdiction cases from general jurisdiction cases. Second, it ensures that the element of causation remains in the forefront of the due process investigation. Most courts share this emphasis on causation, but differ over the proper causative threshold. Generally, courts have gravitated toward one of two familiar tort concepts—"but for" or "proximate cause."

The Ninth Circuit is the most forceful defender of the "but for" test. In *Shute v. Carnival Cruise Lines* (CA9 1990), the court stated that "but for" serves the basic function of relatedness by "preserv[ing] the essential distinction between general and specific jurisdiction." A more stringent standard, the court asserted, "would represent an unwarranted departure from the core concepts of 'fair play and substantial justice,'" because it would preclude jurisdiction in cases where it would be reasonable. In turn, in those cases where "but for" might lead to an unreasonable result, the court predicted that the third prong—the reasonableness inquiry—would guard against unfairness.

...

The Sixth Circuit applies a "substantial connection" standard. The court's discussion in *Lanier v. American Board of Endodontics* (CA6 1988), however, suggests that a "but for" relationship survives the due process inquiry.

Finally, the Seventh Circuit has upheld jurisdiction under the Illinois long-arm statute, and the Due Process Clause, for claims that "lie in the wake of the commercial activities by which the defendant submitted to the jurisdiction of the Illinois courts." See *Deluxe Ice Cream Co. v. R.C.H. Tool Corp.* (CA7 1984) (breach of warranty). Whether this indeterminate standard would encompass tortious negligence committed outside the forum is unknown.

On the other hand, the Second and Eighth Circuits, as well as this one, appear to approve a proximate cause standard. See *Pearrow v. National Life & Accident Ins. Co.* (CA8 1983); *Gelfand v. Tanner Motor Tours, Ltd.* (CA2 1964). ...

This circuit, whether accurately or not, has been recognized as the main proponent of the proximate cause standard. We think the attraction of proximate cause is two-fold. First, proximate or legal cause clearly distinguishes between foreseeable and unforeseeable risks of harm. Foreseeability is a critical component in the due process inquiry, particularly in evaluating purposeful availment, and we think it also informs the relatedness prong. ... Adherence to a proximate cause standard is likely to enable defendants better to anticipate which conduct might subject them to a state's jurisdiction than a more tenuous link in the chain of causation. Certainly, jurisdiction that is premised on a contact that is a legal cause of the injury underlying the controversy ... is presumably reasonable, assuming, of course, purposeful availment.

As our discussion suggests, ... we think the proximate cause standard better comports with the relatedness inquiry because it so easily correlates to foreseeability, a significant component of the jurisdictional inquiry. A "but for" requirement, on the other hand, has in itself no limiting principle; it literally embraces every event that hindsight can logically identify in the causative chain. True, as the Ninth Circuit has noted, courts can use the reasonableness prong to keep Pandora's jar from opening too wide. But to say that the harm that might be done by one factor can be prevented by another is not, after all, an affirmative justification for the former.

That being said, we are persuaded that strict adherence to a proximate cause standard in all circumstances is unnecessarily restrictive. The concept of proximate cause is critically important in the tort context because it defines the scope of a defendant's liability. In contrast, the first prong of the jurisdictional tripartite test is not as rigid.... We see no reason why, in the context of a relationship between a contractual or business association and a subsequent tort, the absence of proximate cause per se should always render the exercise of specific jurisdiction unconstitutional.

When a foreign corporation directly targets residents in an ongoing effort to further a business relationship, and achieves its purpose, it may not necessarily be unreasonable to subject that corporation to forum jurisdiction when the efforts lead to a tortious result. The corporation's own conduct increases the likelihood that a specific resident will respond favorably. If the resident is harmed while engaged in activities integral to the relationship the corporation sought to establish, we think the nexus between the contacts and the cause of action is sufficiently strong to survive the due process inquiry at least at the relatedness stage.

This concept represents a small overlay of "but for" on "proximate cause." ... It may be that other kinds of fact patterns will be found to meet the basic factor of foreseeability, but we have no occasion here to pronounce more broadly.

This case is illustrative of our reasoning. Through its ongoing correspondence with Kiddie Products, Tak How knew that Kiddie Products employees would stay at its hotel, and could easily anticipate that they might use the pool, a featured amenity of the hotel. The district court thoroughly described this connection.

The Hotel's solicitation of Kiddie's business and the extensive back-and-forth resulting in Burke's reserving a set of rooms for Kiddie employees and their spouses set in motion a chain of reasonably foreseeable events resulting in Mrs. Nowak's death. The possibility that the solicitation would prove successful and that one or more of the guests staying at the Hotel as a result would use the pool was in no sense remote or unpredictable; in fact, the Hotel included the pool as an attraction in its promotional materials. While the nexus between Tak How's solicitation of Kiddie Products' business and Mrs. Nowak's death does not constitute a proximate cause relationship, it does represent a meaningful link between Tak How's contact and the harm suffered. Given these circumstances, we think it would be imprudent to reject jurisdiction at this early stage of the inquiry.

By this approach, we intend to emphasize the importance of proximate causation, but to allow a slight loosening of that standard when circumstances dictate. We think such flexibility is necessary in the jurisdictional inquiry: relatedness cannot merely be reduced to one tort concept for all circumstances. ...

We recognize it will not always be easy to apply this flexible approach to particular circumstances, but that is a function of the complexity of this area of the law. ...

DAGESSE & DAGESSE v. PLANT HOTEL N.V.
113 F.Supp.2d 211 (D.N.H. 2000)

BARBADORO, Chief Judge.

Daniel Dagesse contends that he suffered serious injuries when he slipped and fell in his hotel room at the Aruba Marriott Resort. He sued Plant Hotel N.V., the limited liability company that owns the resort, Oranjestad Property Management N.V., Plant Hotel's parent company, Marriott Aruba N.V., the company that manages the resort, and Marriott International, Inc., a corporation that Dagesse claims was an agent and management company for

Plant Hotel and Oranjestad. Elaine Dagesse, Daniel's wife, has sued the same defendants alleging loss of consortium.

In a previous order, I granted Marriott Aruba's motion to dismiss for lack of personal jurisdiction. Plant Hotel and Oranjestad have now filed similar motions.

The Dagesses cite two new jurisdictional facts to support their claim that the court has personal jurisdiction over Plant Hotel and Oranjestad. In addition to the New Hampshire contacts they presented in opposition to Marriott Aruba's motion to dismiss, the Dagesses contend that Marriott International, acting as an agent for Plant Hotel and Oranjestad, (1) maintained an interactive internet web site that was accessible from New Hampshire; and (2) was responsible for television advertisements for the Aruba Marriott Resort that Elaine Dagesse viewed from her New Hampshire home. In the discussion that follows, I consider these new allegations in combination with the jurisdictional facts previously alleged by the Dagesses.

I. *Background*

Daniel and Elaine Degasse made travel arrangements for a trip to Aruba in November 1995. The Dagesses booked their flights through Berlin Travel, a travel agency located in Berlin, New Hampshire, but made their own hotel reservations at the Aruba Marriott Resort in Oranjestad, Aruba. They made and confirmed their hotel reservation from New Hampshire through a representative of Marriott International by calling the company's toll-free telephone reservation line. A Marriott reservations officer accepted and confirmed the reservation and mailed a confirmation letter to the Dagesses's New Hampshire residence. The Dagesses had never been guests at the resort before, but selected it because of Marriott's general reputation for comfort and quality. The Dagesses never contacted the Aruba Marriott Resort directly, and at all times were under the impression that they were dealing with Marriott International. Before the Dagesses made their travel arrangements, Elaine Dagesse saw television advertisements for the Aruba Marriott Resort while at her home in New Hampshire.

The Dagesses made their trip to Aruba in November 1995. On or about November 25, 1995, Daniel Dagesse walked into the bathroom of his guestroom at the resort and slipped and fell in a pool of standing water that apparently had accumulated because of an unspecified plumbing problem. Dagesse allegedly suffered severe injuries as a result of the fall.

The Dagesses claim that Plant Hotel, as the owner of the Aruba Marriott Resort, owed them a duty of care to maintain their guestroom in a reasonably safe condition and to correct or warn them of any dangerous conditions therein. The Dagesses assert that Plant Hotel either knew of the plumbing problem in its guestroom or should have known about it through the exercise of reasonable care. Accordingly, the Dagesses maintain that their injuries are the result of Plant Hotel's negligent maintenance of their guestroom and/or Plant Hotel's failure to warn them of the hazardous conditions present therein.

The Dagesses also claim that Oranjestad, as the parent company of Plant Hotel, owed them a duty to ensure that its subsidiary company maintained the Aruba Marriott Resort in a reasonably safe condition, and that its failure to supervise the business affairs of Plant Hotel ultimately led to the accident. Similarly, the Dagesses claim that defendant Marriott International, the alleged management company for Plant Hotel and Oranjestad, owed them a duty to ensure that the Aruban defendants maintained the Marriott Aruba Resort in a reasonably safe condition, and that its failure to do so ultimately led to the accident.

Plant Hotel is a limited liability company under the laws of Aruba. Plant Hotel has a principal place of business in Palm Beach, Aruba, and is authorized to do business only in Aruba. Oranjestad, Plant Hotel's parent company, is an Aruban corporation that is not authorized to conduct business in the state of New Hampshire. Oranjestad does not have a registered agent in New Hampshire, nor does it have any employees, mailing address, bank account or office in New Hampshire. The Dagesses claim that Marriott International serves as the management company for Plant Hotel and Oranjestad, a claim that Marriott International denies.

The Dagesses also contend that Marriott International maintains an interactive internet web site that is accessible in New Hampshire. According to evidence provided by the Dagesses, the web site advertises the Aruba Marriott Resort, provides a toll-free number for making reservations by telephone, and allows users to make hotel reservations over the internet.

II. *Standard of Review*

When a defendant contests personal jurisdiction under Rule 12(b)(2), the plaintiff bears the burden of showing that a basis for asserting jurisdiction exists. In this case, in which no evidentiary hearing has been held, I hold the Dagesses to a prima facie standard.

To make a prima facie showing of jurisdiction, a plaintiff may not rest on the pleadings. Rather, he or she must "adduce evidence of specific facts" that support jurisdiction. In conducting my analysis, I take the facts offered by the plaintiff as true and construe them in the light most favorable to the plaintiff's jurisdictional claim. ...

III. *Analysis*

For purposes of assessing personal jurisdiction over a nonresident defendant, ... I must determine whether jurisdiction is proper under both the New Hampshire long-arm statute and the due process requirements of the federal constitution. The New Hampshire long-arm statute applicable to foreign corporations has been interpreted to be coterminous with federal constitutional limits on jurisdiction. Therefore, I proceed directly to the constitutional due process analysis.

The due process clause precludes a court from asserting jurisdiction over a defendant unless "the defendant's conduct and connection with the forum State are such that [it] should reasonably anticipate being haled into court there." *World-Wide Volkswagen Corp. v. Woodsen* (1980). ...

The "constitutional touchstone" for personal jurisdiction is "whether the defendant purposefully established 'minimum contacts' in the forum State." *Burger King Corp. v. Rudzewicz* (1985). The inquiry into "minimum contacts" is necessarily fact-specific, "involving an individualized assessment and factual analysis of the precise mix of contacts that characterize each case." *Pritzker v. Yari* (1st Cir. 1994). A defendant cannot be subjected to a forum state's jurisdiction based solely on "random," "fortuitous," or "attenuated" contacts. *Burger King* (quotation omitted). Rather, "it is essential in each case that there be some act by which the defendant purposefully avails itself of the privilege of conducting activities within the forum State, thus invoking the benefits and protections of its laws." *Id.* (quotation omitted).

A court may assert authority over a defendant by means of either general or specific jurisdiction. A defendant who has engaged in continuous and systematic activity in a forum is subject to general jurisdiction in that forum with respect to all causes of action, even those unrelated to the defendant's forum-based activities. A court may exercise specific jurisdiction, by contrast, only when the cause of action arises from, or relates to, the defendant's contacts with the forum.

The First Circuit has developed a tripartite test for determining whether an exercise of specific jurisdiction is consistent with due process. The analysis consists of an inquiry into [(1) purposeful availment, (2) relatedness, and (3) reasonableness.] An affirmative finding on each of these three components is required to support an assertion of specific jurisdiction.

In the present case, I focus my attention on the [second] element of the tripartite test. Under the relatedness requirement, I must determine whether the plaintiff's claim arises out of, or is related to, the defendant's contacts with the forum. The First Circuit has interpreted relatedness to require a connection of proximate cause between the defendant's contacts and the plaintiff's claim. *See Nowak v. Tak How Investments Ltd.* (1st Cir. 1996). This proximate cause standard ... "enable[s] defendants better to anticipate which conduct might subject them to a state's jurisdiction." *Id.* ...

The Dagesses have alleged that Plant Hotel and Oranjestad, acting through their agent Marriott International, had the following contacts with New Hampshire:

1. Marriott International was responsible for television advertisements promoting the Aruba Marriott Resort, which Elaine Dagesse viewed at her New Hampshire home prior to making the decision to travel to Aruba.

2. Marriott International maintained an interactive internet web site, accessible from New Hampshire, that advertised the Aruba Marriott Resort, provided a toll-free telephone number for making hotel reservations, and allowed users to make hotel reservations directly over the internet.

3. The Dagesses made their hotel reservations from their New Hampshire home by telephoning a Marriott International representative in the United States. A Marriott International representative mailed a confirmation of the reservations to the Dagesses at their New Hampshire home.

Based on this evidence, the Dagesses are unable to demonstrate that Marriott International's contacts with New Hampshire were both the factual and legal cause of the injuries for which they seek relief. The Dagesses do not allege that they visited the Marriott web site prior to their trip; thus the web site is not related to their claim even as a matter of factual causation. Moreover, assuming that the television advertisements, the receiving and confirmation of reservations through the toll-free telephone number, and the mailing of the reservation confirmation were factual causes of the injuries suffered by the Dagesses, they were not legal causes of those injuries because they did not make it foreseeable that the Dagesses would be injured by negligent maintenance of their hotel room. *See Nowak* (concluding that plaintiff's wife's fatal injuries were not proximately caused by defendant's forum-related contacts).

The First Circuit has recognized a narrow exception to the proximate cause standard that applies "[w]hen a foreign corporation directly targets residents in an ongoing effort to further a business relationship, and achieves its purpose." *Id.* In *Nowak*, the plaintiff's wife drowned in the swimming pool of a Hong Kong hotel where the couple was staying during the husband's business trip. When the plaintiff brought a wrongful death action against the foreign corporation that owned the hotel, the court found that personal jurisdiction could properly rest upon an extensive series of communications between the defendant corporation and the plaintiff's employer. The court concluded that "[w]hile the nexus between [the defendant's] solicitation of [the plaintiff's employer's] business and [the plaintiff's wife's] death does not constitute a proximate cause relationship, it does represent a meaningful link between [the defendant's] contact and the harm suffered." *Id.*

In the present case, however, the Dagesses have failed to adduce any evidence that either Plant Hotel or Oranjestad, whether acting directly or through Marriott International, targeted them or any other New Hampshire residents in an ongoing and ultimately successful effort to further a business relationship. Simply put, none of the facts produced by the Dagesses suggest the sort of established business relationship that existed between the defendant and the plaintiff's employer in *Nowak*.

...

F. Reasonableness

ASAHI METAL INDUSTRY CO., LTD.
v.
SUPERIOR COURT OF CALIFORNIA
480 U.S. 102 (1987)

JUSTICE O'CONNOR announced the judgment of the Court and delivered the unanimous opinion of the Court with respect to Part I, the opinion of the Court with respect to Part II-B, in which THE CHIEF JUSTICE, JUSTICE BRENNAN, JUSTICE WHITE, JUSTICE MARSHALL, JUSTICE BLACKMUN, JUSTICE POWELL, and JUSTICE STEVENS join, and an opinion with respect to Parts II-A and III, in which THE CHIEF JUSTICE, JUSTICE POWELL, and JUSTICE SCALIA join.

B

The strictures of the Due Process Clause forbid a state court to exercise personal jurisdiction over Asahi under circumstances that would offend "traditional notions of fair play and substantial justice." *International Shoe Co. v. Washington* (1945) (quoting *Milliken v. Meyer* (1940)).

We have previously explained that the determination of the reasonableness of the exercise of jurisdiction in each case will depend on an evaluation of several factors. A court must consider the burden on the defendant, the interests of the forum State, and the plaintiff's interest in obtaining relief. It must also weigh in its determination "the interstate judicial system's interest in obtaining the most efficient resolution of controversies; and the shared interest of the several States in furthering fundamental substantive social policies." *World-Wide Volkswagen Corp. v. Woodsen* (1980) (citations omitted).

A consideration of these factors in the present case clearly reveals the unreasonableness of the assertion of jurisdiction over Asahi, even apart from the question of the placement of goods in the stream of commerce.

Certainly the burden on the defendant in this case is severe. Asahi has been commanded by the Supreme Court of California not only to traverse the distance between Asahi's headquarters in Japan and the Superior Court of California in and for the County of Solano, but also to submit its dispute with Cheng Shin to a foreign nation's judicial system. The unique burdens placed upon one who must defend oneself in a foreign legal system should have significant weight in assessing the reasonableness of stretching the long arm of personal jurisdiction over national borders.

When minimum contacts have been established, often the interests of the plaintiff and the forum in the exercise of jurisdiction will justify even the serious burdens placed on the alien defendant. In the present case, however, the interests of the plaintiff and the forum in California's assertion of jurisdiction over Asahi are slight. All that remains is a claim for indemnification asserted by Cheng Shin, a Tawainese corporation, against Asahi. The transaction on which the indemnification claim is based took place in Taiwan; Asahi's components were shipped from Japan to Taiwan. Cheng Shin has not demonstrated that it is more convenient for it to litigate its indemnification claim against Asahi in California rather than in Taiwan or Japan.

Because the plaintiff is not a California resident, California's legitimate interests in the dispute have considerably diminished. The Supreme Court of California argued that the State had an interest in "protecting its consumers by ensuring that foreign manufacturers comply with the state's safety standards" The State Supreme Court's definition of California's interest, however, was overly broad. The dispute between Cheng Shin and Asahi is primarily about indemnification rather than safety standards. Moreover, it is not at all clear at this point that California law should govern the question whether a Japanese corporation should indemnify a Taiwanese corporation on the basis of a sale made in Taiwan and a shipment of goods from Japan to Taiwan. The possibility of being haled into a California court as a result of an accident involving Asahi's components undoubtedly creates an additional deterrent to the manufacture of unsafe components; however, similar pressures will be placed on Asahi by the purchasers of its components as long as those who use Asahi components in their final products, and sell those products in California, are subject to the application of California tort law.

World-Wide Volkswagen also admonished courts to take into consideration the interests of the "several States," in addition to the forum State, in the efficient judicial resolution of the dispute and the advancement of substantive policies. In the present case, this advice calls for a court to consider the procedural and substantive policies of other *nations* whose interests are affected by the assertion of jurisdiction by the California court. The procedural and substantive interests of other nations in a state court's assertion of jurisdiction over an alien defendant will differ from case to case. In every case, however, those interests, as well as the Federal Government's interest in its foreign relations policies, will be best served by a careful inquiry into the reasonableness of the assertion of jurisdiction in the particular case, and an unwillingness to find the serious burdens on an alien defendant outweighed by minimal interests on the part of the plaintiff or the forum State. "Great care and reserve should be exercised when extending our notions of personal jurisdiction into the international field." *United States v. First National City Bank* (1965) (Harlan, J., dissenting).

Considering the international context, the heavy burden on the alien defendant, and the slight interests of the plaintiff and the forum State, the exercise of personal jurisdiction by a California court over Asahi in this instance would be unreasonable and unfair.

III

Because the facts of this case do not establish minimum contacts such that the exercise of personal jurisdiction is consistent with fair play and substantial justice, the judgment of the Supreme Court of California is reversed, and the case is remanded for further proceedings not inconsistent with this opinion.

NOWAK V. TAK HOW INVESTMENTS LTD
94 F.3d 708 (CA1 1996)

C. The Gestalt Factors

Our conclusion that minimum contacts exist in this case does not end the inquiry. Personal jurisdiction may only be exercised if it comports with traditional notions of "fair play and substantial justice." Out of this requirement, courts have developed a series of factors that bear on the fairness of subjecting a nonresident to a foreign tribunal. These "gestalt factors" are as follows:

5 factors

- (1) the defendant's burden of appearing, (2) the forum state's interest in adjudicating the dispute, (3) the plaintiff's interest in obtaining convenient and effective relief, (4) the judicial system's interest in obtaining the most effective resolution of the controversy, and (5) the common interests of all sovereigns in promoting substantive social policies.

The purpose of the gestalt factors is to aid the court in achieving substantial justice, particularly where the minimum contacts question is very close. In such cases, the gestalt factors may tip the constitutional balance. The Supreme Court's decision in *Asahi Metal Indus. Co. v. Superior Court* (1987) is one such example. In *Asahi*, the question of minimum contacts divided the Court, but eight of the Justices agreed that exercising personal jurisdiction would not comport with notions of fair play and substantial justice. ...

1. The Burden of Appearance. It would undoubtedly be burdensome for Tak How to defend itself in Massachusetts: Tak How's only place of business is in Hong Kong. This Court has recognized, however, that it is almost always inconvenient and costly for a party to litigate in a foreign jurisdiction. Thus for this particular gestalt factor to have any significance, the defendant must demonstrate that exercise of jurisdiction in the present circumstances is onerous in a special, unusual, or other constitutionally significant way. [quotation omitted.] Tak How alleges nothing special or unusual about its situation beyond the ordinary cost and inconvenience of defending an action

so far from its place of business. [I]t simply cannot be the case that every Hong Kong corporation is immune from suit in Massachusetts. We are also persuaded that the burden on Tak How will be minimized by, for example, the availability of transcripts from the Coroner's Court for use in the Massachusetts proceeding.

We have also noted that the burden of appearance is an important gestalt factor primarily because it allows a court to guard against harassing litigation. Were there any indication in the record that the Nowaks brought the present suit to harass Tak How, the burden of appearance in Massachusetts might weigh in Tak How's favor; however, the record does not so indicate.

2. Interest of the Forum. Although a forum state has a significant interest in obtaining jurisdiction over a defendant who causes tortious injury within its borders, that interest is diminished where the injury occurred outside the forum state. Nonetheless, our task is not to compare the interest of the two sovereigns—the place of the injury and forum state—but to determine whether the forum state has an interest. Id. While it is true that the injury in this case occurred in Hong Kong, it is equally true ... that significant events took place in Massachusetts giving it an interest in this litigation. Tak How solicited business in the state. As the district court noted, Massachusetts has a strong interest in protecting its citizens from out-of-state solicitations for goods or services that prove to be unsafe, and it also has an interest in providing its citizens with a convenient forum in which to assert their claims. Given the forum-state activities that took place prior to Mrs. Nowak's death, we conclude that Massachusetts has a strong interest in exercising jurisdiction even though the injury took place in Hong Kong.

3. The Plaintiffs' Convenience. This Court must accord deference to the Nowaks' choice of a Massachusetts forum. Regardless, it is obvious that a Massachusetts forum is more convenient for the Nowaks than another forum, particularly a Hong Kong forum. Further, there exists substantial doubt that the Nowaks could adequately resolve the dispute in Hong Kong: Hong Kong's laws regarding contingency fees and posting of security bonds with the court make litigation economically onerous for plaintiffs, and the future of Hong Kong's political system is also uncertain.

4. The Administration of Justice. This factor focuses on the judicial system's interest in obtaining the most effective resolution of the controversy. Usually this factor is a wash.... Tak How argues that a Massachusetts action would require the application of Hong Kong law, the use of interpreters, and the transportation of key witnesses from Hong Kong that are not subject to compulsory process. On the other hand, the Nowaks point to possible political instability in Hong Kong as the British Colony prepares to revert to Chinese sovereignty. Interpreters and transportation of witnesses would likely also be necessary in Hong Kong. We conclude that the question of efficient

administration of justice favors a Massachusetts forum. Given the likelihood that the Nowaks would face great obstacles in Hong Kong due to possible political instability, as well as Hong Kong laws on contingency fees and security bonds, efficiency concerns require a Massachusetts forum.

5. Pertinent Policy Arguments. The final gestalt factor addresses the interests of the affected governments in substantive social policies. Massachusetts has an interest in protecting its citizens from out-of-state providers of goods and services as well as affording its citizens a convenient forum in which to bring their claims. These interests are best served by the exercise of jurisdiction in Massachusetts. On the other hand, Hong Kong has an interest in protecting visitors to promote and preserve its tourism industry, in protecting its businesses, and in providing all parties with a convenient forum. Only one of Hong Kong's interests—protecting its businesses—might be compromised by a Massachusetts forum, while Massachusetts' primary interest—protecting its citizens—might be compromised by a Hong Kong forum. We thus conclude that the final Gestalt factor tips only slightly in the Nowaks' favor.

On balance, we think the gestalt factors weigh strongly in favor of a Massachusetts forum. When considered in combination with the Nowaks' adequate showing on the first two prongs of the constitutional test, we think that, on the specific facts of this case, the exercise of jurisdiction in Massachusetts is reasonable and does not offend the notions of fair play and substantial justice. The district court therefore properly denied Tak How's Rule 12(b)(2) motion to dismiss for lack of personal jurisdiction.

IV.

For the foregoing reasons, the district court's decision to deny Tak How's motions to dismiss for lack of personal jurisdiction ... is AFFIRMED.

G. General Jurisdiction
PERKINS v. BENGUET CONSOLIDATED MINING CO.
342 U.S. 437 (1952)

MR. JUSTICE BURTON delivered the opinion of the Court.

This case calls for an answer to the question whether the Due Process Clause of the Fourteenth Amendment to the Constitution of the United States precludes Ohio from subjecting a foreign corporation to the jurisdiction of its courts.... The corporation has been carrying on in Ohio a continuous and systematic, but limited, part of its general business. Its president, while engaged in doing such business in Ohio, has been served with summons in this proceeding. The cause of action sued upon did not arise in Ohio and does not relate to the corporation's activities there. For the reasons hereafter stated, we hold that the Fourteenth Amendment leaves Ohio free to take or decline jurisdiction over the corporation.

After extended litigation elsewhere petitioner, Idonah Slade Perkins, a nonresident of Ohio, filed two actions *in personam* in the Court of Common Pleas of Clermont County, Ohio, against the several respondents. Among those sued is the Benguet Consolidated Mining Company, here called the mining company. It is styled a "sociedad anonima" under the laws of the Philippine Islands, where it owns and has operated profitable gold and silver mines. In one action petitioner seeks approximately $68,400 in dividends claimed to be due her as a stockholder. In the other she claims $2,500,000 damages largely because of the company's failure to issue to her certificates for 120,000 shares of its stock.

In each case the trial court sustained a motion to quash the service of summons on the mining company. The Court of Appeals of Ohio affirmed that decision, as did the Supreme Court of Ohio. The cases were consolidated and we granted certiorari in order to pass upon the conclusion voiced within the court below that federal due process required the result there reached.

...

The essence of the issue here, at the constitutional level, is ... one of general fairness to the corporation. Appropriate tests for that are discussed in *International Shoe Co. v. Washington* (1945). The amount and kind of activities which must be carried on by the foreign corporation in the state of the forum so as to make it reasonable and just to subject the corporation to the jurisdiction of that state are to be determined in each case. The corporate activities of a foreign corporation which, under state statute, make it necessary for it to secure a license and to designate a statutory agent upon whom process may be served provide a helpful but not a conclusive test. For example, the state of the forum may by statute require a foreign mining corporation to secure a license in order lawfully to carry on there such functional intrastate operations as those of mining or refining ore. On the other hand, if the same corporation carries on, in that state, other continuous and systematic corporate activities as it did here—consisting of directors' meetings, business correspondence, banking, stock transfers, payment of salaries, purchasing of machinery, etc.—those activities are enough to make it fair and reasonable to subject that corporation to proceedings *in personam* in that state, at least insofar as the proceedings *in personam* seek to enforce causes of action relating to those very activities or to other activities of the corporation within the state.

The instant case takes us one step further to a proceeding *in personam* to enforce a cause of action not arising out of the corporation's activities in the state of the forum. Using the tests mentioned above we find no requirement of federal due process that either *prohibits* Ohio from opening its courts to the cause of action here presented or *compels* Ohio to do so. This conforms to the

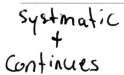

Systmatic
+
Continues

realistic reasoning in *International Shoe*: "... there have been instances in which the continuous corporate operations within a state were thought so substantial and of such a nature as to justify suit against it on causes of action arising from dealings entirely distinct from those activities."

It remains only to consider, in more detail, the issue of whether, as a matter of federal due process, the business done in Ohio by the respondent mining company was sufficiently substantial and of such a nature as to *permit* Ohio to entertain a cause of action against a foreign corporation, where the cause of action arose from activities entirely distinct from its activities in Ohio.

The Ohio Court of Appeals summarized the evidence on the subject. From that summary the following facts are substantially beyond controversy: The company's mining properties were in the Philippine Islands. Its operations there were completely halted during the occupation of the Islands by the Japanese. During that interim the president, who was also the general manager and principal stockholder of the company, returned to his home in Clermont County, Ohio. There he maintained an office in which he conducted his personal affairs and did many things on behalf of the company. He kept there office files of the company. He carried on there correspondence relating to the business of the company and to its employees. He drew and distributed there salary checks on behalf of the company, both in his own favor as president and in favor of two company secretaries who worked there with him. He used and maintained in Clermont County, Ohio, two active bank accounts carrying substantial balances of company funds. A bank in Hamilton County, Ohio, acted as transfer agent for the stock of the company. Several directors' meetings were held at his office or home in Clermont County. From that office he supervised policies dealing with the rehabilitation of the corporation's properties in the Philippines and he dispatched funds to cover purchases of machinery for such rehabilitation. Thus he carried on in Ohio a continuous and systematic supervision of the necessarily limited wartime activities of the company. He there discharged his duties as president and general manager, both during the occupation of the company's properties by the Japanese and immediately thereafter. While no mining properties in Ohio were owned or operated by the company, many of its wartime activities were directed from Ohio and were being given the personal attention of its president in that State at the time he was served with summons. Consideration of the circumstances which, under the law of Ohio, ultimately will determine whether the courts of that State will choose to take jurisdiction over the corporation is reserved for the courts of that State. Without reaching that issue of state policy, we conclude that, under the circumstances above recited, it would not violate federal due process for Ohio either to take or decline jurisdiction of the corporation in this proceeding. This relieves the Ohio courts of the restriction relied upon in the opinion accompanying the syllabus below and which may have influenced the judgment of the court below.

Accordingly, the judgment of the Supreme Court of Ohio is vacated and the cause is remanded to that court for further proceedings in the light of this opinion.

It is so ordered.

MR. JUSTICE BLACK concurs in the result.

MR. JUSTICE MINTON, with whom THE CHIEF JUSTICE joins, dissenting.

HELICOPTEROS NACIONALES DE COLOMBIA, S. A. v. HALL
466 U.S. 408 (1984)

JUSTICE BLACKMUN delivered the opinion of the Court.

We granted certiorari in this case to decide whether the Supreme Court of Texas correctly ruled that the contacts of a foreign corporation with the State of Texas were sufficient to allow a Texas state court to assert jurisdiction over the corporation in a cause of action not arising out of or related to the corporation's activities within the State.

I

Petitioner Helicopteros Nacionales de Colombia, S. A. (Helicol), is a Colombian corporation with its principal place of business in the city of Bogota in that country. It is engaged in the business of providing helicopter transportation for oil and construction companies in South America. On January 26, 1976, a helicopter owned by Helicol crashed in Peru. Four United States citizens were among those who lost their lives in the accident. Respondents are the survivors and representatives of the four decedents.

At the time of the crash, respondents' decedents were employed by Consorcio, a Peruvian consortium, and were working on a pipeline in Peru. Consorcio is the alter ego of a joint venture named Williams-Sedco-Horn (WSH). The venture had its headquarters in Houston, Tex. Consorcio had been formed to enable the venturers to enter into a contract with Petro Peru, the Peruvian state-owned oil company. Consorcio was to construct a pipeline for Petro Peru running from the interior of Peru westward to the Pacific Ocean. Peruvian law forbade construction of the pipeline by any non-Peruvian entity.

Consorcio/WSH needed helicopters to move personnel, materials, and equipment into and out of the construction area. In 1974, upon request of Consorcio/WSH, the chief executive officer of Helicol, Francisco Restrepo, flew to the United States and conferred in Houston with representatives of the three joint venturers. At that meeting, there was a discussion of prices, availability, working conditions, fuel, supplies, and housing. Restrepo represented that Helicol could have the first helicopter on the job in 15 days. The Consorcio/WSH representatives decided to accept the contract proposed by Restrepo. Helicol began performing before the agreement was formally signed in Peru on November 11, 1974. The contract was written in Spanish on official government stationery and provided that the residence of all the parties would be Lima, Peru. It further stated that controversies arising out of the contract would be submitted to the jurisdiction of Peruvian courts. In addition, it provided that Consorcio/WSH would make payments to Helicol's account with the Bank of America in New York City.

Aside from the negotiation session in Houston between Restrepo and the representatives of Consorcio/WSH, Helicol had other contacts with Texas. During the years 1970-1977, it purchased helicopters (approximately 80% of its fleet), spare parts, and accessories for more than $4 million from Bell Helicopter Company in Fort Worth. In that period, Helicol sent prospective pilots to Fort Worth for training and to ferry the aircraft to South America. It also sent management and maintenance personnel to visit Bell Helicopter in Fort Worth during the same period in order to receive "plant familiarization" and for technical consultation. Helicol received into its New York City and Panama City, Fla., bank accounts over $5 million in payments from Consorcio/WSH drawn upon First City National Bank of Houston.

Beyond the foregoing, there have been no other business contacts between Helicol and the State of Texas. Helicol never has been authorized to do business in Texas and never has had an agent for the service of process within the State. It never has performed helicopter operations in Texas or sold any product that reached Texas, never solicited business in Texas, never signed any contract in Texas, never had any employee based there, and never recruited an employee in Texas. In addition, Helicol never has owned real or personal property in Texas and never has maintained an office or establishment there. Helicol has maintained no records in Texas and has no shareholders in that State. None of the respondents or their decedents were domiciled in Texas, but all of the decedents were hired in Houston by Consorcio/WSH to work on the Petro Peru pipeline project.

Respondents instituted wrongful-death actions in the District Court of Harris County, Tex., against Consorcio/WSH, Bell Helicopter Company, and Helicol. Helicol filed special appearances and moved to dismiss the actions for lack of *in personam* jurisdiction over it. The motion was denied. After a consolidated jury trial, judgment was entered against Helicol on a jury verdict of $1,141,200 in favor of respondents.

The Texas Court of Civil Appeals, Houston, First District, reversed the judgment of the District Court, holding that *in personam* jurisdiction over Helicol was lacking. The Supreme Court of Texas, with three justices dissenting, initially affirmed the judgment of the Court of Civil Appeals. Seven months later, however, on motion for rehearing, the court withdrew its prior opinions and, again with three justices dissenting, reversed the judgment of the intermediate court. In ruling that the Texas courts had *in personam* jurisdiction, the Texas Supreme Court first held that the State's long-arm statute reaches as far as the Due Process Clause of the Fourteenth Amendment permits. Thus, the only question remaining for the court to decide was whether it was consistent with the Due Process Clause for Texas courts to assert *in personam* jurisdiction over Helicol.

II

... Due process requirements are satisfied when *in personam* jurisdiction is asserted over a nonresident corporate defendant that has "certain minimum contacts with [the forum] such that the maintenance of the suit does not offend 'traditional notions of fair play and substantial justice.'" International Shoe Co. v. Washington (1945) [quotation omitted]. When a controversy is related to or "arises out of" a defendant's contacts with the forum, the Court has said that a "relationship among the defendant, the forum, and the litigation" is the essential foundation of *in personam* jurisdiction.

Even when the cause of action does not arise out of or relate to the foreign corporation's activities in the forum State, due process is not offended by a State's subjecting the corporation to its *in personam* jurisdiction when there are sufficient contacts between the State and the foreign corporation. *Perkins v. Benguet Consolidated Mining Co.* (1952). In *Perkins*, the Court addressed a situation in which state courts had asserted general jurisdiction over a defendant foreign corporation. During the Japanese occupation of the Philippine Islands, the president and general manager of a Philippine mining corporation maintained an office in Ohio from which he conducted activities on behalf of the company. He kept company files and held directors' meetings in the office, carried on correspondence relating to the business, distributed salary checks drawn on two active Ohio bank accounts, engaged on Ohio bank to act as transfer agent, and supervised policies dealing with the rehabilitation of the corporation's properties in the Philippines. In short, the foreign corporation, through its president, "ha[d] been carrying on in Ohio a continuous and systematic, but limited, part of its general business," and the exercise of general jurisdiction over the Philippine corporation by an Ohio court was "reasonable and just."

All parties to the present case concede that respondents' claims against Helicol did not "arise out of," and are not related to, Helicol's activities within Texas.[10] We thus must explore the nature of Helicol's contacts with the State of Texas to determine whether they constitute the kind of continuous and systematic general business contacts the Court found to exist in *Perkins*. We hold that they do not.

It is undisputed that Helicol does not have a place of business in Texas and never has been licensed to do business in the State. Basically, Helicol's contacts with Texas consisted of sending its chief executive officer to Houston for a contract-negotiation session; accepting into its New York bank account checks drawn on a Houston bank; purchasing helicopters, equipment, and training services from Bell Helicopter for substantial sums; and sending personnel to Bell's facilities in Fort Worth for training.

The one trip to Houston by Helicol's chief executive officer for the purpose of negotiating the transportation-services contract with Consorcio/WSH cannot be described or regarded as a contact of a "continuous and systematic" nature, as *Perkins* described it, and thus cannot support an assertion of *in personam* jurisdiction over Helicol by a Texas court. Similarly, Helicol's acceptance from Consorcio/WSH of checks drawn on a Texas bank is of negligible significance for purposes of determining whether Helicol had sufficient contacts in Texas. There is no indication that Helicol ever requested that the checks be drawn on a Texas bank or that there was any negotiation between Helicol and Consorcio/WSH with respect to the location or identity of the bank on which checks would be drawn. Common sense and everyday experience suggest that, absent unusual circumstances, the bank on which a check is drawn is generally of little consequence to the payee and is a matter left to the discretion of the drawer. Such unilateral activity of another party or a third person is not an appropriate consideration when determining whether a defendant has sufficient contacts with a forum State to justify an assertion of jurisdiction. See *Hanson v. Denckla* (1958).

The Texas Supreme Court focused on the purchases and the related training trips in finding contacts sufficient to support an assertion of jurisdiction. We do not agree with that assessment, for the Court's opinion in *Rosenberg Bros. & Co. v. Curtis Brown Co.* (1923) (Brandeis, J., for a unanimous tribunal), makes clear that purchases and related trips, standing alone, are not a sufficient basis for a State's assertion of jurisdiction.

The defendant in *Rosenberg* was a small retailer in Tulsa, Okla., who dealt in men's clothing and furnishings. It never had applied for a license to do business in New York, nor had it at any time authorized suit to be brought against it there. It never had an established place of business in New York and never regularly carried on business in that State. Its only connection with New York was that it purchased from New York wholesalers a large portion of the merchandise sold in its Tulsa store. The purchases sometimes were made by correspondence and sometimes through visits to New York by an officer of the defendant. The Court concluded: "Visits on such business, even if occurring at regular intervals, would not warrant the inference that the corporation was present within the jurisdiction of [New York]."

This Court in *International Shoe* acknowledged and did not repudiate its holding in *Rosenberg*. In accordance with *Rosenberg*, we hold that mere purchases, even if occurring at regular intervals, are not enough to warrant a State's assertion of *in personam* jurisdiction over a nonresident corporation in a cause of action not related to those purchase transactions. Nor can we conclude that the fact that Helicol sent personnel into Texas for training in connection with the purchase of helicopters and equipment in that State in any way enhanced the nature of Helicol's contacts with Texas. The training was a part of the package of goods and services purchased by Helicol from Bell Helicopter. The brief presence of Helicol employees in Texas for the purpose of attending the training sessions is no more a significant contact than were the trips to New York made by the buyer for the retail store in *Rosenberg*.

III

We hold that Helicol's contacts with the State of Texas were insufficient to satisfy the requirements of the Due Process Clause of the Fourteenth Amendment. Accordingly, we reverse the judgment of the Supreme Court of Texas.

It is so ordered.

[10] Because the parties have not argued any relationship between the cause of action and Helicol's contacts with the State of Texas, we, contrary to the dissent's implication, assert no "view" with respect to that issue.

The dissent suggests that we have erred in drawing no distinction between controversies that "relate to" a defendant's contacts with a forum and those that "arise out of" such contacts. This criticism is somewhat puzzling, for the dissent goes on to urge that, for purposes of determining the constitutional validity of an assertion of specific jurisdiction, there really should be no distinction between the two.

We do not address the validity or consequences of such a distinction because the issue has not been presented in this case. Respondents have made no argument that their cause of action either arose out of or is related to Helicol's contacts with the State of Texas. Absent any briefing on the issue, we decline to reach the questions (1) whether the terms "arising out of" and "related to" describe different connections between a cause of action and a defendant's contacts with a forum, and (2) what sort of tie between a cause of action and a defendant's contacts with a forum is necessary to a determination that either connection exists. Nor do we reach the question whether, if the two types of relationship differ, a forum's exercise of personal jurisdiction in a situation where the cause of action "relates to," but does not "arise out of," the defendant's contacts with the forum should be analyzed as an assertion of specific jurisdiction.

JUSTICE BRENNAN, dissenting.

... Given that Helicol has purposefully availed itself of the benefits and obligations of the forum, and given the direct relationship between the underlying cause of action and Helicol's contacts with the forum, maintenance of this suit in the Texas courts "does not offend [the] 'traditional notions of fair play and substantial justice,'" *International Shoe Co. v. Washington*

(1945) [quotation omitted], that are the touchstone of jurisdictional analysis under the Due Process Clause. I therefore dissent.

...

By asserting that the present case does not implicate the specific jurisdiction of the Texas courts, the Court necessarily removes its decision from the reality of the actual facts presented for our consideration. Moreover, the Court refuses to consider any distinction between contacts that are "related to" the underlying cause of action and contacts that "give rise" to the underlying cause of action. In my view, however, there is a substantial difference between these two standards for asserting specific jurisdiction. Thus, although I agree that the respondents' cause of action did not formally "arise out of" specific activities initiated by Helicol in the State of Texas, I believe that the wrongful-death claim filed by the respondents is significantly related to the undisputed contacts between Helicol and the forum. On that basis, I would conclude that the Due Process Clause allows the Texas courts to assert specific jurisdiction over this particular action.

The wrongful-death actions filed by the respondents were premised on a fatal helicopter crash that occurred in Peru. Helicol was joined as a defendant in the lawsuits because it provided transportation services, including the particular helicopter and pilot involved in the crash, to the joint venture that employed the decedents. Specifically, the respondent Hall claimed in her original complaint that "Helicol is . . . legally responsible for its own negligence through its pilot employee." Viewed in light of these allegations, the contacts between Helicol and the State of Texas are directly and significantly related to the underlying claim filed by the respondents. The negotiations that took place in Texas led to the contract in which Helicol agreed to provide the precise transportation services that were being used at the time of the crash. Moreover, the helicopter involved in the crash was purchased by Helicol in Texas, and the pilot whose negligence was alleged to have caused the crash was actually trained in Texas. This is simply not a case, therefore, in which a state court has asserted jurisdiction over a nonresident defendant on the basis of wholly unrelated contacts with the forum. Rather, the contacts between Helicol and the forum are directly related to the negligence that was alleged in the respondent Hall's original complaint. Because Helicol should have expected to be amenable to suit in the Texas courts for claims directly related to these contacts, it is fair and reasonable to allow the assertion of jurisdiction in this case.

Despite this substantial relationship between the contacts and the cause of action, the Court declines to consider whether the courts of Texas may assert specific jurisdiction over this suit. Apparently, this simply reflects a narrow interpretation of the question presented for review. It is nonetheless possible that the Court's opinion may be read to imply that the specific jurisdiction of the Texas courts is inapplicable because the cause of action did not formally "arise out of" the contacts between Helicol and the forum. In my view, however, such a rule would place unjustifiable limits on the bases under which Texas may assert its jurisdictional power.

... At least since *International Shoe*, the principal focus when determining whether a forum may constitutionally assert jurisdiction over a nonresident defendant has been on fairness and reasonableness to the defendant. To this extent, a court's specific jurisdiction should be applicable whenever the cause of action arises out of *or* relates to the contacts between the defendant and the forum. It is eminently fair and reasonable, in my view, to subject a defendant to suit in a forum with which it has significant contacts directly related to the underlying cause of action. Because Helicol's contacts with the State of Texas meet this standard, I would affirm the judgment of the Supreme Court of Texas.

DAIMLER AG v. BAUMAN
571 U.S. ___ (2014)

JUSTICE GINSBURG delivered the opinion of the Court.

This case concerns the authority of a court in the United States to entertain a claim brought by foreign plaintiffs against a foreign defendant based on events occurring entirely outside the United States. The litigation commenced in 2004, when twenty-two Argentinian residents filed a complaint in the United States District Court for the Northern District of California against DaimlerChrysler Aktiengesellschaft (Daimler), a German public stock company, headquartered in Stuttgart, that manufactures Mercedes–Benz vehicles in Germany. The complaint alleged that during Argentina's 1976–1983 "Dirty War," Daimler's Argentinian subsidiary, Mercedes–Benz Argentina (MB Argentina) collaborated with state security forces to kidnap, detain, torture, and kill certain MB Argentina workers, among them, plaintiffs or persons closely related to plaintiffs. Damages for the alleged human-rights violations were sought from Daimler under the laws of the United States, California, and Argentina. Jurisdiction over the lawsuit was predicated on the California contacts of Mercedes–Benz USA, LLC (MBUSA), a subsidiary of Daimler incorporated in Delaware with its principal place of business in New Jersey. MBUSA distributes Daimler-manufactured vehicles to independent dealerships throughout the United States, including California.

The question presented is whether the Due Process Clause of the Fourteenth Amendment precludes the District Court from exercising jurisdiction over Daimler in this case, given the absence of any California connection to the atrocities, perpetrators, or victims described in the complaint. Plaintiffs invoked the court's general or all-purpose jurisdiction. California, they urge, is a place where Daimler may be sued on any and all claims against it, wherever in the world the claims may arise. For example, as plaintiffs' counsel affirmed, under the proffered jurisdictional theory, if a Daimler-manufactured vehicle overturned in Poland, injuring a Polish driver and passenger, the injured parties could maintain a design defect suit in California. Exercises of personal jurisdiction so exorbitant, we hold, are barred by due process constraints on the assertion of adjudicatory authority.

I

. . . [P]laintiffs asserted claims under the Alien Tort Statute, 28 U.S.C. § 1350, as well as claims for wrongful death and intentional infliction of emotional distress under the laws of California and Argentina. The incidents recounted in the complaint center on MB Argentina's plant in Gonzalez Catan, Argentina; no part of MB Argentina's alleged collaboration with Argentinian authorities took place in California or anywhere else in the United States.

. . . Daimler is a German *Aktiengesellschaft* (public stock company) that manufactures Mercedes–Benz vehicles in Germany and has its headquarters in Stuttgart. At times relevant to this case, MB Argentina was a subsidiary wholly owned by Daimler's predecessor in interest.

Daimler moved to dismiss the action for want of personal jurisdiction. Opposing the motion, plaintiffs submitted declarations and exhibits purporting to demonstrate the presence of Daimler itself in California. Alternatively, plaintiffs maintained that jurisdiction over Daimler could be founded on the California contacts of MBUSA, a distinct corporate entity that, according to plaintiffs, should be treated as Daimler's agent for jurisdictional purposes.

MBUSA, an indirect subsidiary of Daimler, is a Delaware limited liability corporation. MBUSA serves as Daimler's exclusive importer and distributor in the United States, purchasing Mercedes–Benz automobiles from Daimler in Germany, then importing those vehicles, and ultimately distributing them to independent dealerships located throughout the Nation. Although MBUSA's principal place of business is in New Jersey, MBUSA has multiple California-based facilities, including a regional office in Costa Mesa, a Vehicle Preparation Center in Carson, and a Classic Center in Irvine. According to the record developed below, MBUSA is the largest supplier of luxury vehicles to the California market. In particular, over 10% of all sales of new vehicles in the United States take place in California, and MBUSA's California sales account for 2.4% of Daimler's worldwide sales.

The relationship between Daimler and MBUSA is delineated in a General Distributor Agreement, which sets forth requirements for MBUSA's distribution of Mercedes–Benz vehicles in the United States. That agreement established MBUSA as an "independent contracto[r]" that "buy[s] and sell[s] [vehicles] . . . as an independent business for [its] own account." The agreement "does not make [MBUSA] . . . a general or special agent, partner, joint venturer or employee of DAIMLERCHRYSLER or any DaimlerChrysler Group Company"; MBUSA "ha[s] no authority to make binding obligations for or act on behalf of DAIMLERCHRYSLER or any DaimlerChrysler Group Company."

After allowing jurisdictional discovery on plaintiffs' agency allegations, the District Court granted Daimler's motion to dismiss. Daimler's own affiliations with California, the court first determined, were insufficient to support the exercise of all-purpose jurisdiction over the corporation. Next, the court declined to attribute MBUSA's California contacts to Daimler on an agency theory, concluding that plaintiffs failed to demonstrate that MBUSA acted as Daimler's agent.

The Ninth Circuit at first affirmed the District Court's judgment. Addressing solely the question of agency, the Court of Appeals held that plaintiffs had not shown the existence of an agency relationship of the kind that might warrant attribution of MBUSA's contacts to Daimler....

Daimler petitioned for rehearing and rehearing en banc, urging that the exercise of personal jurisdiction over Daimler could not be reconciled with this Court's decision in *Goodyear Dunlop Tires Operations, S.A. v. Brown* (2011). Over the dissent of eight judges, the Ninth Circuit denied Daimler's petition.

We granted certiorari to decide whether, consistent with the Due Process Clause of the Fourteenth Amendment, Daimler is amenable to suit in California courts for claims involving only foreign plaintiffs and conduct occurring entirely abroad.

II

Federal courts ordinarily follow state law in determining the bounds of their jurisdiction over persons. Under California's long-arm statute, California state courts may exercise personal jurisdiction "on any basis not inconsistent with the Constitution of this state or of the United States." California's long-arm statute allows the exercise of personal jurisdiction to the full extent permissible under the U.S. Constitution. We therefore inquire whether the Ninth Circuit's holding comports with the limits imposed by federal due process.

III

...

Since *International Shoe,* "specific jurisdiction has become the centerpiece of modern jurisdiction theory, while general jurisdiction [has played] a reduced role." *Goodyear* [quotation omitted]. *International Shoe*'s momentous departure from *Pennoyer*'s rigidly territorial focus, we have noted, unleashed a rapid expansion of tribunals' ability to hear claims against out-of-state defendants when the episode-in-suit occurred in the forum or the defendant purposefully availed itself of the forum. ...

Our post-*International Shoe* opinions on general jurisdiction, by comparison, are few. ... Most recently, in *Goodyear*, we answered the question: "Are foreign subsidiaries of a United States parent corporation amenable to suit in state court on claims unrelated to any activity of the subsidiaries in the forum State?" That case arose from a bus accident outside Paris that killed two boys from North Carolina. The boys' parents brought a wrongful-death suit in North Carolina state court alleging that the bus's tire was defectively manufactured. The complaint named as defendants not only The Goodyear Tire and Rubber Company (Goodyear), an Ohio corporation, but also Goodyear's Turkish, French, and Luxembourgian subsidiaries. Those foreign subsidiaries, which manufactured tires for sale in Europe and Asia, lacked any affiliation with North Carolina. A small percentage of tires manufactured by the foreign subsidiaries were distributed in North Carolina, however, and on that ground, the North Carolina Court of Appeals held the subsidiaries amenable to the general jurisdiction of North Carolina courts.

We reversed, observing that the North Carolina court's analysis "elided the essential difference between case-specific and all-purpose (general) jurisdiction." Although the placement of a product into the stream of commerce "may bolster an affiliation germane to *specific* jurisdiction," we explained, such contacts "do not warrant a determination that, based on those ties, the forum has *general* jurisdiction over a defendant." As *International Shoe* itself teaches, a corporation's "continuous activity of some sorts within a state is not enough to support the demand that the corporation be amenable to suits unrelated to that activity." Because Goodyear's foreign subsidiaries were "in no sense at home in North Carolina," we held, those subsidiaries could not be required to submit to the general jurisdiction of that State's courts.

... As this Court has increasingly trained on ... specific jurisdiction, general jurisdiction has come to occupy a less dominant place in the contemporary scheme.

IV

With this background, we turn directly to the question whether Daimler's affiliations with California are sufficient to subject it to the general (all-purpose) personal jurisdiction of that State's courts. In the proceedings below, the parties agreed on, or failed to contest, certain points we now take as given. Plaintiffs have never attempted to fit this case into the *specific* jurisdiction category. Nor did plaintiffs challenge on appeal the District Court's holding that Daimler's own contacts with California were, by themselves, too sporadic to justify the exercise of general jurisdiction. While plaintiffs ultimately persuaded the Ninth Circuit to impute MBUSA's California contacts to

Daimler on an agency theory, at no point have they maintained that MBUSA is an alter ego of Daimler.

Daimler, on the other hand, failed to object below to plaintiffs' assertion that the California courts could exercise all-purpose jurisdiction over MBUSA. We will assume then, for purposes of this decision only, that MBUSA qualifies as at home in California.

A

In sustaining the exercise of general jurisdiction over Daimler, the Ninth Circuit relied on an agency theory, determining that MBUSA acted as Daimler's agent for jurisdictional purposes and then attributing MBUSA's California contacts to Daimler. The Ninth Circuit's agency analysis derived from Circuit precedent considering principally whether the subsidiary "performs services that are sufficiently important to the foreign corporation that if it did not have a representative to perform them, the corporation's own officials would undertake to perform substantially similar services."

This Court has not yet addressed whether a foreign corporation may be subjected to a court's general jurisdiction based on the contacts of its in-state subsidiary. Daimler argues, and several Courts of Appeals have held, that a subsidiary's jurisdictional contacts can be imputed to its parent only when the former is so dominated by the latter as to be its alter ego. The Ninth Circuit adopted a less rigorous test based on what it described as an "agency" relationship. Agencies, we note, come in many sizes and shapes: "One may be an agent for some business purposes and not others so that the fact that one may be an agent for one purpose does not make him or her an agent for every purpose." 2A C.J.S., Agency § 43, p. 367 (2013) (footnote omitted).[13] A subsidiary, for example, might be its parent's agent for claims arising in the place where the subsidiary operates, yet not its agent regarding claims arising elsewhere. The Court of Appeals did not advert to that prospect. But we need not pass judgment on invocation of an agency theory in the context of general jurisdiction, for in no event can the appeals court's analysis be sustained.

The Ninth Circuit's agency finding rested primarily on its observation that MBUSA's services were "important" to Daimler, as gauged by Daimler's hypothetical readiness to perform those services itself if MBUSA did not exist. Formulated this way, the inquiry into importance stacks the deck, for it will always yield a pro-jurisdiction answer: "Anything a corporation does through

---

[13] Agency relationships, we have recognized, may be relevant to the existence of *specific* jurisdiction. "[T]he corporate personality," *International Shoe* observed, "is a fiction, although a fiction intended to be acted upon as though it were a fact." As such, a corporation can purposefully avail itself of a forum by directing its agents or distributors to take action there. It does not inevitably follow, however, that similar reasoning applies to *general* jurisdiction.

an independent contractor, subsidiary, or distributor is presumably something that the corporation would do 'by other means' if the independent contractor, subsidiary, or distributor did not exist." (O'Scannlain, J., dissenting from denial of rehearing en banc). The Ninth Circuit's agency theory thus appears to subject foreign corporations to general jurisdiction whenever they have an in-state subsidiary or affiliate, an outcome that would sweep beyond even the "sprawling view of general jurisdiction" we rejected in *Goodyear.*

B

Even if we were to assume that MBUSA is at home in California, and further to assume MBUSA's contacts are imputable to Daimler, there would still be no basis to subject Daimler to general jurisdiction in California, for Daimler's slim contacts with the State hardly render it at home there.

Goodyear made clear that only a limited set of affiliations with a forum will render a defendant amenable to all-purpose jurisdiction there. "For an individual, the paradigm forum for the exercise of general jurisdiction is the individual's domicile; for a corporation, it is an equivalent place, one in which the corporation is fairly regarded as at home." With respect to a corporation, the place of incorporation and principal place of business are "paradig[m] . . . bases for general jurisdiction." Those affiliations have the virtue of being unique—that is, each ordinarily indicates only one place—as well as easily ascertainable. These bases afford plaintiffs recourse to at least one clear and certain forum in which a corporate defendant may be sued on any and all claims.

Goodyear did not hold that a corporation may be subject to general jurisdiction *only* in a forum where it is incorporated or has its principal place of business; it simply typed those places paradigm all-purpose forums. Plaintiffs would have us look beyond the exemplar bases *Goodyear* identified, and approve the exercise of general jurisdiction in every State in which a corporation "engages in a substantial, continuous, and systematic course of business." That formulation, we hold, is unacceptably grasping.

. . . [T]he words "continuous and systematic" were used in *International Shoe* to describe instances in which the exercise of *specific* jurisdiction would be appropriate. Turning to all-purpose jurisdiction, in contrast, *International Shoe* speaks of "instances in which the continuous corporate operations within a state [are] so substantial and of such a nature as to justify suit . . . *on causes of action arising from dealings entirely distinct from those activities.*" Accordingly, the inquiry under *Goodyear* is not whether a foreign corporation's in-forum contacts can be said to be in some sense "continuous and systematic," it is whether that corporation's "affiliations with the State are so 'continuous and systematic' as to render [it] essentially at home in the forum State."[19]

Here, neither Daimler nor MBUSA is incorporated in California, nor does either entity have its principal place of business there. If Daimler's California activities sufficed to allow adjudication of this Argentina-rooted case in California, the same global reach would presumably be available in every other State in which MBUSA's sales are sizable. Such exorbitant exercises of all-purpose jurisdiction would scarcely permit out-of-state defendants "to structure their primary conduct with some minimum assurance as to where that conduct will and will not render them liable to suit." *Burger King Corp.*

It was therefore error for the Ninth Circuit to conclude that Daimler, even with MBUSA's contacts attributed to it, was at home in California, and hence subject to suit there on claims by foreign plaintiffs having nothing to do with anything that occurred or had its principal impact in California.[20]

C

Finally, the transnational context of this dispute bears attention. ...

The Ninth Circuit ... paid little heed to the risks to international comity its expansive view of general jurisdiction posed. Other nations do not share the

---

[19] We do not foreclose the possibility that in an exceptional case, see, *e.g.*, *Perkins*, a corporation's operations in a forum other than its formal place of incorporation or principal place of business may be so substantial and of such a nature as to render the corporation at home in that State. But this case presents no occasion to explore that question, because Daimler's activities in California plainly do not approach that level. It is one thing to hold a corporation answerable for operations in the forum State, quite another to expose it to suit on claims having no connection whatever to the forum State.

[20] To clarify in light of JUSTICE SOTOMAYOR'S opinion concurring in the judgment, the general jurisdiction inquiry does not "focu[s] solely on the magnitude of the defendant's in-state contacts." General jurisdiction instead calls for an appraisal of a corporation's activities in their entirety, nationwide and worldwide. A corporation that operates in many places can scarcely be deemed at home in all of them. Otherwise, "at home" would be synonymous with "doing business" tests framed before specific jurisdiction evolved in the United States. ... JUSTICE SOTOMAYOR would reach the same result, but for a different reason. Rather than concluding that Daimler is not at home in California, JUSTICE SOTOMAYOR would hold that the exercise of general jurisdiction over Daimler would be unreasonable "in the unique circumstances of this case." In other words, she favors a resolution fit for this day and case only. True, a multipronged reasonableness check was articulated in *Asahi*, but not as a free-floating test. Instead, the check was to be essayed when *specific* jurisdiction is at issue. First, a court is to determine whether the connection between the forum and the episode-in-suit could justify the exercise of specific jurisdiction. Then, in a second step, the court is to consider several additional factors to assess the reasonableness of entertaining the case. When a corporation is genuinely at home in the forum State, however, any second-step inquiry would be superfluous . . . .

uninhibited approach to personal jurisdiction advanced by the Court of Appeals in this case. In the European Union, for example, a corporation may generally be sued in the nation in which it is "domiciled," a term defined to refer only to the location of the corporation's "statutory seat," "central administration," or "principal place of business." The Solicitor General informs us, in this regard, that "foreign governments' objections to some domestic courts' expansive views of general jurisdiction have in the past impeded negotiations of international agreements on the reciprocal recognition and enforcement of judgments." Considerations of international rapport thus reinforce our determination that subjecting Daimler to the general jurisdiction of courts in California would not accord with the "fair play and substantial justice" due process demands. *International Shoe.*

* * *

For the reasons stated, the judgment of the United States Court of Appeals for the Ninth Circuit is

Reversed.

JUSTICE SOTOMAYOR, concurring in the judgment.

.... Referring to the "continuous and systematic" contacts inquiry that has been taught to generations of first-year law students as "unacceptably grasping," the majority announces the new rule that in order for a foreign defendant to be subject to general jurisdiction, it must not only possess continuous and systematic contacts with a forum State, but those contacts must also surpass some unspecified level when viewed in comparison to the company's "nationwide and worldwide" activities.

Neither of the majority's two rationales for this proportionality requirement is persuasive. First, the majority suggests that its approach is necessary for the sake of predictability. . . . But there is nothing unpredictable about a rule that instructs multinational corporations that if they engage in continuous and substantial contacts with more than one State, they will be subject to general jurisdiction in each one. The majority may not favor that rule as a matter of policy, but such disagreement does not render an otherwise routine test unpredictable.

Nor is the majority's proportionality inquiry any more predictable than the approach it rejects. If anything, the majority's approach injects an additional layer of uncertainty because a corporate defendant must now try to foretell a court's analysis as to both the sufficiency of its contacts with the forum State itself, as well as the relative sufficiency of those contacts in light of the company's operations elsewhere. Moreover, the majority does not even try to explain just how extensive the company's in-state contacts must be in the context of its global operations in order for general jurisdiction to be proper.

The majority's approach will also lead to greater unpredictability by radically expanding the scope of jurisdictional discovery. Rather than ascertaining the extent of a corporate defendant's forum-state contacts alone, courts will now have to identify the extent of a company's contacts in every other forum where it does business in order to compare them against the company's in-state contacts. That considerable burden runs headlong into the majority's recitation of the familiar principle that "[s]imple jurisdictional rules . . . promote greater predictability."

Absent the predictability rationale, the majority's sole remaining justification for its proportionality approach is its unadorned concern for the consequences. "If Daimler's California activities sufficed to allow adjudication of this Argentina-rooted case in California," the majority laments, "the same global reach would presumably be available in every other State in which MBUSA's sales are sizable."

The majority characterizes this result as "exorbitant," but in reality it is an inevitable consequence of the rule of due process we set forth nearly 70 years ago, that there are "instances in which [a company's] continuous corporate operations within a state" are "so substantial and of such a nature as to justify suit against it on causes of action arising from dealings entirely distinct from those activities," *International Shoe*. In the era of *International Shoe*, it was rare for a corporation to have such substantial nationwide contacts that it would be subject to general jurisdiction in a large number of States. Today, that circumstance is less rare. But that is as it should be. What has changed since *International Shoe* is not the due process principle of fundamental fairness but rather the nature of the global economy. Just as it was fair to say in the 1940's that an out-of-state company could enjoy the benefits of a forum State enough to make it "essentially at home" in the State, it is fair to say today that a multinational conglomerate can enjoy such extensive benefits in multiple forum States that it is "essentially at home" in each one.

In any event, to the extent the majority is concerned with the modern-day consequences of *International Shoe*'s conception of personal jurisdiction, there remain other judicial doctrines available to mitigate any resulting unfairness to large corporate defendants. Here, for instance, the reasonableness prong may afford petitioner relief. In other cases, a defendant can assert the doctrine of *forum non conveniens* if a given State is a highly inconvenient place to litigate a dispute. In still other cases, the federal change of venue statute can provide protection. And to the degree that the majority worries these doctrines are not enough to protect the economic interests of multinational businesses (or that our longstanding approach to general jurisdiction poses "risks to international comity"), the task of weighing those policy concerns belongs ultimately to legislators, who may amend state and federal long-arm statutes in accordance with the democratic process. Unfortunately, the majority short circuits that process by enshrining today's narrow rule of general jurisdiction as a matter of constitutional law.

. . . [Moreover] the majority's approach creates the incongruous result that an individual defendant whose only contact with a forum State is a one-time visit will be subject to general jurisdiction if served with process during that visit, *Burnham v. Superior Court of Cal.* (1990), but a large corporation that owns property, employs workers, and does billions of dollars' worth of business in the State will not be, simply because the corporation has similar contacts elsewhere (though the visiting individual surely does as well).

Finally, it should be obvious that the ultimate effect of the majority's approach will be to shift the risk of loss from multinational corporations to the individuals harmed by their actions. Under the majority's rule, for example, a parent whose child is maimed due to the negligence of a foreign hotel owned by a multinational conglomerate will be unable to hold the hotel to account in a single U.S. court, even if the hotel company has a massive presence in multiple States. Similarly, a U.S. business that enters into a contract in a foreign country to sell its products to a multinational company there may be unable to seek relief in any U.S. court if the multinational company breaches the contract, even if that company has considerable operations in numerous U.S. forums. Indeed, the majority's approach would preclude the plaintiffs in these examples from seeking recourse anywhere in the United States even if no other judicial system was available to provide relief. I cannot agree with the majority's conclusion that the Due Process Clause requires these results. . . .

BNSF RAILROAD CO. v. TYRRELL
581 US ____ (2017)

JUSTICE GINSBURG delivered the opinion of the Court.

The two cases we decide today arise under the Federal Employers' Liability Act (FELA), 45 U. S. C. §51 *et seq.*, which makes railroads liable in money damages to their employees for on-the-job injuries. Both suits were pursued in Montana state courts although the injured workers did not reside in Montana, nor were they injured there. The defendant railroad, BNSF Railway Company (BNSF), although "doing business" in Montana when the litigation commenced, was not incorporated in Montana, nor did it maintain its principal place of business in that State. To justify the exercise of personal jurisdiction over BNSF, the Montana Supreme Court relied on ... state law, under which personal jurisdiction could be asserted over "persons found within ... Montana." Mont. Rule Civ. Proc. 4(b)(1) (2015). BNSF fit that bill, the court stated, because it has over 2,000 miles of railroad track and employs more than 2,000 workers in Montana. Our precedent, however, explains that the Fourteenth Amendment's Due Process Clause does not permit a State to hale an out-of-state corporation before its courts when the corporation is not "at home" in the State and the episode-in-suit occurred elsewhere. We therefore reverse the judgment of the Montana Supreme Court.

I

In March 2011, respondent Robert Nelson, a North Dakota resident, brought a FELA suit against BNSF in a Montana state court to recover damages for knee injuries Nelson allegedly sustained while working for BNSF as a fuel-truck driver. In May 2014, respondent Kelli Tyrrell, appointed in South Dakota as the administrator of her husband Brent Tyrrell's estate, similarly sued BNSF under FELA in a Montana state court. Brent Tyrrell, his widow alleged, had developed a fatal kidney cancer from his exposure to carcinogenic chemicals while working for BNSF. Neither plaintiff alleged injuries arising from or related to work performed in Montana; indeed, neither Nelson nor Brent Tyrrell appears ever to have worked for BNSF in Montana.

BNSF is incorporated in Delaware and has its principal place of business in Texas. It operates railroad lines in 28 States. BNSF has 2,061 miles of railroad track in Montana (about 6% of its total track mileage of 32,500), employs some 2,100 workers there (less than 5% of its total work force of 43,000), generates less than 10% of its total revenue in the State, and maintains only one of its 24 automotive facilities in Montana (4%). Contending that it is not "at home" in Montana, as required for the exercise of general personal jurisdiction under *Daimler AG* v. *Bauman* (2014) (internal quotation marks omitted), BNSF moved to dismiss both suits for lack of personal jurisdiction. Its motion was granted in Nelson's case and denied in Tyrrell's.

After consolidating the two cases, the Montana Supreme Court held that Montana courts could exercise general personal jurisdiction over BNSF. [The] court determined ... Montana law provides for the exercise of general jurisdiction over "[a]ll persons found within" the State. In view of the railroad's many employees and miles of track in Montana, the court concluded, BNSF is both "doing business" and "found within" the State, such that both FELA and Montana law authorized the exercise of personal jurisdiction. The due process limits articulated in *Daimler*, the court added, did not control, because *Daimler* did not involve a FELA claim or a railroad defendant.

...

We granted certiorari to resolve whether ... the Montana courts' exercise of personal jurisdiction in these cases comports with due process.

III

[The] Montana courts' assertion of personal jurisdiction over BNSF here must rest on Mont. Rule Civ. Proc. 4(b)(1), the State's provision for the exercise of personal jurisdiction over "persons found" in Montana. BNSF does not contest that it is "found within" Montana as the State's courts comprehend that rule. We therefore inquire whether the Montana courts' exercise of personal jurisdiction under Montana law comports with the Due Process Clause of the Fourteenth Amendment.

In *International Shoe Co. v. Washington* (1945), this Court explained that a state court may exercise personal jurisdiction over an out-of-state defendant who has "certain minimum contacts with [the State] such that the maintenance of the suit does not offend 'traditional notions of fair play and substantial justice.'" Elaborating on this guide, we have distinguished between specific or case-linked jurisdiction and general or all-purpose jurisdiction. Because neither Nelson nor Tyrrell alleges any injury from work in or related to Montana, only the propriety of general jurisdiction is at issue here.

GoodyearDunlop Tires Operations, S.A. v. Brown (2011) and *Daimler* clarified that "[a] court may assert general jurisdiction over foreign (sister-state or foreign-country) corporations to hear any and all claims against them when their affiliations with the State are so 'continuous and systematic' as to render them essentially at home in the forum State." *Daimler* (quoting *Goodyear*). The "paradigm" forums in which a corporate defendant is "at home," we explained, are the corporation's place of incorporation and its principal place of business. The exercise of general jurisdiction is not limited to these forums; in an "exceptional case," a corporate defendant's operations in another forum "may be so substantial and of such a nature as to render the corporation at home in that State." *Daimler*. We suggested that *Perkins v. Benguet Consol. Mining Co.* (1952) exemplified such a case. *Daimler*. In *Perkins*, war had forced the defendant corporation's owner to temporarily relocate the enterprise from the Philippines to Ohio. Because Ohio then became "the center of the corporation's wartime activities," *Daimler*, suit was proper there.

The Montana Supreme Court distinguished *Daimler* on the ground that we did not there confront "a FELA claim or a railroad defendant." The Fourteenth Amendment due process constraint described in *Daimler*, however, applies to all state-court assertions of general jurisdiction over nonresident defendants; the constraint does not vary with the type of claim asserted or business enterprise sued.

BNSF, we repeat, is not incorporated in Montana and does not maintain its principal place of business there. Nor is BNSF so heavily engaged in activity in Montana "as to render [it] essentially at home" in that State. As earlier noted, BNSF has over 2,000 miles of railroad track and more than 2,000 employees in Montana. But, as we observed in *Daimler*, "the general jurisdiction inquiry does not focus solely on the magnitude of the defendant's in-state contacts" (internal quotation marks and alterations omitted). Rather, the inquiry "calls for an appraisal of a corporation's activities in their entirety"; "[a] corporation that operates in many places can scarcely be deemed at home in all of them." In short, the business BNSF does in Montana is sufficient to subject the railroad to specific personal jurisdiction in that

State on claims related to the business it does in Montana. But in-state business, we clarified in *Daimler* and *Goodyear*, does not suffice to permit the assertion of general jurisdiction over claims like Nelson's and Tyrrell's that are unrelated to any activity occurring in Montana.

IV

Nelson and Tyrrell present a further argument—that BNSF has consented to personal jurisdiction in Montana. The Montana Supreme Court did not address this contention, so we do not reach it.

*　　*　　*

For the reasons stated, the judgment of the Montana Supreme Court is reversed, and the cases are remanded for further proceedings not inconsistent with this opinion.

It is so ordered.

JUSTICE SOTOMAYOR, concurring in part and dissenting in part.

... I continue to disagree with the path the Court struck in *Daimler AG* v. *Bauman* (2014), which limits general jurisdiction over a corporate defendant only to those States where it is "essentially at home." And even if the Court insists on adhering to that standard, I dissent from its decision to apply it here in the first instance rather than remanding to the Montana Supreme Court for it to conduct what should be a fact-intensive analysis under the proper legal framework. Accordingly, I ... dissent from Part III and the judgment.

The Court would do well to adhere more faithfully to the direction from *International Shoe Co.* v. *Washington* (1945), which instructed that general jurisdiction is proper when a corporation's "continuous corporate operations within a state [are] so substantial and of such a nature as to justify suit against it on causes of action arising from dealings entirely distinct from those activities." Under *International Shoe*, in other words, courts were to ask whether the benefits a defendant attained in the forum State warranted the burdens associated with general personal jurisdiction. The majority itself acknowledges that *International Shoe* should govern, describing the question as whether a defendant's affiliations with a State are sufficiently "continuous and systematic" to warrant the exercise of general jurisdiction there. If only its analysis today reflected that directive. Instead, the majority opinion goes on to reaffirm the restrictive "at home" test set out in *Daimler*—a test that, as I have explained, has no home in our precedents and creates serious inequities.

The majority's approach grants a jurisdictional windfall to large multistate or multinational corporations that operate across many jurisdictions. Under its reasoning, it is virtually inconceivable that such corporations will ever be subject to general jurisdiction in any location other than their principal places of business or of incorporation. Foreign businesses with principal places of business outside the United States may never be subject to general jurisdiction in this country even though they have continuous and systematic contacts within the United States. What was once a holistic, nuanced contacts analysis backed by considerations of fairness and reasonableness has now effectively been replaced by the rote identification of a corporation's principal place of business or place of incorporation. The result? It is individual plaintiffs, harmed by the actions of a far-flung foreign corporation, who will bear the brunt of the majority's approach and be forced to sue in distant jurisdictions with which they have no contacts or connection.

...

The majority does even *Daimler* itself a disservice, paying only lipservice to the question the Court purported to reserve there—the possibility of an "exceptional case" in which general jurisdiction would be proper in a forum State that is neither a corporate defendant's place of incorporation nor its principal place of business. Its opinion here could be understood to limit that exception to the exact facts of *Perkins* v. *Benguet Consol. Mining Co.* (1952). That reading is so narrow as to read the exception out of existence entirely; certainly a defendant with significant contacts with more than one State falls outside its ambit. And so it is inevitable under its own reasoning that the majority would conclude that BNSF's contacts with Montana are insufficient to justify the exercise of personal jurisdiction here. This result is perverse. Despite having reserved the possibility of an "exceptional case" in *Daimler*, the majority here has rejected that possibility out of hand.

Worse, the majority reaches its conclusion only by departing from the Court's normal practice. Had it remanded to the Montana Supreme Court to reevaluate the due process question under the correct legal standard, that court could have examined whether this is such an "exceptional case." Instead, with its ruling today, the Court unnecessarily sends a signal to the lower courts that the exceptional-circumstances inquiry is all form, no substance.

A. Diversity
RODRÍGUEZ v. SEÑOR FROG'S DE LA ISLA, INC.
642 F.3d 28 (CA1 2011)

THOMPSON, Circuit Judge.

This is a diversity-based personal-injury case. A jury returned a $450,000 verdict for Paloma Rodríguez against Señor Frog's de la Isla, Inc. ("Señor Frog," for short) in Puerto Rico's federal district court. Señor Frog now appeals, challenging nearly every aspect of the district judge's performance. Unable to find any reversible error in the judge's actions, we affirm.

How It All Began

San Juan, Puerto Rico, early in the predawn morning of December 5, 2004. Cruising in her Mazda 323 on the Muñoz Rivera Expressway, 21-year-old Rodríguez hit a pothole—a collision that cost her two tires and killed the engine. But the worst was yet to come.

Turning her hazards on, Rodríguez somehow got her car to the side of the road, completely out of the way of oncoming traffic. A police officer patrolling that stretch of highway spotted her and pulled over. He left the cruiser's flashing lights on. A tow-truck driver also showed up, parked his truck in front of Rodríguez's car, activated the truck's flashing lights, pointed a spotlight on the work area, and put out cones to caution drivers passing by. As the truck driver lowered the truck's platform, Rodríguez got back into the Mazda either to grab some personal items or to do something to help out with the towing process.

That is when Carlos Estrada closed in, speeding in a Mitsubishi Mirage registered to Señor Frog. His headlights were off. He had a blood-alcohol level nearly double the legal limit in Puerto Rico. And he smashed that Mitsubishi right into the rear of Rodríguez's Mazda. Rodríguez was hurt, and apparently hurt badly. "She was thrown inside the vehicle," the officer later said. Covered in blood, she had no vital signs—"she appeared to be dead." But she survived and sued Señor Frog in district court under diversity jurisdiction, *see* 28 U.S.C. § 1332, alleging negligence and negligent entrustment. ...

...The attorneys later sparred over whether the parties were of diverse citizenship, and the judge ruled that they were, following an evidentiary hearing convened after Rodríguez had rested her case. ...

The Diverse-Citizenship Issue

The diversity-jurisdiction statute empowers federal courts to hear and decide suits between citizens of different states, provided the amount in controversy is more than $75,000. Puerto Rico is a state for diversity-jurisdiction purposes. And Señor Frog is a citizen of Puerto Rico, so Rodríguez's suit is untenable if she was a Puerto Rico citizen when she filed her December 1, 2005 complaint. Señor Frog argues that she *was*, though it did not press this argument until after Rodríguez had rested her case. But after an evidentiary hearing, the judge deemed Rodríguez a citizen of California when she sued, and this conclusion survives clear-error review.

Citizenship for diversity purposes is domicile, and domicile is the place where one is present and intends to stay. As the party invoking diversity jurisdiction, Rodríguez had to prove domicile by a preponderance of the evidence—and she did just that, presenting enough evidence to show that she was a domiciliary (and thus a citizen) of California.

Rodríguez was the only witness at the hearing on the diversity issue— Señor Frog called no one. Rodríguez testified that she had moved from Puerto Rico to California in September 2005, roughly three months before she filed this suit. She was pregnant, and she and her boyfriend Adrian Peralta wanted to start their lives together in the Golden State. Since they had very little money, the couple lived in a San Francisco Bay area home owned by Peralta's grandmother. And by the time she sued Señor Frog, she had fully relocated from Puerto Rico to California: she was physically present in California (with her clothes, books, furniture, household items, *etc.*), had opened up a California bank account (she had no money in any Puerto Rico banks), had gotten a California driver's license and job, and had hired a California lawyer to fight on her behalf. And though she had not registered to vote in California (actually, she was not registered to vote anywhere) and did not attend church there, she had settled on living in the Golden State permanently. *Cf. Bank One, Texas, N.A. v. Montle* (1st Cir. 1992) (holding that factors that can help an inquiring court determine a party's intent include where the party exercises civil and political rights, pays taxes, has real and personal property, has a driver's or other license, has bank accounts, has a job or owns a business, attends church, and has club memberships—for simplicity we call these the "*Bank One* factors").

Post-complaint events cast no doubt on the earnestness of Rodríguez's intent either. Rodríguez told the judge that she gave birth to a baby boy in

California, turned to a California pediatrician to treat him, and put him in a California daycare for a spell. She also enrolled in three California community college courses and got a cell phone with a California area code (she may have acquired the cell phone pre-complaint, but we cannot tell for certain). True, starting in 2007, Rodríguez spent several semesters at the Inter-American University in Puerto Rico (she could get her bachelor's degree faster if she studied there, she said), and she was still taking classes there at the time of trial. But she made clear that she returned to California whenever school was not in session (during winter, spring, and summer breaks, for example), and she provided copies of plane tickets to prove that point. She also reaffirmed that she intended to live in California for the rest of her life (she hoped to land a teaching job there once she got her degree).

Having the exclusive ability to assess Rodríguez's demeanor and tone, the district judge was best positioned to separate true from false testimony. The judge found Rodríguez credible, and after carefully canvassing the testimony, she meticulously detailed findings of fact, which she supported with specific references to the evidence. Because we cannot say that these findings were clearly erroneous, her ruling that there was diverse citizenship must stand.

Undaunted, Señor Frog insists that the district judge botched her ruling in several respects. For openers, Señor Frog protests that Rodríguez did not have enough *Bank One* factors on her side, given that she had not registered to vote in California and had no religious affiliation there. Also, Rodríguez produced no documentary evidence—no bank statements, driving records, college transcripts, *etc.*—to support key claims, and, given the best-evidence rule, the judge had no business accepting her "self-serving" comments about her intent to stay in California indefinitely. Searching for a "gotcha!" moment, Señor Frog notes too that Rodríguez said at trial that she "lived in Mayaguez," Puerto Rico, "all my life"—testimony it says should have caused the judge to dismiss the case for lack of diversity jurisdiction straightaway, without bothering with an evidentiary hearing.

We cannot buy into these arguments. For one thing, a party need not check off *every Bank One* factor to satisfy her burden, and, in any event, Rodríguez checked off more than enough of them—the California bank account, driver's license, job, and personal-property location sync up nicely with key *Bank One* factors.

For another thing, the district judge did not blindly accept Rodríguez's statement that she intended to make California her home. Rather, the judge sifted the testimony and grounded her ruling in facts that *confirmed* Rodríguez's intent claim. And Señor Frog's best-evidence theory changes nothing. With exceptions not relevant here, the best-evidence rule requires a party trying to prove the "content" of a written document to introduce the document itself. Think of a will contest where the will is not in evidence and a witness tries to discuss the document's words from memory—

that is the sort of situation that the rule was designed to address. But that is not our case. Rodríguez never tried to give the exact terms of her California bank account, driver's license, or college transcripts. She simply tried to prove, through her own direct testimony, certain facts that she had direct knowledge of—that she had opened a California bank account, acquired a California license, and taken several California community-college courses pre-complaint. Consequently, this case falls outside the compass of the best-evidence rule.

Last but not least, Rodríguez's trial testimony in no way short-circuited her diverse-citizenship claim. Consider the context. Thrilled beyond words that his daughter had survived the collision, Rodríguez's father hosted a Christmas Day party at his Mayaguez home in 2004—roughly three weeks after Estrada had rear-ended Rodríguez and one year before she filed this action. Rodríguez was deeply depressed, he said, and he thought a small soirée with family and friends might lift her spirits. At trial, Rodríguez's counsel asked her whether any party-goers had come from San Juan (we are not sure why this mattered). "No," she replied, "I *lived in Mayaguez all my life*, so most of my friends are from Mayaguez." Señor Frog makes much of this language, suggesting that it proved her California-domicile claim was a lie—so, the argument goes, the judge should have kicked her case to the curb without further ado. We think not. Again, diversity of citizenship is determined as of the time of suit. And, fairly read, Rodríguez's testimony went to her *pre*-suit living situation, which means that her statement could not and did not sabotage diversity jurisdiction.

... [We] cannot call the judge's diverse-citizenship conclusion clearly wrong ...

COVENTRY SEWAGE ASSOCIATES v. DWORKIN REALTY
71 F.3d 1 (1st Cir. 1995)

STAHL, Circuit Judge.

Appellants, Coventry Sewage Associates ("Coventry") and Woodland Manor Improvement Association ("Woodland") brought a diversity action against appellees, Dworkin Realty Co. ("Dworkin") and The Stop & Shop Supermarket Company ("Stop & Shop"). The United States District Court for the District of Rhode Island found that the amount-in-controversy requirement of 28 U.S.C. § 1332(a) was not met and dismissed the case, pursuant to appellees' motion under Fed.R.Civ.P. 12(b)(1), for lack of subject matter jurisdiction. For the reasons stated below, and because of the unusual facts of this case, we reverse.

I. FACTUAL BACKGROUND AND PRIOR PROCEEDINGS

Coventry and Woodland own and operate a private sewer line and sewage pumping station servicing, among others, a supermarket run by Stop & Shop, located on property owned by Dworkin, a wholly-owned subsidiary of Stop & Shop (hereinafter appellees will be referred to collectively as "Stop & Shop"). In June 1992, Coventry and Woodland (hereinafter, collectively "Coventry") entered into a "Sewer Connection Agreement" with Stop & Shop, whereby Stop & Shop agreed to pay a service fee for sewer-main usage. The service fee was based, in part, upon the number of cubic feet of water consumed on the property. To determine the amount of water consumed, the parties' contract relied on invoices from the Kent County Water Authority ("KCWA"). The KCWA sent these invoices to Stop & Shop, and Stop & Shop in turn forwarded them to Coventry.

Because of a dispute over the reasonableness of an increase in the service fee-an increase Coventry claimed was permitted by the contract-Stop & Shop refused to pay Coventry's bills which accumulated beginning in early 1994. In October 1994, Coventry filed this action seeking recovery of $74,953.00, the amount it claimed to be due based upon water-usage numbers obtained from the KCWA invoices and what Coventry claimed was the correct new service fee rate. Coventry also sought contractual attorneys' fees. It is undisputed that, at the time Coventry commenced the action, it alleged the amount in controversy in the belief that it exceeded the jurisdictional minimum, and not as a ruse to invoke federal jurisdiction.

Shortly after the complaint was filed, but before Stop & Shop filed its answer, Stop & Shop contacted the KCWA about the invoices underlying Coventry's fee calculations. The KCWA then sent an employee to the property who discovered that there had been a misreading of Stop & Shop's water meters, essentially caused by the adding of an extra zero to the number of cubic meters actually consumed. By letter dated November 18, 1994, the KCWA notified Stop & Shop that it was correcting the billing error by changing the amounts of the invoices.

Based upon the KCWA's corrected invoices, Coventry reduced the sum of its bills to Shop & Stop to only $18,667.88, an amount that included the disputed fee increase. Subsequently, Stop & Shop paid the undisputed portion of the fee, $10,182.48, initially withholding the disputed balance of $8,485.40. Stop & Shop ultimately paid this remaining sum as well, reserving the right to recoup the amount should it prevail in its challenge to the reasonableness of the service fee. Stop & Shop, presumably doubting the existence of diversity jurisdiction, asked Coventry to voluntarily dismiss the federal action; Coventry refused, however, apparently because of its intention to pursue in federal court its claim for contractual attorneys' fees.[2]

Stop & Shop moved to dismiss the action under Fed.R.Civ.P. 12(b)(1) for lack of subject matter jurisdiction.[3] The district court granted the motion, finding that, "to a legal certainty," the amount in controversy did not exceed $50,000 as required by 28 U.S.C. § 1332(a). Notwithstanding the small amount actually in controversy, Coventry appeals the dismissal of the action. At oral argument before this court, counsel for Coventry stated that the reason for the insistence upon federal jurisdiction was that the case would get to an earlier trial in federal court (including the appeal proceedings) than if the case were pursued in state court.

II. DISCUSSION

We review de novo the district court's dismissal ...

Coventry argues that at the time it filed the action, it claimed, in good faith, damages in excess of $50,000; thus, the subsequent reduction of the amount in controversy did not divest the district court of jurisdiction. Coventry contends that the KCWA's post-filing discovery of the billing error and changing of the invoice amounts was a "subsequent event" that neither undermined its good faith in filing, nor disturbed the court's jurisdiction once it attached. Shop & Stop argues that the billing error was a mere "subsequent revelation" that proved, to a legal certainty, that the amount in controversy had always been below the jurisdictional minimum and thus the court properly dismissed the case for lack of subject matter jurisdiction.

This case illustrates the competing policies that operate when a court makes an amount-in-controversy determination. On the one hand, a federal court should rigorously enforce the jurisdictional limits that Congress chooses to set in diversity cases. On the other hand, preliminary jurisdictional determinations should neither unduly delay, nor unfairly deprive a party from, determination of the controversy on the merits. As a policy matter, the "which court" determination ought to be made with relative dispatch so that the parties may proceed to resolution of the dispute's merits. For the purpose of establishing diversity jurisdiction, the amount in controversy is determined by looking to the circumstances at the time the complaint is filed. Moreover, it has long been the rule that a court decides the amount in controversy from the face of the complaint, "unless it appears or is in some way shown that the amount stated in the complaint is not claimed 'in good faith.'" *Horton v. Liberty Mutual Ins. Co.* (1961) (quoting *St. Paul Mercury Indem. Co. v. Red Cab Co.* (1938)). When a plaintiff initiates an action in federal court, the plaintiff knows or should know whether the claim surpasses the jurisdictional minimum.

> [The plaintiff's] good faith in choosing the federal forum is open to challenge not only by resort to the face of the complaint, but by the facts disclosed at trial, and if from either source it is clear that his claim never could have amounted to the sum necessary to give jurisdiction, there is no injustice in dismissing the suit.

Id.

Coventry and Stop & Shop both cite passages from the seminal case of *St. Paul* without discussing its facts. We pause to do so here. In *St. Paul*, the plaintiff-employer initiated a state-court action against the defendant-insurer for payment of workers' compensation benefits. The plaintiff alleged an amount of damages sufficient to permit the defendant to remove the case to federal court. Once in federal court, the plaintiff filed two amended complaints. Attached to the second amended complaint, which alleged the same amount of damages as originally claimed, was an exhibit detailing the damages; the exhibit revealed that the total sum of damages was no more than $1,380.89, an amount below the jurisdictional minimum (then $3,000). The court of appeals, sua sponte, took notice of the exhibit and directed a remand of the case, reasoning that the amount in controversy was less than the jurisdictional minimum and that "[t]he court cannot close its eyes to the obvious, nor go ahead with the trial of a cause of which it has no jurisdiction." *St. Paul Mercury Indemnity Co. v. Red Cab Co.* (CA7 1936).

The Supreme Court reversed, noting that there was no evidence that, at the time the action was commenced, the plaintiff could have ascertained the actual sum of the damages, and that the later exhibit setting forth this sum did not undermine plaintiff's initial good faith. Accordingly, the Court reasoned that the case fell comfortably within the rule that "subsequent reduction of the amount claimed cannot oust the district court's jurisdiction."

In a portion of *St. Paul* crucial to the instant case, and from which the parties before us parse their favorite phrases, the Court wrote:

> The intent of Congress drastically to restrict federal jurisdiction in controversies between citizens of different states has always been rigorously enforced by the courts. The rule governing dismissal for want of jurisdiction in cases brought in the federal court is that, unless the law gives a different rule, the sum claimed by the plaintiff controls if the claim is apparently made in good faith. It must appear to a legal certainty that the claim is really for less than the jurisdictional amount to justify dismissal. The inability of plaintiff to recover an amount adequate to give the court jurisdiction does not show his bad faith or oust the jurisdiction. Nor does the fact that the complaint discloses the existence of a valid defense to the claim. But if, from the face of the pleadings, it is apparent, to a legal certainty, that the plaintiff cannot recover the amount claimed or if, from the proofs, the court is satisfied to a like certainty that the plaintiff never was entitled to recover that amount, and that his claim was therefore colorable for the purpose of conferring jurisdiction, the suit will be dismissed. Events occurring subsequent to the institution of suit which reduce the amount recoverable below the statutory limit do not oust jurisdiction.

(footnotes and citations omitted).

The rules gleaned from the foregoing passage may be summarized as follows. First, federal courts must diligently enforce the rules establishing and limiting diversity jurisdiction. Second, unless the law provides otherwise, the plaintiff's damages claim will control the amount in controversy for jurisdictional purposes if it is made "in good faith." If the face of the complaint reveals, to a legal certainty, that the controversy cannot involve the requisite amount, jurisdiction will not attach. Moreover, if later evidence shows, to a legal certainty, that the damages never could have exceeded the jurisdictional minimum such that the claim was essentially feigned (colorable) in order to confer jurisdiction, the action must be dismissed. Finally, if events subsequent to commencement of the action reduce the amount in controversy below the statutory minimum, the federal court is not divested of jurisdiction.

A careful review of *St. Paul* evinces its primary concern for the plaintiff's "good faith" in alleging the amount in controversy. When discerning a plaintiff's good faith, a court may look to whether it "appear[s] to a legal certainty that the claim is really for less than the jurisdictional amount." *St. Paul.*

The parties in the instant case spill much ink over the meaning of "good faith": whether it includes an objective as well as subjective component, and if so, whether "objective" good faith includes "objective facts" as opposed to "actual facts," etc. Stop & Shop argues that the "objective facts" were always the same: that it consumed much less water than originally shown on KCWA's invoices, and that although the claimed amount in controversy was over $50,000 at the time of filing, the "actual" amount in controversy is, indisputably, less than the jurisdictional minimum. Coventry counters that not only did it file with subjective good faith, but, because a wholly independent third party's actions were relied upon (indeed, it was Stop & Shop that forwarded KCWA's invoices to Coventry), there is no reason that Coventry "should have known" about the "actual" amount in controversy and thus, it claimed the damages in "objective" good faith as well.

This court has found that "good faith" in the amount-in-controversy context includes an element of "objective" good faith. ... We find that here, there is no dispute as to good faith, subjective or objective. It is undisputed that Coventry alleged the amount in controversy believing its accuracy at the time. Furthermore, there is no evidence, and Stop & Shop does not argue otherwise, that Coventry had any reason to believe, at the time of filing, that KCWA's invoices, upon which the service fee was calculated, were factually incorrect. We find that, objectively viewed, at the time of its filing, Coventry's claim was worth more than the jurisdictional minimum.

This case fits well within the rule that once jurisdiction attaches, it is not ousted by a subsequent change of events. In *Thesleff v. Harvard Trust Co.* (CA1 1946), we noted that although plaintiff filed remittiturs that reduced the amount in controversy below the jurisdictional minimum, the facts at the time the action was commenced conferred jurisdiction which subsequent events could not divest. ...

In the instant case, Coventry filed the complaint because Stop & Shop refused to pay its bills totalling $74,953.00. The amount in controversy, at the time of filing, exceeded the statutory minimum regardless of the then-unknown "actual facts" of Stop & Shop's water consumption. It was not until Coventry filed the action that Stop & Shop inquired about KCWA's invoices and KCWA subsequently changed them to reflect accurately the amount of water usage. Presumably, had the billing error never been detected, the action would have proceeded on Coventry's damages claim of $74,953.00. The fact that an independent third party's error initially inflated the amount in controversy above the jurisdictional minimum does not lead to the inevitable result that the third party's correction, subsequent to the filing of the complaint, affects the propriety of the jurisdiction once it attached.

Stop & Shop insists that, in this case, we should draw a distinction between "subsequent events" and "subsequent revelations." Stop & Shop argues that the subsequent revelation that the actual amount of damages never met the jurisdictional minimum—as opposed to a subsequent event that reduces that amount—divests the court of jurisdiction, regardless of what the parties knew or should have known at the time of filing. ...

To support this argument, Stop & Shop cites three cases that are factually distinguishable from the instant one, and that, in any event, are not controlling upon this court. First, in *American Mutual Liab. Ins. Co. v. Campbell Lumber Mfg. Corp.* (N.D.Ga. 1971), the plaintiff filed an action for amounts due on insurance contracts. The plaintiff was forced to estimate its damages claim because certain of defendant's records were not available to it. During post-filing discovery, the plaintiff learned that the actual amount in controversy was below the statutory minimum. The court found that the maximum amount recoverable on the plaintiff's theory never varied, and noted that the correct amount in controversy was ascertainable at the time the action was filed. Thus, in dismissing the action, the court reasoned that the plaintiff's realization that its earlier estimation of damages was erroneous was not an "event," under *St. Paul*, that reduced the amount recoverable.

Second, in *Jones v. Knox Exploration Corp.* (CA6 1993), the plaintiffs revealed in their appellate brief that "it was not discovered until this appeal that the amount in controversy is actually less than $50,000." The court acknowledged that subsequent events that reduce the amount in controversy, such as an amendment to the complaint or an application of a post-discovery legal defense, would not oust federal jurisdiction. The court reasoned that "[a] distinction must be made, however, between subsequent events that change the amount in controversy and subsequent revelations that, in fact, the required amount was or was not in controversy at the commencement of the action." The court found that there was no subsequent event that occurred to reduce the amount; instead, there was only a subsequent revelation that, in fact, the required amount was not in controversy at the time the action was filed. Thus, the court ordered dismissal based on lack of subject matter jurisdiction.

Third, in *Tongkook America, Inc. v. Shipton Sportswear Co.* (CA2 1994), the parties realized during pre-trial discovery that, one year prior to filing suit, the plaintiff had drawn a certain amount upon a letter of credit that was erroneously added to the damages claim. The court rejected plaintiff's argument that the discovery of the failure to credit the amount withdrawn was an "event subsequent to the institution of the suit." The court deemed the plaintiff's previous withdrawal upon the letter of credit an "event which preceded the commencement of the suit [that] objectively altered the amount of [plaintiff's] claim." Thus, the sum certain in controversy was lower than the jurisdictional minimum and the court ordered the case dismissed for lack of subject matter jurisdiction.

In the instant case, Coventry did not base its damages claim on a faulty estimation that required recalculation during discovery, as in American Mutual; rather, it alleged the amount in controversy based upon a third-party's information that neither party had any reason to know was erroneous. Unlike the "mere revelation" in Jones that there was never the requisite amount in controversy, the reduction in the amount in controversy here occurred only after KCWA's affirmative acts of checking the water meters and changing the invoice amounts. Finally, although portions of the Tongkook court's reasoning are not entirely consistent with our decision here, we distinguish that case narrowly on the facts; in Tongkook, the parties themselves made the error affecting the amount in controversy approximately one year prior to commencement of the suit. Thus, it appears that the plaintiff in that case should have known that its claim did not exceed the jurisdictional minimum. In the instant case, an independent third party with otherwise no connection to the case made an apparently non-obvious error so that the amount-in-controversy at the time of filing, in fact, exceeded the jurisdictional minimum. Coventry had no reason to know that its claimed amount of damages was in error. Moreover, the reduction of the amount in controversy resulted from acts occurring wholly after the action commenced. We hold that, under these extraordinary circumstances, the district court's jurisdiction was not disturbed by the subsequent reduction of the amount in controversy.

III. CONCLUSION

For the foregoing reasons, we vacate the judgment of the district court, and remand for further proceedings consistent with this opinion. Each party shall bear its own costs.

[2] We note that although attorneys' fees usually will not constitute a portion of the amount in controversy, there is an exception where, as here, the fees are contractual. In this case, Coventry cannot avail itself of this exception as a basis

for federal jurisdiction because, not only are there no specifics in the record as to the amount of such fees, Coventry informed this court at oral argument that its estimation of attorneys' fees was only $10,000.

3 Although the KCWA notified Stop & Shop of the error in November 1994, Stop & Shop raised only a general, boilerplate amount-in-controversy defense in its December 1994 answer, and did not formally move to dismiss on the jurisdictional basis until February 1995.

B. Federal Question

GUNN v. MINTON
568 U.S. ____ (2013)

Chief Justice ROBERTS delivered the opinion of the Court.

Federal courts have exclusive jurisdiction over cases "arising under any Act of Congress relating to patents." 28 U.S.C. § 1338(a). The question presented is whether a state law claim alleging legal malpractice in the handling of a patent case must be brought in federal court.

I

In the early 1990s, respondent Vernon Minton developed a computer program and telecommunications network designed to facilitate securities trading. In March 1995, he leased the system—known as the Texas Computer Exchange Network, or TEXCEN—to R.M. Stark & Co., a securities brokerage. A little over a year later, he applied for a patent for an interactive securities trading system that was based substantially on TEXCEN. The U.S. Patent and Trademark Office issued the patent in January 2000.

Patent in hand, Minton filed a patent infringement suit in Federal District Court against the National Association of Securities Dealers, Inc. (NASD) and the NASDAQ Stock Market, Inc. He was represented by Jerry Gunn and the other petitioners. NASD and NASDAQ moved for summary judgment on the ground that Minton's patent was invalid under the "on sale" bar, 35 U.S.C. § 102(b). That provision specifies that an inventor is not entitled to a patent if "the invention was ... on sale in [the United States], more than one year prior to the date of the application," and Minton had leased TEXCEN to Stark more than one year prior to filing his patent application. Rejecting Minton's argument that there were differences between TEXCEN and the patented system that precluded application of the on-sale bar, the District Court granted the summary judgment motion and declared Minton's patent invalid.

Minton then filed a motion for reconsideration in the District Court, arguing for the first time that the lease agreement with Stark was part of ongoing testing of TEXCEN and therefore fell within the "experimental use" exception to the on-sale bar. The District Court denied the motion.

Minton appealed to the U.S. Court of Appeals for the Federal Circuit. That court affirmed, concluding that the District Court had appropriately held Minton's experimental-use argument waived.

Minton, convinced that his attorneys' failure to raise the experimental-use argument earlier had cost him the lawsuit and led to invalidation of his patent, brought this malpractice action in Texas state court. His former lawyers defended on the ground that the lease to Stark was not, in fact, for an experimental use, and that therefore Minton's patent infringement claims would have failed even if the experimental-use argument had been timely raised. The trial court agreed, holding that Minton had put forward "less than a scintilla of proof" that the lease had been for an experimental purpose. It accordingly granted summary judgment to Gunn and the other lawyer defendants.

On appeal, Minton raised a new argument: Because his legal malpractice claim was based on an alleged error in a patent case, it "aris[es] under" federal patent law for purposes of 28 U.S.C. § 1338(a). And because, under § 1338(a), "[n]o State court shall have jurisdiction over any claim for relief arising under any Act of Congress relating to patents," the Texas court—where Minton had originally brought his malpractice claim—lacked subject matter jurisdiction to decide the case. Accordingly, Minton argued, the trial court's order should be vacated and the case dismissed, leaving Minton free to start over in the Federal District Court.

A divided panel of the Court of Appeals of Texas rejected Minton's argument. Applying the test we articulated in *Grable & Sons Metal Products, Inc. v. Darue Engineering & Mfg.* (2005), it held that the federal interests implicated by Minton's state law claim were not sufficiently substantial to trigger § 1338 "arising under" jurisdiction. It also held that finding exclusive federal jurisdiction over state legal malpractice actions would, contrary to *Grable*'s commands, disturb the balance of federal and state judicial responsibilities. Proceeding to the merits of Minton's malpractice claim, the Court of Appeals affirmed the trial court's determination that Minton had failed to establish experimental use and that arguments on that ground therefore would not have saved his infringement suit.

The Supreme Court of Texas reversed, relying heavily on a pair of cases from the U.S. Court of Appeals for the Federal Circuit. The Court concluded that Minton's claim involved "a substantial federal issue" within the meaning of *Grable* "because the success of Minton's malpractice claim is reliant upon the viability of the experimental use exception as a defense to the on-sale bar." Adjudication of Minton's claim in federal court was consistent with the appropriate balance between federal and state judicial responsibilities, it held, because "the federal government and patent litigants have an interest in the uniform application of patent law by courts well-versed in that subject matter."

... We granted certiorari.

II

"Federal courts are courts of limited jurisdiction," possessing "only that power authorized by Constitution and statute." *Kokkomen v. Guardian Life Ins. Co. of America* (1994). There is no dispute that the Constitution permits Congress to extend federal court jurisdiction to a case such as this one; the question is whether Congress has done so.

As relevant here, Congress has authorized the federal district courts to exercise original jurisdiction in "all civil actions arising under the Constitution, laws, or treaties of the United States," 28 U.S.C. § 1331, and, more particularly, over "any civil action arising under any Act of Congress relating to patents," § 1338(a). Adhering to the demands of "[l]inguistic consistency," we have interpreted the phrase "arising under" in both sections identically, applying our § 1331 and § 1338(a) precedents interchangeably. For cases falling within the patent-specific arising under jurisdiction of § 1338(a), however, Congress has not only provided for federal jurisdiction but also eliminated state jurisdiction, decreeing that "[n]o State court shall have jurisdiction over any claim for relief arising under any Act of Congress relating to patents." § 1338(a) (2006 ed., Supp. V). To determine whether jurisdiction was proper in the Texas courts, therefore, we must determine whether it would have been proper in a federal district court—whether, that is, the case "aris[es] under any Act of Congress relating to patents."

For statutory purposes, a case can "aris[e] under" federal law in two ways. Most directly, a case arises under federal law when federal law creates the cause of action asserted. As a rule of inclusion, this "creation" test admits of only extremely rare exceptions, and accounts for the vast bulk of suits that arise under federal law. Minton's original patent infringement suit against NASD and NASDAQ, for example, arose under federal law in this manner because it was authorized by 35 U.S.C. §§ 271, 281.

But even where a claim finds its origins in state rather than federal law—as Minton's legal malpractice claim indisputably does—we have identified a "special and small category" of cases in which arising under jurisdiction still lies. In outlining the contours of this slim category, we do not paint on a blank canvas. Unfortunately, the canvas looks like one that Jackson Pollock got to first.

In an effort to bring some order to this unruly doctrine several Terms ago, we condensed our prior cases into the following inquiry: Does the "state-law claim necessarily raise a stated federal issue, actually disputed and substantial, which a federal forum may entertain without disturbing any congressionally approved balance of federal and state judicial responsibilities"? *Grable.* That is, federal jurisdiction over a state law claim will lie if a federal issue is: (1) necessarily raised, (2) actually disputed, (3) substantial, and (4) capable of resolution in federal court without disrupting the federal-state balance approved by Congress. Where all four of these requirements are met, we held, jurisdiction is proper because there is a "serious federal interest in claiming the advantages thought to be inherent in a federal forum," which can be vindicated without disrupting Congress's intended division of labor between state and federal courts.

III

Applying *Grable*'s inquiry here, it is clear that Minton's legal malpractice claim does not arise under federal patent law. Indeed, for the reasons we discuss, we are comfortable concluding that state legal malpractice claims based on underlying patent matters will rarely, if ever, arise under federal patent law for purposes of § 1338(a). Although such cases may necessarily raise disputed questions of patent law, those cases are by their nature unlikely to have the sort of significance for the federal system necessary to establish jurisdiction.

A

To begin, we acknowledge that resolution of a federal patent question is "necessary" to Minton's case. Under Texas law, a plaintiff alleging legal malpractice must establish four elements: (1) that the defendant attorney owed the plaintiff a duty; (2) that the attorney breached that duty; (3) that the breach was the proximate cause of the plaintiff's injury; and (4) that damages occurred. In cases like this one, in which the attorney's alleged error came in failing to make a particular argument, the causation element requires a "case within a case" analysis of whether, had the argument been made, the outcome of the earlier litigation would have been different. To prevail on his legal malpractice claim, therefore, Minton must show that he would have prevailed in his federal patent infringement case if only petitioners had timely made an experimental-use argument on his behalf. That will necessarily require application of patent law to the facts of Minton's case.

B

The federal issue is also "actually disputed" here—indeed, on the merits, it is the central point of dispute. Minton argues that the experimental-use exception properly applied to his lease to Stark, saving his patent from the on-sale bar; petitioners argue that it did not. This is just the sort of "dispute ... respecting the ... effect of [federal] law" that *Grable* envisioned.

C

Minton's argument founders on *Grable*'s next requirement, however, for the federal issue in this case is not substantial in the relevant sense. In reaching the opposite conclusion, the Supreme Court of Texas focused on the importance of the issue to the plaintiff's case and to the parties before it. As our past cases show, however, it is not enough that the federal issue be significant to the particular parties in the immediate suit; that will *always* be true when the state claim "necessarily raise[s]" a disputed federal issue, as *Grable* separately requires. The substantiality inquiry under *Grable* looks instead to the importance of the issue to the federal system as a whole.

In *Grable* itself, for example, the Internal Revenue Service had seized property from the plaintiff and sold it to satisfy the plaintiff's federal tax delinquency. Five years later, the plaintiff filed a state law quiet title action against the third party that had purchased the property, alleging that the IRS had failed to comply with certain federally imposed notice requirements, so that the seizure and sale were invalid. In holding that the case arose under federal law, we primarily focused not on the interests of the litigants themselves, but rather on the broader significance of the notice question for the Federal Government. We emphasized the Government's "strong interest" in being able to recover delinquent taxes through seizure and sale of property, which in turn "require[d] clear terms of notice to allow buyers ... to satisfy themselves that the Service has touched the bases necessary for good title." The Government's "direct interest in the availability of a federal forum to vindicate its own administrative action" made the question "an important issue of federal law that sensibly belong[ed] in a federal court."

...

Here, the federal issue carries no such significance. Because of the backward-looking nature of a legal malpractice claim, the question is posed in a merely hypothetical sense: *If* Minton's lawyers had raised a timely experimental-use argument, would the result in the patent infringement proceeding have been different? No matter how the state courts resolve that hypothetical "case within a case," it will not change the real-world result of the prior federal patent litigation. Minton's patent will remain invalid.

Nor will allowing state courts to resolve these cases undermine "the development of a uniform body of [patent] law." *Bonito Boats, Inc. v. Thunder Craft Boats, Inc.* (1989). Congress ensured such uniformity by vesting exclusive jurisdiction over actual patent cases in the federal district courts and exclusive appellate jurisdiction in the Federal Circuit. In resolving the non-hypothetical patent questions those cases present, the federal courts are of course not bound by state court case-within-a-case patent rulings. In any event, the state court case-within-a-case inquiry asks what would have happened in the prior federal proceeding if a particular argument had been made. In answering that question, state courts can be expected to hew closely to the pertinent federal precedents. It is those precedents, after all, that would have applied had the argument been made.

As for more novel questions of patent law that may arise for the first time in a state court "case within a case," they will at some point be decided by a federal court in the context of an actual patent case, with review in the Federal Circuit. If the question arises frequently, it will soon be resolved within the federal system, laying to rest any contrary state court precedent; if it does not arise frequently, it is unlikely to implicate substantial federal interests. The present case is "poles apart from *Grable*," in which a state court's resolution of the federal question "would be controlling in numerous other cases." *Empire Healthchoice Assurance v. McVeigh* (2006).

Minton also suggests that state courts' answers to hypothetical patent questions can sometimes have real-world effect on other patents through issue preclusion. Minton, for example, has filed what is known as a "continuation patent" application related to his original patent. He argues that, in evaluating this separate application, the patent examiner could be bound by the Texas trial court's interpretation of the scope of Minton's original patent. It is unclear whether this is true. The Patent and Trademark Office's Manual of Patent Examining Procedure provides that res judicata is a proper ground for rejecting a patent "only when the earlier decision was a decision of the Board of Appeals" or certain federal reviewing courts, giving no indication that state court decisions would have preclusive effect. In fact, Minton has not identified any case finding such preclusive effect based on a state court decision. But even assuming that a state court's case-within-a-case adjudication may be preclusive under some circumstances, the result would be limited to the parties and patents that had been before the state court. Such "fact-bound and situation-specific" effects are not sufficient to establish federal arising under jurisdiction. *Empire Healthchoice.*

Nor can we accept the suggestion that the federal courts' greater familiarity with patent law means that legal malpractice cases like this one belong in federal court. It is true that a similar interest was among those we considered in *Grable*. But the possibility that a state court will incorrectly resolve a state claim is not, by itself, enough to trigger the federal courts' exclusive patent jurisdiction, even if the potential error finds its root in a misunderstanding of patent law.

There is no doubt that resolution of a patent issue in the context of a state legal malpractice action can be vitally important to the particular parties in that case. But something more, demonstrating that the question is significant to the federal system as a whole, is needed. That is missing here.

D

It follows from the foregoing that *Grable*'s fourth requirement is also not met. That requirement is concerned with the appropriate "balance of federal and state judicial responsibilities." We have already explained the absence of a substantial federal issue within the meaning of *Grable*. The States, on the other hand, have "a special responsibility for maintaining standards among members of the licensed professions." *Ohralik v. Ohio State Bar Assn.* (1978). Their "interest ... in regulating lawyers is especially great since lawyers are essential to the primary governmental function of administering justice, and have historically been officers of the courts." *Goldfarb v. Virginia State Bar* (1975) (internal quotation marks omitted). We have no reason to suppose that

Congress—in establishing exclusive federal jurisdiction over patent cases—meant to bar from state courts state legal malpractice claims simply because they require resolution of a hypothetical patent issue.

* * *

As we recognized a century ago, "[t]he Federal courts have exclusive jurisdiction of all cases arising under the patent laws, but not of all questions in which a patent may be the subject-matter of the controversy." *New Marshall Engine Co. v. Marshall Engine Co.* (1912). In this case, although the state courts must answer a question of patent law to resolve Minton's legal malpractice claim, their answer will have no broader effects. It will not stand as binding precedent for any future patent claim; it will not even affect the validity of Minton's patent. Accordingly, there is no "serious federal interest in claiming the advantages thought to be inherent in a federal forum," *Grable.* Section 1338(a) does not deprive the state courts of subject matter jurisdiction.

The judgment of the Supreme Court of Texas is reversed, and the case is remanded for further proceedings not inconsistent with this opinion.

It is so ordered.

C. Supplemental Jurisdiction
ARTIS v. DISTRICT OF COLUMBIA
__ U.S. __ (2018)

Justice GINSBURG delivered the opinion of the Court.

The Supplemental Jurisdiction statute, 28 U.S.C. § 1367, enables federal district courts to entertain claims not otherwise within their adjudicatory authority when those claims "are so related to claims ... within [federal-court competence] that they form part of the same case or controversy." § 1367(a). Included within this supplemental jurisdiction are state claims brought along with federal claims arising from the same episode. When district courts dismiss all claims independently qualifying for the exercise of federal jurisdiction, they ordinarily dismiss as well all related state claims. A district court may also dismiss the related state claims if there is a good reason to decline jurisdiction. See § 1367(c)(1), (2), and (4). This case concerns the time within which state claims so dismissed may be refiled in state court.

Section 1367(d), addressing that issue, provides:

The period of limitations for any [state] claim [joined with a claim within federal-court competence] shall be tolled while the claim is pending [in federal court] and for a period of 30 days after it is dismissed unless State law provides for a longer tolling period.

The question presented: Does the word "tolled," as used in § 1367(d), mean the state limitations period is suspended during the pendency of the federal suit; or does "tolled" mean that, although the state limitations period continues to run, a plaintiff is accorded a grace period of 30 days to refile in state court post dismissal of the federal case? Petitioner urges the first, or stop-the-clock, reading. Respondent urges, and the District of Columbia Court of Appeals adopted, the second, or grace-period, reading.

In the case before us, plaintiff-petitioner Stephanie C. Artis refiled her state-law claims in state court 59 days after dismissal of her federal suit. Reading § 1367(d) as a grace-period prescription, her complaint would be time barred. Reading § 1367(d) as stopping the limitations clock during the pendency of the federal-court suit, her complaint would be timely. We hold that § 1367(d)'s instruction to "toll" a state limitations period means to hold it in abeyance, i.e., to stop the clock. Because the D.C. Court of Appeals held that § 1367(d) did not stop the D.C. Code's limitations clock, but merely provided a 30-day grace period for refiling in D.C. Superior Court, we reverse the D.C. Court of Appeals' judgment.

I

Section 1367, which Congress added to Title 28 as part of the Judicial Improvements Act of 1990, 104 Stat. 5089, codifies the court-developed pendent and ancillary jurisdiction doctrines under the label "supplemental jurisdiction." The House Report accompanying the Act explains that Congress sought to clarify the scope of federal courts' authority to hear claims within their supplemental jurisdiction, appreciating that "[s]upplemental jurisdiction has enabled federal courts and litigants to ... deal economically — in single rather than multiple litigation — with related matters." H.R. Rep. No. 101-734, p. 28 (1990) (H.R. Rep.). Section 1367(a) provides, in relevant part, that a district court with original jurisdiction over a claim "shall have supplemental jurisdiction over all other claims ... form[ing] part of the same case or controversy."

"[N]ot every claim within the same 'case or controversy' as the claim within the federal courts' original jurisdiction will be decided by the federal court." *Jinks v. Richland County* (2003). Section 1367(c) states:

The district courts may decline to exercise supplemental jurisdiction over a claim under subsection (a) if —

(1) the claim raises a novel or complex issue of State law,

(2) the claim substantially predominates over the claim or claims over which the district court has original jurisdiction,

(3) the district court has dismissed all claims over which it has original jurisdiction, or

(4) in exceptional circumstances, there are other compelling reasons for declining jurisdiction.

If a district court declines to exercise jurisdiction over a claim asserted under § 1367(a) and the plaintiff wishes to continue pursuing it, she must refile the claim in state court. If the state court would hold the claim time barred, however, then, absent a curative provision, the district court's dismissal of the state-law claim without prejudice would be tantamount to a dismissal with prejudice. To prevent that result, § 1367(d) supplies "a tolling rule that must be applied by state courts." *Jinks*. ... This case requires us to determine how § 1367(d)'s tolling rule operates.

Petitioner Artis worked as a health inspector for respondent, the District of Columbia (the "District"). In November 2010, Artis was told she would lose her job. Thirteen months later, Artis sued the District in the United States District Court for the District of Columbia, alleging that she had suffered employment discrimination in violation of Title VII of the Civil Rights Act of 1964. She also asserted three allied claims under D.C. law: retaliation in violation of the District of Columbia Whistleblower Act; termination in violation of the District of Columbia False Claims Ac; and wrongful termination against public policy, a common-law claim. Artis alleged that she had been subjected to gender discrimination by her supervisor, and thereafter encountered retaliation for reporting the supervisor's unlawful activities.

On June 27, 2014, the District Court granted the District's motion for summary judgment on the Title VII claim. Having dismissed Artis' sole federal claim, the District Court, pursuant to § 1367(c)(3), declined to exercise supplemental jurisdiction over her remaining state-law claims. "Artis will not be prejudiced," the court noted, "because 28 U.S.C. § 1367(d) provides for a tolling of the statute of limitations during the period the case was here and for at least 30 days thereafter."

Fifty-nine days after the dismissal of her federal action, Artis refiled her state-law claims in the D.C. Superior Court, the appropriate local court. The Superior Court granted the District's motion to dismiss, holding that Artis' claims were time barred, because they were filed 29 days too late. When Artis first asserted her state-law claims in the District Court, nearly two years remained on the applicable three-year statute of limitations. But two and a half years passed before the federal court relinquished jurisdiction. Unless § 1367(d) paused the limitations clock during that time, Artis would have had only 30 days to refile. The Superior Court rejected Artis' stop-the-clock reading of § 1367(d), reasoning that Artis could have protected her state-law claims by "pursuing [them] in a state court while the federal court proceeding [was] pending." ...

The D.C. Court of Appeals affirmed. That court began by observing that two "competing approaches [to § 1367(d)] have evolved nationally": the stop-the-clock reading and the grace-period reading. ... Following the lead of the

California Supreme Court, the D.C. Court of Appeals determined that Congress had intended to implement a 1969 recommendation by the American Law Institute (ALI) to allow refiling in state court "within 30 days after dismissal."

The D.C. Court of Appeals also concluded that the grace-period approach "better accommodates federalism concerns," by trenching significantly less on state statutes of limitations than the stop-the-clock approach. Construing § 1367(d) as affording only a 30-day grace period, the court commented, was "consistent with [its] presumption favoring narrow interpretations of federal preemption of state law."

To resolve the division of opinion among State Supreme Courts on the proper construction of § 1367(d), we granted certiorari.

II

A

As just indicated, statutes that shelter from time bars claims earlier commenced in another forum generally employ one of two means.

First, the period (or statute) of limitations may be "tolled" while the claim is pending elsewhere. Ordinarily, "tolled," in the context of a time prescription like § 1367(d), means that the limitations period is suspended (stops running) while the claim is *sub judice* elsewhere, then starts running again when the tolling period ends, picking up where it left off. See Black's Law Dictionary 1488 (6th ed. 1990) ("toll," when paired with the grammatical object "statute of limitations," means "to suspend or stop temporarily"). This dictionary definition captures the rule generally applied in federal courts. Our decisions employ the terms "toll" and "suspend" interchangeably. For example, in *American Pipe and Constr. Co. v. Utah* (1974), we characterized as a "tolling" prescription a rule "suspend[ing] the applicable statute of limitations"; accordingly, we applied the rule to stop the limitations clock. We have similarly comprehended what tolling means in decisions on equitable tolling.

In lieu of "tolling" or "suspending" a limitations period by pausing its progression, a legislature might elect simply to provide a grace period. When that mode is adopted, the statute of limitations continues to run while the claim is pending in another forum. But the risk of a time bar is averted by according the plaintiff a fixed period in which to refile. A federal statute of that genre is 28 U.S.C. § 2415. That provision prescribes a six-year limitations period for suits seeking money damages from the United States for breach of contract. § 2415(a). The statute further provides: "In the event that any action ... is timely brought and is thereafter dismissed without prejudice, the action may be recommenced within one year after such dismissal, regardless of whether the action would otherwise then be barred by this section." § 2415(e). Many States have enacted similar grace-period provisions. ...

Tellingly, the District has not identified any federal statute in which a grace-period meaning has been ascribed to the word "tolled" or any word similarly rooted. ...

Turning from statutory texts to judicial decisions, only once did an opinion of this Court employ tolling language to describe a grace period: *Hardin v. Straub* (1989). In *Hardin,* we held that, in 42 U.S.C. § 1983 suits, federal courts should give effect to state statutes sheltering claims from time bars during periods of a plaintiff's legal disability. We there characterized a state statute providing a one-year grace period as "tolling" or "suspend[ing]" the limitations period "until one year after the disability has been removed." This atypical use of "tolling" or "suspending" to mean something other than stopping the clock on a limitations period is a feather on the scale against the weight of decisions in which "tolling" a statute of limitations signals stopping the clock.

B

In determining the meaning of a statutory provision, "we look first to its language, giving the words used their ordinary meaning." *Moskal v. United States* (1990) (citation and internal quotation marks omitted). Section 1367(d) is phrased as a tolling provision. It suspends the statute of limitations for two adjacent time periods: while the claim is pending in federal court and for 30 days postdismissal. Artis urges that the phrase "shall be tolled" in § 1367(d) has the same meaning it does in the statutes cited *supra.* That is, the limitations clock stops the day the claim is filed in federal court and, 30 days postdismissal, restarts from the point at which it had stopped.

The District reads "tolled" for § 1367(d)'s purposes differently. To "toll," the District urges, means to "remove or take away an effect." To "toll" a limitations period, then, would mean to "remov[e] the bar that ordinarily would accompany its expiration." "[T]here is nothing special," the District maintains, "about tolling limitations periods versus tolling any other fact, right, or consequence." But the District offers no reason why, in interpreting "tolled" as used in § 1367(d), we should home in only on the word itself, ignoring the information about the verb's ordinary meaning gained from its grammatical object. Just as when the object of "tolled" is "bell" or "highway traveler," the object "period of limitations" sheds light on what it means to "be tolled."

The District's reading ... is problematic for other reasons as well. First, it tenders a strained interpretation of the phrase "period of limitations." In the District's view, "period of limitations" means "the effect of the period of limitations as a time bar." Second, the first portion of the tolling period, the duration of the claim's pendency in federal court, becomes superfluous under the District's construction. The "effect" of the limitations period as a time bar, on the District's reading, becomes operative only after the case has been dismissed. That being so, what need would there be to remove anything while the claim is pending in federal court?

Furthermore, the District's reading could yield an absurdity: It could permit a plaintiff to refile in state court even if the limitations period on her claim had expired before she filed in federal court. To avoid that result, the District's proposed construction of "tolled" as "removed" could not mean simply "removed." Instead, "removed" would require qualification to express "removed, unless the period of limitations expired before the claim was filed in federal court." In sum, the District's interpretation maps poorly onto the language of § 1367(d), while Artis' interpretation is a natural fit.

D

The District asks us to zero in on § 1367(d)'s "express inclusion" of the "period of 30 days after the claim is dismissed" within the tolling period. Under Artis' stop-the-clock interpretation, the District contends, "the inclusion of 30 days within the tolling period would be relegated to insignificance in the mine-run of cases." (citation and internal quotation marks omitted). In § 1367(d), Congress did provide for tolling not only while the claim is pending in federal court, but also for 30 days thereafter. Including the 30 days within § 1367(d)'s tolling period accounts for cases in which a federal action is commenced close to the expiration date of the relevant state statute of limitations. In such a case, the added days give the plaintiff breathing space to refile in state court.

Adding a brief span of days to the tolling period is not unusual in stop-the-clock statutes. In this respect, § 1367(d) closely resembles 46 U.S.C. § 53911, which provides, in a subsection titled "Tolling of limitations period," that if a plaintiff submits a claim for war-related vessel damage to the Secretary of Transportation, "the running of the limitations period for bringing a civil action is suspended until the Secretary denies the claim, and for 60 days thereafter." § 53911(d). Numerous other statutes similarly append a fixed number of days to an initial tolling period. Thus, the "30 days" provision casts no large shadow on Artis' interpretation.

Section 1367(d)'s proviso, "unless State law provides for a longer tolling period," could similarly aid a plaintiff who filed in federal court just short of the expiration of the state limitations period. She would have the benefit of § 1367(d)'s 30-days-to-refile prescription, or such longer time as state law prescribes. It may be that, in most cases, the state-law tolling period will not be longer than § 1367(d)'s. But in some cases it undoubtedly will. For example, Indiana permits a plaintiff to refile within three years of dismissal. And Louisiana provides that after dismissal the limitations period "runs anew."

* * *

For the reasons stated, we resist unsettling the usual understanding of the word "tolled" as it appears in legislative time prescriptions and court decisions thereon. The judgment of the D.C. Court of Appeals is therefore reversed, and the case is remanded for further proceedings not inconsistent with this opinion.

It is so ordered.

Justice GORSUCH, with whom Justice KENNEDY, Justice THOMAS, and Justice ALITO join, dissenting.

Chesterton reminds us not to clear away a fence just because we cannot see its point. Even if a fence doesn't seem to have a reason, sometimes all that means is we need to look more carefully for the reason it was built in the first place.

The same might be said about the law before us. Section 1367(d) provides that "[t]he period of limitations ... shall be tolled while the claim is pending and for a period of 30 days after it is dismissed unless State law provides for a longer tolling period." 28 U.S.C. § 1367(d). Grown from a rich common law and state statutory tradition, this provision serves a modest role. If a federal court dismisses a party's state law claim without ruling on its merits, the law ensures the party will enjoy whatever time state law allows, or at least 30 days, to refile the claim in state court.

Today the Court clears away this traditional rule because it overlooks the original reasons for it. For the first time in the statute's history the Court now reads the law to guarantee parties not 30 days or whatever state law permits but months or years more to refile their dismissed state law claims in state court. Rather than reading the statute as generally deferring to state law judgments about the appropriate lifespan of state law claims brought in state courts, the Court now reads the statute as generally displacing them in favor of a new federal rule. Indeed, the Court today tells state courts that they must routinely disregard clearly expressed state law defining the appropriate length of time parties should have to sue on state law claims in state tribunals. Under the Court's rule, too, the disregard of state limitations law promises to be not only routine but substantial. The Court's approach will require state courts to entertain state law claims that state law deems untimely not only by weeks or months but by many years, as 24 States, the National Conference of State Legislatures, and the Council of State Governments warn us. And the Court demands all this without offering any rational account why it is necessary or proper to the exercise of one of the federal government's limited and enumerated powers. It may only be a small statute we are interpreting, but the result the Court reaches today represents no small intrusion on traditional state functions and no small departure from our foundational principles of federalism. ...

The Court today clears away a fence that once marked a basic boundary between federal and state power. Maybe it wasn't the most vital fence and maybe we've just simply forgotten why this particular fence was built in the first place. But maybe, too, we've forgotten because we've wandered so far from the idea of a federal government of limited and enumerated powers that we've begun to lose sight of what it looked like in the first place. If the federal government can now, without any rational reason, force States to allow state law causes of action in state courts even though the state law limitations period expired many years ago, what exactly can't it do to override the application of state law to state claims in state court? What boundaries remain then?

I respectfully dissent.

SMITH v. COLONIAL PENN INSURANCE COMPANY
943 F. Supp. 782 (S.D. Tex. 1996)
ORDER DENYING MOTION TO TRANSFER

KENT, District Judge.

This is a breach of contract case based on an insurance contract entered into by Plaintiff and Defendant. Now before the Court is Defendant's October 11, 1996 Motion to Transfer Venue from the Galveston Division to the Houston Division of the United States District Court for the Southern District of Texas pursuant to 28 U.S.C. § 1404(a). For the reasons set forth below, the Motion is DENIED.

Section 1404(a) provides: "For the convenience of parties and witnesses, in the interest of justice, a district court may transfer any civil action to any other district or division where it might have been brought." 28 U.S.C. § 1404(a). The defendant bears the burden of demonstrating to the District Court that it should, in its sound discretion, decide to transfer the action. The Court weighs the following factors to decide whether a transfer is warranted: the availability and convenience of witnesses and parties, the location of counsel, the location of books and records, the cost of obtaining attendance of witnesses and other trial expenses, the place of the alleged wrong, the possibility of delay and prejudice if transfer is granted, and the plaintiff's choice of forum, which is generally entitled to great deference.

Defendant's request for a transfer of venue is centered around the fact that Galveston does not have a commercial airport into which Defendant's employees and corporate representatives may fly and out of which they may be expediently whisked to the federal courthouse in Galveston. Rather, Defendant contends that it will be faced with the huge "inconvenience" of flying into Houston and driving less than forty miles to the Galveston courthouse, an act that will "encumber" it with "unnecessary driving time and expenses." The Court certainly does not wish to encumber any litigant with such an onerous burden. The Court, being somewhat familiar with the Northeast, notes that perceptions about travel are different in that part of the country than they are in Texas. A litigant in that part of the country could cross several states in a few hours and might be shocked at having to travel fifty miles to try a case, but in this vast state of Texas, such a travel distance would not be viewed with any surprise or consternation.[1] Defendant should be assured that it is not embarking on a three-week-long trip via covered wagons when it travels to Galveston. Rather, Defendant will be pleased to discover that the highway is paved and lighted all the way to Galveston, and thanks to the efforts of this Court's predecessor, Judge Roy Bean, the trip should be free of rustlers, hooligans, or vicious varmints of unsavory kind. Moreover, the speed limit was recently increased to seventy miles per hour on most of the road leading to Galveston, so Defendant should be able to hurtle to justice at lightning speed. To assuage Defendant's worries about the inconvenience of the drive, the Court

Court notes that Houston's Hobby Airport is located about equal drivetime from downtown Houston and the Galveston courthouse. Defendant will likely find it an easy, traffic-free ride to Galveston as compared to a congested, construction-riddled drive to downtown Houston. The Court notes that any inconvenience suffered in having to drive to Galveston may likely be offset by the peacefulness of the ride and the scenic beauty of the sunny isle.

The convenience of the witnesses and the parties is generally a primary concern of this Court when considering transfer motions. However, vague statements about the convenience of unknown and unnamed witnesses is insufficient to convince this Court that the convenience of the witnesses and the parties would be best served by transferring venue. In the Court's view, even if all the witnesses, documents, and evidence relevant to this case were located within walking distance of the Houston Division courthouse, the inconvenience caused by retaining the case in this Court would be minimal at best in this age of convenient travel, communication, discovery, and trial testimony preservation. The Galveston Division courthouse is only about fifty miles from the Houston Division courthouse. "[I]t is not as if the key witnesses will be asked to travel to the wilds of Alaska or the furthest reaches on the Continental United States." *Continental Airlines v. American Airlines* (S.D. Tex. 1992).

As to Defendant's argument that Houston might also be a more convenient forum for Plaintiff, the Court notes that Plaintiff picked Galveston as her forum of choice even though she resides in San Antonio. Defendant argues that flight travel is available between Houston and San Antonio but is not available between Galveston and San Antonio, again because of the absence of a commercial airport. Alas, this Court's kingdom for a commercial airport![2] The Court is unpersuaded by this argument because it is not this Court's concern how Plaintiff gets here, whether it be by plane, train, automobile, horseback, foot, or on the back of a huge Texas jackrabbit, as long as Plaintiff is here at the proper date and time. Thus, the Court declines to disturb the forum chosen by the Plaintiff and introduce the likelihood of delay inherent in any transfer simply to avoid the insignificant inconvenience that Defendant may suffer by litigating this matter in Galveston rather than Houston.

For the reasons stated above, Defendant's Motion to Transfer is hereby DENIED. The parties are ORDERED to bear their own taxable costs and expenses incurred herein to date. The parties are also ORDERED to file nothing further on this issue in this Court, including motions to reconsider and the like. Instead, the parties are instructed to seek any further relief to which they feel themselves entitled in the United States Court of Appeals for the Fifth Circuit, as may be appropriate in due course.

IT IS SO ORDERED.

[1] "The sun is 'rize, the sun is set, and we is still in Texas yet!"

[2] Defendant will again be pleased to know that regular limousine service is available from Hobby Airport, even to the steps of this humble courthouse, which has got lights, indoor plummin,' 'lectric doors, and all sorts of new stuff, almost like them big courthouses back East.

SKYHAWKE TECHNOLOGIES, LLC v. DECA INTERNATIONAL CORP.

2011 WL 1806511 (D.Miss. 2011)

ORDER DENYING MOTION TO TRANSFER VENUE

MICHAEL T. PARKER, United States Magistrate Judge.

This matter is before the court on the [20] Motion to Change Venue filed by Defendant DECA International Corporation (DECA). Having duly considered the motion [20], the applicable legal standards, and the other submissions by the parties, the court finds that the motion should be DENIED.

Factual Background

Plaintiff Skyhawke Technologies, LLC (Skyhawke) accuses DECA of infringing on two patents of which Skyhawke is the assignee—Patent No. 6,456,938 (hereinafter the "938 patent"), entitled "Personal DGPS Golf Course Cartographer, Navigator and Internet Web Site with Map Exchange and Tutor", and Patent No. 7,118,498 (hereinafter the "498 patent"), entitled "Personal Golfing Assistant and Method and System for Graphically Displaying Golf Related information and for Collection, Processing and Distribution of Golf Related Data." Skyhawke is a limited liability company with its principal place of business in Ridgeland, Mississippi. DECA is a California corporation with its principal place of business in La Palma, California. DECA is a wholly-owned subsidiary of DECA System Inc., a Korean corporation.

Skyhawke alleges that DECA has made, caused to be made, imported, caused to be imported, used, offered to sell, sold, and caused to be sold products (i.e., the Golfbuddy World Platinum product) in Mississippi, which has infringed, induced infringement, and/or contributed to infringement on the 938 patent and the 498 patent.

In the instant motion [20], DECA asks the court to transfer this case from the Southern District of Mississippi (hereinafter "Southern District") to the Central District of California (hereinafter "Central District").

Transfer of Venue Standard

For the convenience of parties and witnesses and in the interest of justice, a district court may transfer any civil action to any other district or division where it might have been brought. 28 U.S .C.A. § 1404(a). "[T]he plaintiff's choice of forum is clearly a factor to be considered but in and of itself it is neither conclusive nor determinative." *In re Horseshoe Entm't* (CA5 2003).

> [W]hen the transferee venue is not clearly more convenient than the venue chosen by the plaintiff, the plaintiff's choice should be respected. When the movant demonstrates that the transferee venue is clearly more convenient, however, it has shown good cause and the district court should therefore grant the transfer.

In re Volkswagen of Am., Inc. (CA5 2008)(*"Volkswagen II"*). A decision to transfer venue under Section 1404 is committed to the sound discretion of the transferring judge.

The threshold issue is whether the claim could have been filed in the judicial district to which the movant is seeking to transfer the case. *In re Volkswagen AG* (CA5 2004) (*"Volkswagen I"*). Venue is proper in any district in which any defendant resides. 28 U.S.C.A. § 1391(b)(1). A defendant corporation is deemed to reside in any district in which it is subject to personal jurisdiction at the time the action is commenced.

In order to determine the convenience to the parties and witnesses the court applies private and public interest factors. The private interest factors include:

> (1) the relative ease of access to sources of proof; (2) the availability of compulsory process to secure the attendance of witnesses; (3) the cost of attendance for willing witnesses; and (4) all other practical problems that make trial of a case easy, expeditious and inexpensive.

The public interest factors are as follows:

> (1) the administrative difficulties flowing from court congestion; (2) the local interest in having localized interests decided at home; (3) the familiarity of the forum with the law that will govern the case;

and (4) the avoidance of unnecessary problems of conflict of laws of the application of foreign law.

Analysis

The court answers the threshold question of whether suit may have been brought against DECA in the Central District in the affirmative, given that DECA is headquartered in the Central District; thus, transfer of venue to the Central District is permissible under 28 U.S.C. § 1404(a). Accordingly, the court finds it necessary to weigh the applicable private interest and public interest factors to determine whether the Central District is the clearly more convenient venue versus the plaintiff's chosen venue, the Southern District.

Private Interest Factors

(1) *Access to sources of proof*

DECA avers that this factor weighs in its favor because the documents relating to design, development, testing, and marketing of the product at issue, as well as product models and prototypes, are located in its California headquarters. *In re Genentech, Inc* (Fed.Cir. 2009), states: "In patent infringement cases, the bulk of the relevant evidence usually comes from the accused infringer. Consequently, the place where the defendant's documents are kept weighs in favor of transfer to that location." DECA argues that transport of the documents for trial will impose a significant and unnecessary burden.

DECA claims that other sources of proof are located at the facility of DECA System in Bundang, Korea. DECA argues that the Central District is 1,850 miles closer to Korea than the Southern District, and thus, the more convenient forum. Conversely, Skyhawke argues that sources of proof found in Korea are located outside of the Central District, thus this does not weigh in favor of transfer.

DECA also highlights the fact that Skyhawke's 938 patent is for a product developed in Wayne City, Illinois and suggests that all documents relating to this product's development will be found in Illinois—not Mississippi. Skyhawke denies this, and claims all documents related to the 938 patent were transferred to Skyhawke's possession.

Skyhawke further argues that in addition to having its principal place of business in the Southern District and employing ninety-six residents of the Southern District, all documents, records, and other evidence relating to the inventions and prosecution histories of the two Skyhawke patents at issue are located in the Southern District at its Ridgeland facility. Additionally, Skyhawke claims that documents relating to the development of the 498 product, financial records relating to damages incurred, documents relating to the commercial success of the products at issue, and the alleged infringing devices that DECA sold in Mississippi are all located in the Southern District. Accordingly, Skyhawke urges this court to find that this factor does not weigh in DECA's favor where Skyhawke would be equally as inconvenienced should its choice of venue be disturbed.

While the court agrees with the observation in the *Genentech* case that the bulk of the evidence in patent matters is often presented by the alleged infringer—in this case DECA—it is clear that SkyHawke maintains records in the Southern District that will be relevant. Moreover, while DECA has certainly not waived its rights to contest venue by filing an answer and counterclaim, its pleadings suggest that SkyHawke's records will also be relevant. For example, DECA claims, *inter alia*, that the patents at issue are invalid for SkyHawke's failure to satisfy the statutory requirements of 35 U.S.C. §§ 101, et. seq. Records and other evidence regarding SkyHawke's compliance, or lack thereof, with the statutory requirements are more likely to be in SkyHawke's possession.

On balance, this factor is either neutral or very slightly favors DECA.

(2) *Compulsory process*

DECA alleges that this court's subpoena powers will not extend to any of the witnesses in this case, given that a number of their identified witnesses reside in or near the Central District. DECA contends the fact that the Central District is "a venue with usable subpoena power .... weighs in favor of transfer, and not only slightly." Conversely, Skyhawke argues that the Southern District has subpoena power over party witnesses and that the analysis of this factor only applies to non-party witnesses. Skyhawke further asserts that this factor is neutral—and if not, weighs against transfer—because neither the Central District nor the Southern District has compulsory process over any of the identified witnesses from Korea or over Mr. Kent Barnard, the inventor of the 938 patent and a resident of Indiana.

Skyhawke is correct in its assessment that the compulsory process factor involves a factual analysis of non-party witnesses versus party witnesses. It is unclear whether the identified witnesses at the DECA System facility in Korea are non-party witnesses rather than party witnesses. Assuming they are non-party witnesses, neither the Central District nor the Southern District could compel them to appear at trial. The same can be said of the inventor of the 938 patent, an Indiana resident.

Accordingly, this factor is essentially neutral as to both parties. It is worth noting, however, that "if this court cannot compel a witness's attendance at trial, neither party is prevented from using the witness's videotaped deposition at trial." *Symbol Technologies, Inc. v. Metrologic Instruments Inc.* (E.D.Tex. 2006).

(3) *Cost of attendance for witnesses*

This factor has been referred to as the most important private interest. DECA estimates the distance between the two forums to be 1,850 miles, which makes travel for DECA's witnesses inconvenient. The Fifth Circuit has established the "100–mile rule," which states: "When the distance between an existing venue for trial of a matter and a proposed venue under § 1404(a) is more than 100 miles, the factor of inconvenience to witnesses increases in direct relationship to the additional distance to be traveled." *Volkswagen II*.

DECA identified three of its officers as material witnesses on the subjects of design, development, and marketing of the alleged infringing product, all of whom reside in the Central District of California. DECA argues that these witnesses will incur a "dramatic burden in terms of cost, time away from family, and time away from other personal and professional obligations" if required to travel to the Southern District for trial. To the extent that former employees of DECA may be necessary witnesses, those former employees are said to currently reside in the Los Angeles and Seattle, Washington areas—much closer to the Central District than the Southern District. The Fifth Circuit has recognized that witnesses who must travel for trial incur not only a monetary burden, "but also the personal costs associated with being away from work, family, and community." *Volkswagen II*.

DECA argues that the previously identified witnesses who live in Korea will incur greater costs due to a lack of direct flights from Seoul to Jackson, Mississippi. DECA identifies three officers from its parent-corporation DECA System as material witnesses—Junha Park (Software Development Manager), Gisu Lee (Hardware Development Manager), and Suk Chul Ham (Global Marketing Manager)—who may have knowledge regarding the design, development, and/or marketing of the alleged infringing product. According to DECA, the fact that there are no direct flights from Seoul, Korea to Jackson, Mississippi and no direct flights from Los Angeles, California to Jackson, Mississippi should weigh in its favor since this means increased costs and increased travel time for DECA's witnesses.

Additionally, DECA suggests that should the inventor or anyone else involved in securing the patent be identified as necessary third-party witnesses those witnesses would have no connection to the Southern District. As a result, DECA argues that the Southern District would be no more convenient for those potential witnesses than the Central District.

For all of the aforementioned reasons, DECA argues that this factor overwhelmingly weighs in its favor.

Conversely, Skyhawke has identified as material witnesses three of its officers, who are inventors of the 498 product, and who all reside in the Southern District. Skyhawke contends that their witnesses will be equally inconvenienced by traveling to the Central District should venue be changed. Ultimately, Skyhawke argues that where a transfer in venue would simply shift the inconvenience from one party to another, this factor is neutral and does not support granting DECA's motion.

The Fifth Circuit has recognized that pursuant to the 100–mile rule the additional distance to be traveled for trial in a proposed venue "means additional travel time; additional travel time increases the probability for meal and lodging expenses; and additional travel time with overnight stays increases the time which these fact witnesses must be away from their regular employment." *Volkswagen I.* However, where a transfer in venue serves to shift inconvenience from one party to the next, this factor does not weigh in favor of granting the movant's request given that the convenience of all parties and witnesses should be considered. Thus, where DECA has identified three of its officers as essential witnesses and Skyhawke has identified three of its officers as essential witnesses, this factor is neutral given that a transfer of venue would result in transferring the increased costs and inconvenience to Skyhawke.

A typical patent case involves witnesses who come from all over the country or world. With regard to the DECA System witnesses traveling from Korea, the court finds the increased travel time of the witnesses from the DECA System facility in Korea may weigh in DECA's favor, but only slightly, as foreign travel will likely inconvenience these witnesses regardless of whether they are traveling to the Central District or the Southern District. "Thus, regardless of where the trial is held, many witnesses, including third-party witnesses, will likely need to travel a significant distance." [quotation omitted].

(4) *Other Practical Problems*

DECA again argues that all documentary evidence and witnesses in this case are located in either California and Korea and that in granting a transfer to a venue in closer proximity to the relevant witnesses and evidence this court will further the interests of ease, expediency and cost of trial. Conversely, Skyhawke avers that to the extent DECA argues in favor of a transfer because witnesses and evidence from Korea are closer to the Central District, DECA is incorrect as a matter of law.

The factual considerations asserted by DECA in support of its contention that this factor weighs in its favor are essentially restatements of previously asserted facts, namely that the majority of the documents and witnesses in the instant case may be found in or in closer proximity to the Central District. Given that DECA has not made any novel arguments nor identified any other practical problems for the court's consideration, the court finds this factor is neutral.

Public Interest Factors

(1) *Local interest*

DECA argues that its company employs over thirty local residents and has become a prominent presence in the local economy of the Central District— generating $10 million in sales in 2010 alone. DECA emphasizes the fact that promotional events for its product are held in conjunction with local golf retail stores and Southern–California–based golf publications and that it has contributed to various local charitable organizations. DECA contends that because the reputation and business activities of its officers and employees are at issue in this case, the Central District has an interest in the outcome.

According to DECA, the only connection between the accused product and the Southern District is the fact that the product is sold here. DECA purports sales in the Southern District to be less than 0.12% of its nationwide sales in 2010. DECA avers that sale of the allegedly infringing product, without more, is insufficient to demonstrate a local interest for the purposes of a transfer of venue analysis. In support of this argument, DECA cites *In re TS Tech USA Corp.* (Fed.Cir. 2008), a patent infringement case which held that there was no local interest in the original venue merely because the accused product was sold there given that none of the parties had an office in the plaintiff's chosen venue, no witnesses resided there, and no evidence was located there.

Skyhawke argues that its chosen venue is the venue wherein its sole facility was founded in 1998, and as such Skyhawke's presence in the Southern District is not "recent, ephemeral, [or] an artifact of litigation." *In Re Zimmer Holdings, Inc.* (Fed.Cir. 2010). Skyhawke submits that ninety-six residents of the Southern District, as well as all of its officers and directors, work at its Ridgeland facility. Moreover, Skyhawke emphasizes that DECA intended for its infringing product to be sold and used in Mississippi, as evidenced by the digital maps of approximately one-hundred-fifty Mississippi golf courses contained on its product. For all of the aforementioned reasons, Skyhawke argues that there is a strong local interest in prosecuting this matter in the Southern District.

The Federal Circuit in *TS Tech* found no local interest in the plaintiff's chosen venue because the only connection to that venue was that the infringing product was sold there. In so finding, the court noted that there were no witnesses, no principal places of business of any party, and no evidence located in the original venue. Conversely, in the instant case, Skyhawke has a facility in Ridgeland, Mississippi, witnesses reside here, and Skyhawke's physical evidence is located at its facility. Moreover, as pointed to by Skyhawke, DECA has presumably directed its product at Mississippi consumers given that the product contains digital maps of Mississippi golf courses. Accordingly, while DECA makes a valid argument that the Central District has a local interest in this matter, the court finds the Southern District likewise has a local interest that is equal to that of the Central District in that Skyhawke's sole facility, witnesses and documents are located in the Southern District and given that the alleged infringing product is being sold here. Thus, the court finds this factor to be neutral.

(2) *Administrative difficulties*

DECA argues that disposition and trial timelines are slightly shorter in the Central District as opposed to the Southern District. DECA cites Administrative Office of the United States Courts data, which lists the Central District median disposition time as 5.6 months and median time to trial as 18 .5 months. The Southern District's median disposition time is listed as 8.1 months with a median time to trial of 23.9 months. Thus, the Southern District's median time to trial is 5.4 months behind that of the Central District. Skyhawke argues that this slightly shorter time frame should be accorded minimal weight, if any. Moreover, Skyhawke notes that the Federal Circuit has referred to this as the "most speculative" factor in the analysis.

... While recognizing that this factor is clearly the most speculative, the court finds that a difference of approximately five months in average time of disposition is significant enough to slightly weigh in favor of DECA. However, given that the other factors are essentially neutral, the court ... affords this factor little weight.

(3) *Forum's Familiarity with the Governing Law and* (4) *Conflict of Law Problems*

Both parties agree that the two remaining factors in the transfer of venue analysis are neutral as to both parties.

Conclusion

This case could have been brought in either of the two jurisdictions at issue. This is not a case ... where the plaintiff had no real connection with the chosen forum, or ... where a substantial number of material witnesses resided in the transferee venue and no witnesses resided in the original forum. Here, SkyHawke has a substantial presence in this District, a number of witnesses are located in this District and some key records are located in this District.

While not determinative, a plaintiff's choice of venue is afforded deference. DECA has the burden of showing that its preferred venue is clearly more convenient. It failed to meet the burden as most of the factors in the analysis are neutral. Only one or two slightly favor a transfer. A change of venue would simply transfer any inconvenience DECA might suffer to SkyHawke. The plaintiff's choice of forum should be upheld.

Supplemental Materials:
Joinder

A. Interpleader
INDIANAPOLIS COLTS v. MAYOR AND CITY COUNCIL OF BALTIMORE
741 F.2d 954 (CA7 1984)

BAUER, Circuit Judge.

Defendants Mayor and City Council of Baltimore (collectively "Baltimore") appeal from two district court orders entered in this interpleader action Plaintiff Indianapolis Colts filed pursuant to 28 U.S.C. § 1335 (1948). The Colts, a football team owning a National Football League franchise, filed the action claiming interpleader jurisdiction on the ground that Baltimore and the Capital Improvement Board of Managers of Marion County, Indiana (CIB), operators of the Indianapolis Hoosier Dome, had conflicting claims against the team. The district court in Indiana granted the Colts' request for an order restraining Baltimore from pursuing its condemnation action against the Colts, which was pending in a federal district court in Maryland. Two weeks later, the district court also enjoined Baltimore from pursuing a Maryland state court action against the NFL in which Baltimore hoped to stop the Colts from moving to Indianapolis. ... We hold that the district court did not have interpleader jurisdiction to hear this suit, and therefore vacate the orders and remand with instructions to dismiss.

I

Through the 1983 season, the Colts played their home games in Baltimore Memorial Stadium. In February 1984, the Colts and the stadium managers began negotiating a renewal of the Memorial Stadium lease. At the same time, the Colts negotiated with the CIB regarding the possibility of moving the team to the Hoosier Dome.

On March 27, 1984, Colts owner Robert Irsay learned that the Maryland Senate passed a bill granting the City of Baltimore the power to acquire the Colts by eminent domain. Irsay decided to move the team to Indianapolis and promptly executed a lease with the CIB. The Colts fled Baltimore under the cloak of darkness; eight moving vans full of Colts equipment arrived in Indianapolis on March 29.

On March 29, Maryland's governor signed into law the bill authorizing Baltimore to acquire the Colts by condemnation. Baltimore filed a condemnation petition against the Colts on March 30 in Maryland state court. The state court restrained the Colts from transferring any element of the team from Baltimore.

After learning about the condemnation suit by telegram, the Colts took two actions. First, on April 2, the Colts caused removal of the state court condemnation proceeding to federal district court in Maryland. Second, on April 5, the Colts filed this action in the United States District Court for the Southern District of Indiana, claiming that their obligations under the lease with the CIB conflicted with Baltimore's attempts to acquire the team through eminent domain.

II

Our review of this case extends to the question of whether the interpleader was proper. This question is an issue of law entitled to full appellate review....

A

A basic jurisdictional requirement of statutory interpleader is that there be adverse claimants to a particular fund. The CIB and Baltimore are not claimants to the same stake. Baltimore seeks ownership of the Colts franchise, whereas the CIB has no claim to ownership of the franchise. Instead, the CIB has a lease with the Colts that requires the team to play its games in the Hoosier Dome and imposes other obligations to ensure the success of the enterprise.

The Colts argue in part that clause 11 of their lease with the CIB raises an interest in the CIB which conflicts with Baltimore's attempt to obtain the franchise. Clause 11 grants the CIB the first chance to find purchasers for the team if Irsay decides to sell his controlling interest. This right of first refusal is the CIB's contractual guarantee either that Irsay always will control the team or that the CIB will have the right to choose his successor. Yet this provision does not give the CIB a present right to buy the Colts, and thus does not raise a claim against the franchise conflicting with Baltimore's claim.

A successful eminent domain action obviously will defeat the CIB's interests in keeping the Colts in Indianapolis. Nevertheless, interpleader is not designed to aid every plaintiff confronted by one claim which, if successful, would defeat a second claim because the plaintiff has lost the ability to pay damages. Such an interpretation would twist interpleader into protection for defendants from losing the opportunity to recover damages because the plaintiff's resources already have been depleted. Interpleader is warranted only to protect the plaintiff-stakeholder from conflicting liability to the stake.

Interpleader is proper in cases such as a surety confronted by claims of subcontractors and materialmen which exceed the surety's contractual liability, conflicting claims of entitlement to the proceeds of a life insurance policy, or automobile insurers surrendering the maximum sum of their liability to the court for disposition to plaintiffs in an accident case. The issue of whether the interpleaded defendants' claims are adverse does not arise often. The Colts' argument here that the "bottom line" of this case is which city "gets" the Colts clouds the issue of adversity.

Only reasonable legal claims can form the adversity to the plaintiff necessary to justify interpleader. The CIB has no reasonable legal claim to ownership of the franchise sought by Baltimore. For the Colts, losing their franchise to Baltimore may lead to breach of the lease claims by the CIB, but this is not a situation for which interpleader was designed.

B

Interpleader is a suit in equity. Because the sole basis for equitable relief to the stakeholder is the danger of exposure to double liability or the vexation of conflicting claims, the stakeholder must have a real and reasonable fear of double liability or vexatious, conflicting claims to justify interpleader. Even assuming that Baltimore and the CIB are fighting over the same stake, the Colts do not have a reasonable fear of double liability or vexatious claims here. The Colts and the CIB foresaw the likelihood of legal obstacles to prevent the Colts from leaving Baltimore, among which was an eminent domain action. The Colts and the CIB thus specifically contracted that the lease obligations will terminate at the Colts' option if the Colts' franchise is acquired by eminent domain. Clause 21.6 of the lease states in part:

21.6 *Club's Option.*

21.6(a) *Actions.* The parties acknowledge and recognize that at the present time there are pending various lawsuits in the state and federal courts dealing with the issues of the provisions of the Constitution and By-Laws of the League, the Constitution of the United States, and various State Constitutions, state and federal antitrust laws, and state and federal laws of eminent domain and other state and federal laws which may be impact on the provisions of this Agreement. In acknowledgement and contemplation of those lawsuits and of the fact: that certain parties may institute lawsuits of a similar or dissimilar nature, including without limitation those described in the preceding sentence and those seeking injunctive relief to prevent the Club from keeping, observing and/or performing any of this Agreement or keeping, observing or performing any other covenant, agreement or undertaking; or, a strike suit is filed by any person; or, there is any act or action of the League, be it the institution of a suit, disciplinary or other proceedings, or threatening termination or suspension of the Franchise or of a fine as a result of or related to the Club's transfer of its Franchise or the playing of its home games in Indianapolis; or, an eminent domain suit is filed by any governmental authority or any other statutory body capable of instituting said suits, the parties agree that:

* * * * * *

(iii) If Club is ordered by a final order of such court of final appellate jurisdiction to play other than at the Stadium or the Franchise is acquired by eminent domain, this Agreement shall terminate at Club's option, and the parties shall have no further obligations hereunder except as stated in this Paragraph [dealing with a few final financial affairs].

This "escape" clause renders unreasonable the Colts' claim that they will face a second suit over the same stake if Baltimore ultimately succeeds in its eminent domain action....

The distinction in this case between the lack of adverse claims and the lack of fear of double liability or vexatious litigation is slight. Other courts, however, have recognized that even if adverse claims exist in theory, still there may be no real fear of multiple lawsuits. In *Bierman v. Marcus* (3d Cir. 1957), for example, the plaintiffs sought interpleader to resolve claims over a specific sum of money. One claimant asserted a valid claim. The other supposed claimant, however, was a corporation controlled by the plaintiffs. The Third Circuit ruled that the plaintiffs knew that the corporation would make no claim against the money and thus no equitable consideration supported interpleader jurisdiction....

Because the Colts cannot assert a reasonable fear of multiple liability or vexatious, conflicting claims, interpleader jurisdiction was not proper. There is no other basis for federal jurisdiction in the federal district court in Indiana to hear the Colts' action and thus this suit must be dismissed.

III

Because we find that Baltimore and the CIB do not have adverse claims and that the Colts are not exposed to the risk of vexatious litigation, we need not address the merits of Baltimore's other arguments against the maintenance of interpleader jurisdiction. Specifically, we decline to decide whether the Colts and the CIB contrived a conflicting claim by signing the lease in order to create jurisdiction in a more favorable forum. Even if that was their plan, it did not succeed. ...

The district court's orders are vacated and this action is remanded with instructions that it be dismissed. ...

COFFEY, Circuit Judge, dissenting.

The issue in this case is whether the Capital Improvement Board ("CIB") and the City Council of Baltimore ("Baltimore") are adverse claimants to a particular stake held by the Indianapolis Colts. The majority asserts that the

CIB and Baltimore "are not claimants to the same stake" and thus the Indianapolis Colts fail to satisfy the jurisdictional requirement of 28 U.S.C. § 1335 (1982). In the alternative, the majority declares that even if a common stake does exist, the Colts are not presented with conflicting and vexatious claims to that stake. I dissent from the majority's strained attempt to simplify this case as merely involving an eminent domain proceeding in Baltimore, Maryland, and a lease agreement in Indianapolis, Indiana. Rather, as characterized by the district court judge, this action involves a struggle over a very unique stake—"the rights and privileges of the [Colts] franchise and the property rights incident to the operation thereof"—with all of the attending social and economic benefits to be derived by two major metropolitan cities competing for the rights and privileges of the Colts' National Football League franchise. ... Based upon the district court's extensive findings of fact, I am convinced that the CIB and the City of Baltimore are adverse claimants to the same stake and thus the Colts satisfy the jurisdictional requirement of 28 U.S.C. § 1335.

...

The claim asserted by the CIB is not, as the majority contends, a simple contract interest, rather it involves the rights, benefits, and privileges of a National Football League franchise formerly known as the Baltimore Colts. It is this intangible, but very unique, property right that the CIB seeks to control by enforcing the terms of its Lease. A realistic view of the facts at hand reveals that the CIB was organized to improve and expand the greater Indianapolis economic market. ...

The CIB's interest in enforcing the Lease is not simply to turn a profit for the Hoosier Dome but to enhance the prestige and the economic climate of the City of Indianapolis and the County of Marion, Indiana with a coveted National Football League franchise. There are numerous social and economic benefits associated with a professional sports franchise including public entertainment, increased restaurant and hotel revenues, civic pride, favorable media coverage, increased retail expenditures, and national recognition. This point is clearly driven home by Baltimore's all-out efforts to keep the Colts in Baltimore.

The fact that the City of Indianapolis does not own the Colts and the CIB has only entered into a contract with the present owners of the franchise is of no consequence. As the California Supreme Court acknowledged in *City of Oakland v. Oakland Raiders* (Cal. 1982), there may be no substantial legal difference between "managing and owning the facility in which the game is played, and managing and owning the team which plays in the facility." ... The full intent of the CIB as embodied in the Lease is to keep the Colts in Indianapolis and thereby enjoy the rights and privileges of a National Football League franchise. The City of Baltimore also clearly desires these very same rights and privileges and thus, contrary to the majority's simplified analysis, there does exist in this case a common, identifiable stake—the rights and privileges of the Colts' franchise—subject to adverse claims....

B. Intervention

GREAT ATLANTIC & PACIFIC TEA COMPANY, INC. v. TOWN OF EAST HAMPTON

178 F.R.D. 39 (E.D.N.Y. 1998)

MEMORANDUM AND ORDER

WEXLER, District Judge.

In this action challenging the validity of a local zoning law, Group for the South Fork, Inc. (the "Group") requests leave to intervene as defendants either as of right under Fed.R.Civ.P. 24(a)(2), or alternatively, as a matter of discretion under Fed.R.Civ.P. 24(b)(2). For the reasons set forth below, the Group's motion is denied with leave to renew at a later stage of the litigation.

FACTS

In 1996, defendant Town of East Hampton adopted and filed with the State of New York a local zoning law, officially known as Local Law No. 17 of 1996 (the "Superstore Law"), amending Chapter 153 of the East Hampton Town Code to restrict the establishment of very large retail stores within East Hampton outside of the Central Business zone. The Superstore Law provides, *inter alia,* that a building used for a supermarket may not exceed 25,000 square feet in gross floor area and that parking for supermarkets shall be located primarily to the sides or rear of the building. The effect of the Superstore Law was to prevent plaintiff, The Great Atlantic & Pacific Tea Company, Inc. ("A & P"), from proceeding with its proposal to develop a 33,878 square foot supermarket at a site on Montauk Highway formerly occupied by a Stern's department store. The proposed site is in a Neighborhood Business zone.

A & P brings this suit against the Town, seeking a declaratory judgment that the Town's passage of the Superstore Law was beyond its legislative authority, and that the law itself violates the New York and federal constitutions in that it denies A & P due process and equal protection, and interferes with interstate commerce. A & P also asserts that the law violates 42 U.S.C. § 1983 and is an illegal restraint of trade under New York law. The Town has moved to dismiss the complaint for failure to state a claim pursuant to Rule 12(b)(6) of the Federal Rules of Civil Procedure.

Through its president, Robert DeLuca, the Group describes itself as an environmental organization dedicated to preserving the rural character, rural heritage, and natural resources of the South Fork of Long Island, including the East Hampton area. The Group actively supported the Superstore Law, and its members provided extensive testimony during public hearings as well as providing commentary on area planning statements relevant to the law. The Group has also submitted affidavits from some of its members who live near the proposed site of the A & P supermarket, averring that the rural and residential character of the area will be changed to the detriment of their property values.

The Group has filed a proposed answer and proposed memoranda of law in support of its proposed motion to dismiss A & P's complaint. A review of the memoranda of law submitted by the Town and the Group reveals that they raise similar arguments in support of dismissal of plaintiff's complaint. A & P objects to the Group's intervention in this action.

ANALYSIS

I. *Intervention as of Right*

To intervene as of right under Rule 24(a)(2), the would-be intervenor must establish the following:

> (1) a timely motion; (2) an interest relating to the property or transaction that is the subject matter of the action; (3) an impairment of that interest without intervention; and (4) the movant's interest is not adequately represented by the other parties to the litigation.

United States v. Pitney Bowes, Inc. (2d Cir. 1994). Intervention will be denied if any requirement is not met. *Washington Elec. Coop. v. Massachusetts Mun. Wholesale Elec. Co.* (2d Cir. 2990).

A. *Timeliness*

The complaint was filed on November 20, 1996, and the Group's motion to intervene was filed on May 9, 1997. A & P does not contest the timeliness of the motion and the Court finds, absent opposition, that the first element of the *Pitney Bowes* test is met.

B. *The Intervenor's Interest in the Transaction that is the Subject of the Action*

An intervenor's interest must be "direct, substantial, and legally protectable," *New York New, Inc. v. Kheel* (2d Cir. 1992), rather than "remote or contingent." *H.L. Hayden Co. of New York, Inc. v. Siemens Med. Sys., Inc.* (2d Cir. 1986). An organization like the Group has a sufficient interest to support intervention by right where the underlying action concerns legislation previously supported by the organization. This is particularly true where, as here, the personal interests of its members in the continued environmental quality of the area and the continued rural character of East Hampton would be threatened if the Superstore Law is found to be invalid or unconstitutional and A & P proceeds with development of its planned market. The Court finds that the Group has demonstrated a sufficient legal interest in the subject matter of this action to satisfy the second element of the *Pitney Bowes* test.

C. *Effect on Intervenor's Interests*

The third element of the intervention by right standard is met where the intervenors demonstrate that, absent intervention, the disposition of the action may, as a practical matter, impede or impair their interests. Here, the interests of the Group and its members would likely be impaired if the Superstore Law is found to be invalid or unconstitutional.

D. *Adequacy of Representation*

Although the Group's application to intervene passes the first three steps, it founders on the final element, adequacy of representation. An applicant for intervention as of right must show that it may not be adequately represented by a named party. This showing places only a "minimal burden" on the would-be intervenor. *Trbovich v. United Mine Workers of Am.* (1972); *United Postal Serv. v. Brennan* (2d Cir. 1978). Nonetheless, adequate representation is presumed when the would-be intervenor shares the same ultimate objective as a party to the lawsuit. To overcome the presumption of adequate representation in the face of shared objectives, the would-be intervenor must demonstrate collusion, nonfeasance, adversity of interest, or incompetence on the part of the named party that shares the same interest.

On the facts here, adequate representation is presumed because the Group and the Town share the same ultimate objective in this litigation, namely, a declaration that the Superstore Law was validly enacted and is constitutional. The Group does not suggest that the presumption is overcome because of collusion, nonfeasance, or incompetence by the Town in its defense of the validity of the Superstore Law. Rather, the Group contends that the Town will not adequately represent its interests in defending the Superstore Law because the Group is an environmental organization whose concern is focused on protecting the environment and the rural character of the South Fork of Long Island, whereas the Town must concern itself with other interests such as perceived economic growth and stimulation of tax revenues. Consequently, the Group contends, it will argue the environmental rationale for the Superstore Law more vigorously than would the Town.

Even accepting as true the Group's characterization of these differing concerns, the interests of the Group coincide with the interests of the Town in terms of the single legal issue to be determined by this lawsuit, i.e., the validity and constitutionality of the Superstore Law. To prevail on its theory of inadequate representation, the Group would need to demonstrate that it has a legal interest in maintaining the Superstore Law that not only differs from the Town's interest, but would permit the Group to assert a justification for the law that could not be equally asserted by the Town. This demonstration is lacking. The fact that the Group and the Town may have different motives behind their joint interest in defending the statute does not lead to the conclusion that the Town will fail to pursue its defense of the Superstore Law with vigor.

To the extent that the Group, by virtue of its environmental expertise, might be more persuasive than the Town in arguing the environmental justification for the Superstore Law, such a notion is speculative (particularly in light of the cooperation between the Group and the Town in passing the Superstore Law) and unsupported by examination of the Group's proposed briefs submitted in support of the Town's motion to dismiss. Both sets of briefs raise the same issues and offer the same arguments. Even assuming that the Group may be better able than the Town to provide environmental expertise and that a need for such expertise will arise during these proceedings, the Group may seek amicus curiae status to bring its views before the Court.

The Group further contends that it is inadequately represented because the Town might settle the action on terms that the Group would not approve, or because the Town might not appeal an adverse decision. These arguments are unpersuasive. As the Fifth Circuit has noted with respect to possible future settlement of an action:

> The mere possibility that a party may at some future time enter into a settlement cannot alone show inadequate representation. If this were so, the requirement that the would-be intervenor show inadequacy of representation would be effectively written out of the rule, for it is always a possibility that the present parties will settle a lawsuit.

Bush v. Viterna (5ᵗʰ Cir. 1984). Similarly, the mere fact that a party might fail to appeal does not rise to the level of inadequate representation. "If disagreement with an actual party over trial strategy, including whether to challenge or appeal a court order, were sufficient bases for a proposed intervenor to claim that its interests were not adequately represented, the requirement would be rendered meaningless." *United States v. Yonkers Bd. of Educ.* (2d Cir. 1990).

Because the Group has failed to demonstrate that the Town will inadequately represent its interests, the application for intervention as of right pursuant to Rule 24(a)(2) is denied with leave to renew at a later stage of the proceedings in the event the Group can make a factual showing that the Town is not vigorously litigating the case.

II. *Permissive Intervention*

The Group also seeks to intervene pursuant to Rule 24(b)(2). Permissive intervention may be granted "when an applicant's claim or defense and the main action have a question of law or fact in common." This threshold test is clearly met because both the Group and the Town seek a declaration that the Superstore Law is valid and constitutional.

Permissive intervention is a matter left to the discretion of the court. The principal consideration for the court in determining whether or not to allow intervention is "whether the intervention will unduly delay or prejudice the adjudication of the rights of the original parties." *Brennan*. In exercising its discretion, the court may consider other relevant factors, including the nature and extent of the intervenor's interests; whether the intervenor's interests are adequately represented by the parties; and whether the party seeking intervention will significantly contribute to the full development of the underlying factual issues in the suit and to the just and equitable adjudication of the legal question presented.

It is also clear, however, that intervention should not be used as a means to inject collateral issues into an existing action, particularly where it serves to delay and complicate the litigation. After reviewing the affidavits submitted by the Group in support of its motion to intervene, the Court is troubled by the potential for the injection of collateral issues, in particular, the issue of commercial development at the proposed A & P site even where such development would be within the limits imposed by the Superstore Law.

The affidavit submitted by the Group's president, Robert DeLuca, stresses concerns that go far beyond merely validating the Superstore Law and strongly suggests that any major commercial development which changes the present character of the proposed A & P site would be unacceptable to the Group, even if such development fell within the bounds of the Superstore Law. DeLuca states that the site at which plaintiff proposes to build its supermarket was formerly occupied by a Stern's department store. He adds that "[t]he commercial use of the site by Stern's was not apparent from the road [Montauk Highway] and did not adversely impact on the community" because Stern's retained open space, trees, and vegetation on the site, as well as certain older structures, which he describes as "a historic riding academy." He points out that:

> the Group and its members are ... concerned with the numerous *site-specific impacts* of the A & P superstore proposal. The A & P proposal would result in demolishing historic buildings and destroying old field plants, large trees, and open space currently on the site. A & P's proposal, a box-like massive supermarket with parking lot in front, is completely incompatible with the rural and residential character of the area. Further, the A & P proposal would result in greatly increased traffic in the area

The affidavits submitted by other Group members similarly indicate that their concerns are not so much directed to banning superstores in East Hampton areas zoned for Neighborhood Business as they are to banning any major commercial development of the proposed A & P site. ...

After reviewing the affidavits submitted by the Group, the Court is left with the firm impression that the Group will seek to transform this lawsuit from a test of the validity of the Superstore Law into a contest over the propriety of commercial development in East Hampton in general and at the proposed A & P site in particular. The arguments raised in the Group's affidavits are equally applicable to the proposed A & P supermarket and to the establishment of smaller ventures on the site.

Taking the above considerations into account, the Court finds that the nature and extent of the Group's interest in defending the validity of the Superstore Law is identical to that of the Town and both seek the same ultimate outcome. The Town appears ready, willing and able to vigorously defend the validity of the Superstore Law so that the Group's interests are adequately represented. Moreover, the Group's concerns over commercial development at the proposed site, as opposed merely to its concern to defend the validity of the Superstore Law, injects a collateral issue into this lawsuit that can only serve to delay and complicate the proceedings to the prejudice of plaintiff without assisting in the resolution of the central issue before the Court. Such delay is in addition to the unnecessary delay that ensues when a would-be intervenor, as here, "merely underlines issues already raised by the primary parties. Additional parties always take additional time." *British Airways Board v. Port Auth. of N.Y.* (S.D.N.Y. 1982) (internal quotation omitted). Consequently, the Group's motion to intervene pursuant to Rule 24(b)(2) is denied with leave to renew at a later stage of the proceedings in the event the Group can make a factual showing that the Town is not vigorously litigating this action.

CONCLUSION

For the reasons stated above, the Group's motion to intervene is denied with leave to renew at a later stage of the proceedings in the event the Group can make a factual showing that the Town is not vigorously litigating this action.

SO ORDERED.

C. Cross-Claims

HARRISON v. M.S. CARRIERS, INC.

1999 WL 195539 (E.D. La April 7, 1999)

SEAR, District Judge.

... On September 21, 1998, plaintiffs, Mary Gilbert, Cynthia Daniels, and Dave Harrison, Jr., filed suit against defendants as a result of an automobile accident which occurred on September 25, 1997. Plaintiffs allegedly suffered injuries when a car driven by plaintiff Dave Harrison and a M.S. Carriers tractor collided. Plaintiffs seek damages for injuries sustained in connection with the accident.

Plaintiffs originally filed this action in the Civil District Court for the Parish of Orleans ("CDC"). Defendants timely removed this action to this

Court on October 28, 1998, based solely on diversity jurisdiction. I subsequently denied Plaintiffs' motion to remand to the CDC.

On February 4, 1999, plaintiffs then moved to amend their complaint to name their co-plaintiff, Harrison, the driver of the automobile in which they were riding, and his insurer, Guaranty National Insurance Company, as additional defendants. Plaintiffs seek to assert negligence claims against Harrison. Defendants opposed the motion asserting that the proper procedural mechanism by which plaintiffs must assert their claim against co-plaintiff Harrison is a cross claim.

On February 24, 1999, Judge Wilkinson denied plaintiffs' motion to amend their complaint..., but without prejudice to plaintiffs' assertion of a cross claim against Harrison and an amended complaint against his insurer. Plaintiffs Gilbert and Daniels now seek review of this order.

...

Judge Wilkinson ruled that a cross-claim is the proper procedure for asserting a claim against co-plaintiff Harrison. [Gilbert and Daniels] contend that a cross-claim is not proper. To support this contention, movers rely on the Third Circuit's ruling in *Danner v. Anski* (3d Cir.1958).

In *Danner*, the passengers and the driver of one automobile sued the driver of the vehicle with which their vehicle collided. The passenger plaintiffs attempted to file a cross claim against the driver plaintiff. The Third Circuit held that Federal Rule of Civil Procedure 13(g) does not authorize a plaintiff to state as a cross claim against a co-plaintiff for a claim arising out of a transaction or occurrence which is the subject matter of a common complaint against a defendant. The Court reasoned:

> The purpose of rule 13(g) is ... to permit a plaintiff against whom a defendant has filed a counter claim to state as a cross-claim against a co-plaintiff a claim growing out of that transaction or occurrence that is the subject matter of the counter claim or relating to any property that is the subject matter of that counter claim.
>
> * * *
>
> Unless so limited the rule could have the effect of extending the jurisdiction of the district court to controversies not within the federal judicial power in violation of the Constitution...

The clear language of Rule 13(g) does not support the Third Circuit's holding in *Danner*. ... The Fifth Circuit has explained that Rule 13(g) "states two prerequisites for a cross-claim: (1) that it be a claim by one party against a co-party and (2) that the claim arise out of the same transaction or occurrence as the original counterclaim." ... Accordingly, I find that a cross-claim is the proper method of asserting plaintiffs' claim against co-plaintiff Harrison.

Having decided that, it is still necessary that I determine whether Judge Wilkinson properly denied plaintiffs' amendment to the pleadings. In determining whether an amendment to the pleadings should be permitted in a removed case that includes a new nondiverse defendant, Judge Wilkinson relied on the Fifth Circuit's ruling in *Hensgens v. Deere & Co.* (5th Cir.1987).

In *Hensgens,* the Fifth Circuit held that [in such cases the] district court should scrutinize the amendment more closely than an ordinary amendment ...

... Judge Wilkinson concluded that [plaintiffs'] principal motivation in choosing to add the non-diverse co-plaintiff as a defendant in an amended petition, rather than a cross-claim, was to defeat federal jurisdiction. I agree. Judge Wilkinson's ruling gave the plaintiffs what they sought, a procedure to assert their claims against the co-plaintiff Harrison. There appears no other reason to seek review of the Magistrate Judge's Order than to defeat diversity jurisdiction....

I do not find Judge Wilkinson's ruling to be clearly erroneous or contrary to law.

D. Counterclaims

BURLINGTON NORTHERN RAILROAD COMPANY v. STRONG
907 F.2d 707 (CA7 1990)

RIPPLE, Circuit Judge.

John Strong sued his employer, Burlington Northern Railroad Company (Burlington), alleging personal injury tort damages. A jury awarded Mr. Strong $73,000. Thereafter, ... Burlington ... brought a separate suit to recover the funds. Summary judgment in favor of Burlington for the entire amount of the disability funds was entered on November 30, 1988. Mr. Strong appeals from the district court's judgment in the second suit. For the following reasons, we affirm.

I

BACKGROUND

Mr. Strong was a member of the Brotherhood of Maintenance of Way Employees during his employment with Burlington. The union operated under a collective bargaining agreement that applied to all union employees the provisions of the Supplemental Sickness Benefit Agreement of 1973 (1973 Agreement). In turn, the 1973 Agreement provided that the Supplemental Sickness Benefits (SSB) received by employees would not duplicate recovery of lost wages from a disability case.

Mr. Strong was injured in two separate accidents on September 12, 1983 and March 5, 1985 during his employment with Burlington. He brought suit against Burlington to recover for these injuries under the Federal Employers Liability Act (FELA), 45 U.S.C. §§ 51-60. Following a jury trial, Mr. Strong was awarded $73,000 in compensation for the 1983 injury; Burlington was found not liable for the 1985 injury.

...

[Later,], Burlington sued on the contract to recover the SSB payments. Mr. Strong argued that the railroad's suit was barred by *res judicata* because such a claim should have been brought as a compulsory counterclaim to the previous FELA suit. However, the court decided that the railroad's claim was a permissive, not compulsory, counterclaim: "Burlington Northern's right to recoup the disability benefits does not arise out of the same occurrence (the accidents) that gave rise to Strong's lawsuit; it derives from the provisions of the Supplemental Sickness Benefit Agreement of May 12, 1973." The court further decided that, even if the claim could be said to be related to the same occurrence, an exception for claims that had not matured at the time of filing the answer would apply.

... The district court ... granted Burlington's motion for summary judgment.

II

ANALYSIS

In this court, Mr. Strong renews the arguments he submitted to the district court. ...

Mr. Strong argues that Burlington's claim for setoff was a compulsory counterclaim that was waived when Burlington failed to raise it during the first trial (Mr. Strong's FELA trial). *See* Fed.R.Civ.P. 13(a). Rule 13(a) is "in some ways a harsh rule": if a counterclaim is compulsory and the party does not bring it in the original lawsuit, that claim is thereafter barred. But the rule serves a valuable role in the litigation process, especially in conserving judicial resources. As we have noted, Rule 13(a) "is the result of a balancing between competing interests. The convenience of the party with a compulsory counterclaim is sacrificed in the interest of judicial economy." *Martino v. McDonald's Sys., Inc.* (7th Cir. 1979).

In order to be a compulsory counterclaim, Rule 13(a) requires that the claim (1) exist at the time of pleading, (2) arise out of the same transaction or occurrence as the opposing party's claim, and (3) not require for adjudication parties over whom the court may not acquire jurisdiction. There is no dispute that the third element—no required third parties—is met in this case. Our disposition therefore must turn on whether the other two requirements are met. ...

This court has developed a "logical relationship" test to determine whether the "transaction or occurrence" is the same for purposes of Rule 13(a).

> Courts generally have agreed that the words "transaction or occurrence" should be interpreted liberally in order to further the general policies of the federal rules and carry out the philosophy of Rule 13(a).... As a word of flexible meaning, 'transaction' may comprehend a series of many occurrences, depending not so much upon the immediateness of their connection as upon their *logical relationship*. ... [A] counterclaim that has its roots in a separate transaction or occurrence is permissive and is governed by Rule 13(b).

Gilldorn Sav. Ass'n v. Commerce Sav. Ass'n (7th Cir. 1986) (quotation omitted). Despite this liberal construction, we have stressed that our inquiry cannot be a "wooden application of the common transaction label." *Id.* Rather, we must examine carefully the factual allegations underlying each claim to determine if the logical relationship test is met. For example, in *Gilldorn Savings Association*, this court decided that, even in light of this liberal construction, the transactions in that case were not sufficiently close to require that the second suit be barred as a compulsory counterclaim. *Id.* In that case, the first suit related to the 1983 sale of a mortgage company by Commerce to Gilldorn. The second suit related to a 1984 agreement that Commerce exchange a five million dollar subordinated debenture for five million dollars in Gilldorn preferred stock. Commerce alleged that it exchanged its debenture solely on the promise by Gilldorn that Gilldorn would not sue Commerce on a claim associated with the 1983 sale. This court decided that the 1984 stock exchange was "totally unrelated" to the 1983 stock purchase, despite acknowledging that "Commerce's claims technically are related to Gilldorn's in the sense that Commerce's claims may not have accrued until Gilldorn filed the Illinois action." We concluded that the relationship was insufficient to satisfy Rule 13(a) because the two claims were based on different theories and would raise different legal and factual issues. ...

In short, there is no formalistic test to determine whether suits are logically related. A court should consider the totality of the claims, including the nature of the claims, the legal basis for recovery, the law involved, and the respective factual backgrounds.

Even when a counterclaim meets the "same transaction" test, a party need not assert it as a compulsory counterclaim if it has not matured when the party serves his answer. This maturity exception "is derived from the language in the rule limiting its application to claims the pleader has 'at the time of serving the pleading.'" 6 C. Wright, A. Miller & M. Kane, Federal Practice and Procedure § 1411, at 81 (2d ed. 1990). "This exception to the compulsory counterclaim requirement necessarily encompasses a claim that depends upon the outcome of some other lawsuit and thus does not come into existence until the action upon which it is based has terminated." *Id.*

We believe, in light of the foregoing principles, that the district court correctly concluded that Burlington's claim was not a compulsory counterclaim. We agree with the district court that the claims do not arise out of the same transaction. Burlington's right to recoup does not arise out of the same occurrence that gave rise to Mr. Strong's earlier suit. His suit is grounded in the accidents that resulted in his injury. By contrast, Burlington's suit is grounded in the provisions of the Supplemental Sickness Benefit Agreement of May 12, 1973. The two claims "raise different legal and factual issues governed by different bodies of law." *Valencia v. Anderson Bros. Ford* (7th Cir. 1980). ... They "lack any shared realm of genuine dispute." *Id.* (quotation omitted).

We also agree with the district court that, even if we were to assume, *arguendo,* that these claims involve the same transaction, Burlington's claim need not have been brought as a counterclaim. It did not exist until the conclusion of the first suit when Mr. Strong obtained his judgment. Thus, the so-called "maturity exception" would permit the maintenance of this second suit. Accordingly, the district court properly determined that the railroad's claim is a permissive counterclaim that was not waived by Burlington's failure to plead it in the FELA case.

STEWART ORGANIZATION, INC. v. RICOH CORP.
487 U.S. 22 (1988)

JUSTICE MARSHALL delivered the opinion of the Court.

This case presents the issue whether a federal court sitting in diversity should apply state or federal law in adjudicating a motion to transfer a case to a venue provided in a contractual forum-selection clause.

I

The dispute underlying this case grew out of a dealership agreement that obligated petitioner company, an Alabama corporation, to market copier products of respondent, a nationwide manufacturer with its principal place of business in New Jersey. The agreement contained a forum-selection clause providing that any dispute arising out of the contract could be brought only in a court located in Manhattan. Business relations between the parties soured under circumstances that are not relevant here. In September 1984, petitioner brought a complaint in the United States District Court for the Northern District of Alabama. The core of the complaint was an allegation that respondent had breached the dealership agreement, but petitioner also included claims for breach of warranty, fraud, and antitrust violations.

Relying on the contractual forum-selection clause, respondent moved the District Court either to transfer the case to the Southern District of New York under 28 U. S. C. § 1404(a) or to dismiss the case for improper venue under 28 U. S. C. § 1406. The District Court denied the motion. It reasoned that the transfer motion was controlled by Alabama law and that Alabama looks unfavorably upon contractual forum-selection clauses. The court certified its ruling for interlocutory appeal, and the Court of Appeals for the Eleventh Circuit accepted jurisdiction.

On appeal, a divided panel of the Eleventh Circuit reversed the District Court. The panel concluded that questions of venue in diversity actions are governed by federal law, and that the parties' forum-selection clause was enforceable as a matter of federal law. The panel therefore reversed the order of the District Court and remanded with instructions to transfer the case to a Manhattan court. After petitioner successfully moved for rehearing en banc, the full Court of Appeals proceeded to adopt the result, and much of the reasoning, of the panel opinion. ....

II

Both the panel opinion and the opinion of the full Court of Appeals referred to the difficulties that often attend "the sticky question of which law, state or federal, will govern various aspects of the decisions of federal courts sitting in diversity." A district court's decision whether to apply a federal statute such as § 1404(a) in a diversity action, however, involves a considerably less intricate analysis than that which governs the "relatively unguided *Erie* choice." *Hanna* v. *Plumer* (1965) (referring to *Erie R. Co.* v. *Tompkins* (1938)). Our cases indicate that when the federal law sought to be applied is a congressional statute, the first and chief question for the district court's determination is whether the statute is "sufficiently broad to control the issue before the Court." *Walker* v. *Armco Steel Corp.* (1980); *Burlington Northern R. Co.* v. *Woods* (1987). This question involves a straightforward exercise in statutory interpretation to determine if the statute covers the point in dispute.

If the district court determines that a federal statute covers the point in dispute, it proceeds to inquire whether the statute represents a valid exercise of Congress' authority under the Constitution. If Congress intended to reach the issue before the district court, and if it enacted its intention into law in a manner that abides with the Constitution, that is the end of the matter; "[f]ederal courts are bound to apply rules enacted by Congress with respect to matters . . . over which it has legislative power." *Prima Paint Corp.* v. *Flood & Conklin Mfg. Co.* (1967). Thus, a district court sitting in diversity must apply a federal statute that controls the issue before the court and that represents a valid exercise of Congress' constitutional powers.

III

Applying the above analysis to this case persuades us that federal law, specifically [Section 1404(a)], governs the parties' venue dispute.

Section 1404(a) provides: "For the convenience of parties and witnesses, in the interest of justice, a district court may transfer any civil action to any other district or division where it might have been brought." Under the analysis outlined above, we first consider whether this provision is sufficiently broad to control the issue before the court. That issue is whether to transfer the case to a court in Manhattan in accordance with the forum-selection clause. We believe that the statute, fairly construed, does cover the point in dispute.

Section 1404(a) is intended to place discretion in the district court to adjudicate motions for transfer according to an "individualized, case-by-case consideration of convenience and fairness." *Van Dusen* v. *Barrack* (1964). A motion to transfer under § 1404(a) thus calls on the district court to weigh in the balance a number of case-specific factors. The presence of a forum-selection clause such as the parties entered into in this case will be a significant factor that figures centrally in the district court's calculus. In its resolution of the § 1404(a) motion in this case, for example, the District Court will be called on to address such issues as the convenience of a Manhattan forum given the parties' expressed preference for that venue, and the fairness of transfer in light of the forum-selection clause and the parties' relative bargaining power. The flexible and individualized analysis Congress prescribed in § 1404(a) thus encompasses consideration of the parties' private expression of their venue preferences.

Section 1404(a) may not be the only potential source of guidance for the District Court to consult in weighing the parties' private designation of a suitable forum. The premise of the dispute between the parties is that Alabama law may refuse to enforce forum-selection clauses providing for out-of-state venues as a matter of state public policy. If that is so, the District Court will have either to integrate the factor of the forum-selection clause into its weighing of considerations as prescribed by Congress, or else to apply, as it did in this case, Alabama's categorical policy disfavoring forum-selection clauses. Our cases make clear that, as between these two choices in a single "field of operation," *Burlington Northern R. Co.* v. *Woods*, the instructions of Congress are supreme.

It is true that § 1404(a) and Alabama's putative policy regarding forum-selection clauses are not perfectly coextensive. Section 1404(a) directs a district court to take account of factors other than those that bear solely on the parties' private ordering of their affairs. The district court also must weigh in the balance the convenience of the witnesses and those public-interest factors of systemic integrity and fairness that, in addition to private concerns, come under the heading of "the interest of justice." It is conceivable in a particular case, for example, that because of these factors a district court acting under § 1404(a) would refuse to transfer a case notwithstanding the counterweight of a forum-selection clause, whereas the coordinate state rule might dictate the opposite result. But this potential conflict in fact frames an additional argument for the supremacy of federal law. Congress has directed that multiple considerations govern transfer within the federal court system, and a state policy focusing on a single concern or a subset of the factors identified in § 1404(a) would defeat that command. Its application would impoverish the flexible and multifaceted analysis that Congress intended to govern motions to transfer within the federal system. The forum-selection clause, which represents the parties' agreement as to the most proper forum, should receive neither dispositive consideration (as respondent might have it) nor no consideration (as Alabama law might have it), but rather the consideration for which Congress provided in § 1404(a)....

Because § 1404(a) controls the issue before the District Court, it must be applied if it represents a valid exercise of Congress' authority under the Constitution. The constitutional authority of Congress to enact § 1404(a) is not subject to serious question. As the Court made plain in *Hanna*, "the constitutional provision for a federal court system . . . carries with it congressional power to make rules governing the practice and pleading in those courts, which in turn includes a power to regulate matters which, though falling within the uncertain area between substance and procedure, are rationally capable of classification as either." Section 1404(a) is doubtless capable of classification as a procedural rule, and indeed, we have so classified it in holding that a transfer pursuant to § 1404(a) does not carry with it a change in the applicable law. It therefore falls comfortably within Congress' powers under Article III as augmented by the Necessary and Proper Clause.

We hold that federal law, specifically 28 U. S. C. § 1404(a), governs the District Court's decision whether to give effect to the parties' forum-selection clause and transfer this case to a court in Manhattan. We therefore affirm the Eleventh Circuit order reversing the District Court's application of Alabama law. The case is remanded so that the District Court may determine in the first instance the appropriate effect under federal law of the parties' forum-selection clause on respondent's § 1404(a) motion.

It is so ordered.

[Concurring opinion of JUSTICE KENNEDY omitted.]

JUSTICE SCALIA, dissenting.

I agree with the opinion of the Court that the initial question before us is whether the validity between the parties of a contractual forum-selection clause falls within the scope of 28 U. S. C. § 1404(a). I cannot agree, however, that the answer to that question is yes. Nor do I believe that the federal courts can, consistent with the twin-aims test of *Erie R. Co.* v. *Tompkins* (1938), fashion a judge-made rule to govern this issue of contract validity.

When a litigant asserts that state law conflicts with a federal procedural statute or formal Rule of Procedure, a court's first task is to determine whether the disputed point in question in fact falls within the scope of the federal statute or Rule. In this case, the Court must determine whether the scope of § 1404(a) is sufficiently broad to cause a direct collision with state law or implicitly to control the issue before the Court, *i.e.*, validity between the parties of the forum-selection clause, thereby leaving no room for the operation of state law. I conclude that it is not.

Although the language of § 1404(a) provides no clear answer, in my view it does provide direction. The provision vests the district courts with authority to transfer a civil action to another district "[f]or the convenience of parties and witnesses, in the interest of justice." This language looks to the present and the future. As the specific reference to convenience of parties and witnesses suggests, it requires consideration of what is likely to be just in the future, when the case is tried, in light of things as they now stand. Accordingly, the courts in applying § 1404(a) have examined a variety of factors, each of which pertains to facts that currently exist or will exist: *e. g.*, the forum actually chosen by the plaintiff, the current convenience of the parties and witnesses, the current location of pertinent books and records, similar litigation pending elsewhere, current docket conditions, and familiarity of the potential courts with governing state law. In holding that the validity between the parties of a forum-selection clause falls within the scope of § 1404(a), the Court inevitably imports, in my view without adequate textual foundation, a new *retrospective* element into the court's deliberations, requiring examination of what the facts were concerning, among other things, the bargaining power of the parties and the presence or absence of overreaching at the time the contract was made.

...

Second, § 1404(a) was enacted against the background that issues of contract, including a contract's validity, are nearly always governed by state law. It is simply contrary to the practice of our system that such an issue should be wrenched from state control in absence of a clear conflict with federal law or explicit statutory provision. ... It is difficult to believe that state contract law was meant to be pre-empted by [a] provision that we have said "should be regarded as a federal judicial housekeeping measure[.]" *Van Dusen* v. *Barrack* (1964).... It seems to me the generality of its language— "[f]or the convenience of parties and witnesses, in the interest of justice"—is plainly insufficient to work the great change in law asserted here.

Third, it has been common ground in this Court since *Erie*, that when a federal procedural statute or Rule of Procedure is not on point, substantial uniformity of predictable outcome between federal and state courts in adjudicating claims should be striven for. ...Thus, in deciding whether a federal procedural statute or Rule of Procedure encompasses a particular issue, a broad reading that would create significant disuniformity between state and federal courts should be avoided if the text permits. As I have shown, the interpretation given § 1404(a) by the Court today is neither the plain nor the more natural meaning; at best, § 1404(a) is ambiguous. I would therefore construe it to avoid the significant encouragement to forum shopping that will inevitably be provided by the interpretation the Court adopts today.

...

For the reasons stated, I respectfully dissent.

KHALIK v. UNITED AIR LINES
671 F.3d 1188 (10th Cir. 2012)

McKAY, Circuit Judge.

This is an employment-discrimination case the district court dismissed pursuant to Federal Rule of Civil Procedure 12(b)(6) for failure to state a claim. Plaintiff Fedwa Khalik appeals the dismissal, and we affirm.

Plaintiff is an Arab-American, born in Kuwait, who practices Islam. Defendant United Air Lines hired her in 1995, and she rose to the position of Business Services Representative before Defendant terminated her position in 2009. Plaintiff's complaint asserts claims under Title VII of the Civil Rights Act of 1964 for retaliation and discrimination because of race, religion, national origin, and ethnic heritage. Plaintiff's complaint also brings a retaliation claim under the Family and Medical Leave Act (FMLA). Plaintiff also alleged state law claims for discrimination, retaliation, breach of contract, promissory estoppel, and wrongful termination in violation of Colorado public policy.

Since this case turns on the sufficiency of the facts set forth in the complaint, we will now set forth those alleged facts. Plaintiff "was born in Kuwait and is an Arab-American. Both of her parents are Palestinian." "Plaintiff's religion is Islam." Defendant first employed Plaintiff in 1995, and "[s]he performed her job well at all times."' "She rose to the job title of Business Services Representative." "She was physically assaulted in the office (grabbed by the arm) after being subjected to a false investigation and false criticism of her work. She was targeted because of her race, religion, national origin, and ethnic heritage." "Plaintiff complained internally about both discrimination at United Air Lines and being denied FMLA leave." "She complained about an email sent by a United Air Lines employee discussing a possible sexual liaison with an underage girl (which constituted a threat of criminal violation endangering the public)." Defendant's "reasons given for plaintiff's termination and other mistreatment as described herein were exaggerated and false, giving rise to a presumption of discrimination, retaliation and wrongful termination."

More than two months after Defendant filed its motion to dismiss and three weeks after the deadline to amend pleadings had passed, Plaintiff sought to amend her complaint by adding the following sentence: "The above-stated actions against plaintiff were taken because of plaintiff's race, religion, national origin, ethnic heritage and in retaliation for reporting discrimination, seeking an FMLA leave, and reporting a criminal act by a United Air Lines employee that endangered the public." The district court denied Plaintiff's motion to amend as futile and untimely and granted Defendant's motion to dismiss the federal claims for failure to state a claim. ... This appeal followed.

DISCUSSION

We review a district court's dismissal under Federal Rule of Civil Procedure 12(b)(6) de novo. Under Federal Rule of Civil Procedure 8(a)(2), a pleading must contain "a short and plain statement of the claim showing that the pleader is entitled to relief." Recently, the Supreme Court clarified this pleading standard in *Bell Atlantic Corp. v. Twombly* (2007) and *Ashcroft v. Iqbal* (2009): to withstand a Rule 12(b)(6) motion to dismiss, a complaint must contain enough allegations of fact, taken as true, "to state a claim to relief that is plausible on its face." *Twombly*. A plaintiff must "nudge [his] claims across the line from conceivable to plausible" in order to survive a motion to dismiss. *Id.*

The Court explained two principles underlying the new standard: (1) when legal conclusions are involved in the complaint "the tenet that a court must accept as true all of the allegations contained in a complaint is inapplicable to [those] conclusions," *Iqbal*, and (2) "only a complaint that states a plausible claim for relief survives a motion to dismiss," *id*. Thus, mere "labels and conclusions" and "a formulaic recitation of the elements of a cause of action" will not suffice. *Twombly*. Accordingly, in examining a complaint under Rule 12(b)(6), we will disregard conclusory statements and look only to whether the remaining, factual allegations plausibly suggest the defendant is liable.

There is disagreement as to whether this new standard requires minimal change or whether it in fact requires a significantly heightened fact-pleading standard. ... In applying this new, refined standard, we have held that plausibility refers "to the scope of the allegations in a complaint: if they are so general that they encompass a wide swath of conduct, much of it innocent, then the plaintiffs 'have not nudged their claims across the line from conceivable to plausible.'" *Robbins v. Oklahoma* (10th Cir. 2008) (quoting *Twombly*). Further, we have noted that "[t]he nature and specificity of the allegations required to state a plausible claim will vary based on context." *Kansas Penn v. Collins* (10th Cir. 2011). Thus, we have concluded the *Twombly/Iqbal* standard is "a middle ground between heightened fact pleading, which is expressly rejected, and allowing complaints that are no more than labels and conclusions or a formulaic recitation of the elements of a cause of action, which the Court stated will not do." *Robbins* (internal quotation marks and citations omitted).

In other words, Rule 8(a)(2) still lives. There is no indication the Supreme Court intended a return to the more stringent pre-Rule 8 pleading requirements. ...

While the 12(b)(6) standard does not require that Plaintiff establish a prima facie case in her complaint, the elements of each alleged cause of action help to determine whether Plaintiff has set forth a plausible claim. Thus, we start by discussing the elements a plaintiff must prove to establish a claim for discrimination and retaliation under Title VII and the FMLA.

Title VII makes it unlawful "to discharge any individual, or otherwise to discriminate against any individual with respect to his compensation, terms, conditions, or privileges of employment, because of such individual's race, color, religion, sex, or national origin." A plaintiff proves a violation of Title VII either by direct evidence of discrimination or by following the burden-shifting framework of *McDonnell Douglas Corp. v. Green* (1973). Under *McDonnell Douglas*, a three-step analysis requires the plaintiff first prove a prima facie case of discrimination. To set forth a prima facie case of discrimination, a plaintiff must establish that (1) she is a member of a protected class, (2) she suffered an adverse employment action, (3) she qualified for the position at issue, and (4) she was treated less favorably than others not in the protected class. The burden then shifts to the defendant to produce a legitimate, non-discriminatory reason for the adverse employment action. If the defendant does so, the burden then shifts back to the plaintiff to show that the plaintiff's protected status was a determinative factor in the employment decision or that the employer's explanation is pretext.

Title VII also makes it unlawful for an employer to retaliate against an employee "because [s]he has opposed any practice made an unlawful employment practice by this subchapter." A plaintiff can similarly establish retaliation either by directly showing that retaliation played a motivating part in the employment decision, or indirectly by relying on the three-part *McDonnell Douglas* framework. To state a prima facie case for retaliation under Title VII, a plaintiff must show "(1) that [s]he engaged in protected opposition to discrimination, (2) that a reasonable employee would have found the challenged action materially adverse, and (3) that a causal connection existed between the protected activity and the materially adverse action." *Id.* (internal quotation marks omitted) (alteration in original).

The FMLA makes it unlawful for an employer to retaliate against an employee for exercising her rights to FMLA leave. Retaliation claims under the FMLA are also subject to the burden-shifting analysis of *McDonnell Douglas*. And again, to establish a prima facie case of retaliation under the FMLA, a plaintiff must show (1) she engaged in protected activity, (2) the employer took a materially adverse action, and (3) there is a causal connection between the two.

We now turn to whether Plaintiff's complaint sufficiently stated plausible claims for relief. As we stated earlier, while Plaintiff is not required to set forth a prima facie case for each element, she is required to set forth plausible claims. We agree with the district court that Plaintiff's allegations are the type of conclusory and formulaic recitations disregarded by the Court in *Iqbal*. Plaintiff's general assertions of discrimination and retaliation, without any details whatsoever of events leading up to her termination, are insufficient to survive a motion to dismiss. ...

Plaintiff's arguments, particularly as framed at oral argument, accuse the district court of having erroneously applied a heightened pleading standard. If true, this would be a troublesome development, especially because in employment discrimination cases where the employers are large corporations, the employee may not know who actually fired her or for what reason. But, the *Twombly/Iqbal* standard recognizes a plaintiff should have at least some relevant information to make the claims plausible on their face.

In this case, several of Plaintiff's allegations are not entitled to the assumption of truth because they are entirely conclusory, including her allegations that: (1) she was targeted because of her race, religion, national origin and ethnic heritage; (2) she was subjected to a false investigation and false criticism; and (3) Defendant's stated reasons for the termination and other adverse employment actions were exaggerated and false, giving rise to a presumption of discrimination, retaliation, and wrongful termination.

Striking those conclusory allegations leaves us with the following facts, which we take as true: (1) Plaintiff is an Arab-American who was born in Kuwait; (2) Plaintiff's religion is Islam; (3) Plaintiff performed her job well; (4) Plaintiff was grabbed by the arm in the office; (5) Plaintiff complained internally about discrimination; (6) Plaintiff also complained internally about being denied FMLA leave; (7) Plaintiff complained about an email that described a criminal act; and (8) Defendant terminated Plaintiff's employment position. These facts do not sufficiently allege discrimination or retaliation. There is no context for when Plaintiff complained, or to whom. There are no allegations of similarly situated employees who were treated differently. There are no facts relating to the alleged discrimination. There is no nexus between the person(s) to whom she complained and the person who fired her. Indeed, there is nothing other than sheer speculation to link the arm-grabbing and/or termination to a discriminatory or retaliatory motive. And finally, Plaintiff alleges nothing that would link her request for FMLA leave, which she provides no details about, to her termination.

While we do not mandate the pleading of any specific facts in particular, there are certain details the Plaintiff should know and could properly plead to satisfy the plausibility requirement. For instance, Plaintiff should know when she requested FMLA leave and for what purpose. She should know who she requested leave from and who denied her. She should know generally when she complained about not receiving leave and when she was terminated. She should know details about how Defendant treated her compared to other non-Arabic or non-Muslim employees. She should know the reasons Defendant gave her for termination and why in her belief those reasons were pretextual. She should know who grabbed her by the arm, what the context for that action was, and when it occurred. She should know why she believed that action was connected with discriminatory animus. She should know who she complained to about the discrimination, when she complained, and what the response was. She should know who criticized her work, what that criticism was, and how she responded. But in fact, Plaintiff offers none of this detail. To be sure, we are not suggesting a court necessarily require each of the above facts. But a plaintiff must include some further detail for a claim to be plausible. Plaintiff's claims are based solely on the fact that she is Muslim and Arab-American, that she complained about discrimination, that she complained about the denial of FMLA leave, and that Defendant terminated her. Without more, her claims are not plausible under the *Twombly/Iqbal* standard.

CONCLUSION

For the foregoing reasons, we AFFIRM the district court's dismissal.

HAHN v. OFFICE & PROFESSIONAL EMPLOYEES INTERNATIONAL UNION, AFL–CIO
107 F.Supp.3d 379 (S.D.N.Y. 2015)
OPINION AND ORDER

JOHN G. KOELTL, District Judge:

The plaintiff, John J. Hahn, brings this action against Office and Professional Employees International Union, AFL–CIO (the "International Union") and Office and Professional Employees International Union, Local 153 ("Local 153"), alleging two claims pursuant to the Family Medical Leave Act ("FMLA" or "Act"), 29 U.S.C. § 2601 et seq. The International Union now moves to dismiss for failure to serve process pursuant to Federal Rules of Civil Procedure 12(b)(5) and 4(m)....

I.

The following factual allegations are construed in the light most favorable to the plaintiff.

The plaintiff is an individual and a resident of Staten Island, New York. The International Union is a labor union, the Office and Professional Employees International Union ("OPEIU"), with its principal place of business in New York. Local 153 is a local member of OPEIU with its principal place of business in New York.

In October, 2000, Michael Goodwin, the President of the International Union, interviewed Hahn in the International Union's offices. Goodwin assigned Hahn to be a Business Representative at Local 153. Hahn worked in this position with a strong level of commitment until he fell ill in January 2010.

During his employment, Hahn was required to have contact with both Goodwin and Richard Lanigan, who was the Vice President of the International Union and Secretary–Treasurer of Local 153. The International Union and Local 153 shared the same office space, support staff, mail room, supply room, break room, and printers. Goodwin and Lanigan each exercised common management over both unions, and were both aware of all financial and other business-related issues of each union. Goodwin and Lanigan also provided guidance to, established policies for, and were responsible for discipline of the employees assigned to Local 153. Both unions had a pension plan overseen by the same individual, and Goodwin co-chaired the Pension Plan and the Health Plan for Local 153. The two unions held monthly staff meetings in Goodwin's International Union office, where Goodwin was kept up to date on the business activities of Local 153. From time to time, Goodwin instructed Hahn to attend political events on behalf of both the International Union and Local 153, and on one occasion, assigned Hahn to work temporarily for another Local OPEIU division in Southern California. The International Union and Local 153, together, employed more than 50 people working within 75 miles of Mr. Hahn's place of employment.

As a result of his illness, during January and early February of 2010, Hahn was frequently absent from work and was ultimately terminated on or about February 10, 2010…. Hahn … brought an action in this Court against Local 153 on February 8, 2013. Local 153 moved for summary judgment on the basis that it did not employ enough employees to fall within the FMLA's reach. … The Court granted the plaintiff the opportunity to file an amended complaint, which the plaintiff did in August 2014. The Amended Complaint, filed on August 15, 2014, named the International Union as an additional defendant and alleged joint employer. Local 153 then moved to dismiss the amended complaint for failure to state a claim. The Court denied that motion.

The plaintiff never served the International Union in the 120–day period after filing the Amended Complaint. Indeed, the plaintiff only served the International Union with the summons and amended complaint in May 2015. The International Union now moves to dismiss pursuant to Rule 12(b)(5) of the Federal Rules of Civil Procedure for failure to serve process.

II.

Rule 12(b)(5) provides for dismissal of a complaint for insufficient service of process. In deciding such a motion, the Court must refer to Rule 4(m), which provides:

> If a defendant is not served within 120 days after the complaint is filed, the court ... must dismiss the action without prejudice against the defendant or order that service be made within a specified time. But if the plaintiff shows good cause for the failure, the court must extend the time for service for an appropriate period.

Fed.R.Civ.P. 4(m). ... If the plaintiff has failed to effectuate service in accordance with Rule 4(m), a court has the discretion to grant an extension of time to serve the defendant with or without good cause. *Zapata v. The City of New York* (2nd Cir. 2007). However, where the allegations against the defendant fail to state a viable claim, an extension would be futile and should not be granted.

III.

In this case, the plaintiff gives no indication of even attempting to serve process on the International Union for almost nine months after amending its complaint to include the International Union as a defendant, and the plaintiff offers no excuse for his failure to do so. Ordinarily in these circumstances, Rule 4(m) would counsel a dismissal of the claims against the International Union without prejudice. But because the claims against the International Union would likely be time-barred if the plaintiff asserted them again, the parties dispute the proper course for the Court to take. The plaintiff requests an extension of time to serve the International Union, and the International Union argues that the claims should be dismissed with prejudice. For the reasons that follow, the Court dismisses the claims against the International Union without prejudice.

A.

"Dismissal for failure to serve within the time period is without prejudice. It may, however, operate as a dismissal with prejudice when the action will be time-barred." *Putnam v. Morris* (citing *Lovelace v. Acme Markets, Inc.,* 820 F.2d 81, 85 (3d Cir. 1987). The statute of limitations for an FMLA claim is two years, or three years for an intentional violation. Even assuming the three-year statute of limitations applies in this case, it ended two days after the plaintiff filed the original complaint on February 8, 2013. Therefore, the statute of limitations has long since run, and if this Court were to dismiss the plaintiff's claims against the International Union without prejudice, the plaintiff could still not reassert them because they would be time-barred.

"Where, as here, good cause is lacking, but the dismissal without prejudice in combination with the statute of limitations would result in a dismissal *with* prejudice ... the district court [should] weigh[ ] the impact that a dismissal or extension would have on the parties." *Zapata* (emphasis in original). As such, the plaintiff requests an extension of time to serve to avoid the statutes of limitations problems that would result from dismissal. But it would be improper for the Court to grant such a request if the plaintiff's claims against the International Union were already time-barred when he first added the International Union as a party in his Amended Complaint on August 15, 2014. By August 15, 2014, the three-year statute of limitations had already run. Therefore, the Court will not extend time for the plaintiff to serve the International Union unless, pursuant to Federal Rule of Civil Procedure 15(c)(1), the amended complaint against the International Union relates back to the original complaint filed against Local 153.

B.

Federal Rule of Civil Procedure [15(c)(1)] lays out three situations in which an amendment to a pleading relates back to the original pleading:

      (A) The law that provides the applicable statute of limitations allows relations back;

      (B) the amendment asserts a claim or defense that arose out of the conduct, transaction, or occurrence set out—or attempted to be set out—in the original pleading; or

      (C) the amendment changes the party or the naming of the party against whom a claim is asserted, if Rule 15(c)(1)(B) is satisfied and if, within the period provided by Rule 4(m) for serving the summons and complaint, the party to be brought in by amendment:

      (i) received such notice of the action that it will not be prejudiced in defending on the merits; and

      (ii) knew or should have known that the action would have been brought against it, but for a mistake concerning the proper party's identity.

Because the FMLA statute of limitations does not provide for relation back, Rule 15(c)(1)(A) is inapplicable to this case. Additionally, Rule 15(c)(1)(B) is applicable only in the sense that it is incorporated into Rule 15(c)(1)(C), which is the proper rule under which the Court makes a relation-back determination for an amendment that changes or adds parties. Accordingly, in order for the claims against the International Union to relate back to the original complaint, both notice requirements of Rule 15(c)(1)(C) must be satisfied.

To satisfy the notice requirement under Rule 15(c)(1)(C)(i), a plaintiff may plead that two defendants are so "closely related in their business activities or linked in their corporate structure" as to have an "identity of interest"; in such a case, "the institution of an action against one party will constitute imputed notice" to the related party later named in an amended complaint. *In re Allbrand Appliance & Television Co., Inc.* (2d Cir. 1989). Although the Court of Appeals in *Allbrand Appliance* analyzed the "identity of interest exception" without deciding if it is valid, courts within the Second Circuit have generally held that it is a valid manner of showing imputed notice to a prospective defendant. A showing of identity of interest requires "substantial structural and corporate identity, such as shared organizers, officers, directors, and offices." *Allbrand Appliance*. In this case, the plaintiff alleges that the International Union and Local 153 shared offices, staff, organizers, and officers, and were generally intertwined in their organizational structures. Accordingly, the plaintiff has shown that notice of this action may be imputed to the International Union for purposes of Rule 15(c)(1)(C)(i).

Rule 15(c)(1)(C)(ii) is more problematic in this case. The plaintiff must show that the International Union knew or should have known that the action would have been brought against it but for a mistake by the plaintiff concerning the "proper party's identity." In *Krupski v. Costa Crociere, S.p.A.* (2010), the Supreme Court explained the requirements of this subsection and held that the key question hinges not on the plaintiff's knowledge, but whether the prospective defendant "knew or should have known that it would have been named as a defendant but for an error" by the plaintiff. If the prospective defendant "understood, or ... should have understood, that he escaped suit during the limitations period only because the plaintiff misunderstood a crucial fact about his identity," then Rule 15(c)(1)(C)(ii) is satisfied. But if "the original complaint and the plaintiff's conduct compel the conclusion that the failure to name the prospective defendant in the original complaint was the result of a fully informed decision as opposed to a mistake concerning the proper defendant's identity, the requirements of Rule 15(c)(1)(C)(ii) are not met."

The plaintiff offers two bases to contend that the International Union should have been aware that the plaintiff intended to bring suit against it. First, the plaintiff argues that the original complaint alleges that Michael Goodwin terminated the plaintiff and Goodwin is the President of the International Union; therefore, the International Union should have known that the plaintiff intended to sue it. But the factual premise of this argument is incorrect: Goodwin does not appear in the original complaint, by name or by title. Although the plaintiff names Goodwin in the Amended Complaint, only the original complaint and any other conduct by the plaintiff in the 120 days after the complaint is filed can put the prospective defendant on notice of a mistake made by the plaintiff.

Second, the plaintiff argues that he mistakenly believed that Local 153 employed eighty-six individuals, when in reality, that number included both Local 153 and International Union employees. However, this argument is overly focused on the plaintiff's knowledge, rather than what the International Union should have known in the 120 days after the complaint was filed. In his original complaint, the plaintiff only mentions the number of Local 153 employees, or the topic of Local 153 employees at all, once, alleging in a generic fashion that Local 153 exceeds the fifty-employee jurisdictional minimum under the FMLA. Local 153 disputed this allegation, and the plaintiff then began gathering documents to support that Local 153 had more than fifty employees. In July 2013, the plaintiff sent a letter to Local 153 listing eighty-six individuals whom the plaintiff mistakenly believed were all employed by Local 153, some of whom were actually employed by the International Union. The plaintiff contends that this letter gave the International Union notice of the plaintiff's mistake. But, even assuming notice of the letter could be imputed to the International Union, the letter was sent after the 120–day period under Rule 4(m).

Moreover, the plaintiff has not identified the type of mistake as to the "proper party's identity" necessary to satisfy Rule 15(c)(1)(C)(ii). In *Krupski*, the plaintiff originally sued a cruise line, which was the wrong party because her passenger ticket stated that only the carrier could be liable. The prospective defendant carrier had reason to know the passenger made a mistake, not only because the defendant corporations were so closely related, but also because they had represented themselves as essentially the same company to the plaintiff, and because the complaint described the carrier's activities and attributed them to the cruise line.

Rather than suing the *wrong* party, as in *Krupski*, "[t]he plaintiff has sued [what he believes is] the right defendant, and simply neglected to sue another defendant who might also be liable." *In re Vitamin C Antitrust Litig.* (E.D.N.Y. 2014). In the original complaint, the plaintiff alleged that he was employed by Local 153, that he worked for Local 153 as a business representative, and that he was unlawfully terminated. As a business representative for Local 153, the plaintiff could be expected to know who his employer was. Indeed, the plaintiff has never suggested that Local 153, who employed and terminated the plaintiff, is not a proper party in this case. Even in instances of a joint-employer relationship, only the primary employer is liable for the FMLA notice violations, and only a firing party is liable for discriminatory firing. With the International Union absent from this case as a defendant, the plaintiff will still be free to argue that Local 153 was his primary employer that terminated him in violation of the FMLA.

Accordingly, the mistake alleged by the plaintiff did not affect his understanding of which one of the two allegedly joint-employers is liable under the FMLA, and the International Union could not have known that, but for a mistake concerning the liable party's identity, the plaintiff would have brought suit against the International Union in the original complaint. Because the plaintiff has not satisfied Rule 15(c)(1)'s requirements, the plaintiff's claims against the International Union were time-barred when he attempted to add the International Union in his Amended Complaint. Therefore, the Court will not exercise its discretion to extend the time for the plaintiff to serve the International Union.

Rule 4(m) provides that if the defendant is not served within 120 days of the filing of the complaint and if the Court does not extend the time for service, the action against the defendant "must" be dismissed "without prejudice." ... Accordingly, the International Union's motion pursuant to Rule 12(b)(5) is granted and the action against the International Union is dismissed without prejudice.

CONCLUSION

The Court has considered all of the arguments raised by the parties. To the extent not specifically addressed, the arguments are either moot or without merit. For the foregoing reasons, the motion to dismiss by the International Union is granted. The amended complaint is dismissed against the International Union without prejudice. The Clerk is directed to close Docket Nos. 59 and 66.

SO ORDERED.

SCHLAGENHAUF v. HOLDER
379 U.S. 104 (1964)

MR. JUSTICE GOLDBERG delivered the opinion of the Court.

This case involves the validity and construction of Rule 35 (a) of the Federal Rules of Civil Procedure as applied to the examination of a defendant in a negligence action. Rule 35 (a) provides:

> Physical and Mental Examination of Persons. (a) Order for examination. In an action in which the mental or physical condition of a party is in controversy, the court in which the action is pending may order him to submit to a physical or mental examination by a physician. The order may be made only on motion for good cause shown and upon notice to the party to be examined and to all other parties and shall specify the time, place, manner, conditions, and scope of the examination and the person or persons by whom it is to be made.

I.

An action based on diversity of citizenship was brought in the District Court seeking damages arising from personal injuries suffered by passengers of a bus which collided with the rear of a tractor-trailer. The named defendants were The Greyhound Corporation, owner of the bus; petitioner, Robert L. Schlagenhauf, the bus driver; Contract Carriers, Inc., owner of the tractor; Joseph L. McCorkhill, driver of the tractor; and National Lead Company, owner of the trailer. Answers were filed by each of the defendants denying negligence.

Greyhound then cross-claimed against Contract Carriers and National Lead for damage to Greyhound's bus, alleging that the collision was due solely to their negligence in that the tractor-trailer was driven at an unreasonably low speed, had not remained in its lane, and was not equipped with proper rear lights. Contract Carriers filed an answer to this cross-claim denying its negligence and asserting "[t]hat the negligence of the driver of the . . . bus [petitioner Schlagenhauf] proximately caused and contributed to . . . Greyhound's damages."

Pursuant to a pretrial order, Contract Carriers filed a letter—which the trial court treated as, and we consider to be, part of the answer—alleging that Schlagenhauf was "not mentally or physically capable" of driving a bus at the time of the accident.

Contract Carriers and National Lead then petitioned the District Court for an order directing petitioner Schlagenhauf to submit to both mental and physical examinations by one specialist in each of the following fields: (1) Internal medicine; (2) Ophthalmology; (3) Neurology; and (4) Psychiatry.

For the purpose of offering a choice to the District Court of one specialist in each field, the petition recommended two specialists in internal medicine, ophthalmology, and psychiatry, respectively, and three specialists in neurology—a total of nine physicians. The petition alleged that the mental and physical condition of Schlagenhauf was "in controversy" as it had been raised by Contract Carriers' answer to Greyhound's cross-claim. This was supported by a brief of legal authorities and an affidavit of Contract Carriers' attorney stating that Schlagenhauf had seen red lights 10 to 15 seconds before the accident, that another witness had seen the rear lights of the trailer from a distance of three-quarters to one-half mile, and that Schlagenhauf had been involved in a prior accident.

The certified record indicates that petitioner's attorneys filed in the District Court a brief in opposition to this petition asserting, among other things, that "the physical and mental condition of the defendant Robert L. Schlagenhauf is not 'in controversy' herein in the sense that these words are used in Rule 35 of the Federal Rules of Civil Procedure; [and] that good cause has not been shown for the multiple examinations prayed for by the cross-defendant . . . ."

While disposition of this petition was pending, National Lead filed its answer to Greyhound's cross-claim and itself "cross-claimed" against Greyhound and Schlagenhauf for damage to its trailer. The answer asserted generally that Schlagenhauf's negligence proximately caused the accident. The cross-claim additionally alleged that Greyhound and Schlagenhauf were negligent "[b]y permitting said bus to be operated over and upon said public highway by the said defendant, Robert L. Schlagenhauf, when both the said Greyhound Corporation and said Robert L. Schlagenhauf knew that the eyes and vision of the said Robert L. Schlagenhauf was [sic] impaired and deficient."

The District Court, on the basis of the petition filed by Contract Carriers, and without any hearing, ordered Schlagenhauf to submit to nine examinations—one by each of the recommended specialists—despite the fact that the petition clearly requested a total of only four examinations.

Petitioner applied for a writ of mandamus in the Court of Appeals against the respondent, the District Court Judge, seeking to have set aside the order requiring his mental and physical examinations. The Court of Appeals denied mandamus.

We granted certiorari to review undecided questions concerning the validity and construction of Rule 35.

IV.

There remains the issue of the construction of Rule 35. We enter upon determination of this construction with the basic premise "that the deposition-discovery rules are to be accorded a broad and liberal treatment," *Hickman v. Taylor* (1947), to effectuate their purpose that "civil trials in the federal courts no longer need be carried on in the dark."

Petitioner contends that even if Rule 35 is to be applied to defendants, which we have determined it must, nevertheless it should not be applied to him as he was not a party in relation to Contract Carriers and National Lead— the movants for the mental and physical examinations —at the time the examinations were sought. The Court of Appeals agreed with petitioner's general legal proposition, holding that the person sought to be examined must be an opposing party *vis-a-vis* the movant (or at least one of them). While it is clear that the person to be examined must be a party to the case, we are of the view that the Court of Appeals gave an unduly restrictive interpretation to that term. Rule 35 only requires that the person to be examined be a party to the "action," not that he be an opposing party *vis-a-vis* the movant. There is no doubt that Schlagenhauf was a "party" to this "action" by virtue of the original complaint. Therefore, Rule 35 permitted examination of him (a party defendant) upon petition of Contract Carriers and National Lead (codefendants), provided, of course, that the other requirements of the Rule were met. Insistence that the movant have filed a pleading against the person to be examined would have the undesirable result of an unnecessary proliferation of cross-claims and counterclaims and would not be in keeping with the aims of a liberal, nontechnical application of the Federal Rules.

While the Court of Appeals held that petitioner was not a party *vis-a-vis* National Lead or Contract Carriers at the time the examinations were first sought, it went on to hold that he had become a party *vis-a-vis* National Lead by the time of a second order entered by the District Court and thus was a party within its rule. This second order, identical in all material respects with the first, was entered on the basis of supplementary petitions filed by National Lead and Contract Carriers. These petitions gave no new basis for the examinations, except for the allegation that petitioner's mental and physical condition had been additionally put in controversy by the National Lead answer and cross-claim, which had been filed subsequent to the first petition for examinations. Although the filing of the petition for mandamus intervened between these two orders, we accept, for purposes of this opinion, the determination of the Court of Appeals that this second order was the one before it and agree that petitioner was clearly a party at this juncture under any test.

Petitioner next contends that his mental or physical condition was not "in controversy" and "good cause" was not shown for the examinations, both as required by the express terms of Rule 35.

The discovery devices sanctioned by Part V of the Federal Rules include the taking of oral and written depositions (Rules 26-32), interrogatories to parties (Rule 33), production of documents (Rule 34), and physical and mental examinations of parties (Rule 35). The scope of discovery in each instance is limited by Rule 26 (b)'s provision that "the deponent may be examined regarding any matter, not privileged, which is *relevant to the subject matter involved* in the pending action" (emphasis added), and by the provisions of Rule 30 (b) permitting the district court, upon motion, to limit, terminate, or otherwise control the use of discovery devices so as to prevent either their use in bad faith or undue "annoyance, embarrassment, or oppression."

It is notable, however, that in none of the other discovery provisions is there a restriction that the matter be "in controversy," and only in Rule 34 is there Rule 35's requirement that the movant affirmatively demonstrate "good cause."

[The] "in controversy" and "good cause" requirements of Rule 35 ... are not met by mere conclusory allegations of the pleadings—nor by mere relevance to the case—but require an affirmative showing by the movant that each condition as to which the examination is sought is really and genuinely in controversy and that good cause exists for ordering each particular examination. Obviously, what may be good cause for one type of examination may not be so for another. The ability of the movant to obtain the desired information by other means is also relevant.

Rule 35, therefore, requires discriminating application by the trial judge, who must decide, as an initial matter in every case, whether the party requesting a mental or physical examination or examinations has adequately demonstrated the existence of the Rule's requirements of "in controversy" and "good cause," which requirements, as the Court of Appeals in this case itself recognized, are necessarily related. This does not, of course, mean that the movant must prove his case on the merits in order to meet the requirements for a mental or physical examination. Nor does it mean that an evidentiary hearing is required in all cases. This may be necessary in some cases, but in other cases the showing could be made by affidavits or other usual methods short of a hearing. It does mean, though, that the movant must produce sufficient information, by whatever means, so that the district judge can fulfill his function mandated by the Rule.

Of course, there are situations where the pleadings alone are sufficient to meet these requirements. A plaintiff in a negligence action who asserts mental or physical injury places that mental or physical injury clearly in controversy and provides the defendant with good cause for an examination to determine the existence and extent of such asserted injury. This is not only true as to a plaintiff, but applies equally to a defendant who asserts his mental or physical condition as a defense to a claim, such as, for example, where insanity is asserted as a defense to a divorce action.

Here, however, Schlagenhauf did not assert his mental or physical condition either in support of or in defense of a claim. His condition was sought to be placed in issue by other parties. Thus, under the principles discussed above, Rule 35 required that these parties make an affirmative showing that petitioner's mental or physical condition was in controversy and that there was good cause for the examination requested. This, the record plainly shows, they failed to do.

The only allegations in the pleadings relating to this subject were the general conclusory statement in Contract Carriers' answer to the cross-claim that "Schlagenhauf was not mentally or physically capable of operating" the bus at the time of the accident and the limited allegation in National Lead's cross-claim that, at the time of the accident, "the eyes and vision of . . . Schlagenhauf was [sic] impaired and deficient."

The attorney's affidavit attached to the petition for the examinations provided:

> That . . . Schlagenhauf, in his deposition . . . admitted that he saw red lights for 10 to 15 seconds prior to a collision with a semi-tractor trailer unit and yet drove his vehicle on without reducing speed and without altering the course thereof.
>
> The only eye-witness to this accident known to this affiant . . . testified that immediately prior to the impact between the bus and truck that he had also been approaching the truck from the rear and that he had clearly seen the lights of the truck for a distance of three-quarters to one-half mile to the rear thereof.
>
> . . . Schlagenhauf has admitted in his deposition. . . that he was involved in a [prior] similar type rear end collision . . . .

This record cannot support even the corrected order which required one examination in each of the four specialties of internal medicine, ophthalmology, neurology, and psychiatry. Nothing in the pleadings or affidavit would afford a basis for a belief that Schlagenhauf was suffering from a mental or neurological illness warranting wide-ranging psychiatric or neurological examinations. Nor is there anything stated justifying the broad internal medicine examination.

The only specific allegation made in support of the four examinations ordered was that the "eyes and vision" of Schlagenhauf were impaired. Considering this in conjunction with the affidavit, we would be hesitant to set aside a visual examination if it had been the only one ordered. However, as the case must be remanded to the District Court because of the other examinations ordered, it would be appropriate for the District Judge to reconsider also this order in light of the guidelines set forth in this opinion.

The Federal Rules of Civil Procedure should be liberally construed, but they should not be expanded by disregarding plainly expressed limitations. The "good cause" and "in controversy" requirements of Rule 35 make it very apparent that sweeping examinations of a party who has not affirmatively put into issue his own mental or physical condition are not to be automatically ordered merely because the person has been involved in an accident —or, as in this case, two accidents—and a general charge of negligence is lodged. Mental and physical examinations are only to be ordered upon a discriminating application by the district judge of the limitations prescribed by the Rule. To hold otherwise would mean that such examinations could be ordered routinely in automobile accident cases. The plain language of Rule 35 precludes such an untoward result.

Accordingly, the judgment of the Court of Appeals is vacated and the case remanded to the District Court to reconsider the examination order in light of the guidelines herein formulated and for further proceedings in conformity with this opinion.

Vacated and remanded.

[opinion of Mr. JUSTICE BLACK concurring in part and dissenting in part omitted.]

MR. JUSTICE DOUGLAS, dissenting in part.

While I join the Court in reversing this judgment, I would, on the remand, deny all relief asked under Rule 35.

... When the defendant's doctors examine plaintiff, they are normally interested only in answering a single question: did plaintiff in fact sustain the specific injuries claimed? But plaintiff's doctors will naturally be inclined to go on a fishing expedition in search of *anything* which will tend to prove that the defendant was unfit to perform the acts which resulted in the plaintiff's injury. And a doctor for a fee can easily discover something wrong with any patient— a condition that in prejudiced medical eyes might have caused the accident. Once defendants are turned over to medical or psychiatric clinics for an analysis of their physical well-being and the condition of their psyche, the effective trial will be held there and not before the jury. There are no lawyers in those clinics to stop the doctor from probing this organ or that one, to halt a further inquiry, to object to a line of questioning. And there is no judge to sit as arbiter. The doctor or the psychiatrist has a holiday in the privacy of his office. The defendant is at the doctor's (or psychiatrist's) mercy; and his report may either overawe or confuse the jury and prevent a fair trial. ...

[Dissenting opinion of JUSTICE HARLAN omitted.]

SPAULDING v. ZIMMERMAN
116 N.W.2d 704 (Minn. 1962)

THOMAS GALLAGHER, Justice.

Appeal from an order of the District Court of Douglas County vacating and setting aside a prior order of such court dated May 8, 1957, approving a settlement made on behalf of David Spaulding on March 5, 1957, at which time he was a minor of the age of 20 years; and in connection therewith, vacating and setting aside releases executed by him and his parents, a stipulation of dismissal, an order for dismissal with prejudice, and a judgment entered pursuant thereto.

The prior action was brought against defendants by Theodore Spaulding, as father and natural guardian of David Spaulding, for injuries sustained by David in an automobile accident, arising out of a collision which occurred August 24, 1956, between an automobile driven by John Zimmerman, in which David was a passenger, and one owned by John Ledermann and driven by Florian Ledermann.

On appeal defendants contend that the court was without jurisdiction to vacate the settlement solely because their counsel then possessed information, unknown to plaintiff herein, that at the time he was suffering from an aorta aneurysm which may have resulted from the accident, because (1) no mutual mistake of fact was involved; (2) no duty rested upon them to disclose information to plaintiff which they could assume had been disclosed to him by his own physicians; (3) insurance limitations as well as physical injuries formed the basis for the settlement; and (4) plaintiff's motion to vacate the order for settlement and to set aside the releases was barred by the limitations provided in Rule 60.02 of Rules of Civil Procedure.[1]

After the accident, David's injuries were diagnosed by his family physician, Dr. James H. Cain, as a severe crushing injury of the chest with multiple rib fractures; a severe cerebral concussion, probably with petechial hemorrhages of the brain; and bilateral fractures of the clavicles. At Dr. Cain's suggestion, on January 3, 1957, David was examined by Dr. John F. Pohl, an orthopedic specialist, who made X-ray studies of his chest. Dr. Pohl's detailed report of this examination included the following: "... The lung fields are clear. The heart and aorta are normal."

Nothing in such report indicated the aorta aneurysm with which David was then suffering. On March 1, 1957, at the suggestion of Dr. Pohl, David was examined from a neurological viewpoint by Dr. Paul S. Blake, and in the report of this examination there was no finding of the aorta aneurysm.

In the meantime, on February 22, 1957, at defendants' request, David was examined by Dr. Hewitt Hannah, a neurologist. On February 26, 1957, the latter reported to Messrs. Field, Arveson, & Donoho, attorneys for defendant John Zimmerman, as follows:

> The one feature of the case which bothers me more than any other part of the case is the fact that this boy of 20 years of age has an aneurysm, which means a dilatation of the aorta and the arch of the aorta. Whether this came out of this accident I cannot say with any degree of certainty .... Of course an aneurysm or dilatation of the aorta in a boy of this age is a serious matter as far as his life. This aneurysm may dilate further and it might rupture with further dilatation and this would cause his death.

> It would be interesting also to know whether the X-ray of his lungs, taken immediately following the accident, shows this dilatation or not. If it was not present immediately following the accident and is now present, then we could be sure that it came out of the accident.

Prior to the negotiations for settlement, the contents of the above report were made known to counsel for defendants Florian and John Ledermann.

The case was called for trial on March 4, 1957, at which time the respective parties and their counsel possessed such information as to David's physical condition as was revealed to them by their respective medical examiners as above described. It is thus apparent that neither David nor his father, the nominal plaintiff in the prior action, was then aware that David was suffering the aorta aneurysm but on the contrary believed that he was recovering from the injuries sustained in the accident.

On the following day an agreement for settlement was reached wherein, in consideration of the payment of $6,500, David and his father agreed to settle in full for all claims arising out of the accident.

Richard S. Roberts, counsel for David, thereafter presented to the court a petition for approval of the settlement, wherein David's injuries were described as: "... severe crushing of the chest, with multiple rib fractures, severe cerebral concussion, with petechial hemorrhages of the brain, bilateral fractures of the clavicles."

Attached to the petition were affidavits of David's physicians, Drs. James H. Cain and Paul S. Blake, wherein they set forth the same diagnoses they had made upon completion of their respective examinations of David as above described. At no time was there information disclosed to the court that David was then suffering from an aorta aneurysm which may have been the result of the accident. Based upon the petition for settlement and such affidavits of Drs.

Cain and Blake, the court on May 8, 1957, made its order approving the settlement.

Early in 1959, David was required by the army reserve, of which he was a member, to have a physical checkup. For this, he again engaged the services of Dr. Cain. In this checkup, the latter discovered the aorta aneurysm. He then reexamined the X rays which had been taken shortly after the accident and at this time discovered that they disclosed the beginning of the process which produced the aneurysm. He promptly sent David to Dr. Jerome Grismer for an examination and opinion. The latter confirmed the finding of the aorta aneurysm and recommended immediate surgery therefor. This was performed by him at Mount Sinai Hospital in Minneapolis on March 10, 1959.

Shortly thereafter, David, having attained his majority, instituted the present action for additional damages due to the more serious injuries including the aorta aneurysm which he alleges proximately resulted from the accident. As indicated above, the prior order for settlement was vacated. In a memorandum made a part of the order vacating the settlement, the court stated:

> The facts material to a determination of the motion are without substantial dispute. The only disputed facts appear to be whether ... Mr. Roberts, former counsel for plaintiff, discussed plaintiff's injuries with Mr. Arvesen, counsel for defendant Zimmerman, immediately before the settlement agreement, and, further, whether or not there is a causal relationship between the accident and the aneurysm.

> Contrary to the ... suggestion in the affidavit of Mr. Roberts that he discussed the minor's injuries with Mr. Arvesen, the Court finds that no such discussion of the specific injuries claimed occurred prior to the settlement agreement on March 5, 1957.

> ... the Court finds that although the aneurysm now existing is causally related to the accident, such finding is for the purpose of the motions only and is based solely upon the opinion expressed by Dr. Cain (Exhibit 'F'), which, so far as the Court can find from the numerous affidavits and statements of fact by counsel, stands without dispute.

The mistake concerning the existence of the aneurysm was not mutual. For reasons which do not appear, plaintiff's doctor failed to ascertain its existence. By reason of the failure of plaintiff's counsel to use available rules of discovery, plaintiff's doctor and all his representatives did not learn that defendants and their agents knew of its existence and possible serious consequences. Except for the character of the concealment in the light of plaintiff's minority, the Court would, I believe, be justified in denying plaintiff's motion to vacate, leaving him to whatever questionable remedy he may have against his doctor and against his lawyer.

That defendants' counsel concealed the knowledge they had is not disputed. The essence of the application of the above rule is the character of the concealment. Was it done under circumstances that defendants must be charged with knowledge that plaintiff did not know of the injury? If so, an enriching advantage was gained for defendants at plaintiff's expense. There is no doubt of the good faith of both defendants' counsel. There is no doubt that during the course of the negotiations, when the parties were in an adversary relationship, no rule required or duty rested upon defendants or their representatives to disclose this knowledge. However, once the agreement to settle was reached, it is difficult to characterize the parties' relationship as adverse. At this point all parties were interested in securing Court approval....

But it is not possible to escape the inference that defendants' representatives knew, or must be here charged with knowing, that plaintiff under all the circumstances would not accept the sum of $6500.00 if he or his representatives knew of the aneurysm and its possible serious consequences. Moreover, there is no showing by defendants that would support an inference that plaintiff and his representatives knew of the existence of the aneurysm but concluded that it was not causally related to the accident.

When the adversary nature of the negotiations concluded in a settlement, the procedure took on the posture of a joint application to the Court, at least so far as the facts upon which the Court could and must approve settlement is concerned. It is here that the true nature of the concealment appears, and defendants' failure to act affirmatively, after having been given a copy of the application for approval, can only be defendants' decision to take a calculated risk that the settlement would be final. ...

To hold that the concealment was not of such character as to result in an unconscionable advantage over plaintiff's ignorance or mistake, would be to penalize innocence and incompetence and reward less than full performance of an officer of the Court's duty to make full disclosure to the Court when applying for approval in minor settlement proceedings.

1. The principals applicable to the court's authority to vacate settlements made on behalf of minors and approved by it appear well established. With reference thereto, we have held that the court in its discretion may vacate such a settlement, even though it is not induced by fraud or bad faith, where it is shown that in the accident the minor sustained separate and distinct injuries which were not known or considered by the court at the time settlement was approved; and even though the releases furnished therein purported to cover both known and unknown injuries resulting from the accident. The court may vacate such a settlement for mistake even though the mistake was not mutual in the sense that both parties were similarly mistaken as to the nature and extent of the minor's injuries, but where it is shown that one of the parties had

additional knowledge with respect thereto and was aware that neither the court nor the adversary party possessed such knowledge when the settlement was approved. As stated in Keller v. Wolf, 239 Minn. 397, 401, 58 N.W.2d 891, 895:

> ... although in Minnesota the mistake need not be "mutual" ... there must be concealment or, at least, knowledge on the part of one party that the other party is laboring under a mistake in order to set aside a release for unilateral mistake. Equity will prevent one party from taking an unconscionable advantage of another's mistake for the purpose of enriching himself at the other's expense.

2. From the foregoing it is clear that in the instant case the court did not abuse its discretion in setting aside the settlement which it had approved on plaintiff's behalf while he was still a minor. It is undisputed that neither he nor his counsel nor his medical attendants were aware that at the time settlement was made he was suffering from an aorta aneurysm which may have resulted from the accident. The seriousness of this disability is indicated by Dr. Hannah's report indicating the imminent danger of death therefrom. This was known by counsel for both defendants but was not disclosed to the court at the time it was petitioned to approve the settlement. While no canon of ethics or legal obligation may have required them to inform plaintiff or his counsel with respect thereto, or to advise the court therein, it did become obvious to them at the time, that the settlement then made did not contemplate or take into consideration the disability described. This fact opened the way for the court to later exercise its discretion in vacating the settlement and under the circumstances described we cannot say that there was any abuse of discretion on the part of the court in so doing under Rule 60.02(6) of Rules of Civil Procedure.

....

Affirmed.

ROGOSHESKE, J., took no part in the consideration or decision of this case.

[1] Rule 60.02 of Rules of Civil Procedure provides in part:

> On motion ... the court may relieve a party ... from a final ... order, or proceeding for the following reasons: (1) Mistake, inadvertence, surprise, or excusable neglect; (2) newly discovered evidence which by due diligence could not have been discovered in time to move for a new trial under Rule 59.03; (3) fraud (whether ... intrinsic or extrinsic), misrepresentation, or other misconduct of an adverse party; ... or (6) any other reason justifying relief from the operation of the judgment. ... This rule does not limit the power of a court to entertain an independent action to relieve a party from a judgment, order, or proceeding, ... or to set aside a judgment for fraud upon the court.

HERNANDEZ-CUEVAS v. TAYLOR
836 F.3d 116 (CA1 2016)

LIPEZ, Circuit Judge.

We revisit here appellant Carlos Hernandez-Cuevas's ("Hernandez") Fourth Amendment claim of malicious prosecution, actionable under *Bivens v. Six Unknown Named Agents of Federal Bureau of Narcotics* (1971). We first encountered Hernandez's case when defendants William Taylor and Steven Martz—both FBI special agents ("SAs")—brought an interlocutory appeal challenging the district court's denial of qualified immunity. We affirmed, concluding that the facts alleged in Hernandez's complaint, viewed in the light most favorable to him, stated a plausible claim that Taylor and Martz violated Hernandez's "Fourth Amendment right to be free from seizure but upon probable cause." The case returned to the district court for trial. After Hernandez presented his evidence, the court granted Taylor and Martz's motion for judgment as a matter of law and dismissed the case with prejudice. We agree that a reasonable jury would not have a legally sufficient evidentiary basis to find for Hernandez, and we detect no other legal error in the district court's decision. We therefore affirm.

I.

Hernandez filed suit against Martz and Taylor on March 2, 2009, alleging that they were responsible for his being held in federal custody for three months without probable cause. Taylor and Martz filed a motion to dismiss the claims against them, arguing that they were entitled to qualified immunity. The district court denied the motion, Taylor and Martz filed an interlocutory appeal, and we affirmed the district court's judgment. ... [W]e reviewed Hernandez's complaint and determined that he had alleged a plausible claim that Taylor and Martz caused him to be held in federal custody without probable cause. We thus remanded the case to the district court for further proceedings.

In district court, the parties began discovery, and Martz and Taylor moved for summary judgment. The magistrate judge denied the defendants' motion, and the case went to trial. After the testimony of only three witnesses—Hernandez, Martz, and Taylor—Hernandez rested his case. The defendants then moved for judgment as a matter of law, under Federal Rule of Civil Procedure 50(a). A court may grant a motion for judgement [*sic*] as a matter of law "[i]f a party has been fully heard on an issue during a jury trial and the court finds that a reasonable jury would not have a legally sufficient evidentiary basis to find for the party on that issue." Fed. R. Civ. P. 50(a)(1).

The magistrate judge granted the motion, concluding that "Plaintiff Hern[a]ndez-Cuevas ha[d] failed to prove that Defendants Taylor and Martz caused a seizure of [Hernandez] pursuant to a legal process unsupported by probable cause." Concerning the first element of a malicious prosecution claim, causation, the magistrate judge found that Hernandez had not presented any evidence to prove that Taylor and Martz "tainted or arranged" the photo array presented to the informant or that Taylor made statements in his affidavit that "amounted to 'deliberate falsehood or reckless disregard for the truth.'" (quotation omitted). The magistrate judge also addressed the civil conspiracy alleged in Hernandez's complaint and concluded that "[n]o evidence was presented of an agreement between agents Taylor and Martz to inflict a wrong against or injury upon [Hernandez]." Hernandez's timely appeal followed.

II.

We review de novo a district court's grant of a Rule 50(a) motion for judgment as a matter of law, taking the evidence in the light most favorable to the nonmovant. ... We review evidentiary rulings for abuse of discretion if the objecting party has preserved the issue.

A. Fourth Amendment Malicious Prosecution Claim

Hernandez argues that he provided sufficient evidence for a reasonable jury to conclude that he established malicious prosecution in violation of the Fourth Amendment. In order to establish such a violation, Hernandez had to demonstrate that Taylor and Martz "(1) caused (2) a seizure of [Hernandez] pursuant to legal process unsupported by probable cause, and (3) criminal proceedings terminated in [Hernandez's] favor." *Hernandez I.*

To satisfy the first element, causation, Hernandez was required to "demonstrate that law enforcement officers were responsible for his continued, unreasonable pretrial detention." *Id.* Such responsibility may be established by showing that the officers "ma[d]e, influence[d], or participate[d] in the decision to prosecute," *Sykes v. Anderson* (6th Cir. 2010) (quotation omitted) by, for example, "(1) 'l[ying] to or misle[ading] the prosecutors'; (2) 'fail[ing] to disclose exculpatory evidence'; or (3) 'unduly pressur[ing] the prosecutor to seek the indictment,'" *Hernandez I* (quotation omitted). Thus, when establishing causation, the plaintiff must demonstrate that the actions or statements of law enforcement officers "amounted to 'deliberate falsehood or ... reckless disregard for the truth.'" *Hernandez I* (quotation omitted).

Hernandez argues on appeal that the photo array "created at the direction of Martz," and "Taylor's fabricated testimony" in his affidavit, provided "sufficient evidence ... to indicate that Defendants made representations that amounted to deliberate falsehoods or reckless disregard for the truth," and thus caused his seizure without probable cause. We take these two allegations of wrongdoing in turn.

1. The Photographic Array

As the parties stipulated before trial, Martz provided the DMV photo of Hernandez to FBI Newark's photo lab, and, "[c]onsistent with FBI policy, the FBI lab created a photo array which contained Hernandez's photograph, along with five other similar looking individuals." In *Hernandez I*, we concluded that

> [a]lthough the complaint does not specify how the co-conspirators tainted the photo array, Hernandez-Cuevas has pled sufficient facts to support a reasonable inference that something was amiss. Specifically, Hernandez-Cuevas has alleged that rather than selecting a photograph of someone matching the description of [the courier]—short, stocky, and nearly sixty—[the informant] picked a photograph of Hernandez-Cuevas, who was tall, thin, and only forty.

At trial, however, Hernandez did not present any evidence to support the allegation that the array was tainted. To the contrary, [the SA's surveillance report]—which describes the courier as "short, stocky, and nearly sixty," and does not closely resemble Hernandez—was not the only available description of the courier. The record established that the DMV description of Hernandez as forty years old, 5'11", of "medio marrón" complexion, and 185 pounds, matched, at least in part, the informant's description of the courier as approximately forty years old, 5'10", black, and having a big stomach. As the parties stipulated before trial, "FBI agents routinely rely on descriptions provided by witnesses, including [confidential informants], who have face to face interactions with the subject of investigation, given their opportunity to observe the physical characteristics of the subjects."

Furthermore, the courier was last seen at 1655 Santa Ana Street, and [an FBI] report identified Hernandez as the only male officially associated with that address. After receiving the DMV description and the photo of Hernandez from FBI San Juan, Martz testified that he "believed we had enough evidence, based on the investigation." Hernandez presented no evidence at trial to rebut this testimony, to establish that Martz tainted the photo array, or to establish that Martz and Taylor worked in concert with the informant to identify Hernandez.

2. Taylor's Affidavit

As for proving that Taylor "either knowingly or with reckless disregard for the truth made [false] sworn statements in a warrant affidavit" that Hernandez was the courier, Hernandez's case again fails. When initially questioned by Hernandez's counsel at trial, Taylor testified that he "gave consideration to" [the] surveillance report describing the courier as in his late fifties, 5'7", and heavy, but that he also looked to "the body wire [recording], the debriefing of the [informant]," as well as "the utilities check, [and] the other spot surveillance" to corroborate the statement made in his affidavit identifying Hernandez as the courier.

When cross-examined by his own attorney, Taylor stated that he believed that the description of the courier provided by the informant "matched remarkably accurately" the DMV description of Hernandez. Taylor testified that his statement in his affidavit as to his knowledge of the facts of the investigation was "[o]ne hundred percent" truthful. On re-direct, Hernandez's attorney questioned Taylor about the August 10 transcription date of Martz's FBI report (detailing the informant's description of the courier) and whether Taylor was in Puerto Rico on the date of the transaction. Neither line of questioning, however, undermined his previous testimony or provided a sufficient basis for a jury to conclude that Taylor deliberately or recklessly included false statements in his affidavit.

In light of Taylor's unrebutted testimony, Hernandez did not establish "a legally sufficient evidentiary basis," Fed. R. Civ. P. 50(a), for a reasonable jury to conclude that Taylor "made statements in the warrant affidavit which amounted to 'deliberate falsehood or ... reckless disregard for the truth.'" *Hernandez I* (quotation omitted).

In sum, although we concluded in *Hernandez I* that Hernandez's complaint provided sufficiently plausible allegations to make out a malicious prosecution *Bivens* claim, the evidence that Hernandez presented at trial did not bear out his original allegations with respect to either Martz or Taylor. To the contrary, the limited evidence presented at trial revealed that the confluence of matching physical features and residence led the agents to Hernandez. Hence, the record is insufficient to permit the jury to conclude "that law enforcement officers were responsible for [Hernandez's] continued, unreasonable pretrial detention," as required by the causation element of a Fourth Amendment malicious prosecution claim. Hence, we need not examine the remaining two elements of Hernandez's claim.

PORN v. NATIONAL GRANGE MUTUAL INSURANCE COMPANY
93 F.3d 31 (CA1 1996)

STAHL, Circuit Judge.

Having successfully sued his insurer, National Grange Mutual Insurance Company ("National Grange"), six months earlier for breach of contract in refusing to pay his claim for underinsured motorist benefits incurred during a July 1990 car accident, plaintiff-appellant Daryl E. Porn brought this diversity action in Maine's federal district court against National Grange seeking additional damages for its alleged mishandling of his underinsured motorist claim. The district court granted summary judgment in favor of National Grange based on ... res judicata (claim preclusion), concluding that an issue underlying one of Porn's claims had been decided in the earlier proceeding and that all of Porn's claims could have been raised therein. Porn appeals the district court's summary judgment order. Finding no error, we affirm.

I.

On July 17, 1990, Porn, a Connecticut resident, was involved in an automobile accident in Portland, Maine, when motorist Lori Willoughby sped through a stop sign and broad-sided his vehicle. Because his damages exceeded Willoughby's $20,000 policy limit, Porn made a claim to National Grange under his automobile policy seeking recovery from the underinsured motorist indorsement to the policy. For reasons not apparent in the record, National Grange refused to pay the claim.

Disgruntled by this refusal, Porn wrote to National Grange accusing it of bad faith in handling his claim and threatening legal action. Porn sent copies of his letter to the insurance commissioners of Connecticut and Massachusetts. National Grange, unimpressed, remained steadfast in its refusal to pay, and in November 1993, Porn filed suit against National Grange in Maine's federal district court for breach of the insurance contract ("first action").

Because Porn's policy with National Grange required a finding of legal liability on the part of the underinsured motorist as a condition precedent to the payment of benefits, the two-day trial before the magistrate judge] focused on the question of Willoughby's negligence and Porn's contributory negligence. Following the completion of the evidence, the magistrate judge entered judgment as a matter of law for Porn on the issue of contributory negligence, and the jury returned a verdict for Porn, finding that Willoughby's negligence had caused him $400,000 worth of damages. After reducing the jury's award to reflect Porn's $300,000 underinsured motorist policy limit and appropriate set-offs, the magistrate judge entered judgment for Porn in the amount of $255,314.40. The magistrate judge denied Porn's motion for prejudgment interest, finding that while Maine law allows prejudgment interest in excess of the policy limit where the insurer acted in bad faith and needlessly prolonged the litigation, Porn had presented no evidence that National Grange exhibited such behavior.

Six months later, Porn commenced this action against National Grange in Maine's federal district court ("second action"). This time Porn alleged that National Grange's conduct in handling his underinsured motorist claim constituted breach of the covenant of good faith, intentional infliction of emotional distress, negligent infliction of emotional distress, and violations of the Connecticut Unfair Insurance Practices Act and the Connecticut Unfair Trade Practices Act. National Grange moved for summary judgment, arguing that the judgment in the first action precluded Porn from bringing the second action. The district court accepted that argument and granted summary judgment in favor of National Grange on the grounds that (1) one aspect of Porn's bad-faith claim was barred by issue preclusion and (2) all of Porn's claims were barred by claim preclusion.

In reaching its first holding, the district court explained that the magistrate judge's decision not to award Porn prejudgment interest was based in part on his finding that Porn had presented no evidence to suggest that National Grange acted in bad faith and needlessly prolonged the litigation. Accordingly, the court concluded that the question of National Grange's alleged bad-faith conduct in litigating the first action was raised and decided in the first action, and, therefore, to the extent Porn's bad-faith claim involved National Grange's conduct during the first action, it was barred by issue preclusion.

In reaching its broader holding that all five of Porn's claims were barred by claim preclusion, the district court reasoned that once Porn chose to bring the first action against National Grange for breach of contract, he was required to raise all his claims arising from the breach or else forfeit the right to do so. Because it found that Porn's five tort and statutory claims, like the earlier breach of contract claim, involved National Grange's obligations arising under the insurance policy, the district court concluded that they should have been brought in the first action and therefore were barred by claim preclusion from being raised in the second action.

II.

Porn appeals the district court's grant of summary judgment in favor of National Grange, arguing that the judgment in the first action for breach of contract does not preclude his bad-faith, emotional distress, and statutory unfair practices claims (collectively "bad-faith claim") against National Grange in this action. Specifically, Porn argues that (1) the facts relevant to his bad-faith claim are separate from those relevant to his contract claim, (2) the bad-faith facts do not form a convenient trial unit with the contract facts, (3) treatment of both sets of facts as a unit does not conform to the parties' expectations, and (4) it was inequitable to apply the res judicata bar where, as here, the insurer's conduct in the contract litigation forms part of the bad-faith action. After reciting the standard of review and setting forth the governing res judicata law, we consider each argument in turn.

We review a grant of summary judgment *de novo,* under the same standards that govern the district court, to determine whether "the pleadings, depositions, answers to interrogatories, and admissions on file, together with the affidavits, if any, show that there is no genuine issue as to any material fact and that the moving party is entitled to judgment as a matter of law." Fed.R.Civ.P. 56(c). The applicability of the doctrine of res judicata is a question of law subject to plenary review.

Because the judgment in the first action was rendered by a federal court, the preclusive effect of that judgment in the instant diversity action is governed by federal res judicata principles. Under the federal law of res judicata, a final judgment on the merits of an action precludes the parties from relitigating claims that were raised or could have been raised in that action. For a claim to be precluded, the following elements must be established: (1) a final judgment on the merits in an earlier action, (2) sufficient identity between the causes of action asserted in the earlier and later suits, and (3) sufficient identity between the parties in the two suits. Because there is no dispute that the first and third elements of the test are established, we focus on the second element: whether the causes of action in the two lawsuits are sufficiently identical.

In defining the cause of action for res judicata purposes, this circuit has adopted the "transactional" approach of the Restatement (Second) of Judgments. Under this approach, a valid and final judgment in the first action will extinguish subsequent claims "with respect to all or any part of the transaction, or series of connected transactions, out of which the action arose." *Id.* (quoting Restatement (Second) of Judgments § 24 (1982)). We determine what factual grouping constitutes a "transaction" pragmatically, giving weight to such factors as "whether the facts are related in time, space, origin, or motivation, whether they form a convenient trial unit, and whether their treatment as a unit conforms to the parties' expectations." Restatement § 24. These factors, however, are merely suggestive; they are not intended to be exhaustive, nor is any one factor determinative. Finally, in making this determination, we are mindful that a single transaction may give rise to a multiplicity of claims ....

A. Consideration of the Restatement Factors

With that background, we inquire whether the causes of action asserted in the first and second suits are sufficiently identical, focusing on the three Restatement factors.

1. Relation of the Facts in Time, Space, Origin, or Motivation

The first Restatement factor asks whether the facts underlying the breach of contract and bad-faith claims are related in time, space, origin, or motivation, *i.e.*, whether they arise out of the same transaction, seek redress for essentially the same basic wrong, and rest on the same or a substantially similar factual basis. In this case, our answers to these questions lead us to conclude that the facts underlying the two claims are closely related.

First, we find that both the bad-faith claim and the contract claim derive from the same occurrence: National Grange's refusal to pay Porn the proceeds of his underinsured motorist policy for the July 17, 1990, accident. Second, although the two claims present different legal theories, one sounding in contract and the other in tort, they both seek redress for essentially the same basic wrong. For instance, Porn's contract action sought redress for National Grange's refusal to pay the policy proceeds, while his bad-faith action sought redress for its unreasonable refusal to pay the proceeds. Third, a comparison of the two complaints illustrates that the two claims rest on a similar factual basis. Both complaints, in their factual allegations, outline the circumstances of the accident, the particulars of the insurance policy, and National Grange's conduct in refusing to pay. In sum, the facts underlying the two claims are closely related in time, space, origin, and motivation.

Porn expends considerable effort characterizing the instant action as arising out of a transaction separate from that giving rise to the first action. In particular, Porn maintains that the bad-faith action stems from National Grange's conduct in handling his insurance claim, whereas the contract action stems from the circumstances surrounding the car accident. Porn's definition of the two transactions out of which the claims arise, however, is artificially narrow. For instance, the contract claim arises out of more than the car accident alone. It arises out of the accident in conjunction with National Grange's refusal to pay under the policy. Indeed, without the refusal to pay, no contract breach could exist. Similarly, the factual basis of Porn's bad-faith claim cannot be limited to National Grange's conduct in handling Porn's insurance claim. In this case, the facts of the car accident are also probative of National Grange's reasonableness in refusing to pay Porn's claim. For instance, if, as Porn suggests, the facts of the accident present a clear picture that Willoughby was the legal cause of the accident and Porn was not contributorily negligent, National Grange would have had less reason to contest the claim and therefore its refusal to pay appears less reasonable.

Admittedly, each legal theory relies more heavily on some of the underlying facts than others. The accident facts, for example, will likely receive more emphasis in proving the contract claim, while the facts regarding National Grange's conduct in handling Porn's insurance claim will be more focal in proving the bad-faith claim. However, the Restatement makes clear that merely because two claims depend on different shadings of the facts or emphasize different elements of the facts, we should not color our perception of the transaction underlying them, creating multiple transactions where only one transaction exists. By focusing exclusively on the facts most critical to each claim, Porn has ignored the other facts underlying each claim. Accordingly, we reject Porn's grouping of the facts underlying the two claims into separate transactions.

2. Trial Convenience

The second Restatement factor directs us to determine whether the facts underlying the contract and bad-faith claims form a convenient trial unit. This factor, aimed at conserving judicial resources, provides that where the witnesses or proof needed in the second action overlap substantially with those used in the first action, the second action should ordinarily be precluded. We conclude that Porn's bad-faith claim would use much of the same evidence produced in the first action for breach of the insurance contract, and therefore it would have been convenient and efficient for the district court to have heard the two claims in the same action.

Testimony and exhibits about the circumstances of the accident are relevant to both the contract and bad-faith claims. To establish that National Grange breached the insurance policy in not paying his claim, Porn had to prove that Willoughby's negligence caused the accident and that he was not contributorily negligent. Accordingly, in the first action, Porn presented evidence detailing the circumstances of the accident. This evidence would likely have been repeated in a second action for bad faith, as Porn would have sought to portray the accident facts as so plainly establishing Willoughby's negligence that National Grange had no credible reason for refusing to pay his claim.

The evidence in the contract action and the second action would also overlap as to the terms of Porn's underinsured motorist policy and National Grange's refusal to pay his claim. To prove breach of contract, Porn had to establish that National Grange refused to pay his claim where the terms of the policy so required. Likewise, the reasonableness of National Grange's refusal to pay, *i.e.*, whether it acted in bad faith, depends on what the policy required.

Rather than addressing the degree to which the evidence supporting each claim overlaps, Porn challenges the convenience of bringing the claims together on two other grounds. First, Porn argues that evidence relevant to the bad-faith claim, specifically evidence of the amount of insurance available and the fact of settlement offers and negotiations, would prejudice the insurer's defense of the contract claim, and therefore the two claims do not form a convenient trial unit. However, we agree with the district court that any potential prejudice could be resolved by bifurcating the trial. With bifurcation, the evidence common to both claims, which was considerable, could have been presented at once and not "in separate lawsuits commenced at a distance of months or years." *Porn v. National Grange Mut. Ins. Co.* (D.Me. Sept. 27, 1995).

Second, Porn argues that he had to procure a judgment that National Grange breached the insurance contract before the cause of action for bad faith could accrue and therefore the bad-faith and contract claims could not be joined in the same action. Porn bases this contention on an assumption that, although a Connecticut court has yet to decide this issue, it would follow jurisdictions like Florida and require a judgment of contract breach as a condition precedent to the pursuit of a bad-faith claim. The district court correctly observed, however, that the Connecticut Supreme Court rejected this contention in *Duhaime v. American Reserve Life Ins. Co.* (1986). Invoking the doctrine of res judicata, the Connecticut Supreme Court held that Duhaime's earlier action for breach of the insurance policy barred a subsequent action for bad faith. In so holding, the court implicitly acknowledged that a bad-faith action can accrue without a separate judgment of contract breach. Although *Duhaime* involved disability insurance and the instant case involves underinsured motorist insurance, we see nothing unique about underinsured motorist insurance that would preclude *Duhaime*'s holding from governing here.

3. Parties' Expectations

The final Restatement factor is whether treating the underlying facts as a trial unit conforms to the parties' expectations. For the following reasons, we conclude that it does.

When he brought his contract suit in November 1993, Porn knew the facts necessary for bringing a bad-faith claim. He knew that National Grange had refused to pay; he knew its alleged reasons for so refusing; and he knew the extent of the delay in payment attributable to the refusal. Therefore, because the two claims arose in the same time frame out of similar facts, one would reasonably expect them to be brought together. Indeed, in February 1993, nine months before filing the first action, Porn wrote a letter to National Grange in which he made a demand for his policy proceeds and concomitantly threatened to sue for bad faith. In light of this letter, it would not have been unreasonable for National Grange to expect that any subsequent lawsuit that Porn initiated would include claims for both breach of contract and bad faith. Finally, bringing related claims together is arguably more conducive to settlement and therefore, at least in this case, may have had some pragmatic appeal.

In sum, applying the Restatement's transactional test to this case, we conclude that the two lawsuits involved sufficiently identical causes of action. Because the cause of action should not have been split into two lawsuits, Porn's bad-faith claim is barred by claim preclusion.

B. Equitable Exception

As his final argument, Porn contends that even if we find that res judicata applies, equity demands its suspension in this case. Specifically, Porn argues that because National Grange's decision to proceed to judgment in the contract action with no evidence to support its defense ("litigation conduct") is probative of bad faith, the full nature of National Grange's bad-faith tort was not revealed until judgment was entered in the contract action. Therefore, Porn argues, it would be premature and unfair to require him to bring his bad-faith claim together with his contract claim.

The Supreme Court has counselled us to adhere to traditional principles of res judicata and not to make any "ad hoc determination of the equities in a particular case." *Federated Dep't Stores, Inc. v. Moitie* (refusing to condone an exception to an application of res judicata that would bar relitigation of an unappealed adverse judgment where other plaintiffs in similar actions against common defendants successfully appealed the judgments against them). In a post-*Moitie* decision, however, this court has suggested that an "occasional exception to claim preclusion" may still exist in instances of "unusual hardship." *See Kale v. Combined Ins. Co. of Am.* (1st Cir.), *cert. denied* (1991) (quotation omitted). Assuming *arguendo* that *Moitie* did not foreclose the possibility of an equitable exception, we find that, in the context of this case, requiring the bad-faith claim to be brought in the first action creates no unusual hardship for Porn and therefore the exception does not apply.

First, we challenge Porn's assumption that requiring the two claims to be brought together would necessarily preclude as support for the bad-faith claim any evidence about National Grange's decision to proceed to judgment in the contract action with no evidence to support its defense. Had the contract and bad-faith claims been brought together, the district court would likely have bifurcated the trial into two phases. By the time of the bad-faith phase of the trial, the contract phase would already have been completed and Porn would know both the quality of evidence National Grange presented to defend the contract claim and that the magistrate judge had granted judgment as a matter of law for Porn on the issue of contributory negligence. Accordingly, we see nothing that would have prevented Porn from presenting this evidence in the bad-faith phase of the trial and arguing to the jury that National Grange's refusal to settle the contract action despite insufficient evidence of a meritorious defense was more evidence of its bad faith.

Moreover, assuming *arguendo* that Porn's assumption was correct and that at the time he brought the contract action he was unaware of the litigation conduct that would occur therein, we nonetheless conclude that Porn was aware of other conduct by National Grange sufficient to support a bad-faith claim. Indeed, of the ten factual allegations supporting Porn's bad-faith complaint, nine were known to Porn at the time he instituted the first action. For instance, the second complaint alleged that National Grange failed to act on the claim for nine months; failed to make an offer on the claim for sixteen months; failed to allow Porn to settle with Willoughby's carrier for the available liability proceeds for two years; justified delays with the possibility of other insurance coverage when it knew no such insurance existed; made Porn investigate the possibility of other coverage; failed to investigate the claim; repeatedly lied to Porn about the policy's terms; and instructed its claims personnel to withhold helpful information about the policy from Porn. Because the events underlying these allegations had occurred by the time Porn brought his first action, we find that Porn had ample opportunity to litigate the bad-faith claim therein, and his asserted inability to present evidence of National Grange's litigation conduct as additional support for his bad-faith claim does not present an unusual hardship.

III.

For the reasons stated above, we *affirm* the district court's grant of summary judgment in favor of National Grange.

2019 Federal Rules of Civil Procedure
Table of Contents

AS AMENDED THROUGH DECEMBER 1, 2018

Selected Rules

Title I – Scope of Rules; Form of Action (Rules 1 and 2)

Rule 1 – Scope and Purpose

These rules govern the procedure in all civil actions and proceedings in the United States district courts, except as stated in **Rule 81**. They should be construed, administered, and employed by the court and the parties to secure the just, speedy, and inexpensive determination of every action and proceeding.

Rule 2 – One Form of Action

There is one form of action—the civil action.

Title II – Commencing an Action; Service of Process; Pleadings, Motions, and Orders (Rules 3-6)

Rule 3 – Commencing an Action

A civil action is commenced by filing a complaint with the court.

Rule 4 – Summons

(a) **Contents; Amendments**.

(1) CONTENTS. A summons must:

(A) name the court and the parties;

(B) be directed to the defendant;

(C) state the name and address of the plaintiff's attorney or–if unrepresented–of the plaintiff;

(D) state the time within which the defendant must appear and defend;

(E) notify the defendant that a failure to appear and defend will result in a default judgment against the defendant for the relief demanded in the complaint;

(F) be signed by the clerk; and

(G) bear the court's seal.

(2) AMENDMENTS. The court may permit a summons to be amended.

(b) **Issuance**. On or after filing the complaint, the plaintiff may present a summons to the clerk for signature and seal. If the summons is properly completed, the clerk must sign, seal, and issue it to the plaintiff for service on the defendant. A summons–or a copy of a summons that is addressed to multiple defendants–must be issued for each defendant to be served.

(c) **Service**.

(1) IN GENERAL. A summons must be served with a copy of the complaint. The plaintiff is responsible for having the summons and complaint served within the time allowed by Rule 4(m) and must furnish the necessary copies to the person who makes service.

(2) BY WHOM. Any person who is at least 18 years old and not a party may serve a summons and complaint.

(3) BY A MARSHAL OR SOMEONE SPECIALLY APPOINTED. At the plaintiff's request, the court may order that service be made by a United States marshal or deputy marshal or by a person specially appointed by the court. The court must so order if the plaintiff is authorized to proceed in forma pauperis under 28 U.S.C. §1915 or as a seaman under 28 U.S.C. §1916.

(d) **Waiving Service**.

(1) REQUESTING A WAIVER. An individual, corporation, or association that is subject to service under Rule 4(e), (f), or (h) has a duty to avoid unnecessary expenses of serving the summons. The plaintiff may notify such a defendant that an action has been commenced and request that the defendant waive service of a summons. The notice and request must:

(A) be in writing and be addressed:

(i) to the individual defendant; or

(ii) for a defendant subject to service under Rule 4(h), to an officer, a managing or general agent, or any other agent authorized by appointment or by law to receive service of process;

(B) name the court where the complaint was filed;

(C) be accompanied by a copy of the complaint, 2 copies of the waiver form appended to this Rule 4, and a prepaid means for returning the form;

(D) inform the defendant, using the form appended to this Rule 4, of the consequences of waiving and not waiving service;

(E) state the date when the request is sent;

(F) give the defendant a reasonable time of at least 30 days after the request was sent—or at least 60 days if sent to the defendant outside any judicial district of the United States—to return the waiver; and

(G) be sent by first-class mail or other reliable means.

(2) FAILURE TO WAIVE. If a defendant located within the United States fails, without good cause, to sign and return a waiver requested by a plaintiff located within the United States, the court must impose on the defendant:

(A) the expenses later incurred in making service; and

(B) the reasonable expenses, including attorney's fees, of any motion required to collect those service expenses.

(3) TIME TO ANSWER AFTER A WAIVER. A defendant who, before being served with process, timely returns a waiver need not serve an answer to the complaint until 60 days after the request was sent—or until 90 days after it was sent to the defendant outside any judicial district of the United States.

(4) RESULTS OF FILING A WAIVER. When the plaintiff files a waiver, proof of service is not required and these rules apply as if a summons and complaint had been served at the time of filing the waiver.

(5) JURISDICTION AND VENUE NOT WAIVED. Waiving service of a summons does not waive any objection to personal jurisdiction or to venue.

(e) **Serving an Individual Within a Judicial District of the United States**. Unless federal law provides otherwise, an individual—other than a minor, an incompetent person, or a person whose waiver has been filed—may be served in a judicial district of the United States by:

(1) following state law for serving a summons in an action brought in courts of general jurisdiction in the state where the district court is located or where service is made; or

(2) doing any of the following:

(A) delivering a copy of the summons and of the complaint to the individual personally;

(B) leaving a copy of each at the individual's dwelling or usual place of abode with someone of suitable age and discretion who resides there; or

(C) delivering a copy of each to an agent authorized by appointment or by law to receive service of process.

(f) **Serving an Individual in a Foreign Country**. Unless federal law provides otherwise, an individual—other than a minor, an incompetent person, or a person whose waiver has been filed—may be served at a place not within any judicial district of the United States:

(1) by any internationally agreed means of service that is reasonably calculated to give notice, such as those authorized by the Hague Convention on the Service Abroad of Judicial and Extrajudicial Documents;

(2) if there is no internationally agreed means, or if an international agreement allows but does not specify other means, by a method that is reasonably calculated to give notice:

(A) as prescribed by the foreign country's law for service in that country in an action in its courts of general jurisdiction;

(B) as the foreign authority directs in response to a letter rogatory or letter of request; or

(C) unless prohibited by the foreign country's law, by:

(i) delivering a copy of the summons and of the complaint to the individual personally; or

(ii) using any form of mail that the clerk addresses and sends to the individual and that requires a signed receipt; or

(3) by other means not prohibited by international agreement, as the court orders.

(g) **Serving a Minor or an Incompetent Person**. A minor or an incompetent person in a judicial district of the United States must be served by following state law for serving a summons or like process on such a defendant in an action brought in the courts of general jurisdiction of the state where service is made. A minor or an incompetent person who is not within any judicial district of the United States must be served in the manner prescribed by Rule 4(f)(2)(A), (f)(2)(B), or (f)(3).

(h) **Serving a Corporation, Partnership, or Association**. Unless federal law provides otherwise or the defendant's waiver has been filed, a domestic or foreign corporation, or a partnership or other unincorporated association that is subject to suit under a common name, must be served:

(1) in a judicial district of the United States:

(A) in the manner prescribed by Rule 4(e)(1) for serving an individual; or

(B) by delivering a copy of the summons and of the complaint to an officer, a managing or general agent, or any other agent authorized by appointment or by law to receive service of process and-if the agent is one authorized by statute and the statute so requires-by also mailing a copy of each to the defendant; or

(2) at a place not within any judicial district of the United States, in any manner prescribed by Rule 4(f) for serving an individual, except personal delivery under (f)(2(C)(i).

(i) **Serving the United States and its Agencies, Corporations, Officers, or Employees**.

(1) UNITED STATES. To serve the United States, a party must:

(A) (i) deliver a copy of the summons and of the complaint to the United States attorney for the district where the action is brought–or to an assistant United States attorney or clerical employee whom the United States attorney designates in a writing filed with the court clerk–or

(ii) send a copy of each by registered or certified mail to the civil-process clerk at the United States attorney's office;

(B) send a copy of each by registered or certified mail to the Attorney General of the United States at Washington, D.C.; and

(C) if the action challenges an order of a nonparty agency or officer of the United States, send a copy of each by registered or certified mail to the agency or officer.

(2) AGENCY; CORPORATION; OFFICER OR EMPLOYEE SUED IN AN OFFICIAL CAPACITY. To serve a United States agency or corporation, or a United States officer or employee sued only in an official capacity, a party must serve the United States and also send a copy of the summons and of the complaint by registered or certified mail to the agency, corporation, officer, or employee.

(3) OFFICER OR EMPLOYEE SUED INDIVIDUALLY. To serve a United States officer or employee sued in an individual capacity for an act or omission occurring in connection with duties performed on the United States' behalf (whether or not the officer or employee is also sued in an official capacity), a party must serve the United States and also serve the officer or employee under Rule 4(e), (f), or (g).

(4) EXTENDING TIME. The court must allow a party a reasonable time to cure its failure to:

(A) serve a person required to be served under Rule 4(i)(2), if the party has served either the United States attorney or the Attorney General of the United States; or

(B) serve the United States under Rule 4(i)(3), if the party has served the United States officer or employee.

(j) SERVING A FOREIGN, STATE, OR LOCAL GOVERNMENT.

(1) FOREIGN STATE. A foreign state or its political subdivision, agency, or instrumentality must be served in accordance with 28 U.S.C. §1608.

(2) STATE OR LOCAL GOVERNMENT. A state, a municipal corporation, or any other state-created governmental organization that is subject to suit must be served by:

(A) delivering a copy of the summons and of the complaint to its chief executive officer; or

(B) serving a copy of each in the manner prescribed by that state's law for serving a summons or like process on such a defendant.

(k) **Territorial Limits of Effective Service**.

(1) IN GENERAL. Serving a summons or filing a waiver of service establishes personal jurisdiction over a defendant:

(A) who is subject to the jurisdiction of a court of general jurisdiction in the state where the district court is located;

(B) who is a party joined under Rule 14 or 19 and is served within a judicial district of the United States and not more than 100 miles from where the summons was issued; or

(C) when authorized by a federal statute.

(2) FEDERAL CLAIM OUTSIDE STATE-COURT JURISDICTION. For a claim that arises under federal law, serving a summons or filing a waiver of service establishes personal jurisdiction over a defendant if:

(A) the defendant is not subject to jurisdiction in any state's courts of general jurisdiction; and

(B) exercising jurisdiction is consistent with the United States Constitution and laws.

(l) **Proving Service**.

(1) AFFIDAVIT REQUIRED. Unless service is waived, proof of service must be made to the court. Except for service by a United States marshal or deputy marshal, proof must be by the server's affidavit.

(2) SERVICE OUTSIDE THE UNITED STATES. Service not within any judicial district of the United States must be proved as follows:

(A) if made under Rule 4(f)(1), as provided in the applicable treaty or convention; or

(B) if made under Rule 4(f)(2) or (f)(3), by a receipt signed by the addressee, or by other evidence satisfying the court that the summons and complaint were delivered to the addressee.

(3) VALIDITY OF SERVICE; AMENDING PROOF. Failure to prove service does not affect the validity of service. The court may permit proof of service to be amended.

(m) **Time Limit for Service**. If a defendant is not served within 90 days after the complaint is filed, the court – on motion or on its own after notice to the plaintiff – must dismiss the action without prejudice against that defendant or order that service be made within a specified time. But if the plaintiff shows good cause for the failure, the court must extend the time for service for an appropriate period. This subdivision (m) does not apply to service in a foreign country under Rule 4(f), 4(h)(2), or 4(j)(1) or to service of a notice under Rule 71.1(d)(3)(A).

(n) **Asserting Jurisdiction Over Property or Assets**.

(1) FEDERAL LAW. The court may assert jurisdiction over property if authorized by a federal statute. Notice to claimants of the property must be given as provided in the statute or by serving a summons under this rule.

(2) STATE LAW. On a showing that personal jurisdiction over a defendant cannot be obtained in the district where the action is brought by reasonable efforts to serve a

summons under this rule, the court may assert jurisdiction over the defendant's assets found in the district. Jurisdiction is acquired by seizing the assets under the circumstances and in the manner provided by state law in that district.

Rule 4.1 – Serving Other Process

(a) **In General.** Process—other than a summons under Rule 4 or a subpoena under Rule 45—must be served by a United States marshal or deputy marshal or by a person specially appointed for that purpose. It may be served anywhere within the territorial limits of the state where the district court is located and, if authorized by a federal statute, beyond those limits. Proof of service must be made under Rule 4(**L**).

(b) **Enforcing Orders: Committing for Civil Contempt.** An order committing a person for civil contempt of a decree or injunction issued to enforce federal law may be served and enforced in any district. Any other order in a civil-contempt proceeding may be served only in the state where the issuing court is located or elsewhere in the United States within 100 miles from where the order was issued.

Rule 5 – Serving and Filing Pleadings and Other Papers

(a) **Service: When Required.**

(1) IN GENERAL. Unless these rules provide otherwise, each of the following papers must be served on every party:

(A) an order stating that service is required;

(B) a pleading filed after the original complaint, unless the court orders otherwise under Rule 5(c) because there are numerous defendants;

(C) a discovery paper required to be served on a party, unless the court orders otherwise;

(D) a written motion, except one that may be heard ex parte; and

(E) a written notice, appearance, demand, or offer of judgment, or any similar paper.

(2) IF A PARTY FAILS TO APPEAR. No service is required on a party who is in default for failing to appear. But a pleading that asserts a new claim for relief against such a party must be served on that party under Rule 4.

(3) SEIZING PROPERTY. If an action is begun by seizing property and no person is or need be named as a defendant, any service required before the filing of an appearance, answer, or claim must be made on the person who had custody or possession of the property when it was seized.

(b) **Service: How Made.**

(1) SERVING AN ATTORNEY. If a party is represented by an attorney, service under this rule must be made on the attorney unless the court orders service on the party.

(2) SERVICE IN GENERAL. A paper is served under this rule by:

(A) handing it to the person;

(B) leaving it:

(i) at the person's office with a clerk or other person in charge or, if no one is in charge, in a conspicuous place in the office; or

(ii) if the person has no office or the office is closed, at the person's dwelling or usual place of abode with someone of suitable age and discretion who resides there;

(C) mailing it to the person's last known address—in which event service is complete upon mailing;

(D) leaving it with the court clerk if the person has no known address;

(E) sending it by electronic means if the person consented in writing—in which event service is complete upon transmission, but is not effective if the serving party learns that it did not reach the person to be served; or

(F) delivering it by any other means that the person consented to in writing—in which event service is complete when the person making service delivers it to the agency designated to make delivery.

(3) USING COURT FACILITIES. If a local rule so authorizes, a party may use the court's transmission facilities to make service under Rule 5(b)(2)(E).

(c) **Serving Numerous Defendants.**

(1) IN GENERAL. If an action involves an unusually large number of defendants, the court may, on motion or on its own, order that:

(A) defendants' pleadings and replies to them need not be served on other defendants;

(B) any crossclaim, counterclaim, avoidance, or affirmative defense in those pleadings and replies to them will be treated as denied or avoided by all other parties; and

(C) filing any such pleading and serving it on the plaintiff constitutes notice of the pleading to all parties.

(2) NOTIFYING PARTIES. A copy of every such order must be served on the parties as the court directs.

(d) **Filing.**

(1) REQUIRED FILINGS; CERTIFICATE OF SERVICE. Any paper after the complaint that is required to be served—together with a certificate of service—must be filed within a reasonable time after service. But disclosures under Rule 26(a)(1) or (2) and the following discovery requests and responses must not be filed until they are used in the proceeding or the court orders filing: depositions, interrogatories, requests for documents or tangible things or to permit entry onto land, and requests for admission.

(2) HOW FILING IS MADE—IN GENERAL. A paper is filed by delivering it:

(A) to the clerk; or

(B) to a judge who agrees to accept it for filing, and who must then note the filing date on the paper and promptly send it to the clerk.

(3) ELECTRONIC FILING, SIGNING, OR VERIFICATION. A court may, by local rule, allow papers to be filed, signed, or verified by electronic means that are consistent with any technical standards established by the Judicial Conference of the United States. A local rule may require electronic filing only if reasonable exceptions are allowed. A paper filed electronically in compliance with a local rule is a written paper for purposes of these rules.

(4) ACCEPTANCE BY THE CLERK. The clerk must not refuse to file a paper solely because it is not in the form prescribed by these rules or by a local rule or practice.

Rule 5.1 – Constitutional Challenge to a Statute

(a) **Notice by a Party**. A party that files a pleading, written motion, or other paper drawing into question the constitutionality of a federal or state statute must promptly:

(1) file a notice of constitutional question stating the question and identifying the paper that raises it, if:

(A) a federal statute is questioned and the parties do not include the United States, one of its agencies, or one of its officers or employees in an official capacity; or

(B) a state statute is questioned and the parties do not include the state, one of its agencies, or one of its officers or employees in an official capacity; and

(2) serve the notice and paper on the Attorney General of the United States if a federal statute is questioned—or on the state attorney general if a state statute is questioned—either by certified or registered mail or by sending it to an electronic address designated by the attorney general for this purpose.

(b) **Certification by the Court**. The court must, under 28 U.S.C. §2403, certify to the appropriate attorney general that a statute has been questioned.

(c) **Intervention; Final Decision on the Merits**. Unless the court sets a later time, the attorney general may intervene within 60 days after the notice is filed or after the court certifies the challenge, whichever is earlier. Before the time to intervene expires, the court may reject the constitutional challenge, but may not enter a final judgment holding the statute unconstitutional.

(d) **No Forfeiture**. A party's failure to file and serve the notice, or the court's failure to certify, does not forfeit a constitutional claim or defense that is otherwise timely asserted.

Rule 5.2 – Privacy Protection for Filings Made with the Court

(a) **Redacted Filings**. Unless the court orders otherwise, in an electronic or paper filing with the court that contains an individual's social-security number, taxpayer-identification number, or birth date, the name of an individual known to be a minor, or a financial-account number, a party or nonparty making the filing may include only:

(1) the last four digits of the social-security number and taxpayer-identification number;

(2) the year of the individual's birth;

(3) the minor's initials; and

(4) the last four digits of the financial-account number.

(b) **Exemptions from the Redaction Requirement**. The redaction requirement does not apply to the following:

(1) a financial-account number that identifies the property allegedly subject to forfeiture in a forfeiture proceeding;

(2) the record of an administrative or agency proceeding;

(3) the official record of a state-court proceeding;

(4) the record of a court or tribunal, if that record was not subject to the redaction requirement when originally filed;

(5) a filing covered by Rule 5.2(c) or (d); and

(6) a *pro se* filing in an action brought under 28 U.S.C. §§2241, 2254, or 2255.

(c) **Limitations on Remote Access to Electronic Files; Social-Security Appeals and Immigration Cases**. Unless the court orders otherwise, in an action for benefits under the Social Security Act, and in an action or proceeding relating to an order of removal, to relief from removal, or to immigration benefits or detention, access to an electronic file is authorized as follows:

(1) the parties and their attorneys may have remote electronic access to any part of the case file, including the administrative record;

(2) any other person may have electronic access to the full record at the courthouse, but may have remote electronic access only to:

(A) the docket maintained by the court; and

(B) an opinion, order, judgment, or other disposition of the court, but not any other part of the case file or the administrative record.

(d) **Filings Made Under Seal**. The court may order that a filing be made under seal without redaction. The court may later unseal the filing or order the person who made the filing to file a redacted version for the public record.

(e) **Protective Orders**. For good cause, the court may by order in a case:

(1) require redaction of additional information; or

(2) limit or prohibit a nonparty's remote electronic access to a document filed with the court.

(f) **Option for Additional Unredacted Filing Under Seal**. A person making a redacted filing may also file an unredacted copy under seal. The court must retain the unredacted copy as part of the record.

(g) **Option for Filing a Reference List**. A filing that contains redacted information may be filed together with a reference list that identifies each item of redacted information and specifies an appropriate identifier that uniquely corresponds to each item listed. The list must be filed under seal and may be amended as of right. Any reference in the case to a listed identifier will be construed to refer to the corresponding item of information.

(h) **Waiver of Protection of Identifiers**. A person waives the protection of Rule 5.2(a) as to the person's own information by filing it without redaction and not under seal.

Rule 6 – Computing and Extending Time; Time for Motion Papers

(a) **Computing Time**. The following rules apply in computing any time period specified in these rules, in any local rule or court order, or in any statute that does not specify a method of computing time.

(1) PERIOD STATED IN DAYS OR A LONGER UNIT. When the period is stated in days or a longer unit of time:

(A) exclude the day of the event that triggers the period;

(B) count every day, including intermediate Saturdays, Sundays, and legal holidays; and

(C) include the last day of the period, but if the last day is a Saturday, Sunday, or legal holiday, the period continues to run until the end of the next day that is not a Saturday, Sunday, or legal holiday.

(2) PERIOD STATED IN HOURS. When the period is stated in hours:

(A) begin counting immediately on the occurrence of the event that triggers the period;

(B) count every hour, including hours during intermediate Saturdays, Sundays, and legal holidays; and

(C) if the period would end on a Saturday, Sunday, or legal holiday, the period continues to run until the same time on the next day that is not a Saturday, Sunday, or legal holiday.

(3) INACCESSIBILITY OF THE CLERK'S OFFICE. Unless the court orders otherwise, if the clerk's office is inaccessible:

(A) on the last day for filing under Rule 6(a)(1), then the time for filing is extended to the first accessible day that is not a Saturday, Sunday, or legal holiday; or

(B) during the last hour for filing under Rule 6(a)(2), then the time for filing is extended to the same time on the first accessible day that is not a Saturday, Sunday, or legal holiday.

(4) "LAST DAY" DEFINED. Unless a different time is set by a statute, local rule, or court order, the last day ends:

(A) for electronic filing, at midnight in the court's time zone; and

(B) for filing by other means, when the clerk's office is scheduled to close.

(5) "NEXT DAY" DEFINED. The "next day" is determined by continuing to count forward when the period is measured after an event and backward when measured before an event.

(6) "LEGAL HOLIDAY" DEFINED. "Legal holiday" means:

(A) the day set aside by statute for observing New Year's Day, Martin Luther King Jr.'s Birthday, Washington's Birthday, Memorial Day, Independence Day, Labor Day, Columbus Day, Veterans' Day, Thanksgiving Day, or Christmas Day;

(B) any day declared a holiday by the President or Congress; and

(C) for periods that are measured after an event, any other day declared a holiday by the state where the district court is located.

(b) **Extending Time**.

(1) IN GENERAL. When an act may or must be done within a specified time, the court may, for good cause, extend the time:

(A) with or without motion or notice if the court acts, or if a request is made, before the original time or its extension expires; or

(B) on motion made after the time has expired if the party failed to act because of excusable neglect.

(2) EXCEPTIONS. A court must not extend the time to act under Rules 50(b) and (d), 52(b), 59(b), (d), and (e), and 60(b).

(c) **Motions, Notices of Hearing, and Affidavits**.

(1) IN GENERAL. A written motion and notice of the hearing must be served at least 14 days before the time specified for the hearing, with the following exceptions:

(A) when the motion may be heard ex parte;

(B) when these rules set a different time; or

(C) when a court order—which a party may, for good cause, apply for ex parte—sets a different time.

(2) SUPPORTING AFFIDAVIT. Any affidavit supporting a motion must be served with the motion. Except as Rule 59(c) provides otherwise, any opposing affidavit must be served at least 7 days before the hearing, unless the court permits service at another time.

(d) **Additional Time After Certain Kinds of Service**. When a party may or must act within a specified time after being served and service is made under Rule 5(b)(2)(C) (mail), (D) (leaving with the clerk), or (F) (other means consented to), 3 days are added after the period would otherwise expire under Rule 6(a).

Title III – Pleadings and Motions (Rules 7-16)
Rule 7 – Pleadings Allowed; Form of Motions and Other Papers

(a) **Pleadings**. Only these pleadings are allowed:

(1) a complaint;

(2) an answer to a complaint;

(3) an answer to a counterclaim designated as a counterclaim;

(4) an answer to a crossclaim;

(5) a third-party complaint;

(6) an answer to a third-party complaint; and

(7) if the court orders one, a reply to an answer.

(b) **Motions and Other Papers**.

(1) IN GENERAL. A request for a court order must be made by motion. The motion must:

(A) be in writing unless made during a hearing or trial;

(B) state with particularity the grounds for seeking the order; and

(C) state the relief sought.

(2) FORM. The rules governing captions and other matters of form in pleadings apply to motions and other papers.

Rule 7.1 – Disclosure Statement

(a) **Who Must File; Contents**. A nongovernmental corporate party must file 2 copies of a disclosure statement that:

(1) identifies any parent corporation and any publicly held corporation owning 10% or more of its stock; or

(2) states that there is no such corporation.

(b) **Time to File; Supplemental Filing**. A party must:

(1) file the disclosure statement with its first appearance, pleading, petition, motion, response, or other request addressed to the court; and

(2) promptly file a supplemental statement if any required information changes.

Rule 8 – General Rules of Pleading

(a) **Claim for Relief**. A pleading that states a claim for relief must contain:

(1) a short and plain statement of the grounds for the court's jurisdiction, unless the court already has jurisdiction and the claim needs no new jurisdictional support;

(2) a short and plain statement of the claim showing that the pleader is entitled to relief; and

(3) a demand for the relief sought, which may include relief in the alternative or different types of relief.

(b) **Defenses; Admissions and Denials**.

(1) *In General*. In responding to a pleading, a party must:

(A) state in short and plain terms its defenses to each claim asserted against it; and

(B) admit or deny the allegations asserted against it by an opposing party.

(2) *Denials—Responding to the Substance*. A denial must fairly respond to the substance of the allegation.

(3) *General and Specific Denials*. A party that intends in good faith to deny all the allegations of a pleading—including the jurisdictional grounds—may do so by a general denial. A party that does not intend to deny all the allegations must either specifically deny designated allegations or generally deny all except those specifically admitted.

(4) *Denying Part of an Allegation*. A party that intends in good faith to deny only part of an allegation must admit the part that is true and deny the rest.

(5) *Lacking Knowledge or Information*. A party that lacks knowledge or information sufficient to form a belief about the truth of an allegation must so state, and the statement has the effect of a denial.

(6) *Effect of Failing to Deny.* An allegation—other than one relating to the amount of damages—is admitted if a responsive pleading is required and the allegation is not denied. If a responsive pleading is not required, an allegation is considered denied or avoided.

(c) **Affirmative Defenses**.

(1) *In General.* In responding to a pleading, a party must affirmatively state any avoidance or affirmative defense, including:

- accord and satisfaction;
- arbitration and award;
- assumption of risk;
- contributory negligence;
- duress;
- estoppel;
- failure of consideration;
- fraud;
- illegality;
- injury by fellow servant;
- laches;
- license;
- payment;
- release;
- res judicata;
- statute of frauds;
- statute of limitations; and
- waiver.

(2) *Mistaken Designation.* If a party mistakenly designates a defense as a counterclaim, or a counterclaim as a defense, the court must, if justice requires, treat the pleading as though it were correctly designated, and may impose terms for doing so.

(d) **Pleading to Be Concise and Direct; Alternative Statements; Inconsistency**.

(1) *In General.* Each allegation must be simple, concise, and direct. No technical form is required.

(2) *Alternative Statements of a Claim or Defense.* A party may set out 2 or more statements of a claim or defense alternatively or hypothetically, either in a single count or defense or in separate ones. If a party makes alternative statements, the pleading is sufficient if any one of them is sufficient.

(3) *Inconsistent Claims or Defenses.* A party may state as many separate claims or defenses as it has, regardless of consistency.

(e) **Construing Pleadings**. Pleadings must be construed so as to do justice.

Rule 9 – Pleading Special Matters

(a) **Capacity or Authority to Sue; Legal Existence**.

(1) IN GENERAL. Except when required to show that the court has jurisdiction, a pleading need not allege:

(A) a party's capacity to sue or be sued;

(B) a party's authority to sue or be sued in a representative capacity; or

(C) the legal existence of an organized association of persons that is made a party.

(2) RAISING THOSE ISSUES. To raise any of those issues, a party must do so by a specific denial, which must state any supporting facts that are peculiarly within the party's knowledge.

(b) **Fraud or Mistake; Conditions of Mind**. In alleging fraud or mistake, a party must state with particularity the circumstances constituting fraud or mistake. Malice, intent, knowledge, and other conditions of a person's mind may be alleged generally.

(c) **Conditions Precedent**. In pleading conditions precedent, it suffices to allege generally that all conditions precedent have occurred or been performed. But when denying that a condition precedent has occurred or been performed, a party must do so with particularity.

(d) **Official Document or Act**. In pleading an official document or official act, it suffices to allege that the document was legally issued or the act legally done.

(e) **Judgment**. In pleading a judgment or decision of a domestic or foreign court, a judicial or quasi-judicial tribunal, or a board or officer, it suffices to plead the judgment or decision without showing jurisdiction to render it.

(f) **Time and Place**. An allegation of time or place is material when testing the sufficiency of a pleading.

(g) **Special Damages**. If an item of special damage is claimed, it must be specifically stated.

(h) **Admiralty or Maritime Claim**.

(1) HOW DESIGNATED. If a claim for relief is within the admiralty or maritime jurisdiction and also within the court's subject-matter jurisdiction on some other ground, the pleading may designate the claim as an admiralty or maritime claim for purposes of Rules 14(c), 38(e), and 82 and the Supplemental Rules for Admiralty or Maritime Claims and Asset Forfeiture Actions. A claim cognizable only in the admiralty or maritime jurisdiction is an admiralty or maritime claim for those purposes, whether or not so designated.

(2) DESIGNATION FOR APPEAL. A case that includes an admiralty or maritime claim within this subdivision (h) is an admiralty case within 28 U.S.C. §1292(a)(3).

Rule 10 – Form of Pleadings

(a) **Caption; Names of Parties**. Every pleading must have a caption with the court's name, a title, a file number, and a Rule 7(a) designation. The title of the complaint must name all the parties; the title of other pleadings, after naming the first party on each side, may refer generally to other parties.

(b) **Paragraphs; Separate Statements**. A party must state its claims or defenses in numbered paragraphs, each limited as far as practicable to a single set of circumstances. A later pleading may refer by number to a paragraph in an earlier pleading. If doing so would promote clarity, each claim founded on a separate transaction or occurrence—and each defense other than a denial—must be stated in a separate count or defense.

(c) **Adoption by Reference; Exhibits**. A statement in a pleading may be adopted by reference elsewhere in the same pleading or in any other pleading or motion. A copy of a written instrument that is an exhibit to a pleading is a part of the pleading for all purposes.

Rule 11 – Signing Pleadings, Motions, and Other Papers; Representations to the Court; Sanctions

(a) **Signature**. Every pleading, written motion, and other paper must be signed by at least one attorney of record in the attorney's name—or by a party personally if the party is unrepresented. The paper must state the signer's address, e-mail address, and telephone number. Unless a rule or statute specifically states otherwise, a pleading need not be verified or accompanied by an affidavit. The court must strike an unsigned paper unless the omission is promptly corrected after being called to the attorney's or party's attention.

(b) **Representations to the Court**. By presenting to the court a pleading, written motion, or other paper—whether by signing, filing, submitting, or later advocating it—an attorney or unrepresented party certifies that to the best of the person's knowledge, information, and belief, formed after an inquiry reasonable under the circumstances:

(1) it is not being presented for any improper purpose, such as to harass, cause unnecessary delay, or needlessly increase the cost of litigation;

(2) the claims, defenses, and other legal contentions are warranted by existing law or by a nonfrivolous argument for extending, modifying, or reversing existing law or for establishing new law;

(3) the factual contentions have evidentiary support or, if specifically so identified, will likely have evidentiary support after a reasonable opportunity for further investigation or discovery; and

(4) the denials of factual contentions are warranted on the evidence or, if specifically so identified, are reasonably based on belief or a lack of information.

(c) **Sanctions**.

(1) IN GENERAL. If, after notice and a reasonable opportunity to respond, the court determines that Rule 11(b) has been violated, the court may impose an

appropriate sanction on any attorney, law firm, or party that violated the rule or is responsible for the violation. Absent exceptional circumstances, a law firm must be held jointly responsible for a violation committed by its partner, associate, or employee.

(2) MOTION FOR SANCTIONS. A motion for sanctions must be made separately from any other motion and must describe the specific conduct that allegedly violates Rule 11(b). The motion must be served under Rule 5, but it must not be filed or be presented to the court if the challenged paper, claim, defense, contention, or denial is withdrawn or appropriately corrected within 21 days after service or within another time the court sets. If warranted, the court may award to the prevailing party the reasonable expenses, including attorney's fees, incurred for the motion.

(3) ON THE COURT'S INITIATIVE. On its own, the court may order an attorney, law firm, or party to show cause why conduct specifically described in the order has not violated Rule 11(b).

(4) NATURE OF A SANCTION. A sanction imposed under this rule must be limited to what suffices to deter repetition of the conduct or comparable conduct by others similarly situated. The sanction may include nonmonetary directives; an order to pay a penalty into court; or, if imposed on motion and warranted for effective deterrence, an order directing payment to the movant of part or all of the reasonable attorney's fees and other expenses directly resulting from the violation.

(5) LIMITATIONS ON MONETARY SANCTIONS. The court must not impose a monetary sanction:

(A) against a represented party for violating Rule 11(b)(2); or

(B) on its own, unless it issued the show-cause order under Rule 11(c)(3) before voluntary dismissal or settlement of the claims made by or against the party that is, or whose attorneys are, to be sanctioned.

(6) REQUIREMENTS FOR AN ORDER. An order imposing a sanction must describe the sanctioned conduct and explain the basis for the sanction.

(d) **Inapplicability to Discovery**. This rule does not apply to disclosures and discovery requests, responses, objections, and motions under Rules 26 through 37.

Rule 12 – Defenses and Objections: When and How Presented; Motion for Judgment on the Pleadings; Consolidating Motions; Waiving Defenses; Pretrial Hearing

(a) **Time to Serve a Responsive Pleading**.

(1) IN GENERAL. Unless another time is specified by this rule or a federal statute, the time for serving a responsive pleading is as follows:

(A) A defendant must serve an answer:

(i) within 21 days after being served with the summons and complaint; or

(ii) if it has timely waived service under Rule 4(d), within 60 days after the request for a waiver was sent, or within 90 days after it was sent to the defendant outside any judicial district of the United States.

(B) A party must serve an answer to a counterclaim or crossclaim within 21 days after being served with the pleading that states the counterclaim or crossclaim.

(C) A party must serve a reply to an answer within 21 days after being served with an order to reply, unless the order specifies a different time.

(2) UNITED STATES AND ITS AGENCIES, OFFICERS, OR EMPLOYEES SUED IN AN OFFICIAL CAPACITY.The United States, a United States agency, or a United States officer or employee sued only in an official capacity must serve an answer to a complaint, counterclaim, or crossclaim within 60 days after service on the United States attorney.

(3) UNITED STATES OFFICERS OR EMPLOYEES SUED IN AN INDIVIDUAL CAPACITY. A United States officer or employee sued in an individual capacity for an act or omission occurring in connection with duties performed on the United States' behalf must serve an answer to a complaint, counterclaim, or crossclaim within 60 days after service on the officer or employee or service on the United States attorney, whichever is later.

(4) EFFECT OF A MOTION. Unless the court sets a different time, serving a motion under this rule alters these periods as follows:

(A) if the court denies the motion or postpones its disposition until trial, the responsive pleading must be served within 14 days after notice of the court's action; or

(B) if the court grants a motion for a more definite statement, the responsive pleading must be served within 14 days after the more definite statement is served.

(b) **How to Present Defenses**. Every defense to a claim for relief in any pleading must be asserted in the responsive pleading if one is required. But a party may assert the following defenses by motion:

(1) lack of subject-matter jurisdiction;

(2) lack of personal jurisdiction;

(3) improper venue;

(4) insufficient process;

(5) insufficient service of process;

(6) failure to state a claim upon which relief can be granted; and

(7) failure to join a party under Rule 19.

A motion asserting any of these defenses must be made before pleading if a responsive pleading is allowed. If a pleading sets out a claim for relief that does not require a responsive pleading, an opposing party may assert at trial any defense to that claim. No defense or objection is waived by joining it with one or more other defenses or objections in a responsive pleading or in a motion.

(c) **Motion for Judgment on the Pleadings**. After the pleadings are closed—but early enough not to delay trial—a party may move for judgment on the pleadings.

(d) **Result of Presenting Matters Outside the Pleadings**. If, on a motion under Rule 12(b)(6) or 12(c), matters outside the pleadings are presented to and not excluded by the court, the motion must be treated as one for summary judgment under Rule 56. All parties must be given a reasonable opportunity to present all the material that is pertinent to the motion.

(e) **Motion for a More Definite Statement**. A party may move for a more definite statement of a pleading to which a responsive pleading is allowed but which is so vague or ambiguous that the party cannot reasonably prepare a response. The motion must be made before filing a responsive pleading and must point out the defects complained of and the details desired. If the court orders a more definite statement and the order is not obeyed within 14 days after notice of the order or within the time the court sets, the court may strike the pleading or issue any other appropriate order.

(f) **Motion to Strike**. The court may strike from a pleading an insufficient defense or any redundant, immaterial, impertinent, or scandalous matter. The court may act:

(1) on its own; or

(2) on motion made by a party either before responding to the pleading or, if a response is not allowed, within 21 days after being served with the pleading.

(g) **Joining Motions**.

(1) RIGHT TO JOIN. A motion under this rule may be joined with any other motion allowed by this rule.

(2) LIMITATION ON FURTHER MOTIONS. Except as provided in Rule 12(h)(2) or (3), a party that makes a motion under this rule must not make another motion under this rule raising a defense or objection that was available to the party but omitted from its earlier motion.

(h) **Waiving and Preserving Certain Defenses**.

(1) WHEN SOME ARE WAIVED. A party waives any defense listed in Rule 12(b)(2)–(5) by:

(A) omitting it from a motion in the circumstances described in Rule 12(g)(2); or

(B) failing to either:

(i) make it by motion under this rule; or

(ii) include it in a responsive pleading or in an amendment allowed by Rule 15(a)(1) as a matter of course.

(2) WHEN TO RAISE OTHERS. Failure to state a claim upon which relief can be granted, to join a person required by Rule 19(b), or to state a legal defense to a claim may be raised:

(A) in any pleading allowed or ordered under Rule 7(a);

(B) by a motion under Rule 12(c); or

(C) at trial.

(3) LACK OF SUBJECT-MATTER JURISDICTION. If the court determines at any time that it lacks subject-matter jurisdiction, the court must dismiss the action.

(i) **Hearing Before Trial**. If a party so moves, any defense listed in Rule 12(b)(1)–(7)—whether made in a pleading or by motion—and a motion under Rule

12(c) must be heard and decided before trial unless the court orders a deferral until trial.

Rule 13 – Counterclaim and Crossclaim

(a) **Compulsory Counterclaim.**

(1) IN GENERAL. A pleading must state as a counterclaim any claim that—at the time of its service—the pleader has against an opposing party if the claim:

(A) arises out of the transaction or occurrence that is the subject matter of the opposing party's claim; and

(B) does not require adding another party over whom the court cannot acquire jurisdiction.

(2) EXCEPTIONS. The pleader need not state the claim if:

(A) when the action was commenced, the claim was the subject of another pending action; or

(B) the opposing party sued on its claim by attachment or other process that did not establish personal jurisdiction over the pleader on that claim, and the pleader does not assert any counterclaim under this rule.

(b) **Permissive Counterclaim.** A pleading may state as a counterclaim against an opposing party any claim that is not compulsory.

(c) **Relief Sought in a Counterclaim.** A counterclaim need not diminish or defeat the recovery sought by the opposing party. It may request relief that exceeds in amount or differs in kind from the relief sought by the opposing party.

(d) **Counterclaim Against the United States.** These rules do not expand the right to assert a counterclaim—or to claim a credit—against the United States or a United States officer or agency.

(e) **Counterclaim Maturing or Acquired After Pleading.** The court may permit a party to file a supplemental pleading asserting a counterclaim that matured or was acquired by the party after serving an earlier pleading.

(f) [Abrogated.]

(g) **Crossclaim Against a Coparty.** A pleading may state as a crossclaim any claim by one party against a coparty if the claim arises out of the transaction or occurrence that is the subject matter of the original action or of a counterclaim, or if the claim relates to any property that is the subject matter of the original action. The crossclaim may include a claim that the coparty is or may be liable to the crossclaimant for all or part of a claim asserted in the action against the crossclaimant.

(h) **Joining Additional Parties.** Rules 19 and 20 govern the addition of a person as a party to a counterclaim or crossclaim.

(i) **Separate Trials; Separate Judgments.** If the court orders separate trials under Rule 42(b), it may enter judgment on a counterclaim or crossclaim under Rule 54(b)when it has jurisdiction to do so, even if the opposing party's claims have been dismissed or otherwise resolved.

Joint & Several
Imdentwer
Contrabution

Rule 14 – Third-Party Practice

(a) **When a Defending Party May Bring in a Third Party**.

(1) TIMING OF THE SUMMONS AND COMPLAINT. A defending party may, as third-party plaintiff, serve a summons and complaint on a nonparty who is or may be liable to it for all or part of the claim against it. But the third-party plaintiff must, by motion, obtain the court's leave if it files the third-party complaint more than 14 days after serving its original answer.

(2) THIRD-PARTY DEFENDANT'S CLAIMS AND DEFENSES. The person served with the summons and third-party complaint—the "third-party defendant":

(A) must assert any defense against the third-party plaintiff's claim under Rule 12;

(B) must assert any counterclaim against the third-party plaintiff under Rule 13a, and may assert any counterclaim against the third-party plaintiff under Rule 13(b) or any crossclaim against another third-party defendant under Rule 13(g);

(C) may assert against the plaintiff any defense that the third-party plaintiff has to the plaintiff's claim; and

(D) may also assert against the plaintiff any claim arising out of the transaction or occurrence that is the subject matter of the plaintiff's claim against the third-party plaintiff.

(3) PLAINTIFF'S CLAIMS AGAINST A THIRD-PARTY DEFENDANT. The plaintiff may assert against the third-party defendant any claim arising out of the transaction or occurrence that is the subject matter of the plaintiff's claim against the third-party plaintiff. The third-party defendant must then assert any defense under Rule 12 and any counterclaim under Rule 13(a), and may assert any counterclaim under Rule 13(b) or any crossclaim under Rule 13(g).

(4) MOTION TO STRIKE, SEVER, OR TRY SEPARATELY. Any party may move to strike the third-party claim, to sever it, or to try it separately.

(5) THIRD-PARTY DEFENDANT'S CLAIM AGAINST A NONPARTY. A third-party defendant may proceed under this rule against a nonparty who is or may be liable to the third-party defendant for all or part of any claim against it.

(6) THIRD-PARTY COMPLAINT IN REM. If it is within the admiralty or maritime jurisdiction, a third-party complaint may be in rem. In that event, a reference in this rule to the "summons" includes the warrant of arrest, and a reference to the defendant or third-party plaintiff includes, when appropriate, a person who asserts a right under Supplemental Rule C(6)(a)(i) in the property arrested.

(b) **When a Plaintiff May Bring in a Third Party**. When a claim is asserted against a plaintiff, the plaintiff may bring in a third party if this rule would allow a defendant to do so.

(c) **Admiralty or Maritime Claim**.

(1) SCOPE OF IMPLEADER. If a plaintiff asserts an admiralty or maritime claim under Rule 9(h), the defendant or a person who asserts a right under Supplemental Rule C(6)(a)(i) may, as a third-party plaintiff, bring in a third-party defendant who may be wholly or partly liable—either to the plaintiff or to the third-party plaintiff— for

remedy over, contribution, or otherwise on account of the same transaction, occurrence, or series of transactions or occurrences.

(2) DEFENDING AGAINST A DEMAND FOR JUDGMENT FOR THE PLAINTIFF. The third-party plaintiff may demand judgment in the plaintiff's favor against the third-party defendant. In that event, the third-party defendant must defend under Rule 12 against the plaintiff's claim as well as the third-party plaintiff's claim; and the action proceeds as if the plaintiff had sued both the third-party defendant and the third-party plaintiff.

Rule 15 – Amended and Supplemental Pleadings

(a) **Amendments Before Trial**.

(1) AMENDING AS A MATTER OF COURSE. A party may amend its pleading once as a matter of course within:

(A) 21 days after serving it, or

(B) if the pleading is one to which a responsive pleading is required, 21 days after service of a responsive pleading or 21 days after service of a motion under Rule 12(b), (e), or (f), whichever is earlier.

(2) OTHER AMENDMENTS. In all other cases, a party may amend its pleading only with the opposing party's written consent or the court's leave. The court should freely give leave when justice so requires.

(3) TIME TO RESPOND. Unless the court orders otherwise, any required response to an amended pleading must be made within the time remaining to respond to the original pleading or within 14 days after service of the amended pleading, whichever is later.

(b) **Amendments During and After Trial**.

(1) BASED ON AN OBJECTION AT TRIAL. If, at trial, a party objects that evidence is not within the issues raised in the pleadings, the court may permit the pleadings to be amended. The court should freely permit an amendment when doing so will aid in presenting the merits and the objecting party fails to satisfy the court that the evidence would prejudice that party's action or defense on the merits. The court may grant a continuance to enable the objecting party to meet the evidence.

(2) FOR ISSUES TRIED BY CONSENT. When an issue not raised by the pleadings is tried by the parties' express or implied consent, it must be treated in all respects as if raised in the pleadings. A party may move—at any time, even after judgment—to amend the pleadings to conform them to the evidence and to raise an unpleaded issue. But failure to amend does not affect the result of the trial of that issue.

(c) **Relation Back of Amendments**.

(1) WHEN AN AMENDMENT RELATES BACK. An amendment to a pleading relates back to the date of the original pleading when:

(A) the law that provides the applicable statute of limitations allows relation back;

(B) the amendment asserts a claim or defense that arose out of the conduct, transaction, or occurrence set out—or attempted to be set out—in the original pleading; or

(C) the amendment changes the party or the naming of the party against whom a claim is asserted, if Rule 15(c)(1)(B) is satisfied and if, within the period provided by Rule 4(m) for serving the summons and complaint, the party to be brought in by amendment:

(i) received such notice of the action that it will not be prejudiced in defending on the merits; and

(ii) knew or should have known that the action would have been brought against it, but for a mistake concerning the proper party's identity.

(2) NOTICE TO THE UNITED STATES. When the United States or a United States officer or agency is added as a defendant by amendment, the notice requirements of Rule 15(c)(1)(C)(i) and (ii) are satisfied if, during the stated period, process was delivered or mailed to the United States attorney or the United States attorney's designee, to the Attorney General of the United States, or to the officer or agency.

(d) **Supplemental Pleadings**. On motion and reasonable notice, the court may, on just terms, permit a party to serve a supplemental pleading setting out any transaction, occurrence, or event that happened after the date of the pleading to be supplemented. The court may permit supplementation even though the original pleading is defective in stating a claim or defense. The court may order that the opposing party plead to the supplemental pleading within a specified time.

Rule 16 – Pretrial Conferences; Scheduling; Management

(a) **Purposes of a Pretrial Conference**. In any action, the court may order the attorneys and any unrepresented parties to appear for one or more pretrial conferences for such purposes as:

(1) expediting disposition of the action;

(2) establishing early and continuing control so that the case will not be protracted because of lack of management;

(3) discouraging wasteful pretrial activities;

(4) improving the quality of the trial through more thorough preparation; and

(5) facilitating settlement.

(b) **Scheduling**.

(1) SCHEDULING ORDER. Except in categories of actions exempted by local rule, the district judge—or a magistrate judge when authorized by local rule—must issue a scheduling order:

(A) after receiving the parties' report under Rule 26(f); or

(B) after consulting with the parties' attorneys and any unrepresented parties at a scheduling conference.

(2) TIME TO ISSUE. The judge must issue the scheduling order as soon as practicable, but unless the judge finds good cause for delay, the judge must issue it within the earlier of 90 days after any defendant has been served with the complaint or 60 days after any defendant has appeared.

(3) CONTENTS OF THE ORDER.

(A) Required Contents. The scheduling order must limit the time to join other parties, amend the pleadings, complete discovery, and file motions.

(B) Permitted Contents. The scheduling order may:

(i) modify the timing of disclosures under Rules 26(a) and 26(e)(1);

(ii) modify the extent of discovery;

(iii) provide for disclosure, discovery, or preservation of electronically stored information;

(iv) include any agreements the parties reach for asserting claims of privilege or of protection as trial-preparation material after information is produced, including agreements reached under Federal Rule of Evidence 502;

(v) direct that before moving for an order relating to discovery, the movant must request a conference with the court;

(vi) set dates for pretrial conferences and for trial; and

(vii) include other appropriate matters.

(4) MODIFYING A SCHEDULE. A schedule may be modified only for good cause and with the judge's consent.

(c) **Attendance and Matters for Consideration at a Pretrial Conference**.

(1) ATTENDANCE. A represented party must authorize at least one of its attorneys to make stipulations and admissions about all matters that can reasonably be anticipated for discussion at a pretrial conference. If appropriate, the court may require that a party or its representative be present or reasonably available by other means to consider possible settlement.

(2) MATTERS FOR CONSIDERATION. At any pretrial conference, the court may consider and take appropriate action on the following matters:

(A) formulating and simplifying the issues, and eliminating frivolous claims or defenses;

(B) amending the pleadings if necessary or desirable;

(C) obtaining admissions and stipulations about facts and documents to avoid unnecessary proof, and ruling in advance on the admissibility of evidence;

(D) avoiding unnecessary proof and cumulative evidence, and limiting the use of testimony under Federal Rule of Evidence 702;

(E) determining the appropriateness and timing of summary adjudication under Rule 56;

(F) controlling and scheduling discovery, including orders affecting disclosures and discovery under Rule 26 and Rules 29 through 37;

(G) identifying witnesses and documents, scheduling the filing and exchange of any pretrial briefs, and setting dates for further conferences and for trial;

(H) referring matters to a magistrate judge or a master;

(I) settling the case and using special procedures to assist in resolving the dispute when authorized by statute or local rule;

(J) determining the form and content of the pretrial order;

(K) disposing of pending motions;

(L) adopting special procedures for managing potentially difficult or protracted actions that may involve complex issues, multiple parties, difficult legal questions, or unusual proof problems;

(M) ordering a separate trial under Rule 42(b) of a claim, counterclaim, crossclaim, third-party claim, or particular issue;

(N) ordering the presentation of evidence early in the trial on a manageable issue that might, on the evidence, be the basis for a judgment as a matter of law under Rule 50(a) or a judgment on partial findings under Rule 52(c);

(o) establishing a reasonable limit on the time allowed to present evidence; and

(P) facilitating in other ways the just, speedy, and inexpensive disposition of the action.

(d) **Pretrial Orders**. After any conference under this rule, the court should issue an order reciting the action taken. This order controls the course of the action unless the court modifies it.

(e) **Final Pretrial Conference and Orders**. The court may hold a final pretrial conference to formulate a trial plan, including a plan to facilitate the admission of evidence. The conference must be held as close to the start of trial as is reasonable, and must be attended by at least one attorney who will conduct the trial for each party and by any unrepresented party. The court may modify the order issued after a final pretrial conference only to prevent manifest injustice.

(f) **Sanctions**.

(1) IN GENERAL. On motion or on its own, the court may issue any just orders, including those authorized by Rule 37(b)(2)(A)(ii)-(vii), if a party or its attorney:

(A) fails to appear at a scheduling or other pretrial conference;

(B) is substantially unprepared to participate-or does not participate in good faith-in the conference; or

(C) fails to obey a scheduling or other pretrial order.

(2) IMPOSING FEES AND COSTS. Instead of or in addition to any other sanction, the court must order the party, its attorney, or both to pay the reasonable expenses—including attorney's fees—incurred because of any noncompliance with this rule, unless the noncompliance was substantially justified or other circumstances make an award of expenses unjust.

Title IV – Parties (Rules 17-25)

Rule 17 – Plaintiff and Defendant; Capacity; Public Officers

(a) **Real Party in Interest**.

(1) DESIGNATION IN GENERAL. An action must be prosecuted in the name of the real party in interest. The following may sue in their own names without joining the person for whose benefit the action is brought:

(A) an executor;

(B) an administrator;

(C) a guardian;

(D) a bailee;

(E) a trustee of an express trust;

(F) a party with whom or in whose name a contract has been made for another's benefit; and

(G) a party authorized by statute.

(2) ACTION IN THE NAME OF THE UNITED STATES FOR ANOTHER'S USE OR BENEFIT. When a federal statute so provides, an action for another's use or benefit must be brought in the name of the United States.

(3) JOINDER OF THE REAL PARTY IN INTEREST. The court may not dismiss an action for failure to prosecute in the name of the real party in interest until, after an objection, a reasonable time has been allowed for the real party in interest to ratify, join, or be substituted into the action. After ratification, joinder, or substitution, the action proceeds as if it had been originally commenced by the real party in interest.

(b) **Capacity to Sue or Be Sued**. Capacity to sue or be sued is determined as follows:

(1) for an individual who is not acting in a representative capacity, by the law of the individual's domicile;

(2) for a corporation, by the law under which it was organized; and

(3) for all other parties, by the law of the state where the court is located, except that:

(A) a partnership or other unincorporated association with no such capacity under that state's law may sue or be sued in its common name to enforce a substantive right existing under the United States Constitution or laws; and

(B) 28 U.S.C. §§754 and 959(a) govern the capacity of a receiver appointed by a United States court to sue or be sued in a United States court.

(c) **Minor or Incompetent Person**.

(1) WITH A REPRESENTATIVE. The following representatives may sue or defend on behalf of a minor or an incompetent person:

(A) a general guardian;

(B) a committee;

(C) a conservator; or

(D) a like fiduciary.

(2) WITHOUT A REPRESENTATIVE. A minor or an incompetent person who does not have a duly appointed representative may sue by a next friend or by a guardian ad litem. The court must appoint a guardian ad litem—or issue another appropriate order—to protect a minor or incompetent person who is unrepresented in an action.

(d) **Public Officer's Title and Name**. A public officer who sues or is sued in an official capacity may be designated by official title rather than by name, but the court may order that the officer's name be added.

Rule 18 – Joinder of Claims

(a) **In General**. A party asserting a claim, counterclaim, crossclaim, or third-party claim may join, as independent or alternative claims, as many claims as it has against an opposing party.

(b) **Joinder of Contingent Claims**. A party may join two claims even though one of them is contingent on the disposition of the other; but the court may grant relief only in accordance with the parties' relative substantive rights. In particular, a plaintiff may state a claim for money and a claim to set aside a conveyance that is fraudulent as to that plaintiff, without first obtaining a judgment for the money.

Rule 19 – Required Joinder of Parties

(a) **Persons Required to Be Joined if Feasible**.

(1) REQUIRED PARTY. A person who is subject to service of process and whose joinder will not deprive the court of subject-matter jurisdiction must be joined as a party if:

(A) in that person's absence, the court cannot accord complete relief among existing parties; or

(B) that person claims an interest relating to the subject of the action and is so situated that disposing of the action in the person's absence may:

(i) as a practical matter impair or impede the person's ability to protect the interest; or

(ii) leave an existing party subject to a substantial risk of incurring double, multiple, or otherwise inconsistent obligations because of the interest.

(2) JOINDER BY COURT ORDER. If a person has not been joined as required, the court must order that the person be made a party. A person who refuses to join as a plaintiff may be made either a defendant or, in a proper case, an involuntary plaintiff.

(3) VENUE. If a joined party objects to venue and the joinder would make venue improper, the court must dismiss that party.

(b) **When Joinder Is Not Feasible**. If a person who is required to be joined if feasible cannot be joined, the court must determine whether, in equity and good conscience, the action should proceed among the existing parties or should be dismissed. The factors for the court to consider include:

(1) the extent to which a judgment rendered in the person's absence might prejudice that person or the existing parties;

(2) the extent to which any prejudice could be lessened or avoided by:

(A) protective provisions in the judgment;

(B) shaping the relief; or

(C) other measures;

(3) whether a judgment rendered in the person's absence would be adequate; and

(4) whether the plaintiff would have an adequate remedy if the action were dismissed for nonjoinder.

(c) **Pleading the Reasons for Nonjoinder**. When asserting a claim for relief, a party must state:

(1) the name, if known, of any person who is required to be joined if feasible but is not joined; and

(2) the reasons for not joining that person.

(d) **Exception for Class Actions**. This rule is subject to Rule 23.

Rule 20 – Permissive Joinder of Parties

(a) **Persons Who May Join or Be Joined**.

(1) PLAINTIFFS. Persons may join in one action as plaintiffs if:

(A) they assert any right to relief jointly, severally, or in the alternative with respect to or arising out of the same transaction, occurrence, or series of transactions or occurrences; and

(B) any question of law or fact common to all plaintiffs will arise in the action.

(2) DEFENDANTS. Persons—as well as a vessel, cargo, or other property subject to admiralty process in rem—may be joined in one action as defendants if:

(A) any right to relief is asserted against them jointly, severally, or in the alternative with respect to or arising out of the same transaction, occurrence, or series of transactions or occurrences; and

(B) any question of law or fact common to all defendants will arise in the action.

(3) EXTENT OF RELIEF. Neither a plaintiff nor a defendant need be interested in obtaining or defending against all the relief demanded. The court may grant judgment to one or more plaintiffs according to their rights, and against one or more defendants according to their liabilities.

(b) **Protective Measures**. The court may issue orders—including an order for separate trials—to protect a party against embarrassment, delay, expense, or other prejudice that arises from including a person against whom the party asserts no claim and who asserts no claim against the party.

Rule 21 – Misjoinder and Nonjoinder of Parties

Misjoinder of parties is not a ground for dismissing an action. On motion _____ own, the court may at any time, on just terms, add or drop a party. The court may also sever any claim against a party.

Rule 22 – Interpleader

(a) **Grounds**.

(1) BY A PLAINTIFF. Persons with claims that may expose a plaintiff to double or multiple liability may be joined as defendants and required to interplead. Joinder for interpleader is proper even though:

(A) the claims of the several claimants, or the titles on which their claims depend, lack a common origin or are adverse and independent rather than identical; or

(B) the plaintiff denies liability in whole or in part to any or all of the claimants.

(2) BY A DEFENDANT. A defendant exposed to similar liability may seek interpleader through a crossclaim or counterclaim.

(b) **Relation to Other Rules and Statutes**. This rule supplements—and does not limit—the joinder of parties allowed by Rule 20. The remedy this rule provides is in addition to—and does not supersede or limit—the remedy provided by 28 U.S.C. §§1335, 1397, and 2361. An action under those statutes must be conducted under these rules.

Rule 23 – Class Actions

(a) **Prerequisites**. One or more members of a class may sue or be sued as representative parties on behalf of all members only if:

(1) the class is so numerous that joinder of all members is impracticable;

(2) there are questions of law or fact common to the class;

(3) the claims or defenses of the representative parties are typical of the claims or defenses of the class; and

(4) the representative parties will fairly and adequately protect the interests of the class.

(b) **Types of Class Actions**. A class action may be maintained if Rule 23(a) is satisfied and if:

(1) prosecuting separate actions by or against individual class members would create a risk of:

(A) inconsistent or varying adjudications with respect to individual class members that would establish incompatible standards of conduct for the party opposing the class; or

(B) adjudications with respect to individual class members that, as a practical matter, would be dispositive of the interests of the other members not parties to the individual adjudications or would substantially impair or impede their ability to protect their interests;

(2) the party opposing the class has acted or refused to act on grounds that apply generally to the class, so that final injunctive relief or corresponding declaratory relief is appropriate respecting the class as a whole; or

(3) the court finds that the questions of law or fact common to class members predominate over any questions affecting only individual members, and that a class action is superior to other available methods for fairly and efficiently adjudicating the controversy. The matters pertinent to these findings include:

(A) the class members' interests in individually controlling the prosecution or defense of separate actions;

(B) the extent and nature of any litigation concerning the controversy already begun by or against class members;

(C) the desirability or undesirability of concentrating the litigation of the claims in the particular forum; and

(D) the likely difficulties in managing a class action.

(c) **Certification Order; Notice to Class Members; Judgment; Issues Classes; Subclasses**.

(1) CERTIFICATION ORDER.

(A) TIME TO ISSUE. At an early practicable time after a person sues or is sued as a class representative, the court must determine by order whether to certify the action as a class action.

(B) DEFINING THE CLASS; APPOINTING CLASS COUNSEL. An order that certifies a class action must define the class and the class claims, issues, or defenses, and must appoint class counsel under Rule 23(g).

(C) ALTERING OR AMENDING THE ORDER. An order that grants or denies class certification may be altered or amended before final judgment.

(2) NOTICE.

(A) FOR (B)(1) OR (B)(2) CLASSES. For any class certified under Rule 23(b)(1) or (b)(2), the court may direct appropriate notice to the class.

(B) FOR (B)(3) CLASSES. For any class certified under Rule 23(b)(3), the court must direct to class members the best notice that is practicable under the circumstances, including individual notice to all members who can be identified through reasonable effort. The notice must clearly and concisely state in plain, easily understood language:

(i) the nature of the action;

(ii) the definition of the class certified;

(iii) the class claims, issues, or defenses;

(iv) that a class member may enter an appearance through an attorney if the member so desires;

(v) that the court will exclude from the class any member who requests exclusion;

(vi) the time and manner for requesting exclusion; and

(vii) the binding effect of a class judgment on members under Rule 23(c)(3).

(3) JUDGMENT. Whether or not favorable to the class, the judgment in a class action must:

(A) for any class certified under Rule 23(b)(1) or (b)(2), include and describe those whom the court finds to be class members; and

(B) for any class certified under Rule 23(b)(3), include and specify or describe those to whom the Rule 23(c)(2) notice was directed, who have not requested exclusion, and whom the court finds to be class members.

(4) PARTICULAR ISSUES. When appropriate, an action may be brought or maintained as a class action with respect to particular issues.

(5) SUBCLASSES. When appropriate, a class may be divided into subclasses that are each treated as a class under this rule.

(d) **Conducting the Action**.

(1) IN GENERAL. In conducting an action under this rule, the court may issue orders that:

(A) determine the course of proceedings or prescribe measures to prevent undue repetition or complication in presenting evidence or argument;

(B) require—to protect class members and fairly conduct the action—giving appropriate notice to some or all class members of:

(i) any step in the action;

(ii) the proposed extent of the judgment; or

(iii) the members' opportunity to signify whether they consider the representation fair and adequate, to intervene and present claims or defenses, or to otherwise come into the action;

(C) impose conditions on the representative parties or on intervenors;

(D) require that the pleadings be amended to eliminate allegations about representation of absent persons and that the action proceed accordingly; or

(E) deal with similar procedural matters.

(2) COMBINING AND AMENDING ORDERS. An order under Rule 23(d)(1) may be altered or amended from time to time and may be combined with an order under Rule 16.

(e) **Settlement, Voluntary Dismissal, or Compromise**. The claims, issues, or defenses of a certified class may be settled, voluntarily dismissed, or compromised only with the court's approval. The following procedures apply to a proposed settlement, voluntary dismissal, or compromise:

(1) The court must direct notice in a reasonable manner to all class members who would be bound by the proposal.

(2) If the proposal would bind class members, the court may approve it only after a hearing and on finding that it is fair, reasonable, and adequate.

(3) The parties seeking approval must file a statement identifying any agreement made in connection with the proposal.

(4) If the class action was previously certified under Rule 23(b)(3), the court may refuse to approve a settlement unless it affords a new opportunity to request exclusion to individual class members who had an earlier opportunity to request exclusion but did not do so.

(5) Any class member may object to the proposal if it requires court approval under this subdivision (e); the objection may be withdrawn only with the court's approval.

(f) **Appeals**. A court of appeals may permit an appeal from an order granting or denying class-action certification under this rule if a petition for permission to appeal is filed with the circuit clerk within 14 days after the order is entered. An appeal does not stay proceedings in the district court unless the district judge or the court of appeals so orders.

(g) **Class Counsel**.

(1) APPOINTING CLASS COUNSEL. Unless a statute provides otherwise, a court that certifies a class must appoint class counsel. In appointing class counsel, the court:

(A) must consider:

(i) the work counsel has done in identifying or investigating potential claims in the action;

(ii) counsel's experience in handling class actions, other complex litigation, and the types of claims asserted in the action;

(iii) counsel's knowledge of the applicable law; and

(iv) the resources that counsel will commit to representing the class;

(B) may consider any other matter pertinent to counsel's ability to fairly and adequately represent the interests of the class;

(C) may order potential class counsel to provide information on any subject pertinent to the appointment and to propose terms for attorney's fees and nontaxable costs;

(D) may include in the appointing order provisions about the award of attorney's fees or nontaxable costs under Rule 23(h); and

(E) may make further orders in connection with the appointment.

(2) STANDARD FOR APPOINTING CLASS COUNSEL. When one applicant seeks appointment as class counsel, the court may appoint that applicant only if the applicant is adequate under Rule 23(g)(1) and (4). If more than one adequate applicant seeks appointment, the court must appoint the applicant best able to represent the interests of the class.

(3) INTERIM COUNSEL. The court may designate interim counsel to act on behalf of a putative class before determining whether to certify the action as a class action.

(4) DUTY OF CLASS COUNSEL. Class counsel must fairly and adequately represent the interests of the class.

(h) **Attorney's Fees and Nontaxable Costs**. In a certified class action, the court may award reasonable attorney's fees and nontaxable costs that are authorized by law or by the parties' agreement. The following procedures apply:

(1) A claim for an award must be made by motion under Rule 54(d)(2), subject to the provisions of this subdivision (h), at a time the court sets. Notice of the motion must be served on all parties and, for motions by class counsel, directed to class members in a reasonable manner.

(2) A class member, or a party from whom payment is sought, may object to the motion.

(3) The court may hold a hearing and must find the facts and state its legal conclusions under Rule 52(a).

(4) The court may refer issues related to the amount of the award to a special master or a magistrate judge, as provided in Rule 54(d)(2)(D).

Rule 24 – Intervention

(a) **Intervention of Right**. On timely motion, the court must permit anyone to intervene who:

(1) is given an unconditional right to intervene by a federal statute; or

(2) claims an interest relating to the property or transaction that is the subject of the action, and is so situated that disposing of the action may as a practical matter impair or impede the movant's ability to protect its interest, unless existing parties adequately represent that interest.

(b) **Permissive Intervention**.

(1) IN GENERAL. On timely motion, the court may permit anyone to intervene who:

(A) is given a conditional right to intervene by a federal statute; or

(B) has a claim or defense that shares with the main action a common question of law or fact.

(2) BY A GOVERNMENT OFFICER OR AGENCY. On timely motion, the court may permit a federal or state governmental officer or agency to intervene if a party's claim or defense is based on:

(A) a statute or executive order administered by the officer or agency; or

(B) any regulation, order, requirement, or agreement issued or made under the statute or executive order.

(3) DELAY OR PREJUDICE. In exercising its discretion, the court must consider whether the intervention will unduly delay or prejudice the adjudication of the original parties' rights.

(c) **Notice and Pleading Required**. A motion to intervene must be served on the parties as provided in Rule 5. The motion must state the grounds for intervention and be accompanied by a pleading that sets out the claim or defense for which intervention is sought.

Rule 25 – Substitution of Parties

(a) **Death**.

(1) SUBSTITUTION IF THE CLAIM IS NOT EXTINGUISHED. If a party dies and the claim is not extinguished, the court may order substitution of the proper party. A motion for substitution may be made by any party or by the decedent's successor or representative. If the motion is not made within 90 days after service of a statement noting the death, the action by or against the decedent must be dismissed.

(2) CONTINUATION AMONG THE REMAINING PARTIES. After a party's death, if the right sought to be enforced survives only to or against the remaining parties, the action does not abate, but proceeds in favor of or against the remaining parties. The death should be noted on the record.

(3) SERVICE. A motion to substitute, together with a notice of hearing, must be served on the parties as provided in Rule 5 and on nonparties as provided in Rule 4. A statement noting death must be served in the same manner. Service may be made in any judicial district.

(b) **Incompetency**. If a party becomes incompetent, the court may, on motion, permit the action to be continued by or against the party's representative. The motion must be served as provided in Rule 25(a)(3).

(c) **Transfer of Interest**. If an interest is transferred, the action may be continued by or against the original party unless the court, on motion, orders the transferee to be substituted in the action or joined with the original party. The motion must be served as provided in Rule 25(a)(3).

(d) **Public Officers; Death or Separation from Office**. An action does not abate when a public officer who is a party in an official capacity dies, resigns, or otherwise ceases to hold office while the action is pending. The officer's successor is automatically substituted as a party. Later proceedings should be in the substituted party's name, but any misnomer not affecting the parties' substantial rights must be disregarded. The court may order substitution at any time, but the absence of such an order does not affect the substitution.

Title V – Disclosures and Discovery (Rules 26-37)

Rule 26 – Duty to Disclose; General Provisions Governing Discovery

(a) **Required Disclosures**.

(1) INITIAL DISCLOSURE.

(A) In General. Except as exempted by Rule 26(a)(1)(B) or as otherwise stipulated or ordered by the court, a party must, without awaiting a discovery request, provide to the other parties:

(i) the name and, if known, the address and telephone number of each individual likely to have discoverable information—along with the subjects of that information—that the disclosing party may use to support its claims or defenses, unless the use would be solely for impeachment;

(ii) a copy—or a description by category and location—of all documents, electronically stored information, and tangible things that the disclosing party has in its possession, custody, or control and may use to support its claims or defenses, unless the use would be solely for impeachment;

(iii) a computation of each category of damages claimed by the disclosing party— who must also make available for inspection and copying as under Rule 34 the documents or other evidentiary material, unless privileged or protected from disclosure, on which each computation is based, including materials bearing on the nature and extent of injuries suffered; and

(iv) for inspection and copying as under Rule 34, any insurance agreement under which an insurance business may be liable to satisfy all or part of a possible judgment in the action or to indemnify or reimburse for payments made to satisfy the judgment.

(B) Proceedings Exempt from Initial Disclosure. The following proceedings are exempt from initial disclosure:

(i) an action for review on an administrative record;

(ii) a forfeiture action in rem arising from a federal statute;

(iii) a petition for habeas corpus or any other proceeding to challenge a criminal conviction or sentence;

(iv) an action brought without an attorney by a person in the custody of the United States, a state, or a state subdivision;

(v) an action to enforce or quash an administrative summons or subpoena;

(vi) an action by the United States to recover benefit payments;

(vii) an action by the United States to collect on a student loan guaranteed by the United States;

(viii) a proceeding ancillary to a proceeding in another court; and

(ix) an action to enforce an arbitration award.

(C) Time for Initial Disclosures—In General. A party must make the initial disclosures at or within 14 days after the parties' Rule 26(f) conference unless a different time is set by stipulation or court order, or unless a party objects during the conference that initial disclosures are not appropriate in this action and states the objection in the proposed discovery plan. In ruling on the objection, the court must determine what disclosures, if any, are to be made and must set the time for disclosure.

(D) Time for Initial Disclosures—For Parties Served or Joined Later. A party that is first served or otherwise joined after the Rule 26(f) conference must make the initial disclosures within 30 days after being served or joined, unless a different time is set by stipulation or court order.

(E) Basis for Initial Disclosure; Unacceptable Excuses. A party must make its initial disclosures based on the information then reasonably available to it. A party is not excused from making its disclosures because it has not fully investigated the case or because it challenges the sufficiency of another party's disclosures or because another party has not made its disclosures.

(2) DISCLOSURE OF EXPERT TESTIMONY.

(A) In General. In addition to the disclosures required by Rule 26(a)(1), a party must disclose to the other parties the identity of any witness it may use at trial to present evidence under Federal Rule of Evidence 702, 703, or 705.

(B) Witnesses Who Must Provide a Written Report. Unless otherwise stipulated or ordered by the court, this disclosure must be accompanied by a written report—prepared and signed by the witness—if the witness is one retained or specially employed to provide expert testimony in the case or one whose duties as the party's employee regularly involve giving expert testimony. The report must contain:

(i) a complete statement of all opinions the witness will express and the basis and reasons for them;

(ii) the facts or data considered by the witness in forming them;

(iii) any exhibits that will be used to summarize or support them;

(iv) the witness's qualifications, including a list of all publications authored in the previous 10 years;

(v) a list of all other cases in which, during the previous 4 years, the witness testified as an expert at trial or by deposition; and

(vi) a statement of the compensation to be paid for the study and testimony in the case.

(C) Witnesses Who Do Not Provide a Written Report. Unless otherwise stipulated or ordered by the court, if the witness is not required to provide a written report, this disclosure must state:

(i) the subject matter on which the witness is expected to present evidence under Federal Rule of Evidence 702, 703, or 705; and

(ii) a summary of the facts and opinions to which the witness is expected to testify.

(D) Time to Disclose Expert Testimony. A party must make these disclosures at the times and in the sequence that the court orders. Absent a stipulation or a court order, the disclosures must be made:

(i) at least 90 days before the date set for trial or for the case to be ready for trial; or

(ii) if the evidence is intended solely to contradict or rebut evidence on the same subject matter identified by another party under Rule 26(a)(2)(B) or (C), within 30 days after the other party's disclosure.

(E) Supplementing the Disclosure. The parties must supplement these disclosures when required under Rule 26(e).

(3) PRETRIAL DISCLOSURES.

(A) In General. In addition to the disclosures required by Rule 26(a)(1) and (2), a party must provide to the other parties and promptly file the following information about the evidence that it may present at trial other than solely for impeachment:

(i) the name and, if not previously provided, the address and telephone number of each witness—separately identifying those the party expects to present and those it may call if the need arises;

(ii) the designation of those witnesses whose testimony the party expects to present by deposition and, if not taken stenographically, a transcript of the pertinent parts of the deposition; and

(iii) an identification of each document or other exhibit, including summaries of other evidence—separately identifying those items the party expects to offer and those it may offer if the need arises.

(B) Time for Pretrial Disclosures; Objections. Unless the court orders otherwise, these disclosures must be made at least 30 days before trial. Within 14 days after they are made, unless the court sets a different time, a party may serve and promptly file a list of the following objections: any objections to the use under Rule 32(a) of a deposition designated by another party under Rule 26(a)(3)(A)(ii); and any objection, together with the grounds for it, that may be made to the admissibility of materials identified under Rule 26(a)(3)(A)(iii). An objection not so made—except for one under Federal Rule of Evidence 402 or 403—is waived unless excused by the court for good cause.

(4) FORM OF DISCLOSURES. Unless the court orders otherwise, all disclosures under Rule 26(a) must be in writing, signed, and served.

(b) **Discovery Scope and Limits**.

(1) SCOPE IN GENERAL. Unless otherwise limited by court order, the scope of discovery is as follows: Parties may obtain discovery regarding any nonprivileged matter that is relevant to any party's claim or defense and proportional to the needs of the case, considering the importance of the issues at stake in the action, the amount in controversy, the parties' relative access to relevant information, the parties' resources, the importance of the discovery in resolving the issues, and whether the burden or expense of the proposed discovery outweighs its likely benefit. Information within this scope of discovery need not be admissible in evidence to be discoverable.

(2) LIMITATIONS ON FREQUENCY AND EXTENT.

(A) When Permitted. By order, the court may alter the limits in these rules on the number of depositions and interrogatories or on the length of depositions under Rule 30. By order or local rule, the court may also limit the number of requests under Rule 36.

(B) Specific Limitations on Electronically Stored Information. A party need not provide discovery of electronically stored information from sources that the party identifies as not reasonably accessible because of undue burden or cost. On motion to compel discovery or for a protective order, the party from whom discovery is sought must show that the information is not reasonably accessible because of undue burden or cost. If that showing is made, the court may nonetheless order discovery from such sources if the requesting party shows good cause, considering the limitations of Rule 26(b)(2)(C). The court may specify conditions for the discovery.

(C) When Required. On motion or on its own, the court must limit the frequency or extent of discovery otherwise allowed by these rules or by local rule if it determines that:

(i) the discovery sought is unreasonably cumulative or duplicative, or can be obtained from some other source that is more convenient, less burdensome, or less expensive;

(ii) the party seeking discovery has had ample opportunity to obtain the information by discovery in the action; or

(iii) the proposed discovery is outside the scope permitted by Rule 26(b)(1).

(3) TRIAL PREPARATION: MATERIALS.

(A) Documents and Tangible Things. Ordinarily, a party may not discover documents and tangible things that are prepared in anticipation of litigation or for trial by or for another party or its representative (including the other party's attorney, consultant, surety, indemnitor, insurer, or agent). But, subject to Rule 26(b)(4), those materials may be discovered if:

(i) they are otherwise discoverable under Rule 26(b)(1); and

(ii) the party shows that it has substantial need for the materials to prepare its case and cannot, without undue hardship, obtain their substantial equivalent by other means.

(B) Protection Against Disclosure. If the court orders discovery of those materials, it must protect against disclosure of the mental impressions, conclusions, opinions, or legal theories of a party's attorney or other representative concerning the litigation.

(C) Previous Statement. Any party or other person may, on request and without the required showing, obtain the person's own previous statement about the action or its subject matter. If the request is refused, the person may move for a court order, and Rule 37(a)(5) applies to the award of expenses. A previous statement is either:

(i) a written statement that the person has signed or otherwise adopted or approved; or

(ii) a contemporaneous stenographic, mechanical, electrical, or other recording— or a transcription of it—that recites substantially verbatim the person's oral statement.

(4) TRIAL PREPARATION: EXPERTS.

(A) Deposition of an Expert Who May Testify. A party may depose any person who has been identified as an expert whose opinions may be presented at trial. If Rule 26(a)(2)(B) requires a report from the expert, the deposition may be conducted only after the report is provided.

(B) Trial-Preparation Protection for Draft Reports or Disclosures. Rules 26(b)(3)(A) and (B) protect drafts of any report or disclosure required under Rule 26(a)(2), regardless of the form in which the draft is recorded.

(C) Trial-Preparation Protection for Communications Between a Party's Attorney and Expert Witnesses. Rules 26(b)(3)(A) and (B) protect communications between the party's attorney and any witness required to provide a report under Rule 26(a)(2)(B), regardless of the form of the communications, except to the extent that the communications:

(i) relate to compensation for the expert's study or testimony;

(ii) identify facts or data that the party's attorney provided and that the expert considered in forming the opinions to be expressed; or

(iii) identify assumptions that the party's attorney provided and that the expert relied on in forming the opinions to be expressed.

(D) Expert Employed Only for Trial Preparation. Ordinarily, a party may not, by interrogatories or deposition, discover facts known or opinions held by an expert who has been retained or specially employed by another party in anticipation of litigation or to prepare for trial and who is not expected to be called as a witness at trial. But a party may do so only:

(i) as provided in Rule 35(b); or

(ii) on showing exceptional circumstances under which it is impracticable for the party to obtain facts or opinions on the same subject by other means.

(E) Payment. Unless manifest injustice would result, the court must require that the party seeking discovery:

(i) pay the expert a reasonable fee for time spent in responding to discovery under Rule 26(b)(4)(A) or (D); and

(ii) for discovery under (D), also pay the other party a fair portion of the fees and expenses it reasonably incurred in obtaining the expert's facts and opinions.

(5) CLAIMING PRIVILEGE OR PROTECTING TRIAL-PREPARATION MATERIALS.

(A) Information Withheld. When a party withholds information otherwise discoverable by claiming that the information is privileged or subject to protection as trial-preparation material, the party must:

(i) expressly make the claim; and

(ii) describe the nature of the documents, communications, or tangible things not produced or disclosed—and do so in a manner that, without revealing information itself privileged or protected, will enable other parties to assess the claim.

(B) Information Produced. If information produced in discovery is subject to a claim of privilege or of protection as trial-preparation material, the party making the claim may notify any party that received the information of the claim and the basis for it. After being notified, a party must promptly return, sequester, or destroy the specified information and any copies it has; must not use or disclose the information until the claim is resolved; must take reasonable steps to retrieve the information if the party disclosed it before being notified; and may promptly present the information to the court under seal for a determination of the claim. The producing party must preserve the information until the claim is resolved.

(c) **Protective Orders**.

(1) IN GENERAL. A party or any person from whom discovery is sought may move for a protective order in the court where the action is pending—or as an alternative on

matters relating to a deposition, in the court for the district where the deposition will be taken. The motion must include a certification that the movant has in good faith conferred or attempted to confer with other affected parties in an effort to resolve the dispute without court action. The court may, for good cause, issue an order to protect a party or person from annoyance, embarrassment, oppression, or undue burden or expense, including one or more of the following:

(A) forbidding the disclosure or discovery;

(B) specifying terms, including time and place or the allocation of expenses, for the disclosure or discovery;

(C) prescribing a discovery method other than the one selected by the party seeking discovery;

(D) forbidding inquiry into certain matters, or limiting the scope of disclosure or discovery to certain matters;

(E) designating the persons who may be present while the discovery is conducted;

(F) requiring that a deposition be sealed and opened only on court order;

(G) requiring that a trade secret or other confidential research, development, or commercial information not be revealed or be revealed only in a specified way; and

(H) requiring that the parties simultaneously file specified documents or information in sealed envelopes, to be opened as the court directs.

(2) ORDERING DISCOVERY. If a motion for a protective order is wholly or partly denied, the court may, on just terms, order that any party or person provide or permit discovery.

(3) AWARDING EXPENSES. Rule 37(a)(5) applies to the award of expenses.

(d) **Timing and Sequence of Discovery**.

(1) TIMING. A party may not seek discovery from any source before the parties have conferred as required by Rule 26(f), except in a proceeding exempted from initial disclosure under Rule 26(a)(1)(B), or when authorized by these rules, by stipulation, or by court order.

(2) EARLY RULE 34 REQUESTS.

(A) Time to Deliver. More than 21 days after the summons and complaint are served on a party, a request under Rule 34 may be delivered:

(i) to that party by any other party, and

(ii) by that party to any plaintiff or to any other party that has been served.

(B) When Considered Served. The request is considered to have been served at the first Rule 26(f) conference.

(3) SEQUENCE. Unless the parties stipulate or the court orders otherwise for the parties' and witnesses' convenience and in the interests of justice:

(A) methods of discovery may be used in any sequence; and

(B) discovery by one party does not require any other party to delay its discovery.

(e) **Supplementing Disclosures and Responses**.

(1) IN GENERAL. A party who has made a disclosure under Rule 26(a)—or who has responded to an interrogatory, request for production, or request for admission—must supplement or correct its disclosure or response:

(A) in a timely manner if the party learns that in some material respect the disclosure or response is incomplete or incorrect, and if the additional or corrective information has not otherwise been made known to the other parties during the discovery process or in writing; or

(B) as ordered by the court.

(2) EXPERT WITNESS. For an expert whose report must be disclosed under Rule 26(a)(2)(B), the party's duty to supplement extends both to information included in the report and to information given during the expert's deposition. Any additions or changes to this information must be disclosed by the time the party's pretrial disclosures under Rule 26(a)(3) are due.

(f) **Conference of the Parties; Planning for Discovery**.

(1) CONFERENCE TIMING. Except in a proceeding exempted from initial disclosure under Rule 26(a)(1)(B) or when the court orders otherwise, the parties must confer as soon as practicable—and in any event at least 21 days before a scheduling conference is to be held or a scheduling order is due under Rule 16(b).

(2) CONFERENCE CONTENT; PARTIES' RESPONSIBILITIES. In conferring, the parties must consider the nature and basis of their claims and defenses and the possibilities for promptly settling or resolving the case; make or arrange for the disclosures required by Rule 26(a)(1); discuss any issues about preserving discoverable information; and develop a proposed discovery plan. The attorneys of record and all unrepresented parties that have appeared in the case are jointly responsible for arranging the conference, for attempting in good faith to agree on the proposed discovery plan, and for submitting to the court within 14 days after the conference a written report outlining the plan. The court may order the parties or attorneys to attend the conference in person.

(3) DISCOVERY PLAN. A discovery plan must state the parties' views and proposals on:

(A) what changes should be made in the timing, form, or requirement for disclosures under Rule 26(a), including a statement of when initial disclosures were made or will be made;

(B) the subjects on which discovery may be needed, when discovery should be completed, and whether discovery should be conducted in phases or be limited to or focused on particular issues;

(C) any issues about disclosure, discovery, or preservation of electronically stored information, including the form or forms in which it should be produced;

(D) any issues about claims of privilege or of protection as trial-preparation materials, including—if the parties agree on a procedure to assert these claims after production—whether to ask the court to include their agreement in an order under Federal Rule of Evidence 502;

(E) what changes should be made in the limitations on discovery imposed under these rules or by local rule, and what other limitations should be imposed; and

(F) any other orders that the court should issue under Rule 26(c) or under Rule 16(b) and (c).

(4) EXPEDITED SCHEDULE. If necessary to comply with its expedited schedule for Rule 16(b) conferences, a court may by local rule:

(A) require the parties' conference to occur less than 21 days before the scheduling conference is held or a scheduling order is due under Rule 16(b); and

(B) require the written report outlining the discovery plan to be filed less than 14 days after the parties' conference, or excuse the parties from submitting a written report and permit them to report orally on their discovery plan at the Rule 16(b) conference.

(g) **Signing Disclosures and Discovery Requests, Responses, and Objections**.

(1) SIGNATURE REQUIRED; EFFECT OF SIGNATURE. Every disclosure under Rule 26(a)(1) or (a)(3) and every discovery request, response, or objection must be signed by at least one attorney of record in the attorney's own name—or by the party personally, if unrepresented—and must state the signer's address, e-mail address, and telephone number. By signing, an attorney or party certifies that to the best of the person's knowledge, information, and belief formed after a reasonable inquiry:

(A) with respect to a disclosure, it is complete and correct as of the time it is made; and

(B) with respect to a discovery request, response, or objection, it is:

(i) consistent with these rules and warranted by existing law or by a nonfrivolous argument for extending, modifying, or reversing existing law, or for establishing new law;

(ii) not interposed for any improper purpose, such as to harass, cause unnecessary delay, or needlessly increase the cost of litigation; and

(iii) neither unreasonable nor unduly burdensome or expensive, considering the needs of the case, prior discovery in the case, the amount in controversy, and the importance of the issues at stake in the action.

(2) FAILURE TO SIGN. Other parties have no duty to act on an unsigned disclosure, request, response, or objection until it is signed, and the court must strike it unless a signature is promptly supplied after the omission is called to the attorney's or party's attention.

(3) SANCTION FOR IMPROPER CERTIFICATION. If a certification violates this rule without substantial justification, the court, on motion or on its own, must impose an appropriate sanction on the signer, the party on whose behalf the signer was acting, or both. The sanction may include an order to pay the reasonable expenses, including attorney's fees, caused by the violation.

Rule 30 – Depositions by Oral Examination

(a) **When a Deposition May Be Taken**.

(1) WITHOUT LEAVE. A party may, by oral questions, depose any person, including a party, without leave of court except as provided in Rule 30(a)(2). The deponent's attendance may be compelled by subpoena under Rule 45.

(2) WITH LEAVE. A party must obtain leave of court, and the court must grant leave to the extent consistent with Rule 26(b)(1) and (2):

(A) if the parties have not stipulated to the deposition and:

(i) the deposition would result in more than 10 depositions being taken under this rule or Rule 31 by the plaintiffs, or by the defendants, or by the third-party defendants;

(ii) the deponent has already been deposed in the case; or

(iii) the party seeks to take the deposition before the time specified in Rule 26(d), unless the party certifies in the notice, with supporting facts, that the deponent is expected to leave the United States and be unavailable for examination in this country after that time; or

(B) if the deponent is confined in prison.

(b) **Notice of the Deposition; Other Formal Requirements**.

(1) NOTICE IN GENERAL. A party who wants to depose a person by oral questions must give reasonable written notice to every other party. The notice must state the time and place of the deposition and, if known, the deponent's name and address. If the name is unknown, the notice must provide a general description sufficient to identify the person or the particular class or group to which the person belongs.

(2) PRODUCING DOCUMENTS. If a subpoena duces tecum is to be served on the deponent, the materials designated for production, as set out in the subpoena, must be listed in the notice or in an attachment. The notice to a party deponent may be accompanied by a request under Rule 34 to produce documents and tangible things at the deposition.

(3) METHOD OF RECORDING.

(A) Method Stated in the Notice. The party who notices the deposition must state in the notice the method for recording the testimony. Unless the court orders otherwise, testimony may be recorded by audio, audiovisual, or stenographic means. The noticing party bears the recording costs. Any party may arrange to transcribe a deposition.

(B) Additional Method. With prior notice to the deponent and other parties, any party may designate another method for recording the testimony in addition to that specified in the original notice. That party bears the expense of the additional record or transcript unless the court orders otherwise.

(4) BY REMOTE MEANS. The parties may stipulate—or the court may on motion order—that a deposition be taken by telephone or other remote means. For the

purpose of this rule and Rules 28(a), 37(a)(2), and 37(b)(1), the deposition takes place where the deponent answers the questions.

(5) OFFICER'S DUTIES.

(A) Before the Deposition. Unless the parties stipulate otherwise, a deposition must be conducted before an officer appointed or designated under Rule 28. The officer must begin the deposition with an on-the-record statement that includes:

(i) the officer's name and business address;

(ii) the date, time, and place of the deposition;

(iii) the deponent's name;

(iv) the officer's administration of the oath or affirmation to the deponent; and

(v) the identity of all persons present.

(B) Conducting the Deposition; Avoiding Distortion. If the deposition is recorded nonstenographically, the officer must repeat the items in Rule 30(b)(5)(A)(i)–(iii) at the beginning of each unit of the recording medium. The deponent's and attorneys' appearance or demeanor must not be distorted through recording techniques.

(C) After the Deposition. At the end of a deposition, the officer must state on the record that the deposition is complete and must set out any stipulations made by the attorneys about custody of the transcript or recording and of the exhibits, or about any other pertinent matters.

(6) NOTICE OR SUBPOENA DIRECTED TO AN ORGANIZATION. In its notice or subpoena, a party may name as the deponent a public or private corporation, a partnership, an association, a governmental agency, or other entity and must describe with reasonable particularity the matters for examination. The named organization must then designate one or more officers, directors, or managing agents, or designate other persons who consent to testify on its behalf; and it may set out the matters on which each person designated will testify. A subpoena must advise a nonparty organization of its duty to make this designation. The persons designated must testify about information known or reasonably available to the organization. This paragraph (6) does not preclude a deposition by any other procedure allowed by these rules.

(c) **Examination and Cross-Examination; Record of the Examination; Objections; Written Questions**.

(1) EXAMINATION AND CROSS-EXAMINATION. The examination and cross-examination of a deponent proceed as they would at trial under the Federal Rules of Evidence, except Rules 103 and 615. After putting the deponent under oath or affirmation, the officer must record the testimony by the method designated under Rule 30(b)(3)(A). The testimony must be recorded by the officer personally or by a person acting in the presence and under the direction of the officer.

(2) OBJECTIONS. An objection at the time of the examination—whether to evidence, to a party's conduct, to the officer's qualifications, to the manner of taking the deposition, or to any other aspect of the deposition—must be noted on the record, but the examination still proceeds; the testimony is taken subject to any objection. An objection must be stated concisely in a nonargumentative and nonsuggestive manner. A person may instruct a deponent not to answer only when necessary to preserve a

privilege, to enforce a limitation ordered by the court, or to present a motion under Rule 30(d)(3).

(3) PARTICIPATING THROUGH WRITTEN QUESTIONs. Instead of participating in the oral examination, a party may serve written questions in a sealed envelope on the party noticing the deposition, who must deliver them to the officer. The officer must ask the deponent those questions and record the answers verbatim.

(d) **Duration; Sanction; Motion to Terminate or Limit**.

(1) DURATION. Unless otherwise stipulated or ordered by the court, a deposition is limited to 1 day of 7 hours. The court must allow additional time consistent with Rule 26(b)(1) and (2) if needed to fairly examine the deponent or if the deponent, another person, or any other circumstance impedes or delays the examination.

(2) SANCTION. The court may impose an appropriate sanction—including the reasonable expenses and attorney's fees incurred by any party—on a person who impedes, delays, or frustrates the fair examination of the deponent.

(3) MOTION TO TERMINATE OR LIMIT.

(A) Grounds. At any time during a deposition, the deponent or a party may move to terminate or limit it on the ground that it is being conducted in bad faith or in a manner that unreasonably annoys, embarrasses, or oppresses the deponent or party. The motion may be filed in the court where the action is pending or the deposition is being taken. If the objecting deponent or party so demands, the deposition must be suspended for the time necessary to obtain an order.

(B) Order. The court may order that the deposition be terminated or may limit its scope and manner as provided in Rule 26(c). If terminated, the deposition may be resumed only by order of the court where the action is pending.

(C) Award of Expenses. Rule 37(a)(5) applies to the award of expenses.

(e) **Review by the Witness; Changes**.

(1) REVIEW; STATEMENT OF CHANGES. On request by the deponent or a party before the deposition is completed, the deponent must be allowed 30 days after being notified by the officer that the transcript or recording is available in which:

(A) to review the transcript or recording; and

(B) if there are changes in form or substance, to sign a statement listing the changes and the reasons for making them.

(2) CHANGES INDICATED IN THE OFFICER'S CERTIFICATE. The officer must note in the certificate prescribed by Rule 30(f)(1) whether a review was requested and, if so, must attach any changes the deponent makes during the 30-day period.

(f) **Certification and Delivery; Exhibits; Copies of the Transcript or Recording; Filing**.

(1) CERTIFICATION AND DELIVERY. The officer must certify in writing that the witness was duly sworn and that the deposition accurately records the witness's testimony. The certificate must accompany the record of the deposition. Unless the court orders otherwise, the officer must seal the deposition in an envelope or package bearing the title of the action and marked "Deposition of [witness's name]" and must

promptly send it to the attorney who arranged for the transcript or recording. The attorney must store it under conditions that will protect it against loss, destruction, tampering, or deterioration.

(2) DOCUMENTS AND TANGIBLE THINGS.

(A) Originals and Copies. Documents and tangible things produced for inspection during a deposition must, on a party's request, be marked for identification and attached to the deposition. Any party may inspect and copy them. But if the person who produced them wants to keep the originals, the person may:

(i) offer copies to be marked, attached to the deposition, and then used as originals—after giving all parties a fair opportunity to verify the copies by comparing them with the originals; or

(ii) give all parties a fair opportunity to inspect and copy the originals after they are marked—in which event the originals may be used as if attached to the deposition.

(B) Order Regarding the Originals. Any party may move for an order that the originals be attached to the deposition pending final disposition of the case.

(3) COPIES OF THE TRANSCRIPT OR RECORDING. Unless otherwise stipulated or ordered by the court, the officer must retain the stenographic notes of a deposition taken stenographically or a copy of the recording of a deposition taken by another method. When paid reasonable charges, the officer must furnish a copy of the transcript or recording to any party or the deponent.

(4) NOTICE OF FILING. A party who files the deposition must promptly notify all other parties of the filing.

(g) **Failure to Attend a Deposition or Serve a Subpoena; Expenses**. A party who, expecting a deposition to be taken, attends in person or by an attorney may recover reasonable expenses for attending, including attorney's fees, if the noticing party failed to:

(1) attend and proceed with the deposition; or

(2) serve a subpoena on a nonparty deponent, who consequently did not attend.

Rule 31 – Depositions by Written Questions

(a) **When a Deposition May Be Taken**.

(1) WITHOUT LEAVE. A party may, by written questions, depose any person, including a party, without leave of court except as provided in Rule 31(a)(2). The deponent's attendance may be compelled by subpoena under Rule 45.

(2) WITH LEAVE. A party must obtain leave of court, and the court must grant leave to the extent consistent with Rule 26(b)(1) and (2):

(A) if the parties have not stipulated to the deposition and:

(i) the deposition would result in more than 10 depositions being taken under this rule or Rule 30 by the plaintiffs, or by the defendants, or by the third-party defendants;

(ii) the deponent has already been deposed in the case; or

(iii) the party seeks to take a deposition before the time specified in Rule 26(d); or

(B) if the deponent is confined in prison.

(3) SERVICE; REQUIRED NOTICE. A party who wants to depose a person by written questions must serve them on every other party, with a notice stating, if known, the deponent's name and address. If the name is unknown, the notice must provide a general description sufficient to identify the person or the particular class or group to which the person belongs. The notice must also state the name or descriptive title and the address of the officer before whom the deposition will be taken.

(4) QUESTIONS DIRECTED TO AN ORGANIZATION. A public or private corporation, a partnership, an association, or a governmental agency may be deposed by written questions in accordance with Rule 30(b)(6).

(5) QUESTIONS FROM OTHER PARTIES. Any questions to the deponent from other parties must be served on all parties as follows: cross-questions, within 14 days after being served with the notice and direct questions; redirect questions, within 7 days after being served with cross-questions; and recross-questions, within 7 days after being served with redirect questions. The court may, for good cause, extend or shorten these times.

(b) **Delivery to the Officer; Officer's Duties**. The party who noticed the deposition must deliver to the officer a copy of all the questions served and of the notice. The officer must promptly proceed in the manner provided in Rule 30(c), (e), and (f) to:

(1) take the deponent's testimony in response to the questions;

(2) prepare and certify the deposition; and

(3) send it to the party, attaching a copy of the questions and of the notice.

(c) **Notice of Completion or Filing**.

(1) COMPLETION. The party who noticed the deposition must notify all other parties when it is completed.

(2) FILING. A party who files the deposition must promptly notify all other parties of the filing.

Rule 32 – Using Depositions in Court Proceedings

(a) **Using Depositions**.

(1) IN GENERAL. At a hearing or trial, all or part of a deposition may be used against a party on these conditions:

(A) the party was present or represented at the taking of the deposition or had reasonable notice of it;

(B) it is used to the extent it would be admissible under the Federal Rules of Evidence if the deponent were present and testifying; and

(C) the use is allowed by Rule 32(a)(2) through (8).

(2) IMPEACHMENT AND OTHER USES. Any party may use a deposition to contradict or impeach the testimony given by the deponent as a witness, or for any other purpose allowed by the Federal Rules of Evidence.

(3) DEPOSITION OF PARTY, AGENT, OR DESIGNEE. An adverse party may use for any purpose the deposition of a party or anyone who, when deposed, was the party's officer, director, managing agent, or designee under Rule 30(b)(6) or 31(a)(4).

(4) UNAVAILABLE WITNESS. A party may use for any purpose the deposition of a witness, whether or not a party, if the court finds:

(A) that the witness is dead;

(B) that the witness is more than 100 miles from the place of hearing or trial or is outside the United States, unless it appears that the witness's absence was procured by the party offering the deposition;

(C) that the witness cannot attend or testify because of age, illness, infirmity, or imprisonment;

(D) that the party offering the deposition could not procure the witness's attendance by subpoena; or

(E) on motion and notice, that exceptional circumstances make it desirable—in the interest of justice and with due regard to the importance of live testimony in open court—to permit the deposition to be used.

(5) LIMITATIONS ON USE.

(A) DEPOSITION TAKEN ON SHORT NOTICE. A deposition must not be used against a party who, having received less than 14 days' notice of the deposition, promptly moved for a protective order under Rule 26(c)(1)(B) requesting that it not be taken or be taken at a different time or place—and this motion was still pending when the deposition was taken.

(B) UNAVAILABLE DEPONENT; PARTY COULD NOT OBTAIN AN ATTORNEY. A deposition taken without leave of court under the unavailability provision of Rule 30(a)(2)(A)(iii) must not be used against a party who shows that, when served with the notice, it could not, despite diligent efforts, obtain an attorney to represent it at the deposition.

(6) USING PART OF A DEPOSITION. If a party offers in evidence only part of a deposition, an adverse party may require the offeror to introduce other parts that in fairness should be considered with the part introduced, and any party may itself introduce any other parts.

(7) SUBSTITUTING A PARTY. Substituting a party under Rule 25 does not affect the right to use a deposition previously taken.

(8) DEPOSITION TAKEN IN AN EARLIER ACTION. A deposition lawfully taken and, if required, filed in any federal- or state-court action may be used in a later action involving the same subject matter between the same parties, or their representatives or successors in interest, to the same extent as if taken in the later action. A deposition previously taken may also be used as allowed by the Federal Rules of Evidence.

(b) **Objections to Admissibility**. Subject to Rules 28(b) and 32(d)(3), an objection may be made at a hearing or trial to the admission of any deposition testimony that would be inadmissible if the witness were present and testifying.

(c) **Form of Presentation**. Unless the court orders otherwise, a party must provide a transcript of any deposition testimony the party offers, but may provide the court with the testimony in nontranscript form as well. On any party's request, deposition testimony offered in a jury trial for any purpose other than impeachment must be presented in nontranscript form, if available, unless the court for good cause orders otherwise.

(d) **Waiver of Objections**.

(1) TO THE NOTICE. An objection to an error or irregularity in a deposition notice is waived unless promptly served in writing on the party giving the notice.

(2) TO THE OFFICER'S QUALIFICATION. An objection based on disqualification of the officer before whom a deposition is to be taken is waived if not made:

(A) before the deposition begins; or

(B) promptly after the basis for disqualification becomes known or, with reasonable diligence, could have been known.

(3) TO THE TAKING OF THE DEPOSITION.

(A) OBJECTION TO COMPETENCE, RELEVANCE, OR MATERIALITY. An objection to a deponent's competence—or to the competence, relevance, or materiality of testimony—is not waived by a failure to make the objection before or during the deposition, unless the ground for it might have been corrected at that time.

(B) OBJECTION TO AN ERROR OR IRREGULARITY. An objection to an error or irregularity at an oral examination is waived if:

(i) it relates to the manner of taking the deposition, the form of a question or answer, the oath or affirmation, a party's conduct, or other matters that might have been corrected at that time; and

(ii) it is not timely made during the deposition.

(C) OBJECTION TO A WRITTEN QUESTION. An objection to the form of a written question under Rule 31 is waived if not served in writing on the party submitting the question within the time for serving responsive questions or, if the question is a recross-question, within 7 days after being served with it.

(4) TO COMPLETING AND RETURNING THE DEPOSITION. An objection to how the officer transcribed the testimony—or prepared, signed, certified, sealed, endorsed, sent, or otherwise dealt with the deposition—is waived unless a motion to suppress is made promptly after the error or irregularity becomes known or, with reasonable diligence, could have been known.

Rule 33 – Interrogatories to Parties

(a) **In General**.

(1) NUMBER. Unless otherwise stipulated or ordered by the court, a party may serve on any other party no more than 25 written interrogatories, including all discrete subparts. Leave to serve additional interrogatories may be granted to the extent consistent with Rule 26(b)(1) and (2).

(2) SCOPE. An interrogatory may relate to any matter that may be inquired into under Rule 26(b). An interrogatory is not objectionable merely because it asks for an opinion or contention that relates to fact or the application of law to fact, but the court

may order that the interrogatory need not be answered until designated discovery is complete, or until a pretrial conference or some other time.

(b) **Answers and Objections**.

(1) RESPONDING PARTY. The interrogatories must be answered:

(A) by the party to whom they are directed; or

(B) if that party is a public or private corporation, a partnership, an association, or a governmental agency, by any officer or agent, who must furnish the information available to the party.

(2) TIME TO RESPOND. The responding party must serve its answers and any objections within 30 days after being served with the interrogatories. A shorter or longer time may be stipulated to under Rule 29 or be ordered by the court.

(3) ANSWERING EACH INTERROGATORY. Each interrogatory must, to the extent it is not objected to, be answered separately and fully in writing under oath.

(4) OBJECTIONS. The grounds for objecting to an interrogatory must be stated with specificity. Any ground not stated in a timely objection is waived unless the court, for good cause, excuses the failure.

(5) SIGNATURE. The person who makes the answers must sign them, and the attorney who objects must sign any objections.

(c) **Use**. An answer to an interrogatory may be used to the extent allowed by the Federal Rules of Evidence.

(d) **Option to Produce Business Records**. If the answer to an interrogatory may be determined by examining, auditing, compiling, abstracting, or summarizing a party's business records (including electronically stored information), and if the burden of deriving or ascertaining the answer will be substantially the same for either party, the responding party may answer by:

(1) specifying the records that must be reviewed, in sufficient detail to enable the interrogating party to locate and identify them as readily as the responding party could; and

(2) giving the interrogating party a reasonable opportunity to examine and audit the records and to make copies, compilations, abstracts, or summaries.

Rule 34 – Producing Documents, Electronically Stored Information, and Tangible Things, or Entering onto Land, for Inspection and Other Purposes

(a) **In General**. A party may serve on any other party a request within the scope of Rule 26(b):

(1) to produce and permit the requesting party or its representative to inspect, copy, test, or sample the following items in the responding party's possession, custody, or control:

(A) any designated documents or electronically stored information—including writings, drawings, graphs, charts, photographs, sound recordings, images, and other data or data compilations—stored in any medium from which information can be obtained either directly or, if necessary, after translation by the responding party into a reasonably usable form; or

(B) any designated tangible things; or

(2) to permit entry onto designated land or other property possessed or controlled by the responding party, so that the requesting party may inspect, measure, survey, photograph, test, or sample the property or any designated object or operation on it.

(b) **Procedure**.

(1) CONTENTS OF THE REQUEST. The request:

(A) must describe with reasonable particularity each item or category of items to be inspected;

(B) must specify a reasonable time, place, and manner for the inspection and for performing the related acts; and

(C) may specify the form or forms in which electronically stored information is to be produced.

(2) RESPONSES AND OBJECTIONS.

(A) Time to Respond. The party to whom the request is directed must respond in writing within 30 days after being served or — if the request was delivered under Rule 26(d)(2) — within 30 days after the parties' first Rule 26(f)conference. A shorter or longer time may be stipulated to under Rule 29 or be ordered by the court.

(B) Responding to Each Item. For each item or category, the response must either state that inspection and related activities will be permitted as requested or state with specificity the grounds for objecting to the request, including the reasons. The responding party may state that it will produce copies of documents or of electronically stored information instead of permitting inspection. The production must then be completed no later than the time for inspection specified in the request or another reasonable time specified in the response.

(C) Objections. An objection must state whether any responsive materials are being withheld on the basis of that objection. An objection to part of a request must specify the part and permit inspection of the rest.

(D) Responding to a Request for Production of Electronically Stored Information. The response may state an objection to a requested form for producing electronically stored information. If the responding party objects to a requested form—or if no form was specified in the request—the party must state the form or forms it intends to use.

(E) Producing the Documents or Electronically Stored Information. Unless otherwise stipulated or ordered by the court, these procedures apply to producing documents or electronically stored information:

(i) A party must produce documents as they are kept in the usual course of business or must organize and label them to correspond to the categories in the request;

(ii) If a request does not specify a form for producing electronically stored information, a party must produce it in a form or forms in which it is ordinarily maintained or in a reasonably usable form or forms; and

(iii) A party need not produce the same electronically stored information in more than one form.

(c) **Nonparties**. As provided in Rule 45, a nonparty may be compelled to produce documents and tangible things or to permit an inspection.

Rule 35 – Physical and Mental Examinations

(a) **Order for an Examination**.

(1) IN GENERAL. The court where the action is pending may order a party whose mental or physical condition—including blood group—is in controversy to submit to a physical or mental examination by a suitably licensed or certified examiner. The court has the same authority to order a party to produce for examination a person who is in its custody or under its legal control.

(2) MOTION AND NOTICE; CONTENTS OF THE ORDER. The order:

(A) may be made only on motion for good cause and on notice to all parties and the person to be examined; and

(B) must specify the time, place, manner, conditions, and scope of the examination, as well as the person or persons who will perform it.

(b) **Examiner's Report**.

(1) REQUEST BY THE PARTY OR PERSON EXAMINED. The party who moved for the examination must, on request, deliver to the requester a copy of the examiner's report, together with like reports of all earlier examinations of the same condition. The request may be made by the party against whom the examination order was issued or by the person examined.

(2) CONTENTS. The examiner's report must be in writing and must set out in detail the examiner's findings, including diagnoses, conclusions, and the results of any tests.

(3) REQUEST BY THE MOVING PARTY. After delivering the reports, the party who moved for the examination may request—and is entitled to receive—from the party against whom the examination order was issued like reports of all earlier or later examinations of the same condition. But those reports need not be delivered by the party with custody or control of the person examined if the party shows that it could not obtain them.

(4) WAIVER OF PRIVILEGE. By requesting and obtaining the examiner's report, or by deposing the examiner, the party examined waives any privilege it may have—in that action or any other action involving the same controversy—concerning testimony about all examinations of the same condition.

(5) FAILURE TO DELIVER A REPORT. The court on motion may order—on just terms—that a party deliver the report of an examination. If the report is not provided, the court may exclude the examiner's testimony at trial.

(6) SCOPE. This subdivision (b) applies also to an examination made by the parties' agreement, unless the agreement states otherwise. This subdivision does not preclude obtaining an examiner's report or deposing an examiner under other rules.

Rule 36 – Requests for Admission

(a) **Scope and Procedure**.

(1) SCOPE. A party may serve on any other party a written request to admit, for purposes of the pending action only, the truth of any matters within the scope of Rule 26(b)(1) relating to:

(A) facts, the application of law to fact, or opinions about either; and

(B) the genuineness of any described documents.

(2) FORM; COPY OF A DOCUMENT. Each matter must be separately stated. A request to admit the genuineness of a document must be accompanied by a copy of the document unless it is, or has been, otherwise furnished or made available for inspection and copying.

(3) TIME TO RESPOND; EFFECT OF NOT RESPONDING. A matter is admitted unless, within 30 days after being served, the party to whom the request is directed serves on the requesting party a written answer or objection addressed to the matter and signed by the party or its attorney. A shorter or longer time for responding may be stipulated to under Rule 29 or be ordered by the court.

(4) ANSWER. If a matter is not admitted, the answer must specifically deny it or state in detail why the answering party cannot truthfully admit or deny it. A denial must fairly respond to the substance of the matter; and when good faith requires that a party qualify an answer or deny only a part of a matter, the answer must specify the part admitted and qualify or deny the rest. The answering party may assert lack of knowledge or information as a reason for failing to admit or deny only if the party states that it has made reasonable inquiry and that the information it knows or can readily obtain is insufficient to enable it to admit or deny.

(5) OBJECTIONS. The grounds for objecting to a request must be stated. A party must not object solely on the ground that the request presents a genuine issue for trial.

(6) MOTION REGARDING THE SUFFICIENCY OF AN ANSWER OR OBJECTION. The requesting party may move to determine the sufficiency of an answer or objection. Unless the court finds an objection justified, it must order that an answer be served. On finding that an answer does not comply with this rule, the court may order either that the matter is admitted or that an amended answer be served. The court may defer its final decision until a pretrial conference or a specified time before trial. Rule 37(a)(5) applies to an award of expenses.

(b) **Effect of an Admission; Withdrawing or Amending It**. A matter admitted under this rule is conclusively established unless the court, on motion, permits the admission to be withdrawn or amended. Subject to Rule 16(e), the court may permit withdrawal or amendment if it would promote the presentation of the merits of the action and if the court is not persuaded that it would prejudice the requesting party in maintaining or defending the action on the merits. An admission under this rule is not an admission for any other purpose and cannot be used against the party in any other proceeding.

Title VI – Trials (Rules 38-53)

Rule 50 – Judgment as a Matter of Law in a Jury Trial; Related Motion for a New Trial; Conditional Ruling

(a) **Judgment as a Matter of Law**.

(1) IN GENERAL. If a party has been fully heard on an issue during a jury trial and the court finds that a reasonable jury would not have a legally sufficient evidentiary basis to find for the party on that issue, the court may:

(A) resolve the issue against the party; and

(B) grant a motion for judgment as a matter of law against the party on a claim or defense that, under the controlling law, can be maintained or defeated only with a favorable finding on that issue.

(2) MOTION. A motion for judgment as a matter of law may be made at any time before the case is submitted to the jury. The motion must specify the judgment sought and the law and facts that entitle the movant to the judgment.

(b) **Renewing the Motion After Trial**; Alternative Motion for a New Trial. If the court does not grant a motion for judgment as a matter of law made under Rule 50(a), the court is considered to have submitted the action to the jury subject to the court's later deciding the legal questions raised by the motion. No later than 28 days after the entry of judgment—or if the motion addresses a jury issue not decided by a verdict, no later than 28 days after the jury was discharged—the movant may file a renewed motion for judgment as a matter of law and may include an alternative or joint request for a new trial under Rule 59. In ruling on the renewed motion, the court may:

(1) allow judgment on the verdict, if the jury returned a verdict;

(2) order a new trial; or

(3) direct the entry of judgment as a matter of law.

(c) **Granting the Renewed Motion; Conditional Ruling on a Motion for a New Trial**.

(1) IN GENERAL. If the court grants a renewed motion for judgment as a matter of law, it must also conditionally rule on any motion for a new trial by determining whether a new trial should be granted if the judgment is later vacated or reversed. The court must state the grounds for conditionally granting or denying the motion for a new trial.

(2) EFFECT OF A CONDITIONAL RULING. Conditionally granting the motion for a new trial does not affect the judgment's finality; if the judgment is reversed, the new trial must proceed unless the appellate court orders otherwise. If the motion for a new trial is conditionally denied, the appellee may assert error in that denial; if the judgment is reversed, the case must proceed as the appellate court orders.

(d) **Time for a Losing Party's New-Trial Motion**. Any motion for a new trial under **Rule 59** by a party against whom judgment as a matter of law is rendered must be filed no later than 28 days after the entry of the judgment.

(e) **Denying the Motion for Judgment as a Matter of Law; Reversal on Appeal**. If the court denies the motion for judgment as a matter of law, the prevailing party may, as appellee, assert grounds entitling it to a new trial should the appellate court conclude that the trial court erred in denying the motion. If the appellate court reverses the judgment, it may order a new trial, direct the trial court to determine whether a new trial should be granted, or direct the entry of judgment.

Title VII – Judgment (Rules 54-63)
Rule 54 – Judgment; Costs

(a) **Definition; Form**. "Judgment" as used in these rules includes a decree and any order from which an appeal lies. A judgment should not include recitals of pleadings, a master's report, or a record of prior proceedings.

(b) **Judgment on Multiple Claims or Involving Multiple Parties**. When an action presents more than one claim for relief—whether as a claim, counterclaim, crossclaim, or third-party claim—or when multiple parties are involved, the court may direct entry of a final judgment as to one or more, but fewer than all, claims or parties only if the court expressly determines that there is no just reason for delay. Otherwise, any order or other decision, however designated, that adjudicates fewer than all the claims or the rights and liabilities of fewer than all the parties does not end the action as to any of the claims or parties and may be revised at any time before the entry of a judgment adjudicating all the claims and all the parties' rights and liabilities.

(c) **Demand for Judgment; Relief to Be Granted**. A default judgment must not differ in kind from, or exceed in amount, what is demanded in the pleadings. Every other final judgment should grant the relief to which each party is entitled, even if the party has not demanded that relief in its pleadings.

(d) **Costs; Attorney's Fees**.

(1) COSTS OTHER THAN ATTORNEY'S FEES. Unless a federal statute, these rules, or a court order provides otherwise, costs—other than attorney's fees—should be allowed to the prevailing party. But costs against the United States, its officers, and its agencies may be imposed only to the extent allowed by law. The clerk may tax costs on 14 days' notice. On motion served within the next 7 days, the court may review the clerk's action.

(2) ATTORNEY'S FEES.

(A) CLAIM TO BE BY MOTION. A claim for attorney's fees and related nontaxable expenses must be made by motion unless the substantive law requires those fees to be proved at trial as an element of damages.

(B) TIMING AND CONTENTS OF THE MOTION. Unless a statute or a court order provides otherwise, the motion must:

(i) be filed no later than 14 days after the entry of judgment;

(ii) specify the judgment and the statute, rule, or other grounds entitling the movant to the award;

(iii) state the amount sought or provide a fair estimate of it; and

(iv) disclose, if the court so orders, the terms of any agreement about fees for the services for which the claim is made.

(C) PROCEEDINGS. Subject to Rule 23(h), the court must, on a party's request, give an opportunity for adversary submissions on the motion in accordance with Rule 43(c) or 78. The court may decide issues of liability for fees before receiving submissions on the value of services. The court must find the facts and state its conclusions of law as provided in Rule 52(a).

(D) SPECIAL PROCEDURES BY LOCAL RULE; REFERENCE TO A MASTER OR A MAGISTRATE JUDGE. By local rule, the court may establish special procedures to resolve fee-related issues without extensive evidentiary hearings. Also, the court may refer issues concerning the value of services to a special master under Rule 53 without regard to the limitations of Rule 53(a)(1), and may refer a motion for attorney's fees to a magistrate judge under Rule 72(b) as if it were a dispositive pretrial matter.

(E) EXCEPTIONS. Subparagraphs (A)–(D) do not apply to claims for fees and expenses as sanctions for violating these rules or as sanctions under 28 U.S.C. §1927.

Rule 55 – Default; Default Judgment

(a) **Entering a Default**. When a party against whom a judgment for affirmative relief is sought has failed to plead or otherwise defend, and that failure is shown by affidavit or otherwise, the clerk must enter the party's default.

(b) **Entering a Default Judgment**.

(1) BY THE CLERK. If the plaintiff's claim is for a sum certain or a sum that can be made certain by computation, the clerk—on the plaintiff's request, with an affidavit showing the amount due—must enter judgment for that amount and costs against a defendant who has been defaulted for not appearing and who is neither a minor nor an incompetent person.

(2) BY THE COURT. In all other cases, the party must apply to the court for a default judgment. A default judgment may be entered against a minor or incompetent person only if represented by a general guardian, conservator, or other like fiduciary who has appeared. If the party against whom a default judgment is sought has appeared personally or by a representative, that party or its representative must be served with written notice of the application at least 7 days before the hearing. The court may conduct hearings or make referrals—preserving any federal statutory right to a jury trial—when, to enter or effectuate judgment, it needs to:

(A) conduct an accounting;

(B) determine the amount of damages;

(C) establish the truth of any allegation by evidence; or

(D) investigate any other matter.

(c) **Setting Aside a Default or a Default Judgment**. The court may set aside an entry of default for good cause, and it may set aside a final default judgment under Rule 60(b).

(d) **Judgment Against the United States**. A default judgment may be entered against the United States, its officers, or its agencies only if the claimant establishes a claim or right to relief by evidence that satisfies the court.

Rule 56 – Summary Judgment

(a) **Motion for Summary Judgment or Partial Summary Judgment**. A party may move for summary judgment, identifying each claim or defense — or the part of each claim or defense — on which summary judgment is sought. The court shall grant summary judgment if the movant shows that there is no genuine dispute as to any material fact and the movant is entitled to judgment as a matter of law. The court should state on the record the reasons for granting or denying the motion.

(b) **Time to File a Motion**. Unless a different time is set by local rule or the court orders otherwise, a party may file a motion for summary judgment at any time until 30 days after the close of all discovery.

(c) **Procedures**.

(1) SUPPORTING FACTUAL POSITIONS. A party asserting that a fact cannot be or is genuinely disputed must support the assertion by:

(A) citing to particular parts of materials in the record, including depositions, documents, electronically stored information, affidavits or declarations, stipulations (including those made for purposes of the motion only), admissions, interrogatory answers, or other materials; or

(B) showing that the materials cited do not establish the absence or presence of a genuine dispute, or that an adverse party cannot produce admissible evidence to support the fact.

(2) OBJECTION THAT A FACT IS NOT SUPPORTED BY ADMISSIBLE EVIDENCE. A party may object that the material cited to support or dispute a fact cannot be presented in a form that would be admissible in evidence.

(3) MATERIALS NOT CITED. The court need consider only the cited materials, but it may consider other materials in the record.

(4) AFFIDAVITS OR DECLARATIONS. An affidavit or declaration used to support or oppose a motion must be made on personal knowledge, set out facts that would be admissible in evidence, and show that the affiant or declarant is competent to testify on the matters stated.

(d) **When Facts Are Unavailable to the Nonmovant**. If a nonmovant shows by affidavit or declaration that, for specified reasons, it cannot present facts essential to justify its opposition, the court may:

(1) defer considering the motion or deny it;

(2) allow time to obtain affidavits or declarations or to take discovery; or

(3) issue any other appropriate order.

(e) **Failing to Properly Support or Address a Fact**. If a party fails to properly support an assertion of fact or fails to properly address another party's assertion of fact as required by Rule 56(c), the court may:

(1) give an opportunity to properly support or address the fact;

(2) consider the fact undisputed for purposes of the motion;

(3) grant summary judgment if the motion and supporting materials — including the facts considered undisputed — show that the movant is entitled to it; or

(4) issue any other appropriate order.

(f) **Judgment Independent of the Motion.** After giving notice and a reasonable time to respond, the court may:

(1) grant summary judgment for a nonmovant;

(2) grant the motion on grounds not raised by a party;or

(3) consider summary judgment on its own after identifying for the parties material facts that may not be genuinely in dispute.

(g) **Failing to Grant All the Requested Relief.** If the court does not grant all the relief requested by the motion, it may enter an order stating any material fact — including an item of damages or other relief — that is not genuinely in dispute and treating the fact as established in the case.

(h) **Affidavit or Declaration Submitted in Bad Faith.** If satisfied that an affidavit or declaration under this rule is submitted in bad faith or solely for delay, the court — after notice and a reasonable time to respond — may order the submitting party to pay the other party the reasonable expenses, including attorney's fees, it incurred as a result. An offending party or attorney may also be held in contempt or subjected to other appropriate sanctions.

Rule 57 – Declaratory Judgment

These rules govern the procedure for obtaining a declaratory judgment under 28 U.S.C. §2201. Rules 38 and 39 govern a demand for a jury trial. The existence of another adequate remedy does not preclude a declaratory judgment that is otherwise appropriate. The court may order a speedy hearing of a declaratory-judgment action.

Rule 58 – Entering Judgment

(a) **Separate Document.** Every judgment and amended judgment must be set out in a separate document, but a separate document is not required for an order disposing of a motion:

(1) for judgment under Rule 50(b);

(2) to amend or make additional findings under Rule 52(b);

(3) for attorney's fees under Rule 54;

(4) for a new trial, or to alter or amend the judgment, under Rule 59; or

(5) for relief under Rule 60.

(b) **Entering Judgment**.

(1) WITHOUT THE COURT'S DIRECTION. Subject to Rule 54(b) and unless the court orders otherwise, the clerk must, without awaiting the court's direction, promptly prepare, sign, and enter the judgment when:

(A) the jury returns a general verdict;

(B) the court awards only costs or a sum certain; or

(C) the court denies all relief.

(2) COURT'S APPROVAL REQUIRED. Subject to Rule 54(b), the court must promptly approve the form of the judgment, which the clerk must promptly enter, when:

(A) the jury returns a special verdict or a general verdict with answers to written questions; or

(B) the court grants other relief not described in this subdivision (b).

(c) **Time of Entry**. For purposes of these rules, judgment is entered at the following times:

(1) if a separate document is not required, when the judgment is entered in the civil docket under Rule 79(a); or

(2) if a separate document is required, when the judgment is entered in the civil docket under Rule 79(a) and the earlier of these events occurs:

(A) it is set out in a separate document; or

(B) 150 days have run from the entry in the civil docket.

(d) **Request for Entry**. A party may request that judgment be set out in a separate document as required by Rule 58(a).

(e) **Cost or Fee Awards**. Ordinarily, the entry of judgment may not be delayed, nor the time for appeal extended, in order to tax costs or award fees. But if a timely motion for attorney's fees is made under Rule 54(d)(2), the court may act before a notice of appeal has been filed and become effective to order that the motion have the same effect under Federal Rule of Appellate Procedure 4 (a)(4) as a timely motion under Rule 59.

Rule 59 – New Trial; Altering or Amending a Judgment

(a) **In General**.

(1) GROUNDS FOR NEW TRIAL. The court may, on motion, grant a new trial on all or some of the issues—and to any party—as follows:

(A) after a jury trial, for any reason for which a new trial has heretofore been granted in an action at law in federal court; or

(B) after a nonjury trial, for any reason for which a rehearing has heretofore been granted in a suit in equity in federal court.

(2) FURTHER ACTION AFTER A NONJURY TRIAL. After a nonjury trial, the court may, on motion for a new trial, open the judgment if one has been entered, take

additional testimony, amend findings of fact and conclusions of law or make new ones, and direct the entry of a new judgment.

(b) **Time to File a Motion for a New Trial**. A motion for a new trial must be filed no later than 28 days after the entry of judgment.

(c) **Time to Serve Affidavits**. When a motion for a new trial is based on affidavits, they must be filed with the motion. The opposing party has 14 days after being served to file opposing affidavits. The court may permit reply affidavits.

(d) **New Trial on the Court's Initiative or for Reasons Not in the Motion**. No later than 28 days after the entry of judgment, the court, on its own, may order a new trial for any reason that would justify granting one on a party's motion. After giving the parties notice and an opportunity to be heard, the court may grant a timely motion for a new trial for a reason not stated in the motion. In either event, the court must specify the reasons in its order.

(e) **Motion to Alter or Amend a Judgment**. A motion to alter or amend a judgment must be filed no later than 28 days after the entry of the judgment.

Rule 60 – Relief from a Judgment or Order

(a) **Corrections Based on Clerical Mistakes; Oversights and Omissions**. The court may correct a clerical mistake or a mistake arising from oversight or omission whenever one is found in a judgment, order, or other part of the record. The court may do so on motion or on its own, with or without notice. But after an appeal has been docketed in the appellate court and while it is pending, such a mistake may be corrected only with the appellate court's leave.

(b) **Grounds for Relief from a Final Judgment, Order, or Proceeding**. On motion and just terms, the court may relieve a party or its legal representative from a final judgment, order, or proceeding for the following reasons:

(1) mistake, inadvertence, surprise, or excusable neglect;

(2) newly discovered evidence that, with reasonable diligence, could not have been discovered in time to move for a new trial under Rule 59(b);

(3) fraud (whether previously called intrinsic or extrinsic), misrepresentation, or misconduct by an opposing party;

(4) the judgment is void;

(5) the judgment has been satisfied, released, or discharged; it is based on an earlier judgment that has been reversed or vacated; or applying it prospectively is no longer equitable; or

(6) any other reason that justifies relief.

(c) **Timing and Effect of the Motion**.

(1) TIMING. A motion under Rule 60(b) must be made within a reasonable time— and for reasons (1), (2), and (3) no more than a year after the entry of the judgment or order or the date of the proceeding.

(2) EFFECT ON FINALITY. The motion does not affect the judgment's finality or suspend its operation.

(d) **Other Powers to Grant Relief**. This rule does not limit a court's power to:

(1) entertain an independent action to relieve a party from a judgment, order, or proceeding;

(2) grant relief under 28 U.S.C. §1655 to a defendant who was not personally notified of the action; or

(3) set aside a judgment for fraud on the court.

(e) **Bills and Writs Abolished**. The following are abolished: bills of review, bills in the nature of bills of review, and writs of coram nobis, coram vobis, and audita querela.

Title VIII – Provisional and Final Remedies (Rules 64-71)
Rule 68 – Offer of Judgment

(a) **Making an Offer; Judgment on an Accepted Offer**. At least 14 days before the date set for trial, a party defending against a claim may serve on an opposing party an offer to allow judgment on specified terms, with the costs then accrued. If, within 14 days after being served, the opposing party serves written notice accepting the offer, either party may then file the offer and notice of acceptance, plus proof of service. The clerk must then enter judgment.

(b) **Unaccepted Offer**. An unaccepted offer is considered withdrawn, but it does not preclude a later offer. Evidence of an unaccepted offer is not admissible except in a proceeding to determine costs.

(c) **Offer After Liability is Determined**. When one party's liability to another has been determined but the extent of liability remains to be determined by further proceedings, the party held liable may make an offer of judgment. It must be served within a reasonable time—but at least 14 days—before the date set for a hearing to determine the extent of liability.

(d) **Paying Costs After an Unaccepted Offer**. If the judgment that the offeree finally obtains is not more favorable than the unaccepted offer, the offeree must pay the costs incurred after the offer was made.

Selected Statutes

28 U.S.C. § 41. Number and composition of circuits.

The thirteen judicial circuits of the United States are constituted as follows:

Circuit	Composition
District of Columbia	District of Columbia.
First	Maine, Massachusetts, New Hampshire, Puerto Rico, Rhode Island.
Second	Connecticut, New York, Vermont.
Third	Delaware, New Jersey, Pennsylvania, Virgin Islands.
Fourth	Maryland, North Carolina, South Carolina, Virginia, West Virginia.
Fifth	District of the Canal Zone, Louisiana, Mississippi, Texas.
Sixth	Kentucky, Michigan, Ohio, Tennessee.
Seventh	Illinois, Indiana, Wisconsin.
Eighth	Arkansas, Iowa, Minnesota, Missouri, Nebraska, North Dakota, South Dakota.
Ninth	Alaska, Arizona, California, Idaho, Montana, Nevada, Oregon, Washington, Guam, Hawaii.
Tenth	Colorado, Kansas, New Mexico, Oklahoma, Utah, Wyoming.
Eleventh	Alabama, Florida, Georgia.
Federal	All Federal judicial districts.

28 U.S.C. § 1331. Federal question.

The district courts shall have original jurisdiction of all civil actions arising under the Constitution, laws, or treaties of the United States.

28 U.S.C. § 1332. Diversity of citizenship; amount in controversy.

(a) The district courts shall have original jurisdiction of all civil actions where the matter in controversy exceeds the sum or value of $75,000, exclusive of interest and costs, and is between—

(1) citizens of different States;

(2) citizens of a State and citizens or subjects of a foreign state, except that the district courts shall not have original jurisdiction under this subsection of an action between citizens of a State and citizens or subjects of a foreign state who are lawfully admitted for permanent residence in the United States and are domiciled in the same State;

(3) citizens of different States and in which citizens or subjects of a foreign state are additional parties; and

(4) a foreign state, defined in section 1603(a) of this title, as plaintiff and citizens of a State or of different States.

(b) Except when express provision therefor is otherwise made in a statute of the United States, where the plaintiff who files the case originally in the Federal courts is finally adjudged to be entitled to recover less than the sum or value of $75,000, computed without regard to any setoff or counterclaim to which the defendant may be adjudged to be entitled, and exclusive of interest and costs, the district court may deny costs to the plaintiff and, in addition, may impose costs on the plaintiff.

(c) For the purposes of this section and section 1441 of this title—

(1) a corporation shall be deemed to be a citizen of every State and foreign state by which it has been incorporated and of the State or foreign state where it has its principal place of business, except that in any direct action against the insurer of a policy or contract of liability insurance, whether incorporated or unincorporated, to which action the insured is not joined as a party-defendant, such insurer shall be deemed a citizen of—

(A) every State and foreign state of which the insured is a citizen;

(B) every State and foreign state by which the insurer has been incorporated; and

(C) the State or foreign state where the insurer has its principal place of business; and

(2) the legal representative of the estate of a decedent shall be deemed to be a citizen only of the same State as the decedent, and the legal representative of an infant or incompetent shall be deemed to be a citizen only of the same State as the infant or incompetent.

(d)(1) In this subsection—

(A) the term "class" means all of the class members in a class action;

(B) the term "class action" means any civil action filed under rule 23 of the Federal Rules of Civil Procedure or similar State statute or rule of judicial procedure authorizing an action to be brought by 1 or more representative persons as a class action;

(C) the term "class certification order" means an order issued by a court approving the treatment of some or all aspects of a civil action as a class action; and

(D) the term "class members" means the persons (named or unnamed) who fall within the definition of the proposed or certified class in a class action.

(2) The district courts shall have original jurisdiction of any civil action in which the matter in controversy exceeds the sum or value of $5,000,000, exclusive of interest and costs, and is a class action in which—

(A) any member of a class of plaintiffs is a citizen of a State different from any defendant;

(B) any member of a class of plaintiffs is a foreign state or a citizen or subject of a foreign state and any defendant is a citizen of a State; or

(C) any member of a class of plaintiffs is a citizen of a State and any defendant is a foreign state or a citizen or subject of a foreign state.

(3) A district court may, in the interests of justice and looking at the totality of the circumstances, decline to exercise jurisdiction under paragraph (2) over a class action in which greater than one-third but less than two-thirds of the members of all proposed plaintiff classes in the aggregate and the primary defendants are citizens of the State in which the action was originally filed based on consideration of—

(A) whether the claims asserted involve matters of national or interstate interest;

(B) whether the claims asserted will be governed by laws of the State in which the action was originally filed or by the laws of other States;

(C) whether the class action has been pleaded in a manner that seeks to avoid Federal jurisdiction;

(D) whether the action was brought in a forum with a distinct nexus with the class members, the alleged harm, or the defendants;

(E) whether the number of citizens of the State in which the action was originally filed in all proposed plaintiff classes in the aggregate is substantially larger than the number of citizens from any other State, and the citizenship of the other members of the proposed class is dispersed among a substantial number of States; and

(F) whether, during the 3-year period preceding the filing of that class action, 1 or more other class actions asserting the same or similar claims on behalf of the same or other persons have been filed.

(4) A district court shall decline to exercise jurisdiction under paragraph (2)—

(A)(i) over a class action in which—

(I) greater than two-thirds of the members of all proposed plaintiff classes in the aggregate are citizens of the State in which the action was originally filed;

(II) at least 1 defendant is a defendant—

(aa) from whom significant relief is sought by members of the plaintiff class;

(bb) whose alleged conduct forms a significant basis for the claims asserted by the proposed plaintiff class; and

(cc) who is a citizen of the State in which the action was originally filed; and

(III) principal injuries resulting from the alleged conduct or any related conduct of each defendant were incurred in the State in which the action was originally filed; and

(ii) during the 3-year period preceding the filing of that class action, no other class action has been filed asserting the same or similar factual allegations against any of the defendants on behalf of the same or other persons; or

(B) two-thirds or more of the members of all proposed plaintiff classes in the aggregate, and the primary defendants, are citizens of the State in which the action was originally filed.

(5) Paragraphs (2) through (4) shall not apply to any class action in which—

(A) the primary defendants are States, State officials, or other governmental entities against whom the district court may be foreclosed from ordering relief; or

(B) the number of members of all proposed plaintiff classes in the aggregate is less than 100.

(6) In any class action, the claims of the individual class members shall be aggregated to determine whether the matter in controversy exceeds the sum or value of $5,000,000, exclusive of interest and costs.

(7) Citizenship of the members of the proposed plaintiff classes shall be determined for purposes of paragraphs (2) through (6) as of the date of filing of the complaint or amended complaint, or, if the case stated by the initial pleading is not subject to Federal jurisdiction, as of the date of service by plaintiffs of an amended pleading, motion, or other paper, indicating the existence of Federal jurisdiction.

(8) This subsection shall apply to any class action before or after the entry of a class certification order by the court with respect to that action.

(9) Paragraph (2) shall not apply to any class action that solely involves a claim—

(A) concerning a covered security as defined under 16(f)(3) 1 of the Securities Act of 1933 (15 U.S.C. 78p(f)(3) 2) and section 28(f)(5)(E) of the Securities Exchange Act of 1934 (15 U.S.C. 78bb(f)(5)(E));

(B) that relates to the internal affairs or governance of a corporation or other form of business enterprise and that arises under or by virtue of the laws of the State in which such corporation or business enterprise is incorporated or organized; or

(C) that relates to the rights, duties (including fiduciary duties), and obligations relating to or created by or pursuant to any security (as defined under section 2(a)(1) of the Securities Act of 1933 (15 U.S.C. 77b(a)(1)) and the regulations issued thereunder).

(10) For purposes of this subsection and section 1453 , an unincorporated association shall be deemed to be a citizen of the State where it has its principal place of business and the State under whose laws it is organized.

(11)(A) For purposes of this subsection and section 1453 , a mass action shall be deemed to be a class action removable under paragraphs (2) through (10) if it otherwise meets the provisions of those paragraphs.

(B)(i) As used in subparagraph (A), the term "mass action" means any civil action (except a civil action within the scope of section 1711(2)) in which monetary relief claims of 100 or more persons are proposed to be tried jointly on the ground that the plaintiffs' claims involve common questions of law or fact, except that jurisdiction shall exist only over those plaintiffs whose claims in a mass action satisfy the jurisdictional amount requirements under subsection (a).

(ii) As used in subparagraph (A), the term "mass action" shall not include any civil action in which—

(I) all of the claims in the action arise from an event or occurrence in the State in which the action was filed, and that allegedly resulted in injuries in that State or in States contiguous to that State;

(II) the claims are joined upon motion of a defendant;

(III) all of the claims in the action are asserted on behalf of the general public (and not on behalf of individual claimants or members of a purported class) pursuant to a State statute specifically authorizing such action; or

(IV) the claims have been consolidated or coordinated solely for pretrial proceedings.

(C)(i) Any action(s) removed to Federal court pursuant to this subsection shall not thereafter be transferred to any other court pursuant to section 1407, or the rules promulgated thereunder, unless a majority of the plaintiffs in the action request transfer pursuant to section 1407.

(ii) This subparagraph will not apply—

(I) to cases certified pursuant to rule 23 of the Federal Rules of Civil Procedure; or

(II) if plaintiffs propose that the action proceed as a class action pursuant to rule 23 of the Federal Rules of Civil Procedure.

(D) The limitations periods on any claims asserted in a mass action that is removed to Federal court pursuant to this subsection shall be deemed tolled during the period that the action is pending in Federal court.

(e) The word "States", as used in this section, includes the Territories, the District of Columbia, and the Commonwealth of Puerto Rico.

28 U.S.C. § 1335. Interpleader.

(a) The district courts shall have original jurisdiction of any civil action of interpleader or in the nature of interpleader filed by any person, firm, or corporation, association, or society having in his or its custody or possession money or property of the value of $500 or more, or having issued a note, bond, certificate, policy of insurance, or other instrument of value or amount of $500 or more, or providing for the delivery or payment or the loan of money or property of such amount or value, or being under any obligation written or unwritten to the amount of $500 or more, if

(1) Two or more adverse claimants, of diverse citizenship as defined in subsection (a) or (d) of section 1332 of this title, are claiming or may claim to be entitled to such money or property, or to any one or more of the benefits arising by virtue of any note, bond, certificate, policy or other instrument, or arising by virtue of any such obligation; and if

(2) the plaintiff has deposited such money or property or has paid the amount of or the loan or other value of such instrument or the amount due under such obligation into the registry of the court, there to abide the judgment of the court, or has given bond payable to the clerk of the court in such amount and with such surety as the court or judge may deem proper, conditioned upon the compliance by the plaintiff with the

future order or judgment of the court with respect to the subject matter of the controversy.

(b) Such an action may be entertained although the titles or claims of the conflicting claimants do not have a common origin, or are not identical, but are adverse to and independent of one another.

28 U.S.C. § 1367. Supplemental Jurisdiction.

(a) Except as provided in subsections (b) and (c) or as expressly provided otherwise by Federal statute, in any civil action of which the district courts have original jurisdiction, the district courts shall have supplemental jurisdiction over all other claims that are so related to claims in the action within such original jurisdiction that they form part of the same case or controversy under Article III of the United States Constitution. Such supplemental jurisdiction shall include claims that involve the joinder or intervention of additional parties.

(b) In any civil action of which the district courts have original jurisdiction founded solely on section 1332 of this title, the district courts shall not have supplemental jurisdiction under subsection (a) over claims by plaintiffs against persons made parties under Rule 14, 19, 20, or 24 of the Federal Rules of Civil Procedure, or over claims by persons proposed to be joined as plaintiffs under Rule 19 of such rules, or seeking to intervene as plaintiffs under Rule 24 of such rules, when exercising supplemental jurisdiction over such claims would be inconsistent with the jurisdictional requirements of section 1332.

(c) The district courts may decline to exercise supplemental jurisdiction over a claim under subsection (a) if—

(1) the claim raises a novel or complex issue of State law,

(2) the claim substantially predominates over the claim or claims over which the district court has original jurisdiction,

(3) the district court has dismissed all claims over which it has original jurisdiction, or

(4) in exceptional circumstances, there are other compelling reasons for declining jurisdiction.

(d) The period of limitations for any claim asserted under subsection (a), and for any other claim in the same action that is voluntarily dismissed at the same time as or after the dismissal of the claim under subsection (a), shall be tolled while the claim is pending and for a period of 30 days after it is dismissed unless State law provides for a longer tolling period.

(e) As used in this section, the term "State" includes the District of Columbia, the Commonwealth of Puerto Rico, and any territory or possession of the United States.

28 U.S.C. § 1391. Venue generally.

(a) Applicability of section. —Except as otherwise provided by law—

(1) this section shall govern the venue of all civil actions brought in district courts of the United States; and

(2) the proper venue for a civil action shall be determined without regard to whether the action is local or transitory in nature.

(b) Venue in general. —A civil action may be brought in—

(1) a judicial district in which any defendant resides, if all defendants are residents of the State in which the district is located;

(2) a judicial district in which a substantial part of the events or omissions giving rise to the claim occurred, or a substantial part of property that is the subject of the action is situated; or

(3) if there is no district in which an action may otherwise be brought as provided in this section, any judicial district in which any defendant is subject to the court's personal jurisdiction with respect to such action.

(c) Residency. —For all venue purposes—

(1) a natural person, including an alien lawfully admitted for permanent residence in the United States, shall be deemed to reside in the judicial district in which that person is domiciled;

(2) an entity with the capacity to sue and be sued in its common name under applicable law, whether or not incorporated, shall be deemed to reside, if a defendant, in any judicial district in which such defendant is subject to the court's personal jurisdiction with respect to the civil action in question and, if a plaintiff, only in the judicial district in which it maintains its principal place of business; and

(3) a defendant not resident in the United States may be sued in any judicial district, and the joinder of such a defendant shall be disregarded in determining where the action may be brought with respect to other defendants.

(d) Residency of corporations in States with multiple districts. —For purposes of venue under this chapter, in a State which has more than one judicial district and in which a defendant that is a corporation is subject to personal jurisdiction at the time an action is commenced, such corporation shall be deemed to reside in any district in that State within which its contacts would be sufficient to subject it to personal jurisdiction if that district were a separate State, and, if there is no such district, the corporation shall be deemed to reside in the district within which it has the most significant contacts.

(e) Actions where defendant is officer or employee of the United States—

(1) In general. —A civil action in which a defendant is an officer or employee of the United States or any agency thereof acting in his official capacity or under color of legal authority, or an agency of the United States, or the United States, may, except as otherwise provided by law, be brought in any judicial district in which (A) a defendant in the action resides, (B) a substantial part of the events or omissions giving rise to the claim occurred, or a substantial part of property that is the subject of the action is situated, or (C) the plaintiff resides if no real property is involved in the action. Additional persons may be joined as parties to any such action in accordance with the Federal Rules of Civil Procedure and with such other venue requirements as would be applicable if the United States or one of its officers, employees, or agencies were not a party.

(2) Service. —The summons and complaint in such an action shall be served as provided by the Federal Rules of Civil Procedure except that the delivery of the summons and complaint to the officer or agency as required by the rules may be made by certified mail beyond the territorial limits of the district in which the action is brought.

(f) Civil actions against a foreign state —A civil action against a foreign state as defined in section 1603(a) of this title may be brought—

(1) in any judicial district in which a substantial part of the events or omissions giving rise to the claim occurred, or a substantial part of property that is the subject of the action is situated;

(2) in any judicial district in which the vessel or cargo of a foreign state is situated, if the claim is asserted under section 1605(b) of this title;

(3) in any judicial district in which the agency or instrumentality is licensed to do business or is doing business, if the action is brought against an agency or instrumentality of a foreign state as defined in section 1603(b) of this title; or

(4) in the United States District Court for the District of Columbia if the action is brought against a foreign state or political subdivision thereof.

(g) Multiparty, multiforum litigation —A civil action in which jurisdiction of the district court is based upon section 1369 of this title may be brought in any district in which any defendant resides or in which a substantial part of the accident giving rise to the action took place.

Catapiller —

28 U.S.C. § 1441. Removal of civil actions.

(a) Generally. —Except as otherwise expressly provided by Act of Congress, any civil action brought in a State court of which the district courts of the United States have original jurisdiction, may be removed by the defendant or the defendants, to the district court of the United States for the district and division embracing the place where such action is pending.

(b) Removal based on diversity of citizenship. — (1) In determining whether a civil action is removable on the basis of the jurisdiction under section 1332(a) of this title, the citizenship of defendants sued under fictitious names shall be disregarded.

(2) A civil action otherwise removable solely on the basis of the jurisdiction under section 1332(a) of this title may not be removed if any of the parties in interest properly joined and served as defendants is a citizen of the State in which such action is brought.

(c) Joinder of Federal law claims and State law claims. — (1) If a civil action includes—

(A) a claim arising under the Constitution, laws, or treaties of the United States (within the meaning of section 1331 of this title), and

(B) a claim not within the original or supplemental jurisdiction of the district court or a claim that has been made nonremovable by statute, the entire action may be removed if the action would be removable without the inclusion of the claim described in subparagraph (B).

(2) Upon removal of an action described in paragraph (1), the district court shall sever from the action all claims described in paragraph (1)(B) and shall remand the severed claims to the State court from which the action was removed. Only defendants against whom a claim described in paragraph (1)(A) has been asserted are required to join in or consent to the removal under paragraph (1).

(d) Actions against foreign States. —Any civil action brought in a State court against a foreign state as defined in section 1603(a) of this title may be removed by the foreign state to the district court of the United States for the district and division embracing the place where such action is pending. Upon removal the action shall be tried by the court without jury. Where removal is based upon this subsection, the time limitations of section 1446(b) of this chapter may be enlarged at any time for cause shown.

(e) Multiparty, multiforum jurisdiction. — (1) Notwithstanding the provisions of subsection (b) of this section, a defendant in a civil action in a State court may remove the action to the district court of the United States for the district and division embracing the place where the action is pending if—

(A) the action could have been brought in a United States district court under section 1369 of this title; or

(B) the defendant is a party to an action which is or could have been brought, in whole or in part, under section 1369 in a United States district court and arises from the same accident as the action in State court, even if the action to be removed could not have been brought in a district court as an original matter.

The removal of an action under this subsection shall be made in accordance with section 1446 of this title, except that a notice of removal may also be filed before trial of the action in State court within 30 days after the date on which the defendant first becomes a party to an action under section 1369 in a United States district court that arises from the same accident as the action in State court, or at a later time with leave of the district court.

(2) Whenever an action is removed under this subsection and the district court to which it is removed or transferred under section 1407(j) has made a liability determination requiring further proceedings as to damages, the district court shall remand the action to the State court from which it had been removed for the determination of damages, unless the court finds that, for the convenience of parties and witnesses and in the interest of justice, the action should be retained for the determination of damages.

(3) Any remand under paragraph (2) shall not be effective until 60 days after the district court has issued an order determining liability and has certified its intention to remand the removed action for the determination of damages. An appeal with respect to the liability determination of the district court may be taken during that 60-day period to the court of appeals with appellate jurisdiction over the district court. In the event a party files such an appeal, the remand shall not be effective until the appeal has been finally disposed of. Once the remand has become effective, the liability determination shall not be subject to further review by appeal or otherwise.

(4) Any decision under this subsection concerning remand for the determination of damages shall not be reviewable by appeal or otherwise.

(5) An action removed under this subsection shall be deemed to be an action under section 1369 and an action in which jurisdiction is based on section 1369 of this title for purposes of this section and sections 1407 , 1697 , and 1785 of this title.

(6) Nothing in this subsection shall restrict the authority of the district court to transfer or dismiss an action on the ground of inconvenient forum.

(f) Derivative removal jurisdiction. —The court to which a civil action is removed under this section is not precluded from hearing and determining any claim in such civil action because the State court from which such civil action is removed did not have jurisdiction over that claim.

28 U.S.C. § 1446. Procedure for removal of civil actions.

(a) Generally. —A defendant or defendants desiring to remove any civil action from a State court shall file in the district court of the United States for the district and division within which such action is pending a notice of removal signed pursuant to Rule 11 of the Federal Rules of Civil Procedure and containing a short and plain statement of the grounds for removal, together with a copy of all process, pleadings, and orders served upon such defendant or defendants in such action.

(b) Requirements; generally. — (1) The notice of removal of a civil action or proceeding shall be filed within 30 days after the receipt by the defendant, through service or otherwise, of a copy of the initial pleading setting forth the claim for relief upon which such action or proceeding is based, or within 30 days after the service of summons upon the defendant if such initial pleading has then been filed in court and is not required to be served on the defendant, whichever period is shorter.

(2)(A) When a civil action is removed solely under section 1441(a) , all defendants who have been properly joined and served must join in or consent to the removal of the action.

(B) Each defendant shall have 30 days after receipt by or service on that defendant of the initial pleading or summons described in paragraph (1) to file the notice of removal.

(C) If defendants are served at different times, and a later-served defendant files a notice of removal, any earlier-served defendant may consent to the removal even though that earlier-served defendant did not previously initiate or consent to removal.

(3) Except as provided in subsection (c), if the case stated by the initial pleading is not removable, a notice of removal may be filed within 30 days after receipt by the defendant, through service or otherwise, of a copy of an amended pleading, motion, order or other paper from which it may first be ascertained that the case is one which is or has become removable.

(c) Requirements; removal based on diversity of citizenship. — (1) A case may not be removed under subsection (b)(3) on the basis of jurisdiction conferred by section 1332 more than 1 year after commencement of the action, unless the district court finds that the plaintiff has acted in bad faith in order to prevent a defendant from removing the action.

(2) If removal of a civil action is sought on the basis of the jurisdiction conferred by section 1332(a), the sum demanded in good faith in the initial pleading shall be deemed to be the amount in controversy, except that—

(A) the notice of removal may assert the amount in controversy if the initial pleading seeks—

(i) nonmonetary relief; or

(ii) a money judgment, but the State practice either does not permit demand for a specific sum or permits recovery of damages in excess of the amount demanded; and

(B) removal of the action is proper on the basis of an amount in controversy asserted under subparagraph (A) if the district court finds, by the preponderance of the evidence, that the amount in controversy exceeds the amount specified in section 1332(a).

(3)(A) If the case stated by the initial pleading is not removable solely because the amount in controversy does not exceed the amount specified in section 1332(a), information relating to the amount in controversy in the record of the State proceeding, or in responses to discovery, shall be treated as an 'other paper' under subsection (b)(3).

(B) If the notice of removal is filed more than 1 year after commencement of the action and the district court finds that the plaintiff deliberately failed to disclose the actual amount in controversy to prevent removal, that finding shall be deemed bad faith under paragraph (1).

(d) Notice to adverse parties and State court. —Promptly after the filing of such notice of removal of a civil action the defendant or defendants shall give written notice thereof to all adverse parties and shall file a copy of the notice with the clerk of such State court, which shall effect the removal and the State court shall proceed no further unless and until the case is remanded.

(e) Counterclaim in 337 proceeding. —With respect to any counterclaim removed to a district court pursuant to section 337(c) of the Tariff Act of 1930, the district court shall resolve such counterclaim in the same manner as an original complaint under the Federal Rules of Civil Procedure, except that the payment of a filing fee shall not be required in such cases and the counterclaim shall relate back to the date of the original complaint in the proceeding before the International Trade Commission under section 337 of that Act.

[(f) Redesignated (e)]

(g) Where the civil action or criminal prosecution that is removable under section 1442(a) is a proceeding in which a judicial order for testimony or documents is sought or issued or sought to be enforced, the 30-day requirement of subsection (b) of this section and paragraph (1) of section 1455(b) is satisfied if the person or entity desiring to remove the proceeding files the notice of removal not later than 30 days after receiving, through service, notice of any such proceeding.

28 U.S.C. § 1447. Procedure after removal generally.

(a) In any case removed from a State court, the district court may issue all necessary orders and process to bring before it all proper parties whether served by process issued by the State court or otherwise.

(b) It may require the removing party to file with its clerk copies of all records and proceedings in such State court or may cause the same to be brought before it by writ of certiorari issued to such State court.

(c) A motion to remand the case on the basis of any defect other than lack of subject matter jurisdiction must be made within 30 days after the filing of the notice of removal under section 1446(a). If at any time before final judgment it appears that the district court lacks subject matter jurisdiction, the case shall be remanded. An order remanding the case may require payment of just costs and any actual expenses, including attorney fees, incurred as a result of the removal. A certified copy of the order of remand shall be mailed by the clerk to the clerk of the State court. The State court may thereupon proceed with such case.

(d) An order remanding a case to the State court from which it was removed is not reviewable on appeal or otherwise, except that an order remanding a case to the State court from which it was removed pursuant to section 1442 or 1443 of this title shall be reviewable by appeal or otherwise.

(e) If after removal the plaintiff seeks to join additional defendants whose joinder would destroy subject matter jurisdiction, the court may deny joinder, or permit joinder and remand the action to the State court.

42 U.S.C. § 1981. Equal rights under the law.

(a) Statement of equal rights

All persons within the jurisdiction of the United States shall have the same right in every State and Territory to make and enforce contracts, to sue, be parties, give evidence, and to the full and equal benefit of all laws and proceedings for the security of persons and property as is enjoyed by white citizens, and shall be subject to like punishment, pains, penalties, taxes, licenses, and exactions of every kind, and to no other.

(b) "Make and enforce contracts" defined

For purposes of this section, the term "make and enforce contracts" includes the making, performance, modification, and termination of contracts, and the enjoyment of all benefits, privileges, terms, and conditions of the contractual relationship.

(c) Protection against impairment

The rights protected by this section are protected against impairment by nongovernmental discrimination and impairment under color of State law.

42 U.S.C. § 1983. Civil action for deprivation of rights.

Every person who, under color of any statute, ordinance, regulation, custom, or usage, of any State or Territory or the District of Columbia, subjects, or causes to be subjected, any citizen of the United States or other person within the jurisdiction thereof to the deprivation of any rights, privileges, or immunities secured by the Constitution and laws, shall be liable to the party injured in an action at law, suit in equity, or other proper proceeding for redress, except that in any action brought against a judicial officer for an act or omission taken in such officer's judicial capacity, injunctive relief shall not be granted unless a declaratory decree was violated or declaratory relief was unavailable. For the purposes of this section, any Act of Congress applicable exclusively to the District of Columbia shall be considered to be a statute of the District of Columbia.

42 U.S.C. § 1988. Proceedings in vindication of civil rights.

(a) Applicability of statutory and common law

The jurisdiction in civil and criminal matters conferred on the district courts by the provisions of titles 13, 24, and 70 of the Revised Statutes for the protection of all persons in the United States in their civil rights, and for their vindication, shall be exercised and enforced in conformity with the laws of the United States, so far as such laws are suitable to carry the same into effect; but in all cases where they are not adapted to the object, or are deficient in the provisions necessary to furnish suitable remedies and punish offenses against law, the common law, as modified and changed by the constitution and statutes of the State wherein the court having jurisdiction of such civil or criminal cause is held, so far as the same is not inconsistent with the Constitution and laws of the United States, shall be extended to and govern the said courts in the trial and disposition of the cause, and, if it is of a criminal nature, in the infliction of punishment on the party found guilty.

(b) Attorney's fees

In any action or proceeding to enforce a provision of sections 1981 , 1981a , 1982 , 1983 , 1985 , and 1986 of this title, title IX of Public Law 92-318 [20 U.S.C.A. § 1681 et seq.], the Religious Freedom Restoration Act of 1993 [42 U.S.C.A. § 2000bb et seq.], the Religious Land Use and Institutionalized Persons Act of 2000 [42 U.S.C.A. § 2000cc et seq.], title VI of the Civil Rights Act of 1964 [42 U.S.C.A. § 2000d et seq.], or section 13981 of this title, the court, in its discretion, may allow the prevailing party, other than the United States, a reasonable attorney's fee as part of the costs, except that in any action brought against a judicial officer for an act or omission taken in such officer's judicial capacity such officer shall not be held liable for any costs, including attorney's fees, unless such action was clearly in excess of such officer's jurisdiction.

(c) Expert fees

In awarding an attorney's fee under subsection (b) of this section in any action or proceeding to enforce a provision of section 1981 or 1981a of this title, the court, in its discretion, may include expert fees as part of the attorney's fee.

Venue 13:91 - p 311 & 312
14:04 - Proper
14:06 - Improper
Removal 14:41 p 313 -
Skyhel4 factors

Joinder 19 & 20
Indespoble parts 19₂ Can move forward without th
Pur misive Party

Impleder :
Joint & Seval
Imdemady
Contrubutións

Made in the USA
Middletown, DE
29 August 2019